D0783223

Framing medieval bodies

edited by Sarah Kay & Miri Rubin

Framing
medieval
bodies

MANCHESTER
UNIVERSITY PRESS
Manchester and New York

distributed exclusively in the USA and Canada by St. Martin's Press

Published by Manchester University Press
Oxford Road, Manchester M13 9NR, UK
and Room 400, 175 Fifth Avenue,
New York, NY 10010, USA

Distributed exclusively in the USA and Canada
by St. Martin's Press, Inc.,
175 Fifth Avenue, New York, NY 10010, USA

British Library Cataloguing-in-Publication Data
A catalogue record is available from the British Library

Library of Congress Cataloging-in-Publication Data
Framing medieval bodies / edited by Sarah Kay and Miri Rubin.
    p.   cm.
    ISBN 0-7190-3615-1 (hardback)
    1. Human body—Social aspects—History. 2. Civilization, Medieval. I. Kay, Sarah.
    II. Rubin, Miri, 1956–
    GT495.F73   1994
    391′.6—dc20   93–35902

ISBN 0 7190 5010 3 *paperback*

Paperback edition published 1996, reprinted 1997

Typeset by Graphicraft Typesetters Ltd., Hong Kong
Printed in Great Britain
by Biddles Limited, Guildford and King's Lynn

Contents

Figures

Contributors

Anna Sapir Abulafia Fellow, College Lecturer and Director of Studies in History, Lucy Cavendish College, Cambridge

Sarah Beckwith Assistant Professor of Medieval Literature, Department of English, University of Pittsburgh, Pittsburgh, Pennsylvania

Michael Camille Associate Professor, Department of Art History, University of Chicago

Mark Chinca Lecturer, Department of German, University of Cambridge

Rita Copeland Associate Professor of English, University of Minnesota, Twin Cities, Minneapolis

Roberta Gilchrist Lecturer in Archaeology, Centre of East Anglian Studies, University of East Anglia, Norwich

Sarah Kay Lecturer, Department of French, University of Cambridge

Robin Kirkpatrick Lecturer, Department of Italian, University of Cambridge

Miri Rubin Tutorial Fellow, Pembroke College, Oxford, and Lecturer in Modern History, Oxford University

Shulamith Shahar Professor in the Department of History, Tel Aviv University

Walter Simons Assistant Professor, Department of History, Dartmouth College, Hanover, New Hampshire

Jocelyn Wogan-Browne Lecturer, Department of English, University of Liverpool

We are all born with bodies, but although they are thus native to us, and we innate to them, they are not thereby 'natural', distanced as they are from 'nature' by a multiplicity of psychic, sexual, social and political codes. This systematic coding of bodies means that they are as much the product, as the site, of experience. They can, of course, be spoken of as 'natural' entities (biological, anatomical, or material), but only because the discourses of biology, anatomy and materialism exist within our culture, offering intellectual conceptualisations (or 'frames') in the same way as do the manifestly less naturalistic discourses of fashion or asceticism (to take just two examples).

Historians' interests have converged on the body from a variety of theoretical and historical directions in the last fifteen years. Studies inspired by cultural anthropology have centred on the rituals and symbolic gestures of acting bodies, perceived as carriers of potent symbolic value; as interacting in formulae of ritual events; or as expressing and interpreting symbolic traditions. The derided body in *charivari*, the bodies of actors in mystery plays, the intricate language of gesture at prayer, and even the body of a cat, have become familiar stepping stones on one of the paths leading towards a historical understanding of embodiment.[1] The impact of the thought of Michel Foucault, as well as the remnants of a functionalist sociology seeking to define normative and deviant contours for societies, have pointed in their different ways towards the contexts in which bodies – different, deviant, criminal, resistant to law and order – were branded, mutilated, tortured or disgraced.

Another significant historical impetus to the study of the body has been scholarly excitement over the field of female mysticism, which preceded the rise of intellectual feminism but has taken fresh impetus from it. This area of study has habitually chronicled the uses of bodies, in flights of mystical transcendence, as objects of discipline and as conduits for religious exploration which even the humblest possessed.[2] It has been crowned by the most authoritative study of the bodily performance of religious women in the Middle Ages, Caroline Walker Bynum's *Holy Feast and Holy Fast*.[3]

The subtly established hegemony of an intellectual agenda which can be identified generally with 'social history' and more specifically with the history of material life and everyday life (which German scholars call *Realienkunde* or *Alltagsgeschichte*) has led to the investigation of the underlying conditions of life which informed a variety of social practices: diet, sexual mores, physical environment, and the rhythms of household formation. These conditions provided the grounding for a series of practices and entitlements experienced through the body, whether in public, in private, or within the family, in what seemed to be a shared and necessary life-provision. A further, and related, area of inquiry is the field of popular medicine, such as surgical practice, or the magical know-how which so often worked through bodily ingestion, or bodily gesture and adornment.

The approaches adopted by historians of literature have overlapped to a large degree with those of historians proper. Two other theoretical impulses, however, have had a major impact on literary studies: psychoanalysis and poststructuralism. Psychoanalytic theory is inevitably attentive to the embodied nature of consciousness and its development. The very young child, according to Lacan, is unaware of his body as an ordered totality. The drifting, disconnected members of this unbounded and fragmented infant body (the *corps morcelé* in Lacan's terminology) are perceived as cohering together only when the ego begins to form.[4] The ego develops as a kind of precipitation from identifications with other people (notably the mother), on whom the infant gazes, and from identification of himself as just such another person; it also results from the infant's growing need to regulate his own relation to his body, controlling the amount of excitation and tension generated by its sensations in order to maximise his own well-being. For Lacan, the ego manifests itself in the so-called mirror stage: the staging, or stadium (*le stade du miroir*), of the body as a unity.

From then on, bodily coherence may be a valuable achievement, but it is also a spectacle produced and directed by this emergent impresario, the ego. In *The Ego and the Id*,[5] Freud contends that there is a reciprocal relation between the outline form of this body as now represented, and the ego, that part of the mind where sense perceptions are recorded and policed. The outer surface of the body, where these perceptions arise, is what shapes potential 'consciousness'. The outline of the body sustains the ego's sense of the outlines of the person – the structured wholeness of itself. Thus the ego is in some degree the product of the body. But at the same time, the ego censors or promotes bodily perceptions differentially. For example, different zones of the body are unequally invested with sexual value, and not because those zones are themselves inherently and automatically erotogenic. Hence Freud hypothesises a migration of libidinal energy from mouth to anus to genitals, and argues for the deflection of that energy on to other body parts as the expression of neurotic symptoms. This investment of the body by the psyche illustrates to what extent, in psychoanalytic thought, the body is not 'natural', or even 'real', but fantasised. Our sexual drives are geared to the mechanisms of this psychically ordered body, determining our sexual orientation and erotic tastes.

If the *body* as a totality is the product of a psychic investment, the concept of *the* body, in the singular, is one of (a totalising) ideology, and one which has increasingly been challenged by poststructuralism. From within a predominantly structuralist framework, Mary Douglas asserted, at the beginning of *Natural Symbols*,[6] that the body is something that we all have in common. If so, it is only in the sense of the joke about the British and Americans being separated by a common language. It is a standing point of disagreement between poststructuralists and traditional psychoanalysis that the masters of the latter discipline seek to impose a single body image: one organised around the phallus, or its lack. Hence the insistence in the writings of Luce Irigaray on the distinctiveness of the female body;[7] feminist poststructuralists in Europe and the Anglo-Saxon world have voiced a united attack on the traditional concept of the *body* in the singular as a cover for masculinist privileging of the male embodied subject. In their attack on Freudian and post-Freudian psychoanalysis, Gilles Deleuze and Félix Guattari seek to restore the importance of the fragmented body, claiming all its diverse dynamics and flows as the activities of so many 'desiring machines' – mouth, breast, eyes – so that the phallus no longer enjoys a unique position of privilege, and the body is no longer hierarchised.[8] If each of us has a *corps morcelé* and a fantasised body, we also have the bodies assigned to us by social, political or scientific discourses; and while these stage for each person a series of different bodies, they also discriminate between the bodies of different persons. Thus another intellectual gain of the poststructuralist enterprise has been the recognition of the way *bodies* (in the plural) are constructed discursively, in the symbolic order.[9]

In this volume, we seek to address the intersection between these various historical and literary-theoretical perspectives. They have given rise to two powerful trends in epistemology: the rethinking of human experience as refracted through gender; and the destabilising of the category of the centred person. These trends have come to influence the work of medievalists, who so often shy away from theoretical discussion and doubt the ability of the sources at their disposal to generate new, intimate, resistant meanings. Other scholarly initiatives have already explored specific theoretical[10] and subject[11] areas. In this volume, we have cast our net more widely, contributing a range of different approaches and topics.

It should be clear, then, why the title of this volume refers to *bodies*. And because the body is capable of such plastic conceptualisation, we have spoken of it as having many *frames*. The frame is what shapes a visual image. In this volume, Michael Camille considers how bodies are represented as pictures, and as a pictorial means to understand other phenomena. Frames also serve to exhibit and display, as bodies from the mirror stage are displayed. The desire to flaunt and display bodies, as well as to confine them, is discussed here in relation to lepers and nuns by Roberta Gilchrist; to the frenzies and levitations of beguines by Walter Simons; and Jocelyn Wogan-Browne shows how the enclosure of anchoresses, whilst cutting them off from the society without, also provides them with an alternative, and sustaining, female community within the 'frame'. Frames may serve mainly to delimit and confine. Thus, for example, Anna Abulafia contends that identification with the body is a means of denigrating Jews in the Middle Ages; and Shulamit Shahar shows how the aged body is likewise depreciated and set apart. It is, however, helpful to distinguish between degrees of framing. As many of the essays in this volume point out, frames are not always very secure. Robin Kirkpatrick and Miri Rubin both contest, in different ways, the efficacy of frames: Robin Kirkpatrick in the light of Dante's relentless concentration on the particular, which means that his attention to the body eludes the generality of any frame; Miri Rubin in face of the dissolution of frames which restores to circulation freaks, viscera, and other body parts (in the manner of the *corps morcelé*). Frames may challenge and even undermine one another; thus Sarah Kay suggests that competing epistemologies trouble the framing of gender, and Mark Chinca exposes the contradictions generated by social frames, such as the centre–periphery opposition.

It is evident that the notion of framing invoked here is inherently historical, since the discourses and perceptions that frame bodies are themselves produced by, and produce, historically situated subjects. Some of the essays in this volume attend to quite specific historical moments; Paris in the 1270s (Sarah Kay), York in the early 1400s (Sarah Beckwith). Others, whilst taking on a broader canvas, remain historically delimited in space and time (for Mark Chinca thirteenth-century Germany; for Anna Abulafia twelfth-century texts in the Jewish–Christian debate). All our contributors are attentive to particular medieval texts or circumstances: is there any way in which medieval bodies are distinctively different from modern ones?

Mary Douglas suggests that some cultures give the lie to Lévi-Strauss's fundamental contention that the opposition which founds society is that between 'nature' and 'culture': that between 'body' and 'spirit' may, she proposes, in some cases be more crucial.[12] The European Middle Ages would surely be a good example to illustrate her view. Some of these essays discuss this familiar opposition as a founding hierarchy, used to articulate other hierarchies, such as Jew to Christian (Anna Abulafia) or feminine to masculine (Sarah Kay), deviance and correction (Rita Copeland), inside and outside (Miri Rubin). Others of the essays collected here re-explore the metaphorical use of the body – within the concept of the body politic – in the discourses of political privilege and legitimation (Sarah Beckwith, Mark Chinca).

Clearly when the body is used in either of these two ways, for the constructing of normative hierarchies and political systems, the bodily concept at work is not the fragmented body, nor the desire- and fantasy-torn body, but the serenely assembled and staged Narcissistic body of the ego, translated into a variety of symbolic discourses. Yet, since such 'bodies' are forever challenged by their disorderly or fragmented counter-parts, our essays demonstrate the extent to which the fictions of bodily control are contested within the very texts that promote them. The body may be a familiar context for cultural inquiry, an obvious point of departure for explorations of political, social and psychic meaning. This volume, however, seeks to break new ground in its emphasis on lack as well as on content, on contestation as well as on control.

The body/soul opposition was deployed regularly in medieval rhetoric to denote a troubling proximity of incommensurable, yet coexisting enti-ties.[13] Such is the use made of it by Humbert of Romans in his sermon *ad status* aimed at nobles (*Ad omnes nobiles*). A fine, noble body is not always coupled with a fine, noble person; why, even a rabble can be endowed with corporal nobility 'because robbers, killers, blasphemers and criminals of all kinds often have them [noble bodies]'.[14] In mid-twelfth-century French literature, physical nobility and nobility of character habitually coincide,[15] but in later texts the status of bodily 'signs' becomes increasingly open to deviant readings. The succession of contrasting glosses on the body of the heroine of Jean Renart's *Guillaume de Dole*, for example, provides much of the substance of this thirteenth-century romance.[16] The relation-ship posited between body and soul was subject to constant redefinition, with the thirteenth century forming a crucial stage in both learned and literary texts.[17] And as G. S. Rousseau and Roy Porter have recently observed, even when these were disapproving and untrusting of the human condition of embodiment, the body never ceased to fascinate and comfort as the site of all possible self-expression and example.[18]

Inasmuch as the human body was both an outer, misleading shell, and a psychosomatic whole, authority over the body was contested between physicians and priests,[19] between the clergy and the laity, and between men and women. The body was a privileged site, vehicle, and metaphor of political struggle. Thus, when we consider the familiar use of the body as a metaphor for good and just government, we must bear in mind the exact context of application. Ostensibly it is the language of privilege, of ruling groups (and their writers) in justification of the order which has endowed them with power. See, for example, the powerful deployment of the image in the records of the York Corpus Christi fraternity in 1408, a statement of intent for a new national patrician club centred in York. The power of office drawn from the 'naturalness' of the bodily order, and even more, from the majesty of Christ's body, is present in the symbolism and the celebrations of Corpus Christi in that city, in which the fraternity played an important part. Their fraternity was to be a haven of peace, harmonious like the mystical body:

> In this fraternal union all brethren will be the members of Christ, from the union of which is a cause for joy just as the divisiveness of sins is cause for sadness. From which follows that just as the attraction of the members of the human body is natural, so will be the reciprocal love of all the brethren in Christ.

And sympathy with Christ is likened to the sympathy felt by the whole body, if the eye or a leg, for example, is in pain.[20]

Yet this language of the body politic is one that can also be turned against its users, the hierarchies it seems to enforce being reversed or deconstructed. Thus the body, as well as endorsing regimes of power, is also a challenge to the dichotomies and hierarchies of established categories. As contributions to this volume demonstrate, we need to transcend – or deconstruct – the classification by male–female, nature–culture, elite–popular, body–soul, matter–spirit, even as we carefully delineate the contours of the very discourses which sustained such oppositions.

The body both produces knowledge and is shaped by it, both is determined by it and colludes with it. For within the social field, even though apparently obscured by it, fantasy and desire run their course.[21] The body is after all *the* tool of desire, the *tool* of desire. The self is ultimately an imaginary construction within the world, invested in the body that a person becomes after the primary link to the mother has been lost. From creatures in the world, dependent, unassuming, we grow into selves whose bodily frame changes as it ages, is adorned, is owned, works, dreams and claims its place among others. So in any person's being there is an overhanging shadow, an ambiguity, an emptiness between the sense of discrete selfhood and a *ressentiment* of a wholeness or togetherness which is only partially incorporated into the self through desire. Within medieval culture it is possible to discern traces of this desire in fantasies of incorporation, or in religious symbolism of transcendence, for instance. The corollary to this desire is the dialectically related process of ordered division, through schemes of knowledge and systematic hierarchies, many of which depend on a gendered division of the world. But the move of the self within these fields is unstable and fraught with anxiety that such bodies may, after all, result from pretence or illusion. The tension to which this gives rise, within the seemingly unchanging frame of the body, becomes clear whenever we take a closer look at attempts to 'frame' that body – or to frame that 'body'.

Thus, whilst the essays in this volume are concerned to elucidate historically-specific conceptualisations of the body, they are, for the most part, also necessarily reliant on modern, theoretical frames: Marxism, feminism, race and gender theory, deconstruction. We have tried to develop in different ways an *embodied understanding* of subjects who perceive through their bodies, and are accountable through their bodies. We thus explore embodied relations, experience and knowledge. We can never fully know another person's body, even though we persist in making analogies to our own bodies, as a means to knowing others.[22] Merleau-Ponty has probably left us with the most explicit acknowledgement of the embodied nature of consciousness, and the subjectivity of intention, enacted through a body only knowable through language and social relations. He posits meaning in the reality of unknowability, likening it to an interaction, and locates value in the very perception of the Other's body as a dynamic engagement which defines being.[23] Such perception is contained within discourses, like the language of work and production traced by Sarah Beckwith or the discourse on knowledge and gender traced by Sarah Kay, in the fluidity of sexual identity and pain discerned by Miri Rubin, or in the transcendent states of embodied consciousness described by Walter Simons. A variety of languages, a series of frames which medieval people entered and exited in the specific contexts of their lives and texts are here recovered. Embodied persons, embodied relations, emerge from the following pages, and these will suggest many other contexts for embodied understanding.[24] As both external and internal, personal and public, life-giving and vulnerable, the body leads to alternative ways of establishing priorities, and perceiving the human person.[25] Bodily gestures communicate between persons, and these can also be a subject of self-fashioning, even of life-conversion, as old gestures are discarded in favour of new ones, in an attempt to remake *corporeal style*.[26] To attempt to identify the variety of experiences of bodies and of selves need not result in babble, unfathomable and shapeless information, but rather turn into a kaleidoscope pattern as different idioms and ways of being compete and interact in the social and psychic fields.

In conclusion, then, we have tried to assemble here vantage points as well as discursive frames, and thus we have collected pieces which are often theoretically informed and yet which are grounded in particular texts, or in a variety of specific traces of the medieval past. While we have tried to be explicit in introducing the concepts applied, the contributors have also felt free to move between medieval terms and theoretical positions and ideas related to current intellectual discussions. Medievalists will, we hope, appreciate the variety of materials and contexts explored here, while non-medievalists interested in concepts and approaches relating to the body will benefit from the fresh encounter with familiar concerns refracted by an unfamiliar and defamiliarising textual environment.

NOTES

1 N. Z. Davis, 'Women on Top', in *Society and Culture in Early Modern France*, 1976, reprinted Cambridge, 1987, pp. 124–51; R. C. Trexler, *The Christian at Prayer: An Illustrated Prayer Manual Attributed to Peter the Chanter (d.1197)*, Binghamton (NY), 1987; J.-C. Schmitt, *La Raison des gestes dans l'Occident medieval*, Paris, 1990. For the cat and some comments on it see R. Darnton, *The Great Cat Massacre and Other Episodes in French Cultural History*, New York, 1984, chapter 2; D. La Capra, 'Chartier, Darnton, and the great symbol massacre', *Journal of modern history*, LXIX, 1988, pp. 95–112; J. W. Fernandez, 'Historians tell tales: of Cartesian cats and Gallic cockfights', *Journal of modern history*, LXIX, 1988, pp. 113–27.

2 S. Beckwith, ' "A Very Material Mystic": the Medieval Mysticism of Margery Kempe', in *Medieval Literature: Criticism, Ideology and History*, ed. D. Aers, Brighton, 1986, pp. 34–57.

3 Berkeley (CA), 1987.

4 Jacques Lacan, 'The Mirror Stage as Formative of the Function of the I', in *Ecrits. A Selection*, trans. Alan Sheridan, London, 1977, pp. 1–7.

5 Sigmund Freud, *The Ego and the Id*, 1923, trans. James Strachey, *Standard Edition*, XIX, pp. 12–59. See also Freud's essay 'On Narcissism: an Introduction', 1914a, *Standard Edition*, XIV, pp. 67–104.

6 Mary Douglas, *Natural Symbols. Explorations in Cosmology*, 2nd edn, London, 1973, p. 11.

7 Luce Irigary, *Speculum: Of The Other Woman*, trans. Gillian Gill, Ithaca, 1985.

8 Gilles Deleuze and Félix Guattari, *Anti-Oedipus. Capitalism and Schizophrenia*, trans. Robert Hurley, Mark Seem and Helen R. Lane, Minneapolis, 1990.

9 An example of this approach is Julia Kristeva's *Powers of Horror: An Essay on Abjection*, trans. Leon S. Roudiez, New York, 1982.

10 *Feminist Approaches to the Body in Medieval Literature*, L. Lomperis and S. Stanbury (eds.), Philadelphia (PA), 1993.

11 For example, a new international journal has just been founded: *Micrologus: natura, scienze e società medievali*, edited by Cecilia Panti and Agostino Paravicini Bagliani, and published by Brepols (Turnholt). Its first volume (1993) reflects an interest in the discourses of science, medicine and religion and the location of bodies within them.

12 Mary Douglas, *Natural Symbols*, p. 17, and cf. pp. 94–5.

13 See R. W. Ackerman, 'The debate of the body and the soul and parochial Christianity', *Speculum*, XXXVII, 1962, pp. 541–65.

14 'Nam raptores, homicidae, sacrilegi, et omni genere vitiorum scelerati, hanc habent frequenter', Humbert of Romans, *Sermones*, Venice, 1603, sermon 80, pp. 78b–79b, at p. 79a.

15 Alice M. Colby-Hall, *The Portrait in Twelfth-century Literature*, Geneva, 1965.

16 Jean Renart, *Le Roman de la Rose ou de Guillaume de Dole*, ed. L. Foulet, Paris, 1969.

17 On the dissemination of these shifting understandings, see D. L. d'Avray, 'Some Franciscan ideas about the body', *Archivum Franciscanum Historicum*, LXXXIV, 1991, pp. 343–63.

18 G. S. Rousseau and R. Porter, 'Introduction: Toward a Natural History of Mind and Body', in *The Languages of Psyche: Mind and Body in Enlightenment Thought*, Berkeley (CA), 1990, p. 20; see also R. Porter, *'Barely Touching*: a Social Perspective on Mind and Body', *ibid.*, pp. 45–80, at p. 50.

19 See on a similar issue N. Siriasi, *Medieval and Early Renaissance Medicine: An Introduction to Knowledge and Practice*, Chicago, 1990, pp. 84–6.

20 'Hac unitate insuper fraternali omnes confratres erunt membra Christi, de quorum unione est summe gaudendum et peccatis divisionis nimie tristandum. Unde, sicut membrorum naturalium hominis ad caput est naturalis compassio, sic omnium confratrum ad Christum erit reciproca amatio . . . quod si oculus vel pes capiatur aliqua aegritudine, totum corpus condolet naturali pietate', *Register of the Guild of Corpus Christi in the City of York*, ed. R. H. Skaife, Surtees Society 57, Durham, 1872, p. 5.

21 Deleuze and Guattari, *Anti-Oedipus*, p. 30, stress the *social* character of fantasy.

22 'Let us assume that another man enters our perceptual sphere . . . Since, in this Nature and this world, my animate organism is the only body that is or can be constituted originally as an animate organism . . . the body over there, which is nevertheless apprehended as an animate organism, must have derived this sense by an *appreciative transfer from my animate organism*, and done so in a manner that excludes an actually direct . . . showing of the predicates belonging to an animate organism specifically . . . only a similarity connecting, within my primordial sphere, that body over there with my body can serve as the motivational basis for the *"analogizing" apprehension* of that body as another animate organism', Edmund Husserl, *Cartesian Meditations: an Introduction to Phenomenology*, trans. D. Cairns, The Hague, 1960, pp. 110–11.

23 *The Phenomenology of Perception and Other Essays*, ed. J. M. Edie, Evanston (IL), 1964, p. 118.

24 See for example the application in the context of medieval poetry, P. Zumthor, *Introduction à la poésie orale*, Paris, 1983, chapter 11: 'Présence du corps', pp. 193–206.

25 These points were emphasised in the context of human gesture in J.-C. Schmitt, 'The Ethics of Gesture', in *Fragments for a History of the Human Body*, ed. M. Feher, R. Naddaff and N. Tazi, New York, 1989, I, pp. 128–47, at p. 136.

26 See for example the case of life-change in entry to monasticism, as recommended by Hugh of St Victor in his guidelines to novices, *Institutio Novitiorum*, c. 12: 'De disciplina servanda in gestu', col. 938–44. For the concept of 'corporeal style' see J. Butler, *Gender Trouble: Feminism and the Subversion of Identity*, New York and London, 1990, pp. 139–41.

Reading a saint's body: rapture and bodily movement in the *vitae* of thirteenth-century beguines

Among the biographies of saintly beguines in the thirteenth-century Low Countries, the Life of Elisabeth of Spalbeek poses some of the most intriguing questions. Scholarly research on the Life came relatively late: although at least ten medieval manuscript copies of the Latin original have been preserved and the Life was translated into Middle English perhaps as early as the fourteenth century[1], demonstrating a certain interest in Elisabeth during the first 200 years after her death, the text was not included in the earliest editions of beguine *vitae* by Chrysostomos Henriquez[2] or by the Bollandists in their *Acta Sanctorum*.[3] Only in the late nineteenth century, when the Latin text and the Middle-English translation were edited almost simultaneously,[4] did the Life become more widely accessible, but even so it provoked little historical reflection until a few years ago.

This may be due in part to the fact that it is not a true *vita*: it is not a more or less comprehensive account of the saint's life and miracles composed after his or her death by the saint's confessor or another clerical admirer, on the basis of personal experience or information gathered from individuals close to the saint. The Life of Elisabeth of Spalbeek is a contemporary report[5] drawn up by Philip, abbot of Clairvaux, on Elisabeth's stigmata – the five wounds of Christ which Elisabeth bore on her hands, feet, and side[6] – and on her periodic re-enactment of the Passion story in her family home in Spalbeek. In the spring of 1267, while visiting the nearby Cistercian monastery of Herkenrode in the diocese of Liège, Philip heard of Elisabeth, then a twenty-year-old woman, and decided to meet her in order to examine the stigmata for himself. He witnessed her spiritual exercises, interviewed local devotees, and, upon his return to Clairvaux, sat down to write a factual, detailed account of his observations, in which he related how his initial scepticism gave way to enchantment when he saw these extraordinary phenomena with his own eyes. The result is a brief, almost journalistic portrait of a living saint that couples surprise and awe with an ethnographer's concern for meticulous description. For all we know, the controversy engendered by her wider fame in the 1270s actually dissuaded others from continuing Philip's work and keeping a record of her further activities. Whether she later went on to embrace the monastic life at Herkenrode, as has been presumed in the past, must remain an open question. A remarkable series of wall paintings (c.1350–1500) in Spalbeek's chapel of Our Lady commemorated her eucharistic piety for local devotees over the centuries, but no one recorded stories of miraculous events at her tomb, and there is very little evidence of sustained liturgical remembrance of her life and death. Finally, while Elisabeth may have been in touch with such prolific authors of mystical works as Hadewijch, she herself left no writings.[7]

The last observation brings us to the core of Elisabeth's religiosity. She did not express her feelings or provide guidance through writing. Her preferred media of communication were oral and visual. In a typical display of true insight, Philip dwells on the ways in which Elisabeth used her body to provide visual instruction. He relates how she showed him her wounds, which bled on Fridays; he narrates in vivid, sometimes gruesome, detail how she observed the Hours by acting out Christ's Passion story, from His capture to the deposition from the cross, and finally how her gestures evoked the stages of her mystical transport. Whatever misgivings he may initially have had, Philip firmly endorses Elisabeth's behaviour. He even adds the following statement, in which he affirms his faith in the authenticity of Elisabeth's stigmata, but also introduces some startling thoughts on the meaning of the miracle itself, and on the nature of Elisabeth's teaching:

> In the male sex, namely in the person of St Francis, God has revealed himself already. So that both sexes not only by the testimony of the Scriptures, but also by living examples of the human condition, may perceive on Christ's cross what should be honoured, venerated, adored, imitated, and loved, and so that no human, whom that Child of the Immaculate Virgin redeemed, can prevaricate, however illiterate and simple he or she may be, and say: 'I cannot understand such profound mysteries, because I am not lettered,' or 'because this is a closed book for me'. For now this illiterate man or woman can read, not in parchments or documents, but in the members and the body of this girl [i.e. Elisabeth], as a vivid and unmistakable Veronica, a living image and an animated history of redemption, as if he or she were literate.[8]

We might consider Philip's interpretation a mere application of Gregory's celebrated dictum, that works of visual art fulfil a didactic function in the Church and may serve as a substitute for reading.[9] Philip goes much further than that, however. He argues that even living individuals, through their bodily appearance, can set an example and preach without words: 'Truly no human can be forgiven for not gaining strength of faith, a desire for charity, and eagerness in devotion, when convinced by arguments that

have come alive and stand bodily before our eyes.'[10] The stigmata testify
to God's special grace and identify Francis and Elisabeth as divinely
chosen exemplars, one for each gender. That Philip deemed such role
models gender-specific may point to typically male assumptions on how
such transferences actually operate. He was certainly convinced of the
power wielded by the visual medium in general and by physical representation in particular; his understanding of gender appears to have en-
hanced rather than diminished his faith in the use of the medium.

Philip's defence of Elisabeth's behaviour frequently reverts to the analogy between her bodily enactment of the Passion story and a priest's
exposition of the Gospel. Rather than reading the Gospel to the faithful
she enacts it. Conversely, as a learned cleric writing for an audience im-
mersed in a written culture, Philip's account provides a running commentary on her behaviour, citing the appropriate verses of the Passion story.
When Elisabeth, standing with her arms extended in the form of the cross
and emulating Christ's last moments, shakes her head in agony, he notes:
'It was as though she explained to us the passage in the Gospel that says
"But the Son of man has nowhere to lay his head" (Matthew 8.20).' She
then cries, sighs, lowers her head on to the shoulder, and Philip again
explains that this 'signifies the words: "He bowed His head and gave up
His spirit" (John 19.30).'[11] How closely Philip identifies Elisabeth's role
with that of the priest in the liturgy of the mass is confirmed by his
concluding remarks:

> From what I have written above it is clear that this virgin, whose entire life is
> a miracle (indeed, her entire body itself is a miracle), with that same body
> represents and explains not only Christ and the Crucifixion, but also the mys-
> tical body of Christ, that is the Church. For in her observance of the Hours she
> personifies the rite of the entire Church divinely instituted and prefigured by
> the words 'Seven times a day do I praise thee' [Psalms 119, 164]; by the stig-
> mata and her penitential exercises she confirms her faith in the Passion; her
> jubilation and joy afterwards signify the Resurrection; her raptures symbolise
> the Ascension; her power, revelations, and spirituality exemplify the mission of
> the Holy Spirit.[12]

But if Elisabeth's role is likened to that of a priest in Philip's description,
and her bodily expression of the Passion story and of the mysteries of the
Church is said to match the power of the word, this leads to a number of
intriguing questions. Scholars tend to agree that around the year 1200
learned Christian discourse re-evaluated the virtues of the human body.[13]
It was increasingly argued that the female body, in particular, could be an
instrument to communicate religious concepts and feelings.[14] However, did
this change allow for a purely physical expression of religious feelings and
the acceptance of 'body language' as a didactic instrument equal to the
written or spoken word, as suggested by Philip? Were word and body now

regarded as competing powers? How coherent, how univocal is this 'body language'? How can it be 'read' (to use Philip's terminology), how is it interpreted?

The Life of Elisabeth of Spalbeek and the hagiographical literature surrounding other beguine saints of the Southern Low Countries during the thirteenth century may help us to answer these questions. Imbued with the well-known bridal mysticism of the period, and deeply rooted in the devotion to Christ's Passion, these stories contain numerous passages in which the body and bodily movement take centre stage, so to speak: bodies give external expression to experiences of mystical transport which spoken or written language did not and could not articulate. This paper examines how hagiographers attempted to translate those external signs, using a terminology and interpretative framework established in early Christianity and refined by twelfth- and early thirteenth-century mysticism. Focusing on their analysis of ecstasy and its aftermath we will understand, however, the inevitable limitations of their textual approach.

Early Christian thought perceived the body and all bodily activity with profound distrust. It added to the classical, non-Christian, renunciation of the body its own fascination with ascetic heroism; fueled by the gnostic association of evil with the body and its attachment to the material world, it proposed the abandonment of bodily pleasures[15] and redefined the body's function as the 'temple of the Holy Spirit'.[16] Partly in revulsion from the static human body, partly because the dynamic body invariably recalled pagan or Jewish religious practices, early Christianity renounced the use of dance in worship. Whether confronted with Germanic fertility charms or with survivals of the classical spectacle, the Christian mind identified dance as a pagan reminiscence, possibly even as anti-ritual, the domain of black magic.[17] From the early Middle Ages onwards church councils prohibited dancing in churches or in religious ceremonies; the endless repetition of these decrees must prove that such dances were not unusual, however, and some texts appear to single out women as the prime suspects.[18] In the later Middle Ages women repeatedly joined in dance as a means of participating in worship. The famous visitation record kept by Eudes of Rigaud, archbishop of Rouen (1248–75), shows that the Benedictine nuns of Villarceaux used to celebrate Holy Innocents' Day and the Feast of the Magdalene by (choral) dances, referring, in their defence before the archbishop, to David's dance before the Ark of the Covenant (2 Samuel 6).[19] Nevertheless late-medieval preachers and moralists continued to reject dance, not only as a manifestation of praise for God but even as secular rituals of socialisation and as recreation.

If dance could not be a legitimate part of worship, other forms of bodily movement, on the other hand, might be appropriate or even praiseworthy. A priest celebrating mass would naturally mark and illustrate stages in the liturgy to the faithful by gestures. His performance could very well be likened to that of a classical actor, mimicking dramatic development by gesture, as in Honorius Augustodunensis's *Gemma Animae*:

> Those who recited tragedies in theatres represented the deeds of fighters to the people by their gestures. In the same way our tragic actor, the priest, represents by his gestures the battle of Christ to the Christian people in the theatre of the church.[20]

Augustine's influential semiology dominated the interpretation of liturgical gestures. Such movements could be understood as signs, 'visible words', but they could also convey emotions and intentions. They are therefore complex and in constant need of clarification, even in the liturgy, where the priest's gestures are explained by words and context. These are no 'natural' gestures; their interpretation is a matter of convention.[21]

Outside the liturgy the external appearance of the body would similarly convey the inner state of the soul, to be interpreted by convention.[22] 'A state of mind is perceived in the comportment of the body . . . Hence a motion of the body is like an expression of the soul', in the words of Ambrose.[23] The consequences of this widely held view (informed by Greek as well as Scriptural thought) for the regulation of bodily movement were extensive. The subordination of the body to the soul required its regulation; conversely, moderation of the body might help to achieve greater control over the soul. The true Christian should therefore always obey the ancient precept of moderation, honouring restraint and dignity. This idea is underscored in Augustine's rule for monastic life, in which the famous injunction was given 'to avoid in gait and posture, in all your movements, all that may offend the gaze of anyone: you will comport yourself as demanded by your saintliness'.[24]

The same elements (conventional agreement, respect for the general *habitus* of the body) figure prominently in instructions for prayer which circulated from the twelfth century on, as well as in manuals for novices. Like many other treatises produced in this age of reappraisal, the manuals systematised Christian thought on the body's appearance and behaviour. Works like Hugh of St Victor's *De Institutione Novitiorum*[25] or the prayer manual attributed to Peter the Chanter[26] also argued that the body's appearance reflects a person's inner spirituality. Within the framework of a general discipline of the body they helped to distinguish between 'proper', well-controlled bodily movements or postures appropriate in worship, on the one hand, and improper ones, pertaining to the domain of 'gesticulation'. Prayer manuals prescribed such postures at the *inclinatio* (the inclination of the bust), *genuflectio* (genuflexion, with the bust held straight, or inclined), and *prostratio* (which could take the form of complete prostration of the body stretched out on the ground); such later manuals as the short

Dominican treatise known as *The Nine Ways of Prayer of St Dominic*,[27] written between 1260 and 1288, could include flagellation, but it is unclear whether this ancient penitential custom was generally classified as a mode of prayer.[28]

The beguine *vitae* of the thirteenth century similarly assume that a saint's appearance demonstrates grace and moderation, but conventional modes of prayer fulfil only a minor role in the saint's body language. Her example plays on a wider range of motions and postures than those prescribed in manuals. The Lives even include irregular modes of bodily behaviour which, in the Augustinian understanding, are ambivalent; as we shall see, they may depart from the ideal of moderation. Such are, of course, the demands of the hagiographical genre itself:[29] the lives record unusual deeds and derive their persuasive power precisely from extraordinary situations in which actions may deviate from the norms. As James of Vitry warns in his famous Life of Marie d'Oignies: 'When we read about what certain saints have done through the familiar counsel of the Holy Spirit, let us rather admire than imitate.'[30]

The *vitae* agree with the manuals that the inner state of the saint shines through her outer appearance. That is why James, in the first book of the Life of Marie, commented on her 'external appearance' after his chapters on her good works, her manual labour, her fasting, prayer, and penance. All of these represent activities that were externally visible and signified her inner grace.

> Her outward body demonstrated the composure of her inward mind [*interiorem mentis ejus compositionem*] . . . Thus the holy grace of the Spirit was reflected in her face from the fullness of her heart, so that many were spiritually refreshed by her appearance, moved to tears by her devotion, and, reading the unction of the Spirit in her face as if they were reading from a book, they knew what virtue came from her.[31]

Similarly Thomas of Cantimpré, the author of the Life of Lutgard of Aywières, reminds his readers that 'the body draws an exterior likeness from the intellectual consideration of the inward mind'.[32] More often than not the beguine saint's mind enjoys a state of total harmony. Of Juliana of Mont-Cornillon we are told: 'One very religious and holy man claimed that, during more than thirty years he could not remember seeing her move a member of her body even once without cause.' And her biographer exclaims: 'Her speech, her gait, her gestures, her expression . . . , what was not edifying and admirable in all of these?'[33]

When Philip of Clairvaux relates how Elisabeth of Spalbeek enacts the Passion story and reveals her stigmata to her audience, he hastens to add that 'there was never in her behaviour anything indecent or that could offend the eye . . . Even when she threw herself in a whirl involving her whole body, . . . nothing impudent was ever shown.' Philip is not thinking only of nudity, as the modern reader might suppose. There was *nihil incompositum*, he says, nothing 'out or order, out of control'.[34] James of Vitry asserts of Marie d'Oignies that he never heard her speak an idle word, nor was there ever 'any disorder in her appearance; she never displayed any dishonourable habit of the body . . . ; she never manifested any indecorous or disordered movement of the body.'[35]

The ideal appearance of the saint externalises her inner harmony. Yet dramatic lapses occur when the saint moves into the mode of rapture. If the saint shocks her audience by her often convulsive, catatonic, even violent behaviour that veers so widely from the overarching model of control, it is only when divine grace allows her to experience ecstasy. At that time, conventional body language seems suspended. Mystical transport naturally falls outside the range of conventional human behaviour. Nevertheless, the authors distinguish between gestures and postures that are extravagant but legitimised (and therefore conventionally interpretable) because they help to achieve mystical transport, and others that *signify* or 'express' ecstasy.

Since the earliest experiments of Christian asceticism a wide range of exercises were at the disposal of the supplicant to induce mystical transport: fasting and vigils, repeated genuflexion, the repetition of words. They had been practised in the monastic world for centuries, and beguines were familiar with them. It is possible, however, that they preferred other means to gradually shut out the sensual world. In his Life of Marie d'Oignies James recalls how Marie intoned a chant that lasted three days, commencing her final union with God on her death-bed:

> She rhythmically wove in sweet harmony the most sweet song about God . . .
> At first she began her antiphon in a very high and then even higher tone and
> . . . she sang praise for a very long time and inserted marvellous and, as it were,
> ineffable things into her song.[36]

Songs vibrate throughout many of these Lives, and in Ida of Louvain's ascent to ecstasy her tongue is called 'the mellifluous harp, the cymbals and tambourine . . . with which she sings over and over again the same song'.[37] Undoubtedly the textual metaphors are drawn from the sensual imagery of the Song of Songs, but rhythmical incantation and percussive sounds are common aids to ecstasy in non-Christian cultures and their effective use by medieval mystics cannot be excluded.[38]

Once ecstasy has set in, the saint's exterior aspect changes entirely. Ravishment is described as a moment frozen in time, in which no movement at all is made, the saint existing without feeling or breathing, immobile, 'abstracted from sensible things'.[39] The saint is 'rapt', literally 'taken away'. Lutgard becomes 'blind, blinded externally, for inwardly in her whole mind she was borne along in light', a classic example of the way in which the spiritual senses would compensate for the blocked, external senses. 'Who doubts', her biographer Thomas exclaims at this point, 'that the highest spiritual power of the mind is dulled by images of sensual things?'[40] And in his scientific work, the *De Natura Rerum*, he explains that 'the soul may see itself through itself, when it withdraws itself from all corporeal senses'.[41] The saint is now 'quiet, and her eyes were closed as if she were sleeping'.[42] Beatrice of Nazareth, upon receiving the Eucharist:

> lost the use of her outward senses so she could neither walk nor do any work with her hands . . . But why wonder at this? Just as wax melts before the fire [Psalm 67.3] . . . so her spirit melted before the deifying Sacrament, and her body before the spiritual joy flowing out from her interior and diffusing itself throughout her members with a wonderful sweetness.[43]

Most hagiographers portray the rapt saint 'outside the senses'. James of Vitry narrates Marie's transport under the heading of 'The Spirit of Understanding', referring to her final, deeper knowledge of God, devoid of physical sense perception:

> She was dried out in all humours of the senses and, purged of the cloud of all corporeal images and from every kind of imagination, she received in her soul simple and divine forms as in a mirror. Having cast aside sensible forms, the undivided and unchangeable species from above heaven reached her mind more purely as she approached more closely the highest, simple, and unchanging Majesty. When her subtle and enfeebled spirit, reduced to ashes by the fire of holy love, penetrated above the heavens . . . , there she finally found sublime rest, there she remained fixed without motion.[44]

This corresponds, naturally, to the very external definition of trance used by scholars of comparative religion: a condition of dissociation, characterised by the lack of voluntary movement, often accompanied by visions.

Total immobility, as described in the Life of Elisabeth[45] and in the many other examples cited above, signifies trance, that seems certain. But is this the only external manifestation of rapture? The body is said to be 'freed', 'overjoyed', and the saint experiences a sense of floating (levitation), or might lapse into dance, as in the 'mystical jubilus', a jubilant song of praise of cosmic dimension.[46] 'When she [a devout women known to James of Vitry] returned to herself, she was filled with such joy that once on a feast day when she was occupied with the rest of her thoughts, she was driven to show her inner joy by clapping her hands and by jumping up and down, like David before the Ark.'[47] Christina Mirabilis feels 'unchained', and then proceeds to dance in praise of the Lord.[48] This is the spiritual *tripudatio* which Beatrice performs as 'the delight breaking out in all members of her body, like an inebriating nectar, made her move excitedly'.[49] Elsewhere, 'affected by the sweetness of heavenly delight', she is said to 'be gesturing and dancing'.[50] Ida of Louvain, her senses returning after a beautiful vision of the Virgin and Child, 'expressed her feelings with bodily gestures as if exceedingly drunk'.[51] The forces overpowering the saint cannot be restrained. 'Whether she willed it or not,' Beatrice's biographer claims, 'the interior jubilation of her mind would betray itself outwardly either in laughter or dancing, in a gesture or in some other external manner.'[52]

Sometimes these powers seem to pose a threat. Juliana of Mont-Cornillon feels her body overflow with grace, but fears 'that it would burst and split down the middle'.[53] Once trance sets in, the textual metaphors split the body in parts or evoke its swelling and elongation. Proportion is lost, the very sign of disharmony. The Life of Ida of Louvain offers a 'marvellous' example. One night, Ida shares her bed with a young beguine who came to visit her in attendance of the feast of Epiphany:

> At twilight, both took to a bed that had been made up, and the beguine curled up for some rest. Ida, however, found those lingering thoughts of the Saviour's infancy making too strong and abrupt an impact on her mind to allow her eyes any sleep or her eyelids any slumber [Psalm 131.4]. In fact, her spirit leapt into such an abyss of eternal joyousness that the confines of her heart could not contain the abounding sweetness and delight – so much so that the individual members of her body began wondrously to swell to so monstrous a hugeness that one of her feet succumbed under the weight and burst asunder, leaving a wound as lasting tell-tale evidence of the hurt. Just imagine how Ida would then have crowded and squeezed her bedfellow, had the latter not shrunk aside and left the whole bed to her! How puzzled she must have been as to the meaning of so sudden a corpulence, as she confined herself to the extreme edge of the bed and carefully watched to see how the miracle would end. This did not take long, for Ida, who just now had been commandeering the whole width of the bed for her bloated self, barely allowing her fellow that tiny extremity, forthwith and wondrously so disappeared and so withdrew her bodily companionship as to leave empty the bed she had thus filled.[54]

The body loses its form altogether in the Life of Christina Mirabilis, whose

> limbs were gathered together into a ball as if they were hot wax and all that one could perceive of her was a round mass. Only after her physical senses had restored her limbs to their proper places [i.e. after trance], like a hedgehog her rolled up body returned to its proper shape and the limbs that had been bent formlessly once again were spread out.[55]

Such scenes occurred repeatedly in this Life, whenever, in fact, Christina is subject to rapture: 'When ravished she would roll and whirl around like a hoop. She would roll and whirl with such extreme violence that the individual limbs of her body could not be distinguished.'[56] After coming to her senses, the individual limbs would be restored to their proper place, and quiet would descend upon her again. Interpretation of these movements therefore tended to relate the conflict between the intake of God's grace and the terrible forces it releases. The onset of ecstasy arrests the saint's normally controlled demeanour. Once the mind is filled with the full power of the experience, that power will manifest itself outwardly in dancing and jumping about, or in kinaesthetic or other extraordinary behaviour of the limbs.[57] We do see an internal logic, a 'grammar' of movement to be perceived outwardly, but its translation required more than visual perception. How to interpret the extraordinary movement depended on inside knowledge of mystical theory as well as on a more general assessment of the saint's action. It proved to be extremely difficult, if not impossible, to ascertain whether divine intervention or demonic possession produced the sort of convulsive behaviour described above. Even experienced observers of beguine mysticism could fail to distinguish between the two. In the Life of Lutgard of Aywières, Thomas of Cantimpré mentions the case of a nun whose limbs and mouth contracted by what he assumed was diabolical possession,[58] but James of Vitry, in his Life of Marie d'Oignies, regards very similar behaviour as a sign of the woman's great devotion.[59] Great confusion beset the clergy of the southern Low Countries during the so-called dance-craze of 1374, when groups of wild dancers roamed the region. Madeleine Braekman has shown how their frenetic movements puzzled ecclesiastical authorities, who in the end assumed that these men and women were possessed by demons, yet refrained from condemning them.[60]

No consistent Christian code emerged to read movement of the body outside liturgy and prayer. Extravagant bodily behaviour could only be judged and interpreted by a sympathetic observer whose initial stance would be defined in a larger context: it would take into account a wider range of phenomena than the trance state alone or its immediate physical expression. 'Speaking in tongues', prophesying, clairvoyance, the transmission of messages beyond death, and, of course, miraculous healing, all of these entered the Christian matrix of saintly behaviour and framed the saint's bodily appearance. It was on those grounds, ultimately, that Christians tended to judge whether a person's abnormal behaviour indicated grace or demonic possession. Only after extensive dealings with Elisabeth, after interrogating the local clergy who testified to her saintliness and her powers of clairvoyance, and finally, persuaded by the miracle of the stigmata, did Philip condone Elisabeth's behaviour.

She may not have been the only beguine saint whose extravagant motions drew comments from those around her. Few are the beguines who managed to escape the eyes of their companions. Even though she might feel outraged by the attention bestowed upon her, as a semi-religious not living in monastic enclosure she was subject to constant public scrutiny. Her most private ecstasies could turn into a 'performance'. But reading her movements 'correctly' also required a privileged interpreter, the hagiographer.

The body language of the *vitae* contained elements of conventional prayer postures and reaffirmed the conviction that the saint's appearance expressed the composure of her inner spiritual harmony. Ecstasy and its immediate response, however, resulted in action that involved a very different scale of gestures. This behaviour, too, could be read by the observer, and translated into words by an interpreter familiar with their mystical underpinnings. Nevertheless, ambiguity loomed large when the body ventured into the world of rapture. Harmony gave way to disorder, proportion to distortion, and Christian affinity with the body staked its boundaries.

NOTES

Early versions or portions of this essay were given at the 1991 Congress of the Medieval Institute at Kalamazoo, Michigan, the Harvard Divinity School (October 1991), the conference at the Algemeen Rijksarchief in Brussels on Late Medieval Spirituality organised by the Belgian Committee for Comparative Church History and the Belgian Historical Institute in Rome (November 1992), and the 1993 Congress of the Centre for Medieval Studies in Toronto; I am grateful to Rosemary Hale and Ludo Milis for their kind invitations and comments, and to Jeffrey Hamburger, Susan Rodgers and Robert Sweetman for their invaluable suggestions. As will be evident from the notes, the essay is greatly indebted to the research on the Life of Elisabeth of Spalbeek which I have undertaken jointly with Joanna E. Ziegler, to whom, as always, I extend my warmest thanks.

1 The textual tradition is currently being re-examined. For a preliminary check-list of manuscripts, see Patricia Deery Kurtz, 'Mary of Oignies, Christine the Marvelous, and Medieval Heresy,' *Mystics Quarterly*, XIV, 1988, pp. 186–96 (especially pp. 195–6) and Amandus Bussels, 'Was Elisabeth van Spalbeek Cisterciënserin in Herkenrode?', *Cîteaux in de Nederlanden*, II, 1951, pp. 43–54 (p. 43, note 1).
2 *Quinque prudentes virgines*, Antwerp, 1630.
3 See, however, the note on the saint's cult in *Acta Sanctorum* (*AA.SS.*) October, VIII, Paris, 1866, p. 384. Elisabeth's feast-day was locally established on 19 November rather than 19 October; the *Acta Sanctorum* only reaches 10 November.
4 *Vita Elizabeth sanctimonialis in Erkenrode, Ordinis Cisterciensis, Leodiensis dioecesis*, in *Catalogus codicum hagiographicorum bibliothecae Regiae Bruxellensis*, I, Brussels, 1886, pp. 362–78 (henceforth cited as *VE*), and K. Horstmann, 'Prosalegenden: Die Legenden des Ms. Douce 114', *Anglia*, VIII, 1885, pp. 102–95, in particular pp. 107–18.
5 See Simone Roisin, *L'Hagiographie cistercienne dans le diocèse de Liège au XIIIe siècle*, Louvain and Brussels, 1947, pp. 70–2, and on the notion of living sainthood, Aviad M. Kleinberg, *Prophets in Their Own Country: Living Saints and the Making of Sainthood in the Later Middle Ages*, Chicago and London, 1992.
6 In Elisabeth's case the stigmata also included the marks left by the crown of thorns (*VE*, p. 376).
7 See Walter Simons and Joanna E. Ziegler, 'Phenomenal Religion in the Thirteenth Century and its Image: Elisabeth of Spalbeek and the Passion Cult', *Studies in Church History*, XXVII, 1990, pp. 117–26, with a brief discussion of the paintings in the Spalbeek chapel and observations on the controversial nature of Elisabeth's *stigmata*. G. Hendrix, 'Hadewijch benaderd vanuit de tekst over de 22e volmaakte,' *Leuvense Bijdragen*, LXVII, 1978, pp. 129–45 reviews the possibility that Hadewijch and Elisabeth knew each other. We may

assume that Elisabeth's fame as a visionary suffered from her ambiguous testimony in the so-called 'affair of Pierre de la Broce' (1276–77), a bizarre intrigue at the court of Philippe III of France following the sudden death of the dauphin, when her powers of clairvoyance failed to give satisfactory information. For the documents in the case, see J. de Gaulle, 'Documents historiques', *Bulletin de la Société de l'Histoire de France*, I, 1844, pp. 87–100; the most recent, though not always accurate, account is by Richard Kay, 'Martin IV and the Fugitive Bishop of Bayeux', *Speculum*, XL, 1965, pp. 460–83.

8 *VE*, p. 373.

9 A recent stating of the problem of Gregory's saying and its history in the Middle Ages may be found in Lawrence G. Duggan, 'Was Art Really the "Book of the Illiterate"' *Word and Image*, V, 1989, pp. 227–51. See also Celia M. Chazelle, 'Pictures, Books, and the Illiterate: Pope Gregory I's Letters to Serenus of Marseilles', *ibid.*, VI, 1990, pp. 138–53; David Freedberg, *The Power of Images: Studies in the History and Theory of Response*, Chicago and London, 1989, pp. 161–7, 398–402, and, for the thirteenth-century tendency to represent rather than imagine elements of faith, Hans Belting, *Das Bild und sein Publikum im Mittelalter: Form und Funktion früher Bildtafeln der Passion*, Berlin, 1981, pp. 126–41. For Gregory's principle of 'teaching through word and *deed* (rather than image)', and especially its understanding in the twelfth century, see Caroline Walker Bynum, *Docere Verbo et Exemplo: An Aspect of Twelfth-Century Spirituality*, Harvard Theological Studies 31, Missoula, Montana, 1979, pp. 15–18, and *passim*.

10 *VE*, p. 378.

11 *VE*, p. 370.

12 *VE*, p. 378.

13 The literature on this subject is abundant. See for instance David L. d'Avray, 'Some Franciscan Ideas About the Body', *Archivum Franciscanum Historicum*, LXXXIV, 1991, pp. 343–63; Caroline Walker Bynum, 'Material Continuity, Personal Survival, and the Resurrection of the Body: A Scholastic Discussion in Its Medieval and Modern Contexts', *History of Religions*, XX, 1990, pp. 51–85, reprinted (with some changes and illustrations) in her collection *Fragmentation and Redemption: Essays on Gender and the Human Body in Medieval Religion*, New York, 1991, pp. 239–97.

14 See most recently Caroline Walker Bynum, 'The Female Body and Religious Practice in the Later Middle Ages', in *Fragments for a History of the Human Body*, I, New York, 1989, pp. 160–219, reprinted in *Fragmentation and Redemption*, pp. 181–238.

15 Aline Rousselle, *Porneia: de la maîtrise du corps à la privation sensorielle, Ile–IVe siècles de l'ère Chrétienne*, Paris, 1983; Peter Brown, *The Body and Society: Men, Women, and Sexual Renunciation in Early Christianity*, New York, 1988.

16 See especially Robert Markus, *The End of Ancient Christianity*, Cambridge, 1990, pp. 81–3.

17 Teresa Berger, *Liturgie und Tanz: anthropologische Aspekte, historischen Daten, theologische Perspektiven*, St Ottilien, 1985, pp. 15–29 with references to the most important texts. Yet Christian authors continued to adopt dance imagery as metaphors of religious feeling; see the remarkable work by James Miller, *The Cosmic Dance in Classical and Christian Antiquity*, Toronto, 1985.

18 Pierre Riché, 'Danses profanes et religieuses dans le haut Moyen Age', in *Histoire sociale, sensibilités collectives et mentalités. Mélanges Robert Mandrou*, Paris, 1985, pp. 159–67 (with older bibliography); Jeannine Horowitz, 'Les danses cléricales dans les églises au Moyen Age', *Le Moyen Age*, XCV, 1989, pp. 279–92; Jean-Claude Schmitt, *La Raison des gestes dans l'Occident médiéval*, Paris, 1990, pp. 90–1.

19 T. Bonnin, ed., *Regestrum Visitationum archiepiscopi Rothomagensis: Journal des visites pastorales d'Eude Rihaud, archevêque de Rouen 1248–1269*, Rouen, 1852, p. 471. Cf. Horowitz, 'Les danses', p. 285. On David's dance in Christianity, see Miller, *The Cosmic Dance*, pp. 389–92, and for the dance metaphor as a sign of mystical joy, see below p. 17

20 *Gemma Animae*, I, 83, ed. Jean-Paul Migne, *Patrologia Latina* (henceforth *PL*), CLXXII, col. 570, cited by Karl F. Morrison, *History as a Visual Art in the Twelfth-Century Renaissance*, Princeton, 1990, p. 68. Honorius goes on to explain the specific gestures of the priest

during mass; elsewhere in the same work (*Gemma Animae*, I, p. 139; *PL*, CLXXII, col. 587) he argues in defence of sacred dance, see Horowitz, 'Les danses', p. 281.

21 Schmitt, *La Raison des gestes*, 79–84. Cf. Morisson, *History as a Visual Art*, p. 46.

22 See Dilwyn Knox, '*Disciplina:* The Monastic and Clerical Origins of European Civility', in John Monfasani and Ronald G. Musto, eds., *Renaissance Society and Culture: Essays in Honor of Eugene F. Rice Jr*, New York, 1991, pp. 107–35, especially pp. 107–14, and Schmitt, *La Raison des gestes*, pp. 68–79.

23 *De officiis*, 1.108, ed. *PL*, XVI, col. 16.

24 *Praeceptum*, 4.3, ed. L. Verheijen, *La Règle de Saint Augustin*, Paris, 1967, I, p. 423. During the Gregorian Reform the *Praeceptum* became an influential guideline for the regulation of collective religous life for both men and women.

25 *PL*, CLXXVI, cols. 925–52.

26 Richard Trexler, ed, *The Christian at Prayer: An Illustrated Prayer Manual Attributed to Peter the Chanter (d.1197)* Binghamton, New York, 1987.

27 Simon Tugwell, 'The Nine Ways of Prayer of St Dominic: A Textual Study and Critical Edition', *Mediaeval Studies*, XLV, 1985, pp. 1–124.

28 Cf. Louis Gougaud, 'Les gestes de la prière', and 'La discipline, instrument de pénitence', in his *Dévotions et pratiques ascétiques du Moyen Age*, Paris, 1925, pp. 1–42 and pp. 175–99.

29 Cf. Trexler, *The Christian at Prayer*, p. 39, on the parallel between the Chanter's Manual and his Life of St Lucian, in which, on one occasion, he described the saint's gestures as (intentionally) 'deformed, irregular, and . . . uncomposed'.

30 *Vita B. Mariae Oigniacensis*, ed. in *AASS*, June V, pp. 542–72 (henceforth cited as *VM*), quotation from I, 1, § 12, p. 550. I have used, with some emendations, the translation by Margot H. King, *The Life of Marie d'Oignies by Jacques de Vitry*, Saskatoon, Saskatchewan, 1986. For the exemplary function of the Life of Christina Mirabilis, see Robert Sweetman, 'Christine of Saint-Trond's Preaching Apostolate: Thomas of Cantimpré's Hagiographical Method Revisited,' *Vox Benedictina*, LX, 1992, pp. 67–97.

31 *VM*, I, 4, § 38, p. 556. Cf. King, *The Life of Marie d'Oignies*, p. 40, where *compositio* is translated more literally. We note, in passing, that James's comment includes Philip of Clairvaux's book metaphor, and that he, too, claims that the body can be 'read'.

32 *Vita Lutgardis*, ed. in *AASS*, June III, 187–210 (henceforth *VL*), quotation from I, 2, § 23, p. 201. Here, too, my translation differs somewhat from that by Margot H. King, *The Life of Lutgard of Aywières by Thomas of Cantimpré*, Toronto, 1987.

33 *Vita B. Julianae Corneliensis*, ed. in *AASS*, April I, pp. 435–75 (henceforth cited as *VJ*), quotation from II, 5, § 25, p. 465, as translated by Barbara Newman, *The Life of Juliana of Mont-Cornillon*, Toronto, 1987, p. 110.

34 *VE*, p. 373.

35 *VM*, I, 2, § 20, p. 551. The passage echoes St Ambrose's *On Virgins*, 2.2, § 7, ed. *PL*, XVI, col. 209, on the Virgin Mary: 'There was nothing presumptuous in her glance, nothing insolent in her speech, nothing unseemly in her acts. There was not a frivolous movement, not an unrestrained step, nor was her voice petulant; as the nature of the body reflects the mind, she was the very image of modesty.'

36 *VM*, II, 11, § 99–101, pp. 569–70.

37 *Vita B. Idae de Lovanio*, ed. in *AASS*, April II, pp. 156–89 (henceforth *VI*), quotation from I, 5, § 28, p. 166. I have used, with minor changes, the translation by Martinus Cawley, *Ida of Louvain*, Lafayette, Oregon, 1990. Cf. *VE*, p. 365.

38 See the influential article by Rodney Needham, 'Percussion and Transition,' *Man*, II, 1967, pp. 606–14, and Gilbert Rouget, *Music and Trance: A Theory of the Relations Between Music and Possession*, Chicago and London, 1985.

39 *VM*, I, 2, § 25, p. 552.

40 *VL*, III, 1, 1, p. 204. For the concept of the spiritual senses, see Mariette Canévet, 'Sens spirituel,' in *Dictionnaire de Spiritualité*, XIV, Paris, 1990, cols. 598–617.

41 *Thomas Cantimpratensis Liber De Natura Rerum*, 2.3.5, ed. H. Boese, I, Berlin and New York, 1973, p. 84. Cf. King, *The Life of Lutgard*, p. 210.

42 Thomas of Cantimpré, *Vita S. Christinae Mirabilis, Virginis Trudonopolitanae*, ed. in *AASS*, July V, pp. 637–60 (henceforth *VC*), quotation from 3, § 36, p. 656. See also the translation by Margot H. King, *The Life of Christina of Saint-Trond by Thomas of Cantimpré*, Saskatoon, Saskatchewan, 1986.

43 *Vita Beatricis de Nazareth*, 1.80, ed. L. Reypens, originally published as *Vita Beatricis: De autobiografie van de Z. Beatrijs van Tienen O. Cist., 1200–1268*, Antwerp, 1964, reprinted with an introduction and parallel English translation in Roger DeGanck, *The Life of Beatrice of Nazareth 1200–1268*, Kalamazoo, 1991 (henceforth *VB*), p. 102.

44 *VM*, II, 9, § 81.

45 *VE*, pp. 365, 369.

46 See Jeffrey F. Hamburger, *The Rothschild Canticles: Art and Mysticism in Flanders and the Rhineland circa 1300*, New Haven and London, 1990, pp. 58–9, 100, on joyful dance as a metaphor for a stage in mystical ascent or an expression of mystical union; Gertrud Jaron Lewis, 'The Mystical Jubilus,' *Vox Benedictina*, I, 1984, pp. 237–47; II, 1986, pp. 327–37; V, 1988, pp. 164–74; and Roger DeGanck, *Towards Unification with God: Beatrice of Nazareth in Her Context*, Kalamazoo, 1991, pp. 389–90.

47 *VM*, prologue, § 7, p. 548.

48 *VC*, 3, § 36, p. 658.

49 *VB*, I, 79, p. 102.

50 *VB*, III, 205, p. 236.

51 *VI*, I, 33, p. 166.

52 *VB*, I, 74, p. 96.

53 *VJ*, I, 4, § 19, p. 449.

54 *VI*, I, 31, pp. 166–7 (I have followed closely the clever translation by Cawley, *Ida of Louvain*, p. 22). On the capacity of bodies to be 'flooded' by the beatific vision, see Joseph Goering, 'The *De Dotibus* of Robert Grosseteste,' *Mediaeval Studies*, XLIV, 1982, pp. 83–109; Sweetman, 'Christine of Saint-Trond's Preaching Apostolate,' 81.

55 *VC*, 2, § 16, p. 653.

56 *VC*, 3, § 36, p. 656.

57 Cf. Schmitt, *La Raison des gestes*, p. 319.

58 *VL*, II, 1, § 10, p. 198.

59 *VM*, prologue, § 7, p. 548.

60 'La dansomanie de 1374: hérésie ou maladie?', *Revue du Nord*, LXVI, 1981, pp. 339–55; see also Paul Fredericq, *De Secten der geeselaars en der dansers in de Nederlanden tijdens de XIVe eeuw*, Brussels, 1897.

Chaste bodies: frames and experiences

The textual construction of the chaste body, which (despite such important male models of chastity as Christ, St John, Galahad and Perceval) is
predominantly that of the chaste female body, has a long history.[1] At first
sight, it seems both a depressing history and one without change. Medieval treatises, letters and *vitae* continue to reiterate and develop themes
and images from patristic accounts of chastity and virginity in a relatively
stable literary repertoire.[2] Virgin and chaste women are represented as
sealed away from the world, whether in convent, chamber, cell or
anchorhold, awaiting a future in the court of heaven as brides of the
Lamb. In historical practice, as in representation, such women's bodies
are placed within the custody of their own internalised vigilance, decorum
and shame, and within the physical enclosure of veiling and claustration.[3]
Chaste female spirituality is, moreover, located in bodies without histories,
locked away both from outer event and physiological change. The ideal of
virginity as the supreme form of chastity occludes the bodily history of
biological wives, mothers, widows, who must aspire to the condition of a
virginity imaged in bodies without menstrual and menopausal phases.[4]
This writing-out of women is part of a thematic preoccupation with their
death in the literature of chastity. The chaste and enclosed woman is
frequently represented as entombed in her chamber or cell, and the ideal
virgin's life reserved until her death and entry to the court of heaven. In
innumerable exemplary biographies throughout the Middle Ages and
in later times, the chief business of the narrative heroine of chastity, the
virgin martyr, is to die, tortured and dismembered in the *passio* of loyalty
to her bridegroom, Christ.[5] From the celebration of the exhumed intact
bodies of Anglo-Saxon virgin princesses to medieval and later narratives
of virgin martyrs, the best virgin, it seems, is always a dead virgin: 'What
her virtue [mægen] was, was more fully made known after her death
[ma æfter hire deaðe gecyðed wæs].'[6] A review of virginity's long history
of representation and social practice might well conclude that the literature
of female chastity is the literature of textual oppression and misogyny, of
the containment of women and their absence from history. But such an
argument is plausible only at a level of generality which evades historicisa-
tion. It simplifies the complexity with which these representations operate

in practice and neglects women's readings and reactions to the textual construction of female chaste bodies. I want here to look at an important post-Norman Conquest chastity text, in its context and in the light of these concerns.

The chaste body's death to the world and its containment have seldom been more powerfully imaged than in a famous group of vernacular English texts, the early thirteenth-century *Guide for Anchoresses (Ancrene Wisse)*, and the saints' lives, homilies, and meditations associated with it.[7] As with nuns, virginity was desirable and chastity compulsory for anchoresses (who might be laywomen or professed religious). Anchoritism, especially prevalent in twelfth- and thirteenth-century Britain, and particularly undertaken by upper-class English and Anglo-Norman women, makes containment and burial especially explicit as the proper state of the chaste body.[8] Having taken vows (of stability and obedience as well as chastity), anchoresses were often enclosed to the ritual accompaniment of the Office for the Dead.[9] The intensity with which the *Guide* represents female chastity as bodily enclosure is sometimes seen as fundamentally misogynistic.[10] This may be understandable but is not satisfactory: such a position neglects the whole discursive matrix of text and audience in favour of the viewpoint of the author, and makes inadequate allowance for the subject positions and responses of the readers. It also obscures the respect and admiration repeatedly displayed by the author for his audience, as well as the difficulties and ambivalences of our own response. As Anne Savage has pointed out, 'love, respect and admiration [for his audience on the *Guide* author's part] are confusing when we cannot simply reject them as hatred in disguise'.[11] Moreover, as I shall argue, to attend to the undoubted force and power with which the *Guide* images the anchoritic life as a contained and sealed-up female body *only* as a successful expression of misogyny is to reiterate the image's power without allowing for all that it does not contain.

It is useful first of all to remember the inherent theoretical and practical mobility of medieval virginity. Where modern virginity is undifferentiated absence – 'a mere preamble, or waiting-room to be got out of as soon as possible,'[12] medieval virginity has bodily presence and a theoretical morphology. An important image of virginity, as Barbara Newman and Clarissa Atkinson have pointed out, is that of balsam in a fragile vessel.[13] In the *Guide*,

If anyone were carrying a precious liquid, a costly drink such as balsam is, in a delicate vessel, balm in a brittle glass, would she not, unless she were foolish, keep away from the crowd? *We have this treasure in earthen vessels, says the Apostle* (2 Corinthians 4.7). This frail vessel, that is, woman's flesh, although the balm, the balsam contained in it is virginity (or, after the loss of virginity, chaste cleanness), this frail vessel is as fragile as any glass, for once it is broken it may never be mended to its former wholeness any more than glass can ... if you lived in the world's crowd, you might, at a slight encounter, lose altogether [virginity and cleanness in your frail flesh], like some miserable wretches in the world who clash together, break their vessels, and shed their purity.[14]

Like other accounts of virginity, this passage reiterates the construction of the female chaste body as a sign of fallen humanity's alienation from its own properly angelic nature (the treasure is in an earthen vessel), and values female virginity as a reminder and a promise of pre-lapsarian and post-Resurrection integrity.[15] That virginity should be a preservative balsam seems appropriate, for the passage also legitimates the enclosure of women and the value of entombing them: since only dead virgins can with security be declared to have successfully borne their balsam in a vessel unshattered by time and history, the fragile vessel must itself be contained.

Yet the passage both insists on the bodily absoluteness of virginity ('once it is broken, it may never be mended'), *and* asserts its applicability to more than the technically intact among its audience ('the balsam contained in it is virginity, or *after the loss of virginity*, chaste cleanness'). In the same way, medieval theory of the three estates of the flesh (marriage, chastity, virginity) positions virginity as both unique and the best of the three in a graded hierarchy.[16] Conceptually and pragmatically virginity is not as fixed and absolute a state as its images strive to suggest. Even for the *virgo intacta*, virginity is made both a matter of absolute bodily inscription and of negotiation: it can be undermined and negated by lustful thoughts or even by spiritual pride in being a virgin. So Christina of Markyate, after years of sustained resistance in which she preserved her virginity against parental violence and enforced betrothal before finally escaping into her religious career, is still, on the verge of profession, anxious as to

what she should say, when the bishop enquired during the ceremony of consecration about her virginity. For she was mindful of the thoughts and stings of the flesh with which she had been troubled, and even though she was not conscious of having fallen either in deed or in desire, she was chary of asserting that she had escaped unscathed.[17]

The virginity of a virgin is not simply technical intactness, and devotional and prescriptive texts for women are careful not to exclude the wedded and widowed (often the most economically powerful) from their audiences. Such texts prescribe virginity, but address chastity, frequently reinscribing marriage and maternity in the spiritual life of all women even as they offer virgins as role models to mothers and widows. Though these manoeuvres carry their own essentialising implication of confining women to the body, it is not a simple or undifferentiated confinement, and neither in theory or practice is it successfully absolute and definitive.

The *Guide* invokes virginity as superior but says nothing inapplicable to chastely married or widowed women. Its primary construction of the chaste body applies to all three states: in the ordering and relation of its eight sections, the *Guide* enacts the confinement of the anchoress in her cell and thus generalises enclosure and sealing to the entire person rather than being more narrowly concerned with the hymen.[18] If her seclusion from the world is to be sustainable, the recluse must have a servant, who will fetch food and fuel; similarly, in her *Guide*, the 'handmaiden' rule – an outer rule of advice on practical matters – serves the inner spiritual rule – 'the lady rule': the outer rule 'is only an instrument in the building of this work; it is like the handmaid (þuften), serving the lady (þe leafdi) in the governance of the heart (to riwlin þe heorte)'.[19] Between the handmaiden 'Outer Rule' in Part Eight and Part One's prescription of hours and devotions, the *Guide* progresses from the custody of the anchoress's senses, to her inner feelings, to her temptations, confession, penance and, climactically, in Part Seven, to the anchoress's heart and her love for her suitor, Christ. Her *Guide* is thus itself a body model, structuring the anchoress's physical and spiritual existence as a series of enclosures: her cell and her body enclosing her heart and her soul, her heart 'God's chamber'.[20]

Of course every *regula* in some sense constructs an ideal body which all members of a community accept as their own template body, and many *regulae* distinguish between inner and outer rules as, respectively, rules of crucial spiritual formation which must be observed and pragmatic daily prescriptions which can be adjusted according to need and circumstance. But the *Guide*'s series of enclosures mapped on to a female body-cell is uniquely explicit.[21] Contained and containing, the recluse's body-boundaries are as intensely regulated as those of the cell itself, and form a frontier across which significant egresses and entrances may occur. In Part One, she must be 'wiðute blinde', blind to the outer world, while the tiny window of her cell is veiled with the same intricate rhetorical care as is devoted to the custody of her eyes.[22] In Part Two, she must 'remain inside, firmly enclosed, not only bodily, for that is least important, but with regard to your five senses and above all, with regard to your heart in which is the life of the soul'.[23] In Part Six, the anchorhold and the anchoress's penitential life within it are identified with Christ's suffering and the Virgin's womb:

> for the womb is a narrow dwelling, where our Lord was a recluse . . . If you then suffer bitterness in a narrow place, you are his fellows, recluse as he was in Mary's womb. Are you imprisoned within four walls? And he in a narrow cradle, nailed on the cross, enclosed tight in a stone tomb. Mary's womb and this tomb were his anchorhouses . . . you too will go out of both your anchorhouses as he did, without a break, and leave them both whole. That will be when the spirit goes out in the end, without break or blemish, from its two houses. One of them is the body, the other is the outer house, which is like the wall around a castle.[24]

In its body-cell homologies, the *Guide* unites allegorical and medical traditions. It conflates the neo-Galenic body and its permeable fluid systems with the long-standing image of the body as figurative edifice, an image newly intense and prevalent in late twelfth- and early thirteenth-century culture.[25] The body as building and the body as vessel reinforce each other in a powerful and complex account of the container con-tained.[26] The virtuoso development of synaesthetic metaphor into con-vincing conceptual and affective enclosure is typical.[27] So, to take just one example, in the following passage from Part Two on the custody of the senses, the devil's march down the throat, the floating heart, the smell of the voice and God's ear near the tongue help form a refigured sensory universe within the recluse's enclosure such as makes attention to the world outside supererogatory:

> The enemy from hell with his army goes all the way through a mouth which is always open, into the heart . . . Often, when we start to say something, we mean to speak few and well-placed words. But the tongue is slippery, for it wades in wetness, and slides lightly from few words into many . . . from a drop, [speech] grows into a great flood which drowns the soul. For with such floating words the heart also floats away, so that for a long time afterwards she cannot be properly gathered back to herself . . . 'The nearer our mouth is to worldly speech, the farther it is from God when it speaks to him, and prays any prayers to him.' It is for this reason that we often cry out to him and he turns himself away from our voice and will not hear it: because it smells to him of all the world's babbling and her jabbering. Whoever, then, wants God's ear near her tongue, let her turn from the world, or she may be crying out for a long time before God hears her.[28]

Much of the *Guide*'s account of sense experience focuses on entry and impermeability, enclosure and leakage, sealing and opening. Throughout the *Guide*, the recluse is offered a bodily self of intense sensory vividness, imaged in gesture, 'felunge', smell, taste, fluids and kinetic impulse, blushing, blazing and flaming with shame and desire, messily bound to the pot of the belly, straining towards the mobility and lightness which will be the soul's bride-gifts in heaven.[29] The recluse's bodily experience in the cell is represented as a constant struggle for regulation of these permeabilities: the winds and floods of sin and redemption whistle and pour through her body–cell, the beasts of temptation prowl round and through it, and the devil and Christ woo and assault the castle of her body-heart. In a culminating image in Part Seven, love becomes the liquid incendiary of medieval siege and naval warfare, to be poured out by the recluse in defence of her castle even as it kindles her response to Christ.[30]

In her fecund tomb, 'dead to þe worlde & cwic þah to Criste', the consecrated anchoress ('smiriet ancre') is encouraged to be as one of the three Marys bringing 'aromaz [Christ's] bodi forte smirien', by offering the 'swotnesse of deuot heorte' to her soul's bridegroom.[31] Neither the anointed anchoress nor the anointed Christ are dead to each other: Christ 'stretches himself towards us as one who is anointed (ismiret), and makes himself smooth and soft to touch', and the anchoress is to 'touch him with as much love as [she has] once felt for any special person with the promise that he will be "þin to don wið al þt tu wilnest"'.[32] This mobility of response in the tomb may stand in a sense for the anchoress's life as constructed by the *Guide*. Questing within the boundaries of her cell for ever greater internalised regulation of this physiology and psyche in union with her suitor Christ, the stasis of complete control over the fluids and impulses of her body must elude the anchoress before physical death, even as she strives to live a death to the world. Her stable and chaste enclosure, like her body, is dynamic, held in place by the tension of fixture within an economy of unconquerable drives and sensations matched by an imperatively-enjoined volition to control and transcendence. Daily reading of the *Guide* (enjoined in Part Eight's 'Outer Rule', pp. 148/9–10) constantly reiterates this aspiration and its difficulties. Like virginity, stable chastity of the body recedes the more intensely it is sought; as the *Guide* itself asks, 'In the middle of delights and ease and fleshly comforts, who was ever chaste?'[33]

It is important to note, however, that the forcefulness of this account cannot simply be ascribed to dualist, flesh-hating misogyny, accurate as such terms may seen at certain moments in the *Guide*. In Part Four, for example, the anchoress is asked

> from your flesh's vessel, does there come the smell of aromas or sweetbalm? . . . Your flesh – what fruit does it bear in all its orifices? Amid the nobility of your face, which is the fairest part, between the taste of your mouth and the smell of your nose, do you not carry as it were two privy-holes? Are you not come from foul slime? Are you not a vessel of filth? *Philosophus: Sperma es fluidum, vas stercorum, esca vermium.*[34]

Concern with the promiscuously fluid contents of the body–vessel seems here as disgusted as anything in the *Guide*'s *contemptus mundi* source materials.[35] But the context is that of a complexly developed remedy against pride, a meditation on the body's filth and weakness, to be used in specific ways against temptation. Although carnality and uses of the senses deemed sinful are routinely spoken of as filthy, the flesh is presented as essentially filthy only here and more briefly in one other passage (each time carefully qualified and contextualised),[36] while in its practical directions for the body in Part Eight, the ascetic practice of not washing is specifically discouraged by the *Guide*: 'Wash yourselves wherever necessary as often as you wish, and your things as well. Filth (fulðe) was never dear to God, although poverty and plainness of dress are pleasing to him.'[37]

As significant as *contemptus mundi* treatment of the flesh is Part Four's insistence that soul and body are not to be separated:

Now, one of you may at some time say, 'I will love his or her soul well but not in any way his body.' But this is not the thing to say. The soul and the body make but a single person, and to both of them comes a single judgement. Will you divide in two (dealen o twa) what God has joined as one (to an isompnet)? He forbids it, and says, *Quod Deus coniunxit homo non separet* [Matthew 19.6] – 'Let no one be so mad as to divide the thing that God has fastened together.'[38]

This explicit hylomorphism prefaces Part Four's treatment of 'inner' and 'outer' temptations as sent by God, the flesh and the devil. Even as the *Guide* author goes on to note the 'strange mockery' by which the flesh is able to 'entice so high a thing as the soul' into sin, he insists that 'however weak [the flesh] is, it is so joined (icuplet) and so tightly fixed (se feste ifeiet) to our precious soul, God's own image, that we could easily kill the one with the other'.[39] The flesh's role, in this argument, is to be a clod of earth tied to the soul as one puts 'a hobble on a cow' or any other straying animal;[40] it is treated as intimate, potentially ridiculous, familiar, less a thing of sensationalised horror than a foe or friend to spiritual welfare depending on how well it is managed. In Part Six, it is a garment, banner, sign, capable of bearing God's mark or the devil's, and martyred saints tear it up like spoilt children destroying garments supplied by a rich father, confidently expecting the new and better garment of their resurrection.[41]

Although the flesh is seen as a problematic border zone – the territory where the senses and the volition can be led astray – it is the border zone to a body which is both sinful and capable of redemption. The sins of the flesh – lechery, gluttony and sloth – are imaged as foot-wounds, and the spiritual sins of pride, envy, anger and covetousness are imaged as breast-wounds, so that the sinning body itself is as permeable and wounded as the redemptive body of Christ.[42] Christ's body is a dovecot in which the anchoress may hide, its openings and exudings, its five streams of blood positively valued as redemptive bodily suffering.[43] The argument that there is a gap between, on the one hand, the feared 'perviousness of the female body' and the intense need for it to be sealed up and, on the other, the high value placed on the exudings and openings of Christ's body, is not always true, or true in the same way.[44] The *Guide* for example *links* Christ's bleeding to *some* of the anchoress's bodily experiences: Christ is the tireless worker who late in his life still labours bleeding on the cross and yet rises early from death to life in a reproach against sloth; 'others, when they have had blood let from their arms, take rest, hide from the light in their rooms and shut themselves away'.[45] Bloodletting is part of the recluse's physical regimen, prescribed four times a year 'and if necessary more often', to be carefully followed by three days of recreation and recovery.[46] Such links can be made across gender, as in Part Seven's image of Christ as a mother providing a bath of blood to save her sick child.[47]

The thematics of the entombed body and its living death obviously echo *contemptus mundi* traditions of suspicion of the flesh but should also be seen in the context of a historically-specific increased concern with the enclosure of women. The *Guide*'s injunction that the anchoress's white hands should each day scrape up earth from the grave in which they will one day rot has its counterpart in the reminder to the courtly heroine that 'when the turuf is [her] tur' and the pit her bower, only worms will 'enjoy her white throat'.[48] The intensity of these images is not only a function of fear and hatred of the flesh on the part of the clerics who pen them. The *Guide* offers a particularly striking image of the contained female body, but one paralleled in both secular and devotional post-Norman Conquest sources. Pious virgins and widows are represented as longing for heavenly nuptial chambers, and/or retaining their virginity and prosecuting their studies within earthly ones, whether professed religious like Etheldreda (Audrée) or pious noblewomen like Queen Edith or Adela of Blois.[49] The related figure of the repentant harlot undertakes reclusion in the cell (Thaïs) or a cave (the Magdalen at Marseilles).[50] In Grosseteste's *Château d'Amour*, the Virgin herself is a tower and a castle, whilst the courtly heroine is besieged, in hagiography as in romance, by suitors in her tower, bower, and cell.[51] Images of enclosed women are present throughout Christian tradition, but have particular intensity and meaning in the high Middle Ages against the new marriage patterns of the twelfth and thirteenth centuries, and an increased concern with the movement and control of women in changing kinship structures and patterns of household formation.[52] Inflections of containment and control specific to religious lives may also be seen in the context of the monastic orders' restrictions on the development of female houses at the end of the twelfth century.[53] The complex processes by which these changing secular and professed forms of life produce newly isolative and feminised notions of the individual have been discussed in modern scholarship and are further illuminated by the *Guide*.[54]

The force and effectiveness with which the *Guide* valorises the containment of women is manifest. A range of medieval audiences seized on its strenuous form of spirituality as importantly representative, translating the *Guide* from English into French and Latin, and adapting it for textual communities not only non-anchoritic, but lay, and in some cases male.[55] The notion of the solitary recluse itself becomes an important image of the person. Feminised chaste enclosure (feminised at this period both in the gender of the enclosed body and in terms of anchoritism's recruits) becomes an important model for men to think with too. So for instance in a fourteenth-century adaptation of the *Guide*:

Now vnderstondeþ þt a mannes body is cleped in holy wrytt sumtyme an hous. and sumtyme a Citee and sumtyme goddes temple and holy chirche. Þan riȝth as ȝee see þat an Ancre is bischett in an hous and may nouȝth out, riȝth so is

vche mannes soule bischett in his body as an Ancre. And þerfore vche man lered
and lewed if he wil queme [please, be pleasing to] god and be his deciple helde
hym in his hous. Schete his dores and his wyndowes fast þat ben his fyue wyttes.
þat he take no likyng to synne ne to worldelich þinges. and þan he is an Ancre.[56]

The question of what this might mean in terms of empowerment or
containment for the original and subsequent audiences of anchoresses
and other women is, however, a complex one. The *Guide*'s version of the
body as figurative edifice is both containing and dynamic: in its powerful
and absorbing spirituality, the recluse is simultaneously empowered and
immobilised, given high status and occluded visibility. In practice, reclusion was chosen (sometimes as an active preference) by powerful and
wealthy women for whom it was not the only option, as well as by women
from humbler social backgrounds.[57] Rank and prestige seem to have
characterised the imagery and the social status accorded to anchoritism,
whilst some of its recruits already had these things in the world or aspired
to them in undertaking reclusion. So the *Guide* warns that 'it is quite unreasonable to come into an anchorhouse, into God's prison, readily and
willingly into a place of discomfort, in order to look for ease there, and
more mastery and ladyship than she could have in the world . . . such
things would be unfitting for the lady of a castle; it is a contemptible and
unreasonable thing that an anointed anchoress (smiret ancre), and an
anchoress buried (ancre biburiet) – for what is an anchorhouse but her
grave (burinesse)? – wishes to be more graciously regarded than the lady
of a house.'[58] The anchoress is dead to the world, but still signifies to it,
just as the *Guide* has a continuing history beyond its immediate occasion
in the request of three well-born sisters.

Apart from embroidery, weeping, and prayer, the activity most often
envisaged for the woman enclosed in cell or bower is that of reading. In
the *Guide* reading is valued equally with prayer: 'reading is good prayer . . . as
you read, when the heart is pleased, a devotion arises which is worth many
prayers'.[59] Devotional reading in English and French is a regular part of
the recluse's day in addition to her *horarium*, as is reading of the *Guide*
itself.[60] The cell-body, body-soul homologies of her *Guide* insist, as Elizabeth Robertson has noted, that the anchoress is also reading her body,
using it 'as a guide to contemplation', and incorporating the physical and
corporeal existence vigorously refigured to her by the *Guide* as a continuing term of her spiritual life.[61] Focused on the ideal bridegroom,
sustaining and comforting in a penitential life, its parameters of desire
and denial mapped on her body, the recluse's reading also looks very like
modern romance reading as studied by Radway, Modleski and others,
where reading both consoles and reinforces the containment and solitude
of the housewife.[62] As she reads towards the climactic assault of Christ the
lover-knight (who in Part Seven enters the anchoress's cell and heart in

person with a wooing speech of considerable intensity and considerable emotional blackmail), it is possible to see in the anchoress and bride of Christ an early example of romance-reading.[63] As much or more than individual texts of medieval romance, the *Guide* offers women formation in the new high medieval politics of romance and household, [hetero]-sexuality and subordination, in a combination of 'reactionary [social and cultural] structures and private sexual radicalism' such as has been argued to inform some modern mass-produced romance.[64]

Yet reading the body, as Bynum and others have argued for later sources, is not merely the *faute de mieux* product of what misogyny may prescribe for women, particularly not when, as in the *Guide*, the ideal body is complexly distributed between the anchoress's own enclosed body and the beautiful young wooer who is also the embodied and sometimes maternal Christ, suffering, exuding, sweating and bleeding.[65] The anchoresses' way of life is specifically identified as crucifixion with Christ, hanging on the cross with him in 'suffering and shame'.[66] That this suffering might be internalised as a punitively penitential inscription on the body is suggested by the prohibitions of the outer rule in Part Eight: 'Nobody should . . . wear anything made of iron or hair or hedgehog skins, or beat herself with them, or with a scourge weighted with lead, with holly, or with thorns, or draw blood, without her confessor's permission. She should not sting herself anywhere with nettles, or scourge the front of her body, or mutilate herself with cuts, or take excessively severe disciplines at any one time, in order to subdue temptations.'[67] Yet in some contexts, identification with Christ's suffering empowers: reading is an uncontainable as well as a highly scripted activity. Anchoritic identification with Christ's suffering does not lead in thirteenth-century England to such public and vocal representation as contemporary continental religious women's inscription of Christ on their bodies, but not even female anchoritic reading is always solitary, still less silent.[68] As Arlyn Diamond and others have shown for medieval romance, medieval reading is as likely to involve female community as female solitude.[69] In the *Guide*, the anchoresses exchange 'edifying stories' in common during their blood-letting, they read aloud to their servants and though they each have copied out their own service books for individual use will probably have had the *Guide* in a single shared manuscript.[70] The image of the enclosed, self-containing chaste reader of her own body is powerful but not exclusive in the *Guide*, just as the solitude of the anchoress is itself a powerful but partial representation.

This solitude, in the case of female recluses, might be better understood as 'unappendedness'. By this I mean that because she is not perceived as being in the custody of a [literal] husband, the anchoress is perceived (and as discussed above, pp. 27–9, powerfully imaged) as a solitary. Yet, partly because solitary unenclosed women could not survive as hermitesses, most anchorholds are not only situated in a social network of beneficiaries and patrons but are themselves miniature female communities. It is unsurprising that a woman with other women can be argued to be solitary or reclusive; the body most occluded in medieval as in modern thought about chastity is the corporate female body.[71] The heavenly choir and court of virgin brides of the Lamb may be an image valued by different writers (female as well as male) in various ways, but defers the society and sociability of women beyond death. Whether secular or religious, representations of female courts and communities are always to some extent hypotheses, the stuff of experiment and inversion, since however far they encode socio-political functions of intercession, they also do not encode actual rule by women.[72] In the *Guide*, awareness of female community is subordinate to the writing of ideal female solitude, but is none the less not absent. For all its creation of a solitary enclosed body, the *Guide* is a 'riwle (rule)' or 'wisse (guide)' for *ancrene* (anchoresses, genitive plural). Not only is the anchoress's servant present in the very conception of an anchoritic guide (see p. 27 above) but the *Guide*'s particular anchorhold is, from its inception, inhabited by three anchoresses. On the *Guide*'s own evidence we should see here not only a single enclosed female body, but a miniature female community. Even the *Guide*'s solitary body is a miniature household presided over by the lady of the soul, rather than a unitary modern 'solitary self' ('[her servants are] the five senses, which should be at home and serve their lady'), and the recluse is not in fact solitary in terms of the physical and social organisation which supports her, nor in the daily conditions of her life.[73]

The *Guide*'s early manuscripts address three sisters, then twenty; the initial anchorhold has at least three cells, a parlour, perhaps some kind of yard or garden, possibly a servant's room.[74] In interpolations in the revised manuscript, the *Guide* refers to the convents which have developed from the original community, while in its account of confession the women envisaged include nuns, anchoresses, married women and virgins.[75] The body whose boundaries may in its essentialised version be fetishised and sealed off is in fact permeable and labile as a corporate community. The fluidity of conceptual and social distinction between virgins, wives and widows is repeated between anchoresses, nuns and laywomen, as it is in the history of female communal foundations. The informality which the *Guide* perceives and makes explicit (and which has been adduced as evidence for misogynistic contempt) addresses the actual conditions of post-Norman Conquest female communities. As Sally Thompson has shown, except for the surviving Anglo-Saxon royal foundations these are frequently under-funded and insecure, unstable in their assignation to and support by particular orders, fluid and informal in their development, and, with a few privileged exceptions, without long and stable institutional histories.[76]

Roberta Gilchrist has further shown that the very materials of female community are often impermanent compared with monastic corporate building programmes (sometimes, as one hagiographer notes of Queen Edith's assistance to the nuns of Wilton, all the more readily finished, because of their modesty, than grander projects such as the rebuilding of St Peter's, Westminster, simultaneously undertaken by Edith's husband, Edward the Confessor, and still incomplete when her chapel at Wilton was consecrated).[77]

Among the many medieval textual communities which used one or other of the *Guide*'s manuscripts and versions, it is especially striking that the *Guide* served as a foundation text for the community established before 1285 by Matilda, or Maud, Countess of Gloucester, at Minchenleigh (*munchene*, genitive plural, 'nuns').[78] That community has been occluded to some extent by reference to it in modern scholarship as Canonsleigh.[79] But the canons were in fact ejected by Maud to make way for her new female community, suggesting that the *Guide* should not be too readily associated with passivity and silence on the part of medieval women. The seductive image of the entombed woman obscures the activities of women to which these texts also testify and of which, even though written by men, they are the product. (Anchorholds in post-Norman Conquest Britain are repeatedly the founding site of communities, textual and social, but even now Christina of Markyate is remembered as a recluse rather than a foundress and prioress.)[80]

Even as the powerful post-Conquest ideology of containment for women is enunciated in the *Guide*'s enclosed female body, there are slippages in how completely this represents or articulates the experience of the women addressed. That women also saw opportunities here is suggested by the response of Maud de Clare, as by the multiplication of the *Guide*'s initial textual community and its manuscripts. This text after all, not only provides images of the chaste body enclosed in the death-clasp of the cell, but glimpses of small groups of women surviving tough lives together. The enclosure of the chaste body, whether solitary or collective, is not only a perennially fascinating idea of theoretical and practical concern to clerics, but a history of lived female lives.

NOTES

1 I am grateful to Sarah Kay and Miri Rubin for patient and helpful editing and to Anne Savage and Simon Gaunt for generously allowing me to see in manuscript, respectively, a forthcoming paper on anchoritic works and chapters of a forthcoming book on *Genre and Gender in Medieval Literature*.

2 For a lucid account of these continuities see Bella Millett, ed., *Hali Meiðhad*, EETS OS 284, Oxford, 1982, 'The Theological Background', pp. xxiv–xlv: more extended studies are John Bugge, *Virginitas: the History of a Medieval Ideal*, The Hague, 1986, Matthäus

Bernards, *Speculum Virginum: Geistigkeit und Seelenleben der Frau im Hochmittelalter*, Forschungen zur Volkskunde 36/38, Cologne, 1955.

3 See Jane Tibbetts Schulenberg, 'Strict Active Enclosure and its Effects on the Female Monastic Experience (ca. 500–1100)', in *Distant Echoes, Medieval Religious Women*, I, ed. John A. Nichols and Lillian T. Shank, Kalamazoo, 1984, pp. 51–86.

4 So, for example, Aldhelm's *De virginitate* acknowledges ageing only to deny it to virginity: 'O excellent grace of virginity, which like a rose grown from thorny shoots blushes with a crimson flower and never withers with the defect of dread mortality, and although the tired fragility of the moribund flesh droops and ages with stooping and bent senility as the terminus of death approaches, virginity alone in the manner of happy youth continually flourishes and is constantly growing', trans. M. Lapidge, *Aldhelm: The Prose Works*, Ipswich, 1979, p. 74.

5 Though variously supplemented at different periods by other types of women saints (queens, abbesses, mothers and widows, pastoral workers) the prevalence of the virgin martyr, especially the retellings of legendary virgin martyr passions, is a constant of medieval and later exemplary biography. The most recent virgin martyr is Maria Goretti (1890–1902, canonised 1950): see D. H. Farmer, *The Oxford Dictionary of Saints*, Oxford, 1978, repr. 1982, *s.v. Goretti* and, for a recent account and bibliography, Giovanni Alberti, *Maria Goretti: Storia di un piccolo fiore di campo*, 2nd edn, Rome, 1990. For a theoretical analysis of gender, violence and representation, see Teresa de Lauretis, 'The Violence of Rhetoric; Considerations on Representation and Gender' in her *Technologies of Gender* Bloomington and Indianapolis, 1987, pp. 31–50, repr. in *The Violence of Representation*, ed. Leonard Tennenhouse and Nancy Armstrong London, 1989.

6 T. Miller, ed., *The Old English Version of Bede's Ecclesiastical History of the English People*, EETS OS 95, London, 1890, repr. 1959, p. 176.

7 For editions, see note 14 below. For modern scholarship on these works, see the bibliography by Roger Dahood, '*Ancrene Wisse*, the Katherine Group and the *Wohunge* Group' in *Middle English Prose: A Critical Guide to Major Authors and Genres*, ed. A. S. G. Edwards, New Brunswick, NJ, 1984. An updated bibliography, edited by Bella Millett, is forthcoming.

8 The fundamental modern study is by Ann K. Warren, *Anchorites and Their Patrons in Medieval England*, Berkeley, Los Angeles, 1985; still of interest is Rotha M. Clay, *The Hermits and Anchorites of England*, London, 1914. For continental anchoresses see Patricia J. F. Rosof, 'The Anchoress in the Twelfth and Thirteenth Centuries', in *Peace Weavers, Medieval Religious Women II*, ed. John A. Nichols and Lillian T. Shank, Cistercian Fathers Series 72, Kalamazoo, Michigan, 1987. In the thirteenth century (when the greatest number of anchoritic sites are recorded) female anchorites outnumber male by four to one; see Warren, p. 19 and the table on p. 20.

9 On the enclosure ceremony, see Warren, *Anchorites*, pp. 76–77, 97–100; Sharon Elkins, *Holy Women of Twelfth Century England*, Chapel Hill and London, 1988, pp. 151–2.

10 Thus, for example, Elizabeth Robertson, 'The Rule of the Body: the Feminine Spirituality of the *Ancrene Wisse*', in *Seeking the Woman in Late Medieval and Renaissance Writings: Essays in Feminist Contextual Criticism*, ed. Sheila Fisher and Janet E. Halley, Knoxville, 1989, pp. 109–34, which argues that the spirituality of the *Guide* is devalued by being non-hierarchichal and corporeal, rather than abstract, intellectual and male; Howard Bloch, *Medieval Misogyny and the Invention of Western Romantic Love*, Chicago, 1991, p. 100, where the *Guide*, in an unspecified late thirteenth- or early fourteenth-century version, is once more made part of a seamless misogynistic discourse.

11 Anne Savage, 'The Translation of the Feminine: Untranslatable Dimensions of the Anchoritic Works' in *The Medieval Translator*, IV, ed. R. Ellis and R. Evans, Exeter, 1994. See also Nicholas Watson, 'The Methods and Objectives of Thirteenth-Century Anchoritic Devotion', in *The Medieval Mystical Tradition in England: Exeter Symposium IV*, ed. Marion Glasscoe, Cambridge, 1987, pp. 132–53, especially pp. 146–7.

12 Ursula K. Le Guin, 'The Space Crone', *Co-Evolution Quarterly* 1976, repr. in *Women of the Fourteenth Moon: Writings on Menopause*, ed. Dena Taylor and Amber Coverdale Sumrall Freedom, CA, 1991, p. 3.

13 See Barbara Newman, 'Flaws in the Golden Bowl: Gender and Spiritual Formation in the Twelfth Century', *Traditio* XLV, 1989–90, pp. 111–46; Clarissa Atkinson, ' "Precious Balsam in a Fragile Glass": the Ideology of Virginity in the Later Middle Ages', *Journal of Family History*, VIII, 1983, pp. 131–43.

14 *Ancrene Riwle*, trans. M. B. Salu, London, 1955, repr., 1990, pp. 72–3. The manuscripts of *Ancrene Wisse* have been published in diplomatic editions by the Early English Text Society; Middle English quotations here are from *The English Text of the Ancrene Riwle: Ancrene Wisse*, ed. J. R. R. Tolkien, EETS OS 249, London, 1962, by folio and line number, here f. 44b/9–45a/2. For an edition and translation of *Ancrene Wisse*, Parts Seven and Eight, and some of the related texts, see *Medieval English Prose for Women: Ancrene Wisse and the Katherine Group*, ed. and trans. Bella Millett and Jocelyn Wogan-Browne, Oxford, 1990; repr. 1992; for translations of all of *Ancrene Wisse*, the Katherine Group, and the Wooing Group, see *Anchoritic Spirituality: Ancrene Wisse and Associated Works*, trans. Anne Savage and Nicholas Watson, The Classics of Western Spirituality, New York and Mahwah, NJ, 1991. Except for this extract (where Salu's chaste cleanness' and 'virginity' are more continuous with the terms of my own argument than Savage and Watson's 'chaste purity' and 'maidenhood'), translations are normally from Savage and Watson, henceforth referred to as such by page number in the text.

15 So in *Hali Meiðhad*, the virginity letter associated with the *Guide*: 'Angel and maiden are equal in virtue through the power of virginity, though as yet their degrees of blessedness divide them ... in this world which is called "land of unlikeness" [virginity] keeps its nature in the likeness of heavenly nature, although it is an outlaw from there and in a body of clay'. (Millett and Wogan-Browne, pp. 11/21–30). See further E. Gilson, *'Regio dissimilitudinis* de Platon à Saint Bernard', *Mediaeval Studies*, IX (1947), pp. 103–30; R. Javelet, *Image et resemblance au douzième siècle*, Strasbourg, 1967, II, pp. 270–83.

16 On the three estates, see Bernards, *Speculum*, pp. 40–59; Atkinson, ' "Balsam ..." '; Wogan-Browne, 'The Virgin's Tale' in *The Wife of Bath and All Her Sect*, ed. R. Evans and L. Johnson London, forthcoming. Vernacular usage distinguishes between 'virgin' (ME *vergine*, A-N '*virgine*') and (A-N *pucele*, and ME *mayden*) as internalised and technical states of virginity respectively; see H. Kurath and S. M. Kuhn, eds, *Middle English Dictionary*, Ann Arbor, 1956–; L. W. Stone and W. Rothwell, eds, *Anglo-Norman Dictionary*, London, 1977–92.

17 'quid dicendum foret. quando sacraturus eam episcopus de virginitate sua requireret. Recordabatur namque quos impetus cogitacionum quam ignotos carnis sue stimulos sustinuerat nec audebat se profiteri de tantis procellis integram evasisse. et si nusquam meminerit se neque actu neque voluntate lapsam fuisse', C. H. Talbot, ed. and trans., *The Life of Christina of Markyate: A Twelfth Century Recluse*, Oxford, 1959, repr. 1987, p. 126.

18 On the hymen in virginity literature, see further Wogan-Browne, 'Virgin's Tale'.

19 Tolkien, f. 4a/16–17; Savage and Watson, p. 51.

20 Tolkien, f. 23b/25; Savage and Watson, p. 82.

21 One of the *Guide*'s sources, Aelred of Rievaulx's *De institutis inclusarum*, distinguishes inner and outer rules, but does not systematically structure them as enacting the enclosed body or the recluse's relation to her servant. For a list of anchoritic rules, see Warren, *Anchorites*, Appendix 2.

22 See Tolkien, f. 24a/12 (Savage and Watson, p. 82); Tolkien, ff. 12b/21–15b/1 (Savage and Watson, pp. 66–72). See also, for discussion of this passage, Linda Georgianna, *The Solitary Self: Individuality in the Ancrene Wisse*, Cambridge, Mass., 1981, pp. 59–65.

23 'Haldeð ow feast inne, nawt te bodi ane; for þt is þe unwurðest, ah ower fif wittes 7 te heorte ouer al 7 al þer þe sawle lif is' (Tolkien, f. 47a/10–12; Savage and Watson, p. 112).

24 Tolkien, f. 102a/26–102b/12; Savage and Watson, pp. 186–7. In the Dublin Rule, a thirteenth-century anchoritic rule drawing on *Ancrene Wisse* among other texts, the comparable image for men is that of the body as a ship: 'Nam sicut anchor ponitur ne navis inter rupes periclitetur, ita homo includitur ne anima inter seculares periclitetur. Navis vero significat corpus tuum, funis vero spem inter te et Deum, mare temptaciones significat, rupis autem acriores tribulationes significat. Si navis rupe colliditur, necesse est ut funis perduret' ('For as an anchor is put out so that the ship is not emperilled among rocks,

so an enclosed man must not endanger his soul among things of the world. The ship signifies your body, the cable the hope between you and God, the sea signifies temptations, and the rock signifies fiercer trials. If the ship strikes the rock, it is vital that the cable holds'); see L. Oliger, 'Regula tres inclusorum et eremitarum Angliae saec. XIII–XIV et eremitarum Angliae saec. XIII', *Antonianum*, III, 1928, pp. 170–83, p. 175. When the *Guide* gives the etymology of 'ancre', it is related to the recluse's position, not her body; she is 'anchored under a church like an anchor under the side of a ship' (Tolkien, f. 39a/2–7; Savage and Watson, p. 101).

25 See Roberta D. Cornelius, *The Figurative Castle: A Study in the Medieval Allegory of the Edifice with Special Reference to Religious Writings*, Pennsylvania, Bryn Mawr, 1930. On the Galenic 'one-sex' body see Thomas Laqueur, *Making Sex: Body and Gender from the Greeks to Freud* Cambridge, Mass., 1990, chapter 2.

26 On the body as vessel, see Charlotte Morse, *The Pattern of Judgement in the Queste and Cleanness*, Columbia, 1978, chapter 1, 'The Paradigm of the Vessel as an Image of Man'.

27 See Jocelyn Price, 'Inner and Outer: Conceptualizing the Body in *Ancrene Wisse* and Aelred's *De institutione inclusarum*' in *Medieval Ethical and Religious Literature: Essays in Honour of George Russell*, Cambridge, 1986, pp. 192–208.

28 Tolkien, f. 18b/8–19a/26; Savage and Watson, pp. 75–6.

29 Shame and desire are of particular thematic importance throughout Parts Six and Seven respectively. For the pot of the belly, see Part Six (Tolkien, f. 99b/27–100a/2; Savage and Watson, p. 183); for the bridal-gifts of the soul, Part One (Tolkien, f. 7b/28; Savage and Watson, p. 58) and Part Two (Tolkien, f. 24b/17, f. 24b/28–25a/2; Savage and Watson, p. 83). The *Guide*'s imagery has been studied by Janet Grayson, *Structure and Imagery in Ancrene Wisse*, Hanover, New Hampshire, 1974.

30 See Millett and Wogan-Browne, p. 160, n. 122/35.

31 For these phrases see respectively Tolkien, f. 95a/27–8 (Savage and Watson, p. 177); Tolkien, f. 29a/6 (Savage and Watson, p. 88); Tolkien, f. 101b/15–17 (Savage and Watson, p. 184).

32 Tolkien, f. 102a/23–4; Savage and Watson, p. 186; 'yours to do all that you want with', Tolkien, f. 110a/24–5; Savage and Watson, p. 197.

33 'Bitweonen delices. ant eise. ant flesches este. hwa wes eauer chaste?', Tolkien, f. 99b/25–6; Savage and Watson, p. 183.

34 Tolkien, f. 75b/6–14; Savage and Watson, p. 149.

35 See Savage and Watson's informative note, p. 384, n. 110.

36 The flesh is called 'mud and foul earth' ('fen 7 ful eorð', Tolkien, f. 38a/16) in the passage on f. 38a discussed below. For other uses, s.v. *ful, fule, fuleste, fuleð, fulðe, fulðen* in *Concordance to Ancrene Wisse: Ms Corpus Christi College Cambridge, 402*, ed. J. Potts, L. Stevenson and J. Wogan-Browne, Woodbridge, 1993.

37 Millett and Wogan-Browne, p. 140/30–2. For an example of infrequent bathing as a sign of sanctity, see Bede's Life of Etheldreda *Bede's Ecclesiastical History of the English People*, ed. B. Colgrave and R. A. B. Mynors, Oxford, 1991, pp. 4, 19–20.

38 Tolkien, f. 50a/10–16; Savage and Watson, p. 117.

39 Tolkien, f. 38a/8–11; Savage and Watson, p. 100.

40 Tolkien, f. 38a/28; Savage and Watson, p. 100.

41 See Part Six (Tolkien, ff. 98a/14–98b/9, 98b/26–8; Savage and Watson, pp. 181–2) for these images. In Part Two, the five senses are sweet-fleshed kids from which may come stinking goats, and the flatterer is a raven feeding on carrion flesh; in Part Three the ostrich's flesh makes it too heavy to fly in comparison with the pelican's leanness; the flesh is a fat calf, its desires Holofernes; it is meat, a clod, a brittle vessel. In Part Five it flowers anew in confession, in Six it is torn, lacerated and beaten, in Parts Seven and Two it is the sweetness and special livingness of Christ's flesh. (*s.v. flesch, flesches, fleschlich, fleschliche, fleschs, flesliche* in Potts, Stevenson, Wogan-Browne, eds, *Concordance to Ancrene Wisse*).

42 For the sinning body as wounded, see Tolkien, f. 51b/11–12; Savage and Watson, p. 119.

43 For Christ as dovecot, see Tolkien, f. 79b/23–6 (Savage and Watson, p. 155); for the five streams of blood, see Tolkien, f. 70b/8–9 (Savage and Watson, p. 142).

44 See Karma Lochrie, *Margery Kempe and the Translations of the Flesh*, 1991, chapter 1, especially pp. 23–7.

45 Tolkien, f. 70b/4–6; Savage and Watson, p. 142.

46 Millett and Wogan-Browne, p. 140/20–9 (Tolkien, f. 115a/1–12; Savage and Watson, p. 204).

47 For the healing bath of blood, see Tolkien, f. 107/3–16; Savage and Watson, p. 193. A case for a positive perception of female gender and sexuality in the *Guide* and related texts is made by Catherine Innes Parker, 'Virgin Bride and Lover: A Study of the Relationship Between Sexuality and Spirituality in Anchoritic Literature', unpublished Ph.D. dissertation, Memorial University of Newfoundland, 1992.

48 Tolkien, f. 31b/21–5; Savage and Watson, pp. 91–2: for the lyric, see Carleton Brown, ed., *English Lyrics of the Thirteenth Century*, Oxford, 1932, p. 30, n. 54. On the practice of burying anchorites in their cells and the argument that the anchorhold as grave in the *Guide* is figurative and not the literal practice of earlier continental anchoritic rules, see Warren, *Anchorites*, p. 106, n. 32.

49 For a contemporary account of Etheldreda, see Marie (of Chatteris?), *La Vie sainte Audrée, poème anglo-normand du XIIIe siècle*, ed. Ö. Södergaard, Uppsala, 1955, p. 63, ll. 265–80; for Edith, see Aelred's Life of the Confessor, PL 195.737–90, col. 747; Frank Barlow, *The Life of King Edward the Confessor*, London, 1962, Matthew Paris, *La estoire de Seint Aedward le Rei*, ed. Kathryn Young Wallace, ANTS 41, London, Anglo-Norman Text Society, 1983, ll. 1147–76; *La Vie d'Edouard le confesseur, poème anglo-normand du XIIe siècle*, ed. Ö. Södergaard, Uppsala, 1948, ll. 1255–94. In addition to Christina of Markyate's life in a hermitage (see Talbot, cited in n. 17 above), see, for a vivid account of contemporary non-anchoritic enclosure, *The Book of St Gilbert*, ed. R. Foreville and G. Keir, Oxford, 1987, ch. 9, pp. 34–5. For Adela, see the poem on her chamber by Baudri de Bourgueil, Phyllis Abrahams, ed., *Les Oeuvres poétiques de Baudri de Bourgueil 1046–1130*, Paris, 1936, pp. 196–253.

50 For Thaïs, see R. C. Perman, ed., 'Henri d'Arci: the Shorter Works', in *Studies in Medieval French Presented to Alfred Ewart*, ed. E. A. Francis, Oxford, 1961. Here the penitent harlot is enclosed by Paphnutius as if she were an anchoress ('l'us de la celle de plum enseela', l. 66) and told to purge herself (literally and spiritually) in the cell (for the [misused] anchoritic cell as a privy in the *Guide* see Tolkien, f. 75a/22–35b/2, Savage and Watson, pp. 96–7); for Mary Magdalene, see M. A. Klenke, ed., *Three Saints' Lives by Nicholas Bozon*, Franciscan Institute Publications Historical Series 1, St Bonaventure, NY, 1947, pp. 17–18, ll. 319–25. Cell and desert function as versions of each other in the contemporary metaphorics of penance: the *Guide* envisages reclusion as desert solitude throughout its third part, and the figure of a repentant desert harlot, such as Mary of Egypt, has close affinities with the figure of the virtuous anchoress. (See P. Dembowski, ed., *La Vie de sainte Marie l'Egyptienne*, Publications Romanes et Françaises, Geneva, 1977, for Mary of Egypt.) For Middle English versions of these figures, see Charlotte d'Evelyn, 'Individual Legends' in *Manual of the Writings in Middle English 1050–1500*, vol. 2, ed. Albert E. Hartung, New Haven, Connecticut Academy of Arts and Sciences, 1967, pp. 561–635.

51 For Grosseteste, see Kari Sajavaara, ed. *The Middle English Translations of Robert Grosseteste's Château d'amour*, Mémoires de la Sociéte Neophilologique de Helsinki 32, Helsinki, Société Néophilologique, 1967. Also prevalent is the narrative allegory of the soul in its castle fought for by Christ as lover-knight: see for example the exemplum or *conte* 'Du roi ki avoit une amie', where Christ is armed in a maiden's chamber by her giving him an acetoun of 'blaunche chare e pure' and plate-armour of bones before he goes to fight for the soul. Examples (including the *Guide*'s Part Seven exemplum of the soul–lady wooed by Christ) are collected by Wilbur Gaffrey, 'The Allegory of the Christ–Knight in *Piers Plowman*', *PMLA* 46, 1931, pp. 155–68. As an account of marriage as enclosure, Marie

de France's *Yonec* is particularly striking among her *Lais* (see A. Ewert, ed., *Marie de France, Lais*, Oxford, 1969, pp. 82–96).

52 The classic study is Georges Duby, *The Knight, the Lady and the Priest: the Making of Modern Marriage in Medieval France*, trans. Barbara Bray, with an Introduction by Natalie Zemon Davis, London, 1983; see also Anita Guerreau-Jalabert, 'Sur les structures de parenté dans l'Europe médiévale', *Annales* XXXVI, 1981, pp. 1028–49. I am indebted to Simon Gaunt's lucid discussion of these matters as they affect romance and hagiography in the third and fifth chapters of his forthcoming *Genre and Gender in Medieval Literature*. I have discussed the effects of these changes for chastity literature in greater detail in a paper ('Translating Virginity') given to the Associazione di filologia germanica d'Italia in Udine, 1991, (incorporated in a study of post-Conquest female celibacy on which I am currently working, *Authorized Virgins*).

53 See Penny Schine Gold, *The Lady and the Virgin: Image, Attitude and Experience in Twelfth Century France*, Chicago, 1985; Ernest W. McDonnell, *The Béguines and Beghards in Medieval Culture*, New Jersey, Rutgers UP, 1954, repr. New York, 1969, chapter 11, 'Older Monasticism and the *Cura Monialium*'; Elkins, *Holy Women of Twelfth Century England*.

54 See Georgianna, *Solitary Self*; Colin Morris, *The Discovery of the Individual 1050–1200*, London, SPCK, 1972; Caroline Walker Bynum, 'Did the Twelfth Century Discover the Individual?', *Journal of Ecclesiastical History* XXXI, 1980, pp. 1–17 (and see Morris's reply, pp. 195–206); J. F. Benton, 'Consciousness of Self and Perceptions of Individuality' in *Renaissance and Renewal in the Twelfth Century*, ed. R. L. Benson and G. Constable, Oxford, 1982, pp. 263–95.

55 For details of manuscripts and versions, see Salu, *Ancrene Riwle*, pp. xxii–xxv, and for their textual relations, E. J. Dobson, 'The Affiliations of the Manuscripts of *Ancrene Wisse*', in *English and Medieval Studies Presented to J. R. R. Tolkien on the Occasion of his Seventieth Birthday*, ed. Norman Davis and C. L. Wrenn, London, 1962, pp. 128–63.

56 *The Recluse: A Fourteenth-Century Version of the Ancren Riwle*, ed. Joel Påhlsson, Lund, 1918, pp. 47/30–48/3. On the replacement of the ideal nun by the anchoress as an exemplary female figure, see Mary Byrne, *The Tradition of the Nun in Medieval England*, Washington, DC, 1932, pp. 56–7.

57 See further Warren, *Anchorites*, ch. 2, ch. 5, and, for a detailed study of a noble recluse, F. M. Powicke, 'Loretta, Countess of Leicester' in *Historical Essays in Honour of James Tait*, ed. J. Goronwy Edwards *et al.*, Manchester, 1933, pp. 247–71.

58 Tolkien, f. 28b/13–29a/9; Savage and Watson, p. 88. The countess of Leicester was an influential patron of the friars during her forty-four years of reclusion at Hackington near Canterbury, and was consulted by Henry III about the rights and liberties of the earldom and honour of Leicester, see Powicke, 'Loretta', pp. 267–8.

59 Tolkien, f. 78a/15; Savage and Watson, p. 153.

60 For the liturgical day of the anchoress see R. W. Ackermann and Roger Dahood, eds, *Ancrene Riwle: Introduction and Part One*, Medieval and Renaissance Texts and Studies, Binghampton, 1984, and Savage and Watson's helpful Notes to Part I, pp. 342–7. Part Eight recommends daily reading from the *Guide* (Millett and Wogan-Browne, p. 148/9, Savage and Watson, p. 207), while in Part One, daily 'redunge of englisc oðer of frensch' is envisaged together with 'pater nostres & auez on ower ahne wise, salmes 7 ureisuns', 'verseilunge of sawter ... halie meditatiuns' (Tolkien, f. 11a/20–7; Savage and Watson, p. 64).

61 Robertson, 'Rule of the body', p. 128.

62 Janice Radway, *Reading the Romance: Women, Patriarchy, and Popular Literature*, London and New York, 1987; originally published by the University of North Carolina Press, 1984; Tanya Modleski, *Loving with a Vengeance: Mass-Produced Fantasies for Women*, New York, 1984, and for a critique, Anne Cranny-Francis and Patricia Palmer, 'Soap opera and gender training', in *Masculine, Feminine, and Representation*, ed. Terry Threadgold and Anne Cranny-Francis, Sydney and London, 1990, pp. 171–89, especially pp. 183–9.

63 Its closest pre-Conquest predecessor, Goscelin's *Liber confortatorius*, written for the recluse Eve, underlines by contrast the new emphases of the *Guide*: Eve's cell is narrow and constrained but, since not even Caesar's body can occupy more than its own space, provides all the rooms and functions she could want. The cell is not, however, a feminised body-image as in the *Guide* (see C. H. Talbot, ed., *The Liber confortatorius of Goscelin of St Bertin*, *Analecta Monastica*, 3rd ser., ed. M. M. Lebreton, J. Leclercq and C. H. Talbot, Rome, 1955, pp. 77–9).

64 Cora Kaplan, '*The Thornbirds*: Fiction, Fantasy, Femininity', in *Formations of Fantasy* ed. Victor Burgin, London, 1986, pp. 142–66, p. 164. See also Wogan-Browne, 'Virgin's Tale'.

65 For her collected essays around these themes, see Caroline Walker Bynum, *Fragmentation and Redemption*, New York, 1991. See further Jennifer Ash, 'The Discursive Construction of Christ's Body in the Later Middle Ages: Resistance and Autonomy' in *Masculine, Feminine and Representation*, ed. Terry Threadgold and Anne Cranny-Francis, Sydney and London, 1990, pp. 75–105; Vincent Gillespie, 'Lukyng in haly bukes: *Lectio* in some late Medieval Spiritual Miscellanies', *Spätmittelalterliche Geistliche Literatur in der Nationalsprache*, Band 2, Analecta Cartusiana 106, ed. James Hogg, Salzburg, Institut für Anglistik und Amerikanistik, Universität Salzburg, 1984, pp. 1–27.

66 Part Six (Tolkien, f. 95b/1–96a/5; Savage and Watson, pp. 177–8).

67 Millett and Wogan-Browne, p. 136/13–19.

68 On continental sources, see Caroline Walker Bynum, *Holy Feast and Holy Fast: The Religious Significance of Food to Medieval Women*, Berkeley, 1987, and her *Fragmentation and Redemption*; Peter Dinzelbacher, 'Europäische Frauenmystik des Mittelalters', in *Frauenmystik im Mittelalter*, ed. P. Dinzelbacher and D. Bauer, Ostfildern, 1985. British absorption of these sources is later but intense: for a recent selection see Alexandra Barratt, ed., *Women's Writing in Middle English*, London and New York, 1992, pp. 49–101.

69 I regret that at the time of writing I had not seen Roberta Krueger's book on romance reading, *Women Readers and the Ideology of Gender in Old French Verse Romance*, Cambridge, 1993. Arlyn Diamond's paper, 'Female Freedom and Enclosure in the Romance' (International Courtly Literature Society, Seventh Triennial Congress, University of Massachusetts, August, 1992) is to be part of her forthcoming book on romance.

70 'Euchan segge hire ures as ha haueð iwriten ham', Tolkien, f. 6a/2, suggests that the anchoresses have individual service books, but the saint's life named by the author among their reading is referred to as 'your English *book* (singular) about St Margaret' (Tolkien, f. 66a/19). They are to read a section of Part Eight in the *Guide* to their servants each week until it is memorised (Millett and Wogan-Browne, p. 146/7–8). On the anchoresses' reading and literacy, see Bella Millett, 'Women in No Man's Land', in *Women and Literature in Britain, 1150–1500*, ed. Carol Meale, Cambridge, 1993, pp. 86–103. On monastic views of narrative as recreation, see Glending Olson, *Literature as Recreation in the Later Middle Ages*, Ithaca, NY, 1982, ch. 3.

71 See further Margaret Miles, *Carnal Knowledge: Female Nakedness and Religious Meaning in the Christian West*, Boston, 1989, repr. New York, 1991, especially ch. 6. For an account of continued privileging of the image of the nun as solitary and entombed in the decades prior to the first modern edition of the *Guide* in 1853, see Susan P. Casteras, 'Virgin Vows: the Early Victorian Artists' Portrayal of Nuns and Novices', *Victorian Studies* XXIV, 1981, pp. 157–207.

72 For documentation of this argument, which affects even the sovereignty of queens regnant (not only queens consort) in the Middle Ages, see Louise Fradenburg, ed., *Women and Sovereignty*, Edinburgh, 1992.

73 Tolkien, f. 46b/15–17; Savage and Watson, p. 112. The human body as household is extensively developed in *Sawles Warde*, the allegorical homily associated with the *Guide* (see Millett and Wogan-Browne, pp. 86–109; see also Watson, 'Methods and Objectives', cited in n. 11 above, p. 138). For the social context of the recluse, see Warren, *Anchorites, passim* and Powicke, 'Loretta'.

74 On the physical organisation of anchorholds see Warren, *Anchorites*, pp. 29–36; E. J. Dobson (*The Origins of Ancrene Wisse*, Oxford, 1976, pp. 253–5) discusses the households for whom early texts and copies of the *Guide* were created.

75 See Tolkien, f. 69a/7–27; Savage and Watson, pp. 140–1, where 'twenty or more' anchoresses are mentioned. See also Millett and Wogan-Browne, pp. xxxiii–iv and references. (A critical edition of the *Guide* is being prepared by Bella Millett, with a glossary by George Jack.) The affiliation of the original three anchoresses (through their spiritual director) has been thought to be Victorine (Dobson, *Origins*) but a Dominican affiliation now seems more likely; see Bella Millett, '*Ancrene Wisse*: New Answers, New Questions', *Medium Ævum*, VI, 1992, pp. 206–28.

76 *Women Religious: The Founding of English Nunneries After the Norman Conquest*, Oxford, 1991.

77 See Roberta Gilchrist, *The Archaeology of Female Piety*, London, forthcoming, and her article in this volume. For Edith, see Barlow, *Life of King Edward*, p. 46.

78 See E. J. Dobson, ed., *The English Text of the Ancrene Riwle: Edited from BM Cotton MS Cleopatra C.VI*, EETS OS 267, London, 1972, pp. xxv–xxix.

79 I have discussed Maud's founding activities in more detail in 'Re-routing the Dower: *La vie sainte Audrée*' in *Power of the Weak: Women and Authority in the Middle Ages*, ed. Sally-Beth MacLean, University of Illinois Press, forthcoming.

80 On the growth of anchorholds into larger communities, see Elkins, pp. 45–54, Thompson, chapter 2. The countess of Leicester endowed the sisters of the Order of St John at Minchin Buckland, Somerset, after her own enclosure; see Powicke, 'Loretta', p. 271.

Medieval bodies in the material world: gender, stigma and the body

AN ARCHAEOLOGY OF THE BODY

To archaeologists bodies retain an immediate physical presence. Excavated settlements and standing buildings represent the spaces in which real bodies mingled. Mineralised seeds and animal bones are the remains of meals prepared and consumed by real people. Their quality of life and personal hygiene may be reconstructed through insect fauna recovered through excavations. Bodies themselves are revealed in the excavation of medieval churches, where in each case thousands of dead bodies form a pressing and crowded mass – evidence of standards of health, demography and treatment of the body in death. However eloquent these sources are for reconstructing the flesh and blood of medieval bodies, they do not directly reflect contemporary perceptions of the body. Archaeology frequently reifies the human body as an artefact, chronicling physical processes of life, its death, disposal and decay. This essay seeks instead to consider aspects of the social classification of the body within medieval culture and to assess the extent to which this categorisation was accomplished through the medium of physical space. Space forms the arena in which social relationships are negotiated, expressed through the construction of landscapes, architecture and boundaries. The resulting spatial maps represent discourses of power based in the body.

Archaeology encompasses all forms of material culture – buildings, landscapes, artefacts, or real bodies – in an attempt to capture the physical entirety of past societies. Too often the archaeology of literate societies has painted the descriptive backdrop to history which has been written through documentary sources. The archaeology of the later medieval period, in particular, has made little contribution to social history or to the development of new interpretations enriched by modern theoretical approaches. Its major impact has been in the fields of environmental, economic and landscape studies. A traditional approach to history has used archaeology to reconstruct a stage set for the past, whilst documents have been used to breathe life into the characters. During the last decade, however, archaeologists have drawn from structuralist, poststructuralist and feminist thought in order to explore the *active* nature of material culture in relation to personal agency. Developing anthropological and sociological approaches, recent archaeological work asserts that material culture is used to construct, maintain, control and transform social identity.[1] Far from being static or merely reflective scenery, material culture is seen as social discourse.

All people use material culture to express their social identities, in terms of a personal sense of self and membership of wider groups defined according to structural divisions in society, such as family, household, gender, age, social class, occupation, ethnicity, and so on. Self-expression plays a crucial role in signalling identity through speech, posture, facial and physical gestures. Material culture is also used to indicate personal identity, for example through preferences in clothing, food, architecture and choice of commemoration in death. In addition to showing personal preference, material culture can be used to construct and maintain differences between groups or to disrupt and transform social structures. Medieval attempts to control signification through material culture were numerous, ranging from sumptuary laws which aimed to control clothing according to rank, to royal licences to crenellate buildings and thus regulate status according to the right to display emblems of fortification associated with the castle.[2]

The medieval body was central to a process of social classification according to categories of age, health, sex and purity, which were regulated through constructed categories such as stigma and gender.[3] This essay aims to explore the relationship of material culture and the body with reference to medieval settlement space. Two examples of social classification of the body are examined: the construction of the stigmatised body in relation to boundaries, and the constitution of the gendered body through medieval high-status architecture.

SPACE AND THE BODY

The potential for material culture to comment on the body is by no means self-evident. Like any other text, the archaeological record may be seen as a source which must be interpreted. Recent perspectives have examined the idea of material culture as a text 'which breaks free of the context of authorship'. John Barrett, for example, has adopted the metaphor of the text in order to decode patterns of material culture. Yet while accepting that the intentions of the authors of the archaeological record are thus displaced, Barrett suggests that meaning may be recreated by the reader of the archaeological record as text – a text which is made permanent through the processes by which material culture is laid down, transformed and recovered as archaeology.[4] While influenced by poststructuralism, most theoretical archaeologists have resisted its anti-rational, relativist stance, arguing that material culture forms a concrete basis from which to conceptualise past societies. The nature of reading – or interpreting – material culture as text has been considered according to the power relations which operate in the context of production, recovery and subsequent interpretation of the archaeological record.[5] Archaeology may be seen as central to a discourse of space and the body, since space reproduces social order and sometimes acts as a metaphorical extension of the body. Here the constitution of the subject is considered through the relationship of material culture and space to the human body.

All archaeological enquiries are by their very nature spatial, recording the precise dimensions in which settlements, buildings, artefacts, and burials are first deposited, then subject to processes of decay, and finally recovered by archaeological means. Archaeologists first developed methods of formal spatial analysis which measured variability of spatial organisation both within settlements and between settlements, checking relationships in the landscape according to statistical methods.[6] Subsequent studies concentrated on living spaces, developing formal analyses of domestic space based on syntactic spatial languages that were rooted in structural linguistics. Such studies work from the premise that space and social behaviour are mutually dependent, in order to reconstruct a map of social relationships based on archaeological remains.[7] These structuralist approaches are useful in describing the generation of spatial patterns but are limited in a number of respects. Efforts to read space as a language require the application of universal meanings to spatial patterns, such as the assumption that increased segregation will always accompany increased social complexity and will reflect specific degrees of social development.[8] The assumption that space directly *reflects* behaviour fails to consider the dynamic character of space, which develops with, and has the ability to transform, social relationships.

The greatest impact of poststructuralism on archaeology came with the acknowledgement that space, and other forms of material culture, are *active* in social relations. Spatial studies lost their reflective, static character, and began to consider how material reality might differ from mental understanding of space. It became important to assess the way in which space is interpreted by social agents and how the meanings attributed in the process of interpretation will alter with social changes. Particularly important was Henrietta Moore's study of the Marakwet of Kenya, which focused on the nature of the disposal of refuse and the placement of functional areas in relation to living space, with patterns ascribed according to the myths and cultural metaphors specific to the Marakwet, especially those related to gender, sexuality and impurity. Moore's approach drew from the work of Paul Ricoeur in emphasising that the interpretation of space is based in the creative process in which the participant observer refers to the myths and meanings of her or his own culture, and in developing a concept of distanciation which distinguishes between the meaning intended in the production of cultural products and subsequent perceptions of meaning.[9]

Poststructuralist studies emphasise the contextual nature of spatial patterns, rejecting essential meanings by examining the way in which space constitutes the subject and engages with historical specificity. The personal nature of interpretation means that every pattern will be subject to fluid, multiple meanings consistent with the polysemy of symbols. The work of Pierre Bourdieu, in particular, has been useful in understanding the process by which material culture is embedded with meanings which support hierarchical social structures based on classifications of the body, such as age and sex. Bourdieu has outlined a theory of *habitus*, an unconscious, 'learned ignorance' which provides the subject with a practical logic and sense of order. *Habitus* is conveyed socially through a process of enculturation, one which is ordered materially through objects, architecture and space.[10]

Material culture becomes integral to social structure through this process of enculturation. The notion of identity is similarly constructed through a process of self-classification which relies on 'symbolic interaction'.[11] Symbolic gestures are made with reference to the material world – landscapes, buildings, objects, clothing – which socially constitutes the body in relation to self. Thus material culture encourages self-expression, and through enculturation is central in training individuals in the behaviour appropriate to the structural relations of a specific society. Material culture is in addition used to control and maintain distance between social groups, as Michel Foucault showed in his study of the power of discipline and the space of surveillance.[12] The subject, then, is both active in interpreting material culture, and complicit in being conditioned by it. Moreover, the subject constitutes a personal identity while at the same time reproducing the structural relations of society.[13] The active social agent both constructs and reproduces social structures through material culture, but also possesses the power to challenge them through alternative strategies for its use. My archaeological approach to space considers the function, form and meaning of space, according to the construction, control and transformation of some classifications of the body.

THE STIGMATISED BODY

A sense of space is constructed according to the relationship of topographical features in the town and countryside. The pattern in which features are placed creates a map of physical spaces which orientates individuals and helps to provide their own 'space of emplacement'.[14] The positioning of boundaries is particularly powerful in establishing a sense of identity in relation to oppositions such as rural and urban, and secular and religious. The distinction between the medieval town and countryside was delineated by the construction of fortified town walls and gateways which controlled access into towns. These were symbolic and physical boundaries which demarcated different social, economic and administrative traditions. In addition it may be suggested that this boundary achieved the social classification of bodies as healthy or diseased, pious or sinful, through the placement of medieval hospitals.

Hospitals were situated in order to frame medieval towns, at the gates, in suburbs, or in extramural positions on the main arteries into towns, at harbours, bridges, and roads. Hospitals were placed at the major gates of towns such as Norwich, Bury St Edmunds, York, Beverley, Worcester and London. Leper hospitals were placed at a greater distance, beyond the walls at the town boundary. A ring of hospitals formed a boundary around towns which heightened the distinction between urban and rural and fostered a sense of urban identity. Medieval hospitals, particularly *leprosariae*, were in addition placed on rural parish boundaries, such as Ickburgh (Norfolk) where the remains of a medieval *leprosaria* stand on the parish boundary and flank a bridge. But why should hospitals be integral to the spatial definition of boundaries? This question may be addressed through a consideration of the construction of stigma as a form of social classification invested in the body.

The majority of medieval hospitals were almshouses which offered charity to those afflicted by poverty and old age. In addition there were hospices for pilgrims, infirmaries for the sick, and leper hospitals.[15] The poor, aged, infirm, and leprous were to be recipients of welfare, whether they were groups deemed worthy of charity, such as poor priests, or those targeted for welfare of a more corrective nature.[16] Hospitals were only rarely sited within city walls, within depopulated or marginal parishes. Exceptions include particularly early foundations, such as St Leonard's, York, or those associated with major religious houses, such as the Great Hospital, Norwich, with its patronal and spatial relationship to the Cathedral. It has generally been assumed that the suburban situation of hospitals resulted from a sequence of urban growth from the core outwards, with twelfth- and thirteenth-century hospital foundations pushed to the outer limits of urban development at that time. In this scenario it may not be surprising that charitable institutions were relegated to the cheaper, marginal land of the suburbs. The choice of this siting for leper hospitals may appear even less remarkable, given that they have traditionally been assumed to have fulfilled the role of isolation hospitals.[17] But how could the prominent siting of leper hospitals at gates, bridges and along major roads have facilitated a segregation of lepers effective in controlling the spread of disease?

These hospitals possessed well-defined precinct areas marked by embankments or boundary walls, as excavations have shown at SS Stephen and Thomas, New Romney (Kent) and St Nicholas, Fife. Contrary to the belief that these hospitals consisted of individual cells or cottages, archaeological evidence suggests that inmates shared communal accommodation. The earliest chapels seem to have been organised in the manner of an infirmary hall. A twelfth-century apsidal chapel on the outskirts of Dunwich (Suffolk) has the remains of a substantial cross-wall dividing the chancel, or chapel, from the nave, or lepers' hall. The twelfth-century Lazar, to the north of Norwich, appears to have been organised as a two-storey chapel, so that leprous inmates were accommodated in a gallery from which they could view the high altar. Communal halls detached from lepers' chapels were later partitioned into individual cells or almshouses at St Mary Magdalene, Glastonbury, and St Margaret, Taunton. Initially, at least, *leprosariae* were not intended to serve as isolation hospitals. The physical anthropology of skeletons excavated from leper hospitals such as SS James and Mary Magdalene, Chichester, suggests that their populations consisted of the general aged and sick poor in addition to those suffering from lepromatous and tuberculoid leprosy. In medieval society leprosy represented a conflation of diseases of the skin and was accorded a moral, rather than clinical, definition. All disease was viewed to be as much spiritual as physical, but leprosy was believed to be sexually transmitted and was considered to be a punishment for sexual sin. Medieval lepers were stigmatised both by the appalling disfigurement of their disease and by its perceived connection with lascivious behaviour.[18]

Stigma created a social identity for the victims of leprosy, who assumed the role of religious penitents in the face of sexual sin. Indeed the limited medical treatment of lepers involved the use of water in a rite of purification. Rare archaeological evidence for such practices has come from excavation at the hospital of St John the Baptist, Oxford, where immersion tanks in the eastern end of the chapel of the infirmary hall were fed by the River Cherwell. The immersion tanks, together with the dedication of the hospital, suggest that medical treatment was closely bound to the the expiation of sin, in a rite similar to baptism, in which inmates repented and were reborn. Lepers were banished from their families, homes and personal property, and expected to assume the rule and habit of the penitent. They underwent a formalised rite of stigmatisation, which took the form of a symbolic funeral and burial; it is not surprising that their treatment may have involved a symbolic rebirth.[19] The placement of stigmatised groups at the boundaries of towns is certainly consistent with Mary Douglas's observations of the way in which fear of pollution is used to protect boundaries.[20] In the positioning of medieval hospitals, stigma was used to protect and define the boundaries of towns, and the boundaries between social and economic groups.

Foucault commented on the social control achieved through the management of modern medicine and hospital architecture, which created, in effect, a space of surveillance.[21] Medieval hospital space worked more subtly. Hospitals were placed at the point of transition between territories, whether parish boundaries or the interface between urban and rural. The stigmatised body, in particular that of the leper, took on a transitional identity appropriate to this liminality. Like the biblical leper, medieval lepers 'dwelt alone, without the camp'.[22] This liminal area was used to control and observe stigmatised groups, such as the poor, aged and infirm, but was in addition used to *display* bodies classified through stigma.

The prominent siting of hospitals at the edges of towns is best explained through this desire to display stigmatised bodies. Bodies classified through distinctions commenting on health, purity and economic need were displayed to travellers, pilgrims and traders entering and leaving medieval towns. The urban boundary and identity was strengthened while encouraging additional benefits. The founders of hospitals exhibited their pious charity to the largest possible audience, thus attracting additional prayers to their chantries. The inmates of hospitals benefited economically from conspicuous sites through the collection of additional alms. And the spread of contagion may have been checked by the fear of pollution which guards boundaries.

The stigmatised body became a text through which various forms of social tension could be mediated. This is seen in the body of the leper, in whom the tensions of sin and sexuality were resolved through a symbolic death and rebirth. Other social and economic factors were mediated through the classification and spatial emplacement of bodies which were seen as poor, aged and infirm. This process of classification through the body was pivotal to a system of religious charity which required the continued existence of welfare recipients in order to ensure that the privileged donors of charity could attain salvation. Central to this ideology was a topography which linked space and the body.

THE GENDERED BODY

Space is fundamental in the construction of gender, and in the social classification of the bodies of men and women. Social attitudes towards space establish the contexts in which men and women meet, and the domains in which economic and social reproduction is enacted. It is particularly in the context of architectural and settlement space that gender is constituted, in other words, in the rooms and spaces which men and women frequent both within buildings and according to the layout of the wider settlement. Space interacts with the body in the construction of gender, by which I mean the social definition of values for masculinity and femininity. Such values vary according to social status, so that within medieval society the relationship of space and gender varied considerably across the settlement hierarchy, from hamlet or village to royal castle or monastery. Here the process of bodily classification by gender is considered in relation to the space of women in castles and monasteries.

To date, the architectural study of castles has been dominated by consideration of their role in warfare and their development according to changes in military technology. Only recently has the domestic nature of life in castles been considered.[23] But any discussion of women's spaces in castles has remained problematic, as a result of the difficulty in identifying the functions of any rooms other than the hall, chapel, kitchen and latrines. Moreover, the form and function of masonry castles developed throughout the twelfth to fifteenth centuries, and women's spaces altered accordingly.

The invisibility of women is most marked in the earliest masonry castles, the twelfth-century tower keeps which combined the functions of several buildings within one multi-storeyed, highly fortified complex. A feature of square keeps was an off-centre cross-wall which divided the space of each storey into two compartments of different proportions. This subdivision allowed the provision of private suites within the keeps, in addition to the first-floor public hall which was the main focus. In round or polygonal keeps private rooms were formed by partitioning the interiors, by constructing chambers in the thickness of walls, or through the provision of towers. T. A. Heslop has described the six levels of public and private space at Orford Castle (Suffolk), a polygonal keep with three projecting towers [1].[24] Here five private suites were provided, each with latrines and wall fireplaces; in order to achieve privacy, the suite had a door reached by an entrance corridor or staircase. Four suites were in the eastern tower and the fifth was entered from the keep at mezzanine level, where the main staircase led to the chapel (placed over the porch), and then by a corridor to a private chamber with latrine. We know that women were resident in keeps, if only in the main household of the lord. But is it possible to say more than that they resided within one of the private suites?

By the thirteenth century the emphasis of fortification had shifted from the main structure to the curtain walls, or *enceinte*. Accommodation in these enclosure castles was provided through aisled halls, with private apartments sometimes contained in towers linked to the hall. This arrangement can be seen at Helmsley (North Yorkshire), where the first stone castle on the site was built in the late twelfth century by Robert de Roos I [2]. The castle's garrison was focused on the entrances to the inner ward at the south and north barbicans. Administrative and private accommodation was tucked within the western perimeter of the ward. Women of the lord's household would have lived in the West Tower, which was linked to a hall to the north. The West Tower was rebuilt early in the fourteenth century by William de Roos, who updated the accommodation to provide latrines and fireplaces on each floor for the private suites. The women of the household, together with a small number of female servants and companions, would have been restricted to this most private part of Helmsley Castle, which, like any other aristocratic household, was for all intents and purposes male. This masculine character was reflected in the small numbers of women in aristocratic households; for instance, in the fifteenth-century household of the Earl of Northumberland there were nine women and one hundred and sixty-six men. This proportion includes servants of the household who would have been predominantly male, with only a small number of female launderers, chamberers and nursery servants.[25] Like the medieval women who feature in folklore and saints' lives, the women of many medieval castles were confined to their towers.

Women of the highest status had their own households within castles and palaces. For example, at King's Langley (Hertfordshire) Queen Eleanor of Castile had her own cloister, great and middle chambers rebuilt and gardens repositioned nearby (1278–84); Queen Philippa had four chambers, a chapel and tower built at Windsor (1363–65). By the fifteenth century palaces such as Nonsuch (Surrey) had inner courts divided into a king's and queen's side. Indeed after 1447 at Greenwich Queen Margaret of Anjou had separate courtyards constructed for the king and queen, hers overlooking the gardens. In bishops' palaces, self-contained accommodation with a private court or garden was sometimes developed for the queen's visits, at Knole (Kent) in the fifteenth century and at Wolvesey (Winchester) from the fifteenth.[26]

Documents and archaeological excavations combine to indicate the arrangements of the queen's household at Clarendon Palace (Wiltshire). This formed the four most easterly structures of the north range, which was substantially improved for Eleanor of Provence, who married Henry III in 1236.[27] Her household was located to the east of the king's apartments and was housed similarly in two storeys, consisting of a hall, wardrobe and at least three chambers. The buildings were plastered internally and provided with high-quality ceramic tile floors. The main excavated structure was a ground-floor hall and an upper storey with wall fireplace. This is likely to have been the queen's 'high chamber', which was later screened and extended by the addition of a gallery. From here a doorway provided direct access to a building connected to the south, which at this time seems to have housed the queen's chapel in its upper storey, with a

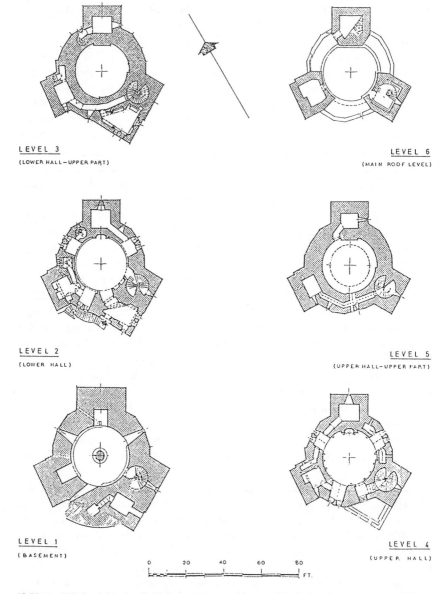

LEVEL 3
(LOWER HALL—UPPER PART)

LEVEL 6
(MAIN ROOF LEVEL)

LEVEL 2
(LOWER HALL)

LEVEL 5
(UPPER HALL—UPPER PART)

LEVEL 1
(BASEMENT)

0   20   40   60   80
FT.

LEVEL 4
(UPPER HALL)

1] Plan of Orford Castle, Suffolk, a polygonal keep with six levels of accommodation

hall below. A building attached at right angles to the others, but without
direct access between, would have formed appropriate accommodation for
the queen's chaplains, who were Franciscan friars. This structure was aligned
east–west, and consisted of two rooms at ground-floor level with hall above.

2] Helmsley Castle, North Yorkshire, from the south. To the right of the picture are the outer ditch and bailey with ruins of the south barbican, the focus of the castle's garrison. To the left is the old hall and its attached west tower which was updated by William de Roos in the fourteenth century to provide latrines and fireplaces on each floor. These most private and comfortable suites were appropriate spaces for the women of the lord's household

The eastern lower room housed an altar, while the western had a raised dais at its eastern end and benches along the walls. The Queen's Tower was near her chamber, and her private garden extended towards the north, forming, in effect, a private ward of the palace.

Occasionally, self-contained female households can be recognised at castles. At Castle Rising (Norfolk) a range of lodgings with chapel was excavated to the south of the keep, and can be linked to a period of occupation by Isabella, widow of Edward II, c.1331–58.[28] At Pickering (North Yorkshire), Countess Alice, wife of Earl Thomas of Lancaster, rebuilt the 'New Hall' in 1314 [3]. This expensive, two-storey hall had a door in its north side which led to a pentice walkway which led in turn to the chapel, where the remains of the Countess's private door can still be seen. This screened passageway allowed privacy for the Countess from the constable's lodging to the north, tower and keep to the east, and prison and barbican to the south. In these examples, increasing status seems to be accompanied by greater segregation of women's quarters, so that residences of the highest status saw the duplication of households for male and female members of the castle. This tendency towards female segregation is apparent even where women appear to have been active in commissioning their quarters, and thus represents an example of the way in which the female subject is both active in interpreting material culture, and complicit with it.

3] Pickering Castle, North Yorkshire. In 1314 Countess Alice, wife of Earl Thomas of Lancaster, rebuilt the 'New Hall', the ruined hall in the left of the picture. The hall was adjacent to the chapel (now reconstructed) to the right. A private pentice walkway was constructed against the north wall of the hall, leading to the Countess's private door into the west end of the chapel

Private accommodation in halls began to be replaced in the later four-teenth century by cellular accommodation provided in continuous ranges or stacked vertically in mural towers within quadrangular castles. By the fifteenth century the notion of cellular accommodation had developed into the ranges of the courtyard house. At Bolton Castle (North Yorkshire), built in the late fourteenth century by Richard Lord Scrope, the courtyard was formed by four three-storey internal ranges, with towers at the junctions between ranges.[28] Services and guards were contained on the ground floor, with the major accommodation in the first and second storeys of the ranges and towers. On the first floor were the garrison, guest hall, state chamber and great hall, the last two open to the roof. The third floor contained the chapel in the south range and the innermost chamber of the castle in the south-western tower, comprising a great chamber and two pairs of inner chambers. This group had direct access to a private pew in the chapel, which formed a west gallery. In addition a buttress tower to the south of the chapel provided three cells for monks from Easby Abbey, who were priests of a chantry established in 1399. On the basis of later planning principles, it is generally assumed that the innermost accommo-dation was reserved for the principal guest and household – the king and queen. The seclusion of this chamber would certainly have been appropriate for the visiting queen. But could this most segregated space have been reserved for women of the household more generally?

Women's accommodation in castles and palaces was situated with an emphasis on privacy and comfort, often including private gardens and facilities for worship. The relationship of women's accommodation to chapels seems pertinent in a number of these cases, including Pickering, Castle Rising, Clarendon and, more tentatively, Bolton. In each case private access to the chapel is apparent, and is likely to have been accompanied by private pews. Most castles had two or more chapels, and many were two-storey chapels which adjoined private chambers. In such cases the relationship of chapels and chambers may be used to consider the position of women's accommodation in the castle. These associations are clear in *Sir Gawain and the Green Knight* (*c.*1400), in which the ladies of the castle have their own *chambre* in the upper reaches of the castle, and share a private pew, or 'cumly closet', in the chapel.[29] Women's quarters were in the most segregated parts of castles, contained in the highest chambers of towers or in halls adjoining chapels. From these observations it may be possible to extrapolate back and re-examine the candidates for women's spaces in early castle-keeps. For instance, might the curious chambers adjoining first-floor chapels within the twelfth-century keeps of Norwich and Castle Rising have been associated with women? The example of Orford, however, remains ambiguous. The proximity of the chapel to the private suite in the keep makes this seem an obvious candidate for women's space, although the greater privacy of the suites in the tower might have been a more appropriate setting for the women's quarters.

Assigning functions to rooms in monasteries is less problematic, in that most monasteries followed a standard Benedictine plan and many were described in detail in inventories taken at the Dissolution. Monasteries of men and women observed similar ordinances in planning, although gender-related differences in ground plan, orientation of the cloister and architectural iconography can be detected.[31] For the purposes of comparison with women's chambers in castles, the spatial situation of dormitories in nunneries seems most pertinent. Female religious are thought to have experienced a stricter degree of monastic enclosure than their male counterparts,[32] a premise which can be tested by means of formal methods of spatial analysis. Comparative degrees of segregation within a building complex can be measured by mapping each room within the complex according to its accessibility from outside and routes of access between rooms [4].[33] This method has been used to compare a sample of sixteen male and female monasteries.[34] The results of the comparison showed an overall tendency for nunneries to have more physical boundaries between the precinct and the heart of the cloister, confirming the greater enclosure

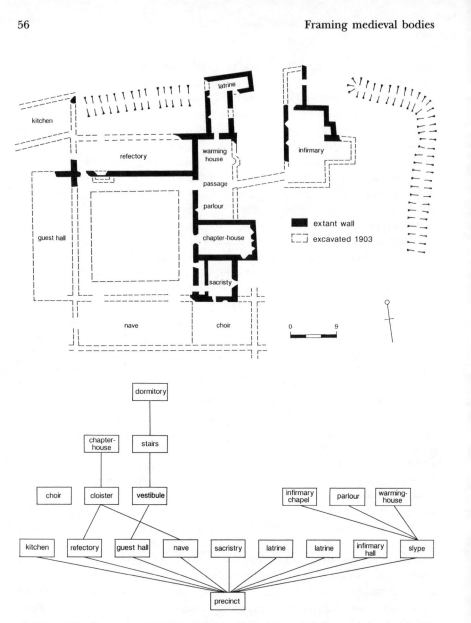

4] Plan of the nunnery of Burnham Abbey (Berkshire) and diagram showing levels of access of each room from the precinct. The most segregated space is the dormitory of the nuns

of religious women. In addition the study showed that the most segregated element of the monastery differed between male and female communities. In nunneries it was the dormitory which occupied the deepest space, whereas in monasteries this space was reserved instead for, or in addition to, the chapter house, the administrative and institutional centre of the monastery. In common with the quarters of secular women in castles, the dormitories of religious women occupied the most secluded space in the cloister. In nunneries monastic space was constructed in relation to the sanctity of the female body, in contrast to monasteries where the corporate body was paramount.

Architectural segregation was fundamental in the process of classifying the female body in monastic and secular contexts. Space was used as a medium in the construction of both sexuality and the conventions for femininity appropriate to high-status medieval women. This gendering of the body was achieved with reference to physical boundaries and architectural spaces, especially the tendencies to link female and religious spaces, and to locate them in the most segregated settings, achieved through boundaries or height; in particular the siting of women's chambers in the upper reaches of towers. Space was used to construct and reinforce a gendering of women's bodies which emphasised chastity and purity. It can be no coincidence that the iconographic representation of chastity was a tower, or that the tower was central in the martyrdom stories of the virgin-saints, in particular St Barbara. Women's chastity was protected through enclosure, but at the same time a notion of femininity was reaffirmed which took fidelity as its prime concern; fidelity to earthly or heavenly bridegrooms. The pivotal role of fidelity in gendering women's bodies can be observed in any number of funerary effigies and brasses, on which the man is represented with a lion at his foot, symbol of fortitude, and the woman appears with a dog at hers, everlasting symbol of marital fidelity in life and death. In funerary monuments material culture can again be seen to establish and maintain personal identities in relation to forms of social classification such as gender.

Like any other form of material culture the architecture of segregation had many meanings, and these were subject to change. The tower, for example, was not always a symbol of power through the control and enclosure of women. In the fifteenth and sixteenth centuries towers came to be expressions of male status and military pretence. For instance at Tattershall (Lincolnshire), Ralph Lord Cromwell demolished a thirteenth-century castle in order to erect an enormous brick tower as his residence, complete with heraldic overmantles to the fireplaces (c.1430–50).[35] Similarly at Fountains Abbey (North Yorkshire), Abbot Marmaduke Huby (1494–1526) constructed a great tower bearing his personal coat of arms. In a similar way, spatial segregation was eventually adopted to define the aristocratic male body through rules of etiquette which determined access according to social rank. This 'axis of honour' was apparent from the late fifteenth century and was fully developed by the seventeenth, when the design of formal houses was determined by a male etiquette which demanded a filtering system of rooms in order to regulate access by status.[36] The meaning of space is historically specific and capable of change in relation to the gendering of men's and women's bodies.

Space is also employed in transforming social relationships. This process may be observed for monastic space in relation to the appearance of *familiae*, households which replaced the communal patterns of dormitory and refectory. This tendency is noted increasingly for both male and female monasteries in records of bishops' visitations from the late thirteenth century, culminating in the fifteenth. It is most marked, however, in nunneries of the highest social status. In certain cases the rejection of formal monastic space is evidenced through standing or excavated remains. For example, at Godstow (Oxfordshire) the walls of the inner court mark an enclosure in which three households replaced the traditional cloister. The households were focused on the southern part of the enclosure towards the chapel, which still remains. The nuns of Godstow used space in transforming their own identities. This involved the rejection of standard male-orientated monastic planning in favour of the household arrangement familiar to women living in castles. For high-ranking women in castles and nunneries, discourses of space and the body were comparable, so that for a nun in Godstow or Countess Alice at Pickering Castle, spatial reference points overlapped, consisting of hall, private chapel and enclosure walls. Moreover, these women appear to have chosen this arrangement of space as their *habitus*, an unconscious, practical logic ordered materially through architecture and space. Their choices reveal the powerful nature of enculturation through material culture. Although this may seem to be a constricting arrangement, the individual or collective female agent chose this spatial pattern in an act of empowerment and transformation. Yet their choice reinforced the wider structural relations of medieval society implied by this gendering of the body through space.

CONCLUSIONS: THE BODY AS TEXT

This paper has illustrated two contrasting examples of the way in which space is employed in discourses of power based on the social classification of the body. In the first example, bodies classified through stigma – according to parameters of age, poverty, health and purity – were constructed in relation to a topography which enabled diseased, leprous and aged bodies to be displayed through the siting of medieval hospitals. In the second example, space was used to achieve precisely the opposite effect. The bodies of high-status women classified through gender were hidden through architectural mechanisms of segregation and enclosure which included towers, private facilities for worship, exclusively female households, and physical boundaries such as walls, gardens and filtering systems which regulated access. Despite these differences, certain similarities can be observed in the use of space in constituting stigma and femininity. Both constructs relied upon notions of boundaries, whether physical, social or ideological. But how were the real and conceptual boundaries between social groups maintained?

To a certain extent fear of pollution may have protected these boundaries. The bodies of lepers and women were considered corrupt in their different ways; lepers through the perceived connection between disease and sexual sin, and women through the essential corporeality attributed to them in theological treatises and biblical exegesis. In a society which elevated the contrasting figures of the Virgin Mary and Mary Magdalene, women were simultaneously idealised and stigmatised, resulting in ambiguity of meaning in relation to the female body. In the aristocratic household, an institution which was overwhelmingly male in composition, courtesy and householding books indicate a hostility towards the presence of any unnecessary women.[37] The central women of the 'inner household', the lord's wife, daughters and their companions, were bounded and protected by a religious ideology which held female chastity and fidelity in high esteem and supported a system of social reproduction in which these characteristics were central to structures of the family and inheritance. A code of chivalric honour was relied upon to protect the inalienability of these particular boundaries, where tension must have been apparent between what Mark Girouard termed 'an island of womanhood and the masculine world that surrounded it'.[38]

Integral to the social classification of bodies by stigma and gender were concepts of purity which interacted with religious belief, in particular notions of sexual sin which surrounded the body of the leper and expectations of purity and sexual fidelity invested in women's bodies. Aspects of material culture were used to construct these classifications of the body, through which social tensions were expressed and mediated. The bodies of lepers and women became texts through the social classification of stigma and gender, a process in which space was active and essential.

NOTES

1 Examples of this influence can be seen in C. Tilley, ed., *Reading Material Culture. Structuralism, Hermeneutics and Post-structuralism*, Oxford, 1990, and J. M. Gero and M. W. Conkey, eds, *Engendering Archaeology. Women and Prehistory*, Oxford, 1991.

2 F. Baldwin, *Sumptuary Legislation and Personal Regulation in England*, Baltimore, 1926; C. Coulson, 'Structural symbolism in medieval castle architecture', *Journal of the British Archaeological Association*, CXXXII, 1979, pp. 73–90.

3 Approaches to the construction of purity and stigma may be found in the standard works: M. Douglas, *Purity and Danger. An Analysis of Concepts of Pollution and Taboo*, Harmondsworth, 1970, and E. Goffman, *Stigma: Notes on the Management of a Spoiled Identity*, Harmondsworth, 1965.

4 J. Barrett, 'Towards an archaeology of ritual', in *Sacred and Profane*, P. Garwood, ed., Oxford, 1991, pp. 1–9.
5 Insights have been brought to the creative role of interpretation by the anthropological work of Clifford Geertz, for instance *The Interpretation of Culture*, New York, 1973. A critique of power relations in the production of archaeological knowledge may be found in M. Shanks and C. Tilley, *Reconstructing Archaeology*, Cambridge, 1987.
6 Examples of this approach include I. Hodder and C. Orton, *Spatial Analysis in Archaeology*, Cambridge, 1976.
7 See in particular B. Hillier and J. Hanson, *The Social Logic of Space*, Cambridge, 1984, and S. Kent, ed., *Domestic Architecture and the Use of Space*, Cambridge, 1990.
8 S. Kent, 'A cross-cultural study of segmentation, architecture and the use of space', *ibid.*, pp. 27–52.
9 H. Moore, *Space, Text and Gender. An Anthropological Study of the Marakwet of Kenya*, Cambridge, 1986; P. Ricoeur, *Hermeneutics and the Human Sciences*, Cambridge, 1981; and H. Moore, 'Paul Ricoeur: action, meaning and text' in C. Tilley, ed., *Reading Material Culture*, pp. 85–120.
10 P. Bourdieu, *Outline of a Theory of Practice*, Cambridge, 1977.
11 M. J. Deegan and M. Hill, eds, *Women and Symbolic Interaction*, Boston, 1987.
12 M. Foucault, *Discipline and Punish*, Harmondsworth, 1979.
13 A. Giddens, *The Constitution of Society*, Cambridge, 1984.
14 M. Foucault, 'Of other spaces', *Diacritics*, XVI, 1986, pp. 22–7.
15 M. Carlin, 'Medieval English Hospitals', in *The Hospital in History*, L. Granshaw and R. Porter, eds, 1989, pp. 21–39. For archaeological elucidation of these types see R. Gilchrist, 'Christian bodies and souls: the archaeology of life and death in later medieval hospitals', in *Death in Towns, 1100–1600*, S. Bassett, ed., Leicester, 1993, pp. 101–13.
16 M. Rubin, 'Development and change in medieval hospitals', in Granshaw and Porter, eds, *Hospital in History*, pp. 41–59.
17 R. M. Clay, *The Medieval Hospitals of England*, London, 1909.
18 Archaeological evidence for New Romney, St Andrew, Fife, and Chichester may be consulted in S. E. Rigold 'Two Kentish Hospitals Re-examined', *Archaeologia Cantiana*, LXXIX, 1964, pp. 31–69; 'Medieval Britain', *Medieval Archaeology*, XXXII, 1988, p. 302, and F. Lee and J. Magilton, 'The cemetery of the Hospital of St James and St Mary Magdalene, Chichester – a case study', *World Archaeology*, XXI, 1989–90, pp. 273–82, respectively. Recent discussions of the social meaning of leprosy include J. Richards, *Sex, Dissidents and Damnation*, London, 1990, and R. I. Moore, *The Formation of a Persecuting Society*, London, 1987.
19 The archaeology of St John the Baptist, Oxford, is discussed in 'Medieval Britain', *Medieval Archaeology*, XXXII, 1988, pp. 270–1. The rite of separation of the leper is printed in Clay, *Medieval Hospitals*, pp. 273–6.
20 Douglas, *Purity and Danger*.
21 Foucault, *Discipline and Punish*.
22 Leviticus 13.45–6.
23 Especially M. W. Thompson, *The Rise of the Castle*, Cambridge, 1991, and *The Decline of the Castle*, Cambridge, 1987; J. R. Kenyon, *Medieval Fortifications*, Leicester, 1990; and T. A. Heslop, 'Orford Castle, nostalgia and sophisticated living', *Architectural History*, XXXIV, 1991, pp. 36–58.
24 Heslop, 'Orford Castle', p. 39.
25 M. Girouard, *Life in the English Country House*, London, 1978, pp. 27–8; and K. Mertes, *The English Noble Household 1250–1600. Good Governance and Political Rule*, Oxford, 1988, pp. 57–8.
26 T. B. James, *The Palaces of Medieval England, c.1050–1550*, London, 1990, pp. 93, 123, 140; P. A. Faulkner, 'Some Medieval Archiepiscopal Palaces', *Archaeological Journal*, CXXVII, 1970, p. 141.

27 The Queen's apartments were excavated in the 1930s. An interpretation by Elizabeth Eames is published in T. B. James and A. M. Robinson, *Clarendon Palace. The History and Archaeology of a Medieval Palace and Hunting Lodge near Salisbury, Wilts*, Society of Antiquaries Report XLV, 1988. Discussion of pertinent documents pp. 17–21; excavation pp. 109–14, where the buildings interpreted as the chamber is referred to as 10a, the chapel 10b, and the chaplains' accommodation 10c/d.

28 Kenyon, *Medieval Fortifications*, p. 137.

29 P. A. Faulkner, 'Castle Planning in the fourteenth century', *Archaeological Journal*, CXX, 1967, pp. 215–35.

30 W. R. J. Barron, trans., *Sir Gawain and the Green Knight*, Manchester, 1974, lines 975, 1373, 933, 938.

31 R. Gilchrist, *Gender and Material Culture, The Archaeology of Religious Women*, London, 1994.

32 J. T. Schulenburg, 'Strict active enclosure and its effect on the female monastic experience', in J. A. Nichols and L. T. Shank, eds, *Medieval Religious Women I. Distant Echoes*, Kalamazoo, 1984, pp. 51–86.

33 This method of syntactic spatial analysis is based on Hillier and Hanson, *Social Logic of Space*.

34 Gilchrist, *Gender and Material Culture*, and summarised in 'The spatial archaeology of gender domains: a case study of medieval English nunneries', *Archaeological Review from Cambridge*, VII, 1988, pp. 21–8.

35 Thompson, *Decline of the Castle*, p. 72.

36 This first appears in the Harleian Regulations, an Elizabethan copy of an apparently late fifteenth-century original, Girouard, *Country House*, pp. 64, 144–6.

37 Mertes, *Noble Household*, p. 57.

38 Girouard, *Country House*, p. 28.

The image and the self: unwriting late medieval bodies

The law constantly writes itself on bodies. It engraves itself on parchment made from the skin of its subjects. It articulates them in a juridicial corpus. It makes its book out of them.[1]

The body hinges open like the pages of a book to be analysed and read in the figures illustrating a mid-fourteenth-century anatomical treatise by the French royal physician Guido da Vigevano [5]. One of the linear developments postulated by the 'old' history of art was that of increasing naturalism in bodily representation, a trajectory in which these early images of human dissection once had a place.[2] But now we assume that nothing is natural, everything is constructed, the body as well as society. The metaphorical power of the body to stand for 'any bounded system' was never more relevant than during the Middle Ages when it served as the locus of a variety of social displacements, intensely-felt religious practices, medical and philosophical debate as well as courtly self-fashioning.[3] Recent historical research exploring these issues has tended to 'read' the body like a book and to view it through a purely textual grid. In what follows I want to map out some of the ways in which a host of competing notions of the body existed in the thirteenth and fourteenth centuries that were articulated, not through texts, but through images. A historian of the body in the French Revolution has written that 'bodies are important because the only experiences that cannot be co-opted by political systems are the inevitably personal bodily experiences of individuals'.[4] This distinctly modern notion of the relation between the somatic and the social does not hold for the medieval period when the human body was the site of intense visual scrutiny and surveillance by the Church, was subject to the bonds of feudal lordship and was at the same time caught in a cosmic network that controlled both its internal and external movements. First I shall look at some of the ways in which the interrelated discourses of cosmology, politics and religion both utilised and were shaped by current visions of corporeality, and then examine how these models served to construct not only communal, but also individual identity in the manic self-imaging of a particular person, a priest and artist whose mind and body broke down

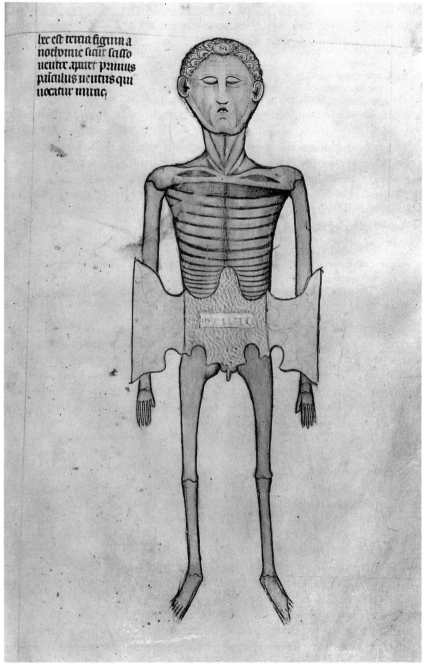

5] The body opened

in March 1334. Only at the end of this essay will we see anything like a personalised body and even then, one caught up in the problem, not of individuality, but of cosmic self-consciousness.

BODY/COSMOS

The most all-encompassing (literally circumscribing, as with a compass) body in later medieval culture was the cosmos itself, that of the *corpus animatum* of the heavens as described by the 'new' philosophy of Aristotle in *De Caelo et Mundo* and illustrated in a tiny marginal drawing made at Oxford University [6]. This pruriently clothed little man is drawn upside-down, his limbs outstretched but not touching the circumference of the circle as in Leonardo da Vinci's famous drawing of Vitruvian man over two hundred years later. However, this is not a representation of the human body as a paradigm of perfect proportion but rather as a site of orientation. As Aristotle explained

> It is in relation to ourselves that we speak of above and below, or right and left, in these objects. We name them either as they correspond with our own right hands (as in augury), or by analogy with our own (as in the right hand of a statue).[5]

This self-referentiality explains why the figure is drawn upside-down in this diagram. It is so that his right hand, pointing *oriens*, or east, corresponds to the viewer's right and the South Pole is under our horizon. If the cosmos is a living thing and the east is its right, then 'the south must be its head'.[6] A hundred years later in 1377 when Aristotle's treatise was translated for King Charles V of France by Nicole Oresme as *Le Livre du ciel et du monde*, the figure of the living body of the heavens is turned so as to be orientated with his head upright and so that the South Pole is now uppermost on the page [7]. East is here on the left so that image and reality are no longer conjoined in the viewing subject but have become separated into subject and object. This figure is now someone else 'out there' – a representation labelled Atlas that we have to invert conceptually in our minds if we are to understand his relation to the four cardinal points and poles. As Oresme's gloss states 'if a picture is placed facing us, its right side is opposite our left side, while its left is opposite our right', concluding that 'these four positional differences, right and left, front and rear, exist in the heavens only by analogy' and that Aristotle's picture of the heavens as 'living body' or *corpus animatum* has to be modified.[7] In its miniature reorientation of the cosmos this drawing is paradigmatic of the new objectivity of the image in the fourteenth century. It no longer maps a subjective position since its right hand is on our left, its left hand on our right. We have to separate it mentally from ourselves as an external representation. To put it more simply, it is now a picture.

6] The body as the model for direction in the cosmos

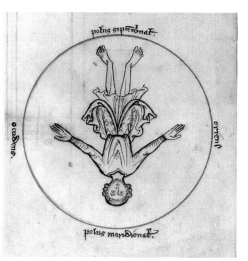

7] The body as the model for direction in the fourteenth-century cosmos

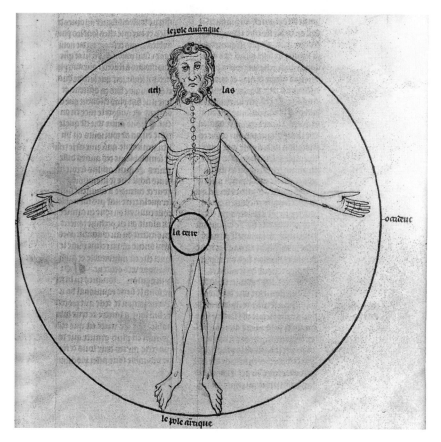

That the human body came into its own as a site of spectacle and metaphorical projection in the fourteenth century is shown in a miniature of the French version of Bartholomeus Anglicus's *Livre des Propriétés des Choses* [8], illustrating Book V 'du corps de l'homme et de ses parties'.[8] In the interior of a fashionable residence a university doctor points out to a fashionably dressed nobleman a picture on the wall above a little dog on a bench, perhaps an indication of man's superior position, even as an image, above the animals. This naked body is one of the earliest examples of what we would call a modern framed painting. It is not a devotional altarpiece nor a narrative fresco cycle. It is the frontal, framed microcosm, man without his universe.

8] The body as a picture in medieval private life

Most medieval people, and not just the readers of treatises by Oresme and Bartholomeus Anglicus, saw an inextricable link between heavenly and earthly bodies. The traditional microcosmic model of the universe, especially popular in the twelfth century, had described influence working in both directions with man as a *minor mundus* or 'lesser world', often illustrated at the centre of things in splendid cosmological diagrams.[9] However, with the revival of astrology in the fourteenth century influence was increasingly seen to go in one direction only. This was from 'superior to inferior things' in St Bonaventure's words,

> because they are nobler bodies and excel in power, just as they excel with
> respect to location. And since the order of the universe is that the more powerful

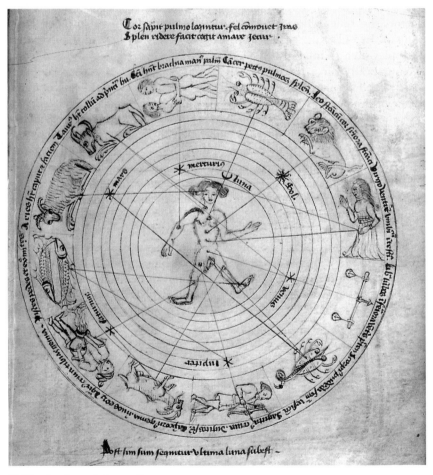

9] The body and the zodiac

and superior should influence the less powerful and inferior, it is appropriate for the order of the universe that the celestial luminaries should influence the elements and elementary bodies.[10]

The stars were tangible bodies which, floating high above, had direct 'lines' to specific parts of one's anatomy and ruled, as did the moon the tides, the waves of humoral fluids within one's body. This is neatly visualised in a diagram from a French medical manuscript in which lines of influence pin down the body's various parts [9]. This anthropomorphic scheme shows both the planets in the inner circles, which ruled the internal organs, and the signs of the moving zodiac in the outer belt, which were believed to affect the external anatomy. Such diagrams, which often placed the zodiacal signs directly on the body and were known as the *homo signorum*, had a very practical and public purpose in showing barber-surgeons and doctors the times when it was auspicious or inauspicious to bleed their patients. In 1427 King Charles VII ordered all the barbers in the kingdom to display such an image in their shops 'pour le bien de la chose publicque et pour pourveoir a la saintete du corps humaine'.[11] If earlier medieval writers like Hildegarde of Bingen (1098–1179) had seen in the microcosmic image of the outstretched human body the splendid Augustinian order of the universe with man as its focus, fourteenth-century thinkers faced a less comforting picture. The little stick-like man in this diagram is more like an insect trapped in a spider's web of fate or a victim strapped to an ever-turning wheel of agonising medical torment than a sign of superiority and centrality.

Vertical hierarchy ruled human physiology too, in which the head, in another illustration from the same medical manuscript, is labelled the *prima regio* [10].[12] The genital area was, by contrast, a site of shame, the uncontrollable Augustinian signal of man's Fall, marked here as the fourth and lowest region.[13] This division of the body into higher nobler parts that were supposed to rule the lower was common in medical and theological discourse but had most influence in political theory, which posited the body, not as a model for heavenly order, but for the structure of earthly society.

BODY/POLITICS

John of Salisbury's metaphor of the state 'as a sort of body' appears in his *Policraticus*, a book of advice for courtiers and princes written in 1159, that has been called the first complete work of political theory written during the Middle Ages.[14] John's picture of political order was not visualised by an artist until the mid-fourteenth century in a vernacular treatise written for a Valois prince where 'la sainte escripture' is cited as the source for the

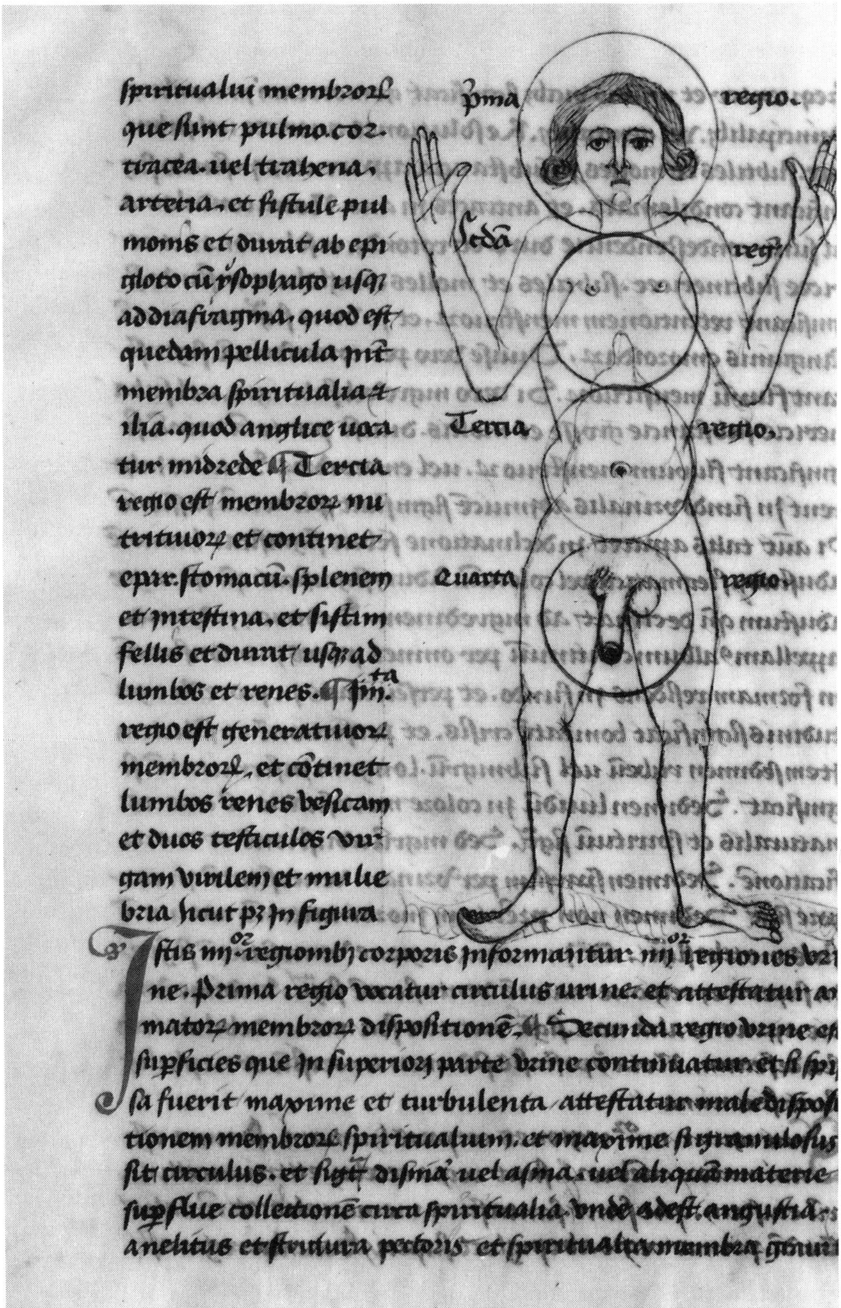

10] The body and its four regions

elegant naked figure [11].[15] Reading further we are told that this image represents how 'the King is head above the subject people'. A crown signifies this royal authority in the image. The rest of the parts of the body politic have to be labelled with scrolls, the eyes 'seneschals', the stomach 'conseilliers', the arms 'chevaliers', the legs, 'marchauntes' and the feet 'laboureurs sur terre'. To understand this representation of the state as a hierarchy of subject members all working in harmony under the rule of the head one has to remember that medieval physiology conceived of the human organism as a union of like and unlike parts in which the central and higher organs controlled the lower ones. Although from the thirteenth century onwards the Aristotelian notion of the heart as the centre of the senses and soul became increasingly influential, this image, like John of Salisbury's 'body politic' image, retains the Neoplatonic notion of vertical authority.[16]

The controversy between the primacy of heart over head was complicated by a more fundamental and crucial dichotomy – that of body and soul. The body politic like the body animal needed a soul, or *pars principans*, in order to move it. John of Salisbury stated that 'just as the soul has rulership of the body so those who are called prefects of religion direct the whole body' making the clergy the incorporeal spiritual leaders of his commonwealth.[17] Medieval artists had a problem when it came to the soul. As a spiritual *pneuma* associated by some medical writers with the breath, it was an invisible force and thus difficult to illustrate. Imbued by God at the moment of creation/conception or freed from the fleshly weight at death as in illustrations of Aristotle's *De Anima*, the soul was only visualised in its movements into and out of the body that it defined [12]. As the Aristotelian 'form of the body' the soul was often pictured in thirteenth- and fourteenth-century art as a miniature repetition of the human form. As the last breath or *spiritus* left the defunct corpse, a little homunculus, representing *through* a body its very antithesis, was shown escaping into the arms of an angel or devil.[18] This also alerts us to the power of the mouth in medieval culture as a dangerous liminal zone, a hole in the crucial barrier between inside and outside. Loaded in earlier medieval art with metaphorical associations of eating and speaking it was also the crucial channel of this animating spirit.[19]

The body politic was also a powerful metaphor for medieval jurists arguing on both sides of the disputes between ecclesiastical and royal authority in the fourteenth century, precisely because it presented an ideal of organic order. In reality there was not one notion of the *corpus* in this period but a host of competing corporealities. The canon-lawyer Hostiensis (d.1271) enumerated a list of the various types of bodies:

> All the faithful might be called a single body of which Christ is the head and we the members. A college or a university are said to be a single body of which

11] The body politic

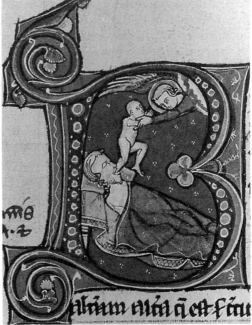

12] The body and the soul

one calls the head the prelate and the members the college. One calls a body
that which gives grace to a soul (*spiritus*) like a tree or a man. Or still that which
holds the parts together like a house. Or where the parts are distinct, one from
another like a troop or a people or a college. Finally man and woman form but
one body.[20]

Seals were the most common forms of collective representation in this
period. Belonging to various lay and ecclesiastical communities and institutions these public visual signs represented through pre-eminent body
types, the frontal vested bishop and the equestrian knight in profile, the
two controlling orders of society.[21] Those who had no control over their
bodies – the serfs – initially had no seals. This meant that in representa-
tional terms they also lacked bodies. When in France during the fourteenth
century the third estate began to use seals, these usually showed the tools
of the trades or name-punning emblems rather than the figures of their
owners.

Hostiensis describes any materialisation or union of discrete parts as a
body, even including the coming together in marriage. An unusual image
of this union of the sexes into a bicephalous creature sharing one body
occurs in a late thirteenth-century northern French treatise on moral
philosophy [13]. Crucial to the metaphor of the body politic was the
stability and normative nature of the human organism which can only
have one head, as the two sides of the papal/imperial disputes constantly
reminded one another. To have pope and emperor equally powerful in
the state, some argued, is to create a monster, an *animal biceps*. The
anomalous body of any kind, whether it be that of those born deformed
or later twisted and crippled by disease, was taboo in medieval society. Yet
increasingly in the later Middle Ages the multiheaded aberration which
had been such a ubiquitous sign of the multiplicity of evil and even Antichrist in twelfth-century art could be appropriated to represent central
dogmas of the Catholic faith, such as the Trinity [14]. The three-headed
Trinity, like the minute Christ-child flying down from God the Father in
scenes of the Annunciation, or the popular statues of the Virgin Mary
whose belly opened to reveal the inner workings of salvation, were sometimes attacked by orthodox churchmen as being 'in error' precisely because they located theological truths in that most radically ductile and
dangerous thing – the body.[22]

To use such visually complex and fantastic images for Christian image-
making was also dangerous because in Gothic art such image aberrations
were usually associated with what had been excluded from the Church
and the sacred body. Excremental images of monstrosity, bifurcation and
multiplicity of parts were available to a wide range of beholders, significantly at the margins.[23] It was here, projecting from monasteries, cathe-
drals, houses and at the edges of textiles and luxury objects, as well as of

13] The body of two lovers united

14] The body of three angels appearing to Abraham *in figura trinitatis*

sacred and secular texts, that the engorging, farting, defecating and sala-
ciously erect bodies of creatures mingling human with animal and vegeta-
ble parts had their legitimate site [15]. This site of image-making more
than any other reminds us of the anti-spiritual current in medieval culture, in which all the fecund and fluid eroticism of what Bakhtin called
'the lower bodily strata' presented a real alternative to the vertical hierarchy of the body/soul previously described. Focusing on the liminal
boundaries of the body – mouth and anus – these images allowed the
artist to pun on and poke holes in the sacred page. They are the anti-
bodies of Christ at the centre. But as we shall see, during the fourteenth
century even His body began to assimilate some of the liquidity and
liminality of these monstrous things.

BODY/CHRIST

The first and most important of all the bodies listed by Hostiensis was that
belonging to God. The body's powerful place in Christianity relied upon
this fact of Word becoming flesh. During the very period when artists
began to depict this fleshiness of God in his suffering on the cross, the
word *corpus* was taking on wider political resonance. The phrase 'mystical
body' which had once stood for the eucharist itself, came to signify the
whole Catholic Church, which found such metaphors crucial to emphasising
its supreme position among various new institutions and heretical frac-
tures and splits in the body of the faithful during the thirteenth century.[24]
A way of underlining the Church's concrete as well as its divine preroga-
tive, Christ's body, exalted in the Dogma of Transubstantiation (1215)
and the Feast of Corpus Christi (1264) had a unique place within the body
politic, separate, above and yet simultaneously within it.[25] New devotional
image-types, like the Man of Sorrows which emphasised the bodily suffering of the Saviour [16] were first imported from Byzantium in the form
of icons and panel paintings. These focused the viewer's gaze on Christ's
body during and after the Passion and, as Hans Belting has shown, were
the stimulus to new doctrinal ideas, theological transformations and poetic
texts, and not merely their result.[26] The image, not the Word, mediated
most powerfully between God and the believer in late medieval spirituality.
Images 'not made by human hands' like the Veronica were taken direct
from the prototype itself, as imprints of the holy flesh. In the case of the
Man of Sorrows the theme was legitimated not by texts but by a vision of
the suffering saviour experienced by Pope Gregory the Great as he
celebrated mass at Santa Croce in Gerusalemme in Rome and recorded in
a miracle-working icon there.[27]

As a professional imager the medieval artist was not creating 'art' in our

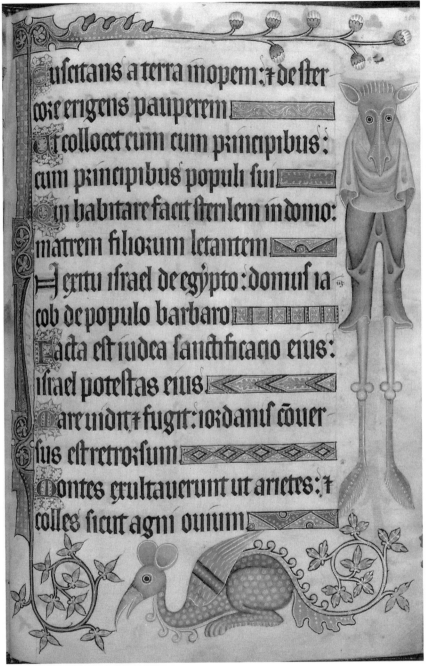

15] The body in the margins

16] The body of the Man of Sorrows

sense of the word, but visual propaganda aimed at an increasingly volatile mass of semi-illiterates yearning for access to the Word through the flesh of the image. The tendency to see late medieval devotional attitudes as intensely personal, expressive and increasingly private has resulted in our overlooking important links between the sacred and the social. This can be seen in a fifteenth-century English miniature illustrating Lydgate's *Fall of Princes*, where Christ's central near-naked body is surrounded by a mandorla of the various orders of society [17]. His feet are associated with ploughman and labourer and his head crowned by those above even the clergy, the princes of the world, at whose pomp and empty glory this text was aimed. The message is clear without even reading the text; that the stable centre of all things is contained in the body of Christ, around which revolves the social hierarchy of the world and its differentiated estates. Until recently art historians tended to separate late medieval devotional images into some transcendent realm apart from the political forces that shaped society. This image reminds us that prayer too can be political; that we are always situating God's body somewhere and looking at Him from a privileged position, often within the image itself, where a small donor-viewer provides an internal empathising focus.

Christ's body in the increasingly somatised private devotions of the fourteenth century was also represented as interacting with the bodies of viewers. His blood mingles with the milk that squirts from the breast of His mother in an unusual initial in the mid-fourteenth-century *Zouche Hours* [18]. The devotional urge was not merely visionary but involved all the senses, especially touch. In this period which saw the increasing emphasis on sight – the need to see the elevation of the host during mass for example, or the increasing visibility of relics in transparent crystal contain-ers – the yearnings for physical intimacy found new and startling shapes. The image of the Resurrected Christ in the *Zouche Hours* is an eroticised, gender-bending and penetrable body open to flows and fluid desires that signalled danger in other, lesser bodies. Medievalists, recently freed from a tyrannous propriety that for so long obfuscated the body as a site of cultural meaning, are at last able to describe and trace this verbal and visual gender-bending, where parts of Christ's body, such as His wound, as depicted in fourteenth-century Books of Hours, becomes a vast vagina-like object of desire, a transference of the dangerously open body of woman in all her horrifying 'difference'.[28]

BODY/DANGER

On the lintel of the Last Judgement tympanum, carved at Bourges cathe-dral in the mid-thirteenth century, a young female figure pulls off her

17] The body of Christ as the body politic

drapery with one hand while her other both touches and hides her genitals like an ancient statue of Venus [19]. Georges Duby has described this image as representing a newly positive attitude to the medieval body, rehabilitated, 'young, radiant, satisfied, reconciled'.[29] But this body is dead. It stands in a grave awakened by the sound of the last trumpet and precisely for all its charms is on the side of the damned, the sinister side of sinners who will burn in Hell for ever. For medieval viewers the body that is revealed beneath her shroud in all its sensuality was a sign not of promise, but of decay, not of the beauty but the fatal fallen nature of the female body. In a French medical manuscript from the same period this body is

18] The body of Christ and the exchange of fluids

associated with Hell even more directly [20]. A series of scenes from Christ's life are shown in a sequence above two tiers of scenes of doctors at work, usually described as quite separate and distinct from the sacred events above them.[30] However, at the moment of Christ's burial in the black shape of a tomb in the top centre, a male practitioner delves deep into a girl's inverted body below. Next, as Christ leads Adam and Eve from the jaws of Hell she opens her legs in an unusual scene of gynaecological exploration.[31] Diseased male sexual organs are also exhibited at the bottom of the page but the exegetical emphasis in these images is upon the old associations between the female body and death. Recent studies by Caroline Walker Bynum and others have tried to show how women used their bodies as powerful conduits of devotional display during the Middle Ages and how, particularly for cloistered women, the somatic could be a more positive form of self-expression. But this should not blind us to the misogynistic roots of medieval culture that relegated most women to an inferior status medically, socially and spiritually.[32] The traditional image of *luxuria*, which in the twelfth century appears carved on many portals and

19] The beautiful body of the damned woman

doorways, represented a woman suffering in Hell by having those parts of her body through which she sinned in life bitten by serpents. In an amazingly explicit version of this subject at Toulouse [21] the serpent not only gnaws at the figure's breasts but emerges from, or enters her vagina, like a perverse phallus. In some exegetical traditions Adam and Eve had allowed themselves to be penetrated by the serpent, signifying sodomy and masturbation, sins of the body to which this unusual carving may allude.[33] Attempts by modern historians to diminish differences between the medieval conception of male and female bodies is best exemplified by Thomas Lacquer who argues that during the Middle Ages a 'one sex model' existed, according to which a woman's genitals were seen as only a reversed and interiorised reflection of a man's.[34] But artists clearly distinguished the dangerous female body as different from the more important but also more vulnerable male one, in everything from the scene of the Last Judgement at Bourges, where it is the very voluptuousness of the woman's body that consigns it to the flames, to the horrendous Romanesque *luxuria* [21] whose sexual organs are engorged by the fetishistic phallus of her own desire.

Images located in medical discourse make this point about difference even more strongly. The 'opposite sex' is depicted across the opening of a Provençal medical manuscript in Basle that pictures the woman on the

20] The body of Christ above, the body of woman below

21] The body of *luxuria* and the penis-serpent

left-hand page, not because woman comes first, but because she is a sinister daughter of Eve [22]. These two drawings made *c.*1300 show sexual physiology entering the traditional 'five figure series', a group of drawings depicting the various systems of veins, arteries, bones, nerves and muscles – usually all drawn upon the paradigmatic body of the male.[35] Here for the first time, according to Karl Sudhoff, a woman's body is displayed in the context of this series of medical diagrams. The female body was problematic because of its lack of heat, another reason why it is placed on the cold, left side. On the warm right-hand page the man spreads his legs, as was traditional in the series. By contrast, the female's legs are closer together, Karl Sudhoff thought 'out of propriety'.[36] Yet this is another means of differentiating her constricted and problematic body from that of the male. Whereas his veins and fluids are spread all over his body, including the twin 'V' veins on his forehead, which were thought to be the channel of semen from the brain down to the testes, hers are bounded in particular areas. His penis is thus linked to his brain whereas nothing above her neck serves in her system of procreation. She is all body. Her head is hidden, covered by a hairnet, avoiding the medieval association of long hair and concupiscence. Indeed her whole body is held in by networks of linear control, rendering her passive and waiting, a mere receptacle for male semen. Her breasts are two added appendages. Her only significant organ is the seven-lobed uterus, the crucial sign of her ability to procreate according to the Provençal text here: 'La maire a vii locs ou se pot far enfant. iii de la dreita part e iii de la sinestra e un el mieg' ('The uterus has seven places and can reproduce four children on the right side, three on the left and one in the middle'). Even that most female-coded organ, the uterus, has a right-sided, male bias. The text goes on to describe the woman's body as a jar for cooking a foetus in, for bringing to fruition the seminal idea implanted in her body by the male seed. These two images, differentiating the male and female bodies, articulate the basic Aristotelian notion held throughout the Middle Ages that the male provides the fiery active principle of form, whereas the cold, wet female provides mere matter through her menstrual fluid. Such imbalance in the physical constitution of male and female bodies and its effect upon the roles played by men and women is everywhere visible in medieval art, in the soft, pliant forms and cold wet colours used to delineate female characters as opposed to the bright, rosy and vibrant hues of male protagonists in paintings and polychrome sculpture.

A new physiognomy joins that of the dangerous female body as the site of fear and fantasy in the fourteenth century, a body however that is rendered sexless, without flesh and reduced to its bare bones. The skeleton became a fashionable image in wall paintings of the Three Living and Three Dead and in medical and moralising manuscripts early in the fourteenth century, decades before the Black Death was to make everyone visibly aware of human decay.[37] Here was a socially undifferentiated sign of the radically equalising power of death personified. Art historians have still a lot to learn about the way that burial customs and fashionable funerary practices like embalming and organ burial interact with representations, notably in tomb sculpture. Significantly, the body was not thought to be truly dead, its spirit separated from the body, until a year after burial. Only when all the flesh had left it and it was nothing, nobody, was

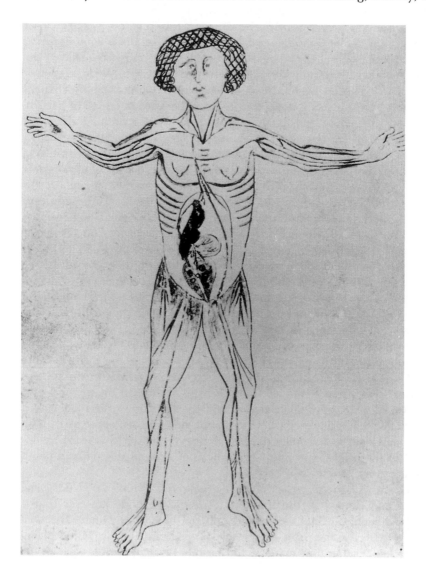

it 'Death'. The fascination with mortification and skeletal display in the funerary art of the late fourteenth century attests to changing attitudes to the body, whose importance did not decline after death but rather continued to haunt the living in sepulcral simulacra long after. Anxieties and debates about the fate of the body after death and its proper reconstitution in the afterlife were especially marked in this period.[38] In a medical manuscript dating from early in the fourteenth century, next to the outline of a male figure who represents Adam holding the forbidden fruit in

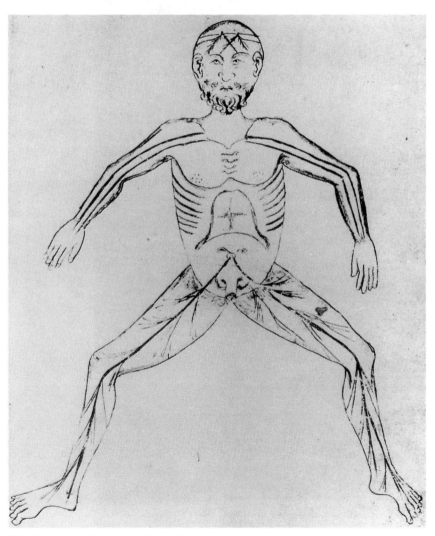

22] The body of woman [*facing*] and the body of man

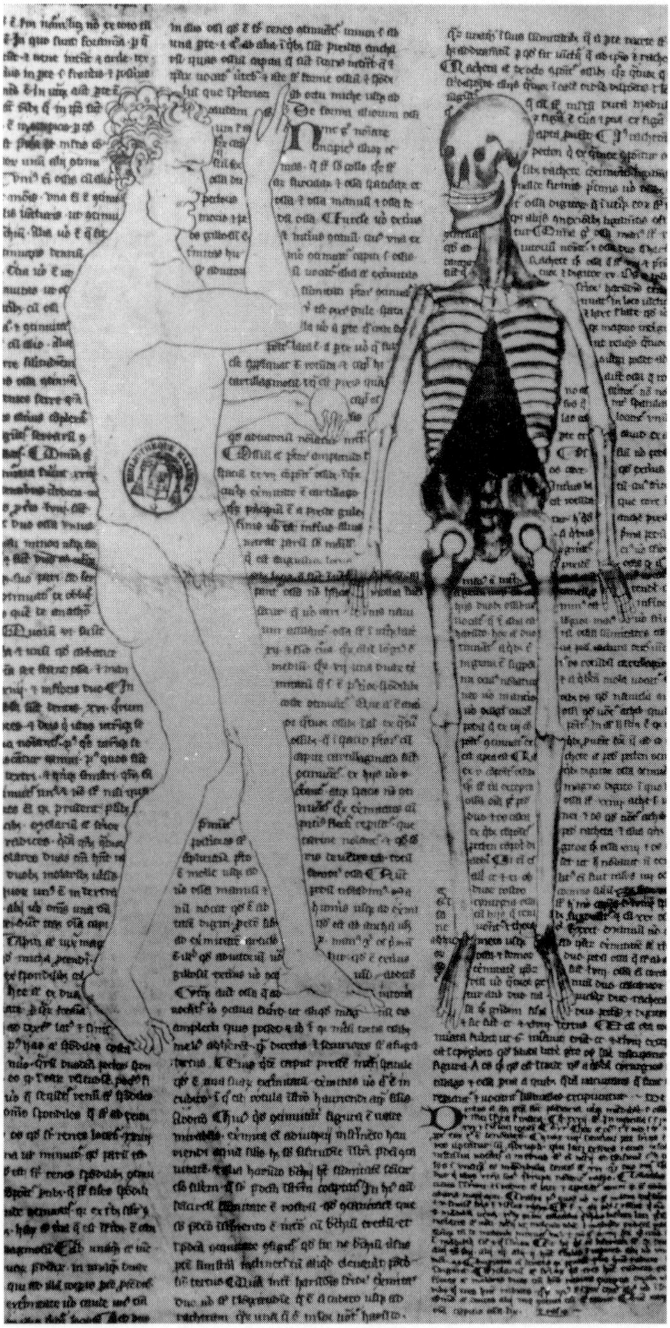

23] The body of death as skeleton

his hand, stands the result of the Fall upon the human body, one of the earliest depictions of a skeleton with a black gaping emptiness in the hollow of his belly [23].[39] Contemplating such images and urged by preachers and poets to remind themselves of their own mortality at every moment, fourteenth-century men and women were attuned to their bodies in a way that it is hard for us to imagine today. Admonished to look at themselves in mirrors which were emblems of the fleeting vanity of fleshly appearance, they saw the grinning skull. The figure facing Adam in the drawing is his *alter ego* or mirror image of what he will become. This same idea of juxtaposing the youthful body with its future double was multiplied through the social hierarchy in the *Dance of the Dead* painted at the Cemetery of the Innocents in Paris in 1426. This was a site for lovers to stroll in and for family outings, where visitors could view charnel-houses piled high with exposed skulls, as well as elaborate tombs and paintings. Cemeteries were thus the earliest museums as well as another crucial site for bodily self-consciousness during this period.

BODY/SELF

Whether located in cemeteries and churches, in painted altarpieces, in illustrations of Latin medical manuscripts or vernacular poems, the images of bodies I have discussed up to now articulated ideas of the universe, of society and of sexual difference that helped shape general ideas and beliefs. But it is more difficult to think about how these representations were sited/sighted by individuals and how they became part of consciousness. Rare evidence of this, of an individual's response to and involvement with some of the images of the body I have described – cosmological diagrams, astrological and medical pictures – has survived in the pictures made by a fourteenth-century artist called Opicinus de Canistris. But whereas the traditional images we have examined [5–10] can be seen as attempts to codify and constitute order by analogies between the microcosm and macrocosm or by defining a strict hierarchy within the body which must exclude certain bodies in preference for others, in Opicinus' works traditional images have an opposite, destabilising effect. It is as if the very strain of maintaining this vast ideological system was too much for him and iconography started to collapse, imploding within his body and exploding into the universe outside it in a series of fantastically obsessive designs that will conclude my discussion [24–7].

Opicinus was born near Pavia in 1296, destined for an ecclesiastical career. After his studies, which, he later tells us, he wasted away by reading French and Italian poetry and, significantly, by drawing, he trained as a book illuminator in Genoa. In 1318 he obtained a chaplaincy at the cathedral of Pavia and entered Holy Orders, becoming a parish priest in 1323

until, oppressed by financial and legal troubles, he fled to Avignon where
he wrote a treatise on the pre-eminence of the spiritual body of the Church
over the secular one. Pope John XXII, to whom the latter timely work was
dedicated, appointed him a *scriptor* in the office of the Apostolic Poenitential
Office at Avignon where he lived out the rest of his life. Opicinus would
be just another of the increasing number of clerical bureacrats serving the
papal cause, most of them lost to history, were it not for the onset of a
strange illness, which he describes in detail in his autobiographical schema
[**24**]:

> On 31 March 1334 I fell sick. I received the sacraments and was near death
> throughout the first of April. When I came to, I found my limbs out of action.
> About this time I dreamed I was in Venice, a city which in fact I know only from
> descriptions. When I opened my eyes, I believed myself to have awakened from
> eternal sleep and to have been reborn into this world. I had forgotten every-
> thing and could not even remember how the world looked outside of our
> dormitory. On 3 June, after Vespers, I saw a vessel in the clouds. In conse-
> quence of the disease I was mute, my right hand was injured and I had lost in
> a miraculous way a great deal of my literal memory. In the night of 15 August
> I saw in a dream the Virgin with the Child in her lap, sadly sitting on the
> ground; and through her merits she has given me back not the *littera* (knowledge)
> but a double spirit. Since 1 February 1335, I began to retire, bit by bit, from
> my work in our office, because of the weakness of my hand. In spiritual work,
> however, this same hand proved stronger than before; since then it has drawn
> all these pictures without any human help. At present [i.e. June 1336] my lost
> literal knowledge is replaced twofold by spiritual knowledge; my right hand is
> weak in wordly work, but strong in spiritual endeavours.[40]

These large pen drawings, done 'in the spirit', like the Apocalyptic visions
of St John, are today extant in two manuscripts in the Vatican Library
which have been the subject of detailed studies by Richard Salomon. They
reveal an individual body inscribed within an overdetermined universe
where everything is burdened with multiple meanings. For Opicinus the
arrangement of pubic hair on his body signifies the arrangement of vine-
yards over the whole European continent. His farts and constipations warn
of troubles in 'the belly of Europe' and a rheumatic pain in his arm which
prevents him touching his shoulder means the failure of a planned German attack against France. He does not recognise where he ends and the
universe outside begins. The boundaries of the self have become bound
up with his remembered schemata for hieratic religious figures, complex
geometrical diagrams, medical illustrations and above all maps.[41]

Bodies within bodies, obscure verbal associations as well as pictorial
associations fill every inch of these diagrams, which have been beautifully
composed with compass and ruler [**24**]. Christ, the Virgin Mary, the saints
and other frontally drawn religious figures are superimposed and combined with other figures and shapes that often overlap or contain one

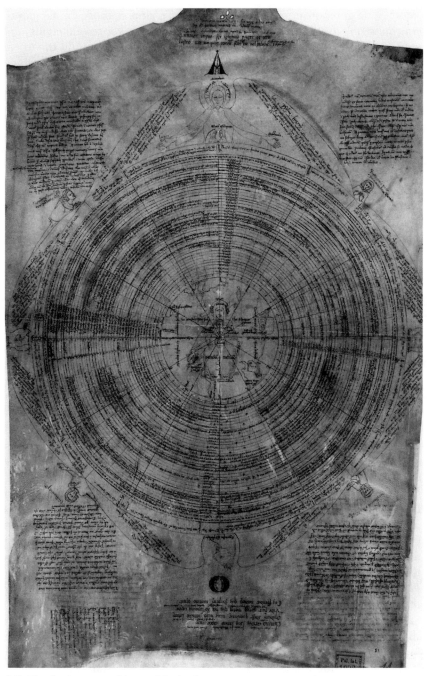

24] The body as autobiographical schema

another. If geometric lines are signs of order and stability for Opicinus, the quivering outlines of the new portolan maps represent chaos and sublunary instability [25]. Maps were a new way of representing the world which Opicinus had learned about in the port city of Genoa and which changed the way we see the world. But he 'medievalises' these maps and, like a geomancer or phrenologist, reads every bump and curve of the land as if it were a human body. Europe becomes a crippled man with a huge beard (Spain) and wobbly leg (Italy) who lends his ear to the large profile of a hag representing Africa. These two figures occur on different scales throughout his work, sometimes as large as half a page [25] and at other times minute and placed inside another body [27]. The misogyny that was part of the general image-repertoire of medieval culture emerges in Opicinus' drawings of this Africa-Woman, who appears again and again as a sign of sexual sin. Between these two figures, 'found' when turned up-side-down, the Mediterranean is drawn as a bearded devil. Water, land, spaces in between – all is analogised and significant in Opicinus' scheme of things. Like many people in the fourteenth century he was devoted to the Virgin Mary and inscribes her as the antithesis of the dark Africa-woman, as the sun-like centre of many images, often opening up her stomach to reveal multiple figures and meanings in her immaculate womb, like a Russian doll.[42] This was quite traditional in contemporary panel paintings and devotional diagrams, but Opicinus goes on to open up many of his figures, not like the new medical anatomist [5] but as a still Augustinian cosmologist seeking worlds within worlds [26]. On this page, below the sun and the *primus homo,* and even smaller than his two chat-tering continents, stand a tiny man and a woman, like Adam and Eve on either side of the tree of knowledge, labelled *causa peccati.* Salomon did not reproduce some of Opicinus' gynaecological drawings which were so explicit that the cleric had to cover them up when visitors came into his cell.[43]

Some of his sources are highly arcane and show him to have been fascinated by new and exotic image types. One example of this which has not hitherto been noted is the non-Western origin of the staring circular face, often representing the sun in Opicinus' personal cosmology, whose minimal oriental features are derived from Persian astrological manuscripts that he probably saw during his training in the commercial city of Genoa [26].[44] In one drawing Opinicus puts himself at the centre of things, arms outstretched, like the traditional image of the cosmological man [27]. Salomon called this a 'painful, confessional self-portrait' in that he has shown himself dressed in the eucharistic vestments of a priest with the inscription 'thus I look outwardly in my pride'.[45] The boundaries between inside and outside are again broken. Like the Virgin Mary who opens to reveal Christ inside her, Opicinus opens himself up to reveal the map of

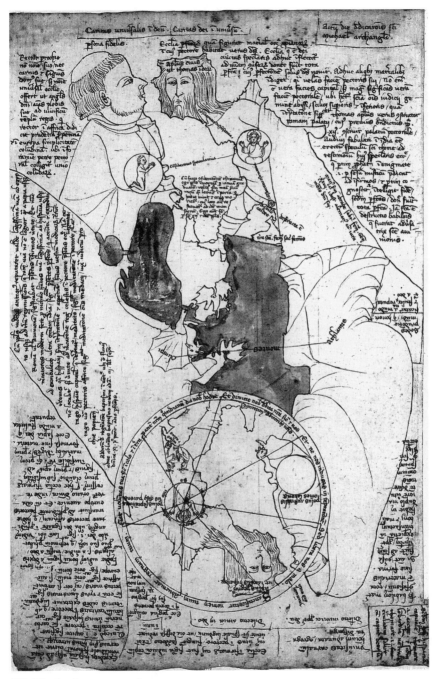

25] The body as map schema

26] The body as cosmological schema

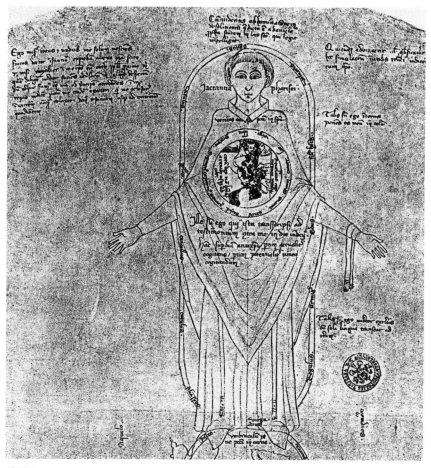

27] The body as self schema

the Africa woman and Europe man, the copulating continents pulsing within his own heart and labelled 'thus I am inwardly in my pride'. The circles and compass-drawn radii of the cosmological diagram, the clear hierarchical divisions between top and bottom of the body, all these are part of the traditional mapping of the body we have seen in other fourteenth-century contexts. Yet Opicinus turns these upside-down and inside out, returning to the Aristotelian notion of the universe as body, but here inscribed upon himself. His is a 'body without organs' in that the emphasis is upon the spiritual signs that elevate his body above its fleshly frame. Whereas the contemporary images in Guido da Vigevano's treatise, with which we began, open the material body up to minute visual analysis, Opicinus' self-portrait opens the spiritual body up to layer upon layer of textual interpretation. In these drawings Opicinus is trying through the power of his own vision to prevent the stripping away of a stratified and unified Augustinian world order by the analytic eye of nominalist science.

The fact that these minutely detailed drawings resemble recent products of the so-called 'art of the insane' suggests how some aspects of the relation of self and body and its sightings/sitings have not changed in five hundred years. The psychoanalyst Ernst Kris in his famous Freudian account of Opicinus as 'a psychotic artist of the Middle Ages' relegates him to the status of a case history. According to Kris, Opicinus' interest in maps is linked to 'delusional inquiries into the human and particularly into the female body' and 'creation and decomposition of the body. At the same time, the play with shapes and the play with words are characteristics of the breakthrough of the primary process and part of the typical symptomatology of schizophrenic production'.[46] However, the danger in accepting the 'scientific facts' of a modern psychoanalytic reading of Opicinus' illness is that by treating the drawings as the result of a pathological condition we force them to conform to the very systematic intellectual order they sought to subvert. Looking at these amazing images it is clear that they are all about body and not mind. Gilles Deleuze and Felix Guattari, in their searing critique of modern notions of the self, describe a postmodern and positive schizophrenic body, one of ever expanding invention, not of withdrawal from the world but of connection with it.[47] These powerful drawings have many of the traits that they associate with this creative, fragmenting schizo-body:

> As for the schizo . . . he plunges further and further into the realm of deterritorialization, reaching the furthest limits of the decomposition of the socius on the surface of his own body without organs . . . He scrambles all the codes and is the transmitter of the decoded flows of desire . . . The schizo . . . goes in the direction of microphysics searching for infinitesimal lines of escape.[48]

Opicinus' meticulously delineated fantasies ultimately need to be explored in terms not of Freudian, but of medieval psychological theory with its pneumatic physiology and priority given to vision. As understood by fourteenth-century commentators on Aristotle and Arabic writers, images were real bodies, tangible signs that were carried through the visible *species* into the mind as *phantasmata*, where they were combined in the imagination and stored in the memory. In this period long before the Cartesian split between mind and body there was much more of a continuum between the two. The body was the receptor and receptacle of sensation and crucial in the process of cognition. All knowledge, even that of the divine, had to be channelled through the body, as is the case with Opicinus' images which are not so much mystical visions as corporeal imprints. As

Deleuze has remarked in relation to Spinoza's adherence to earlier scholastic theories of vision, 'an image is, in the strictest sense, an imprint, a trace or physical impression, an affection of the body itself, the effect of some body on the soft and fluid parts of our own body'.[49]

The importance of Opicinus' drawings is their refusal to be codified or comprehended intellectually as just another sequence of texts in a rational order of history. They are part of the massive fracturing disorder of life that usually goes unrecorded. Opicinus' early twentieth-century Warburgian exegetes saw his drawings as, in Salomon's words, 'lacking logic and coherence', because they expected medieval documents to conform to their own stereotypes of rational textual order and Neoplatonic synthesis.[50] By contrast I would argue that it is precisely because of their incoherence that these images are so significant, both for the history of art and for a consideration of how bodies function in history.

To return to the metaphor with which I began, Opicinus does not make a book out of his body, for all his manic enfolding and scribbling. The objects he left are less like books than relics. These large sheets are, like the Turin shroud, blotted and traced with hardly visible, indecipherable marks, all of which alert us to the ways in which men and women in the past struggled to leave behind signs, not only in words, but also in the impact of their own bodies upon matter. As we look at these vast vellum sheets we can almost touch Opicinus and feel the quick movements of that miraculously deft, diseased hand that produced the most memorable relics of individual sensation, pain and corporeality to have come down to us from the Middle Ages – recording the bodily disintegration, not of a saint or a god, but ironically, of an artist.

NOTES

1 Michel de Certeau, *The Practice of Everyday Life*, trans. Steven Rendell, Berkeley, 1988, p. 140.

2 Ernest Wickersheimer, *Anatomies de Mondino dei Luzzi et de Guido de Vigevano*, Paris, 1926 reproduces all 18 of the full-page pictures from the Chantilly MS with a full commentary. See also Gundolf Keil, 'Ortolfs chirurgischer Traktat und das Aufkommen der medizinischen Demonstrationszeichnung', in *Text und Bild, Bild und Text*, ed. Wolfgang Harms, Stuttgart, 1988, pp. 147–9.

3 Mary Douglas, *Purity and Danger: an Analysis of Concepts of Pollution and Taboo*, London, 1970. See also the useful essay by Arthur W. Frank, 'For a Sociology of the Body: an Analytic Review', in *The Body: Social Process and Cultural Theory*, ed. M. Featherstone, M. Hepworth and B. S. Turner, London, 1991. A short but very useful discussion of medieval theories of the body is Alan E. Bernstein, 'Political Anatomy', in *University Publishing*, Winter, 1978, pp. 8–9. Two crucial aspects of the visualisation of the body that I am not going to touch upon in this general essay but which have received attention recently are bodily gesture, studied by Jean-Claude Schmitt, *La Raison des Gestes dans l'Occident Médievale*, Paris, 1990, and clothing, for which see Dyan Elliott, 'Dress as a Mediator between inner and outer self in the Pious Matron of the High and Later Middle Ages', *Medieval Studies*, LIII, 1991, pp. 270–308.

4 Dorinda Outram, *The Body and the French Revolution: Sex, Class and Political Culture*, New Haven, 1989, p. 5. Rather than textual, the basis of body imaging is visual, as discussed by Jacques Lacan when he describes how any object 'is always more or less structured as the image of the body of the subject', *The Seminar of Jacques Lacan, Book II: The Ego in Freud's Theory and in the Technique of Psychoanalysis, 1954–55*, New York, 1988, p. 199.

5 Aristotle, *De Caelo et Mundo*, trans. W. K. C. Guthrie, Cambridge, 1939, p. 147.

6 A useful discussion of the impact of Aristotle's theories of cosmological direction on late medieval culture is J. Freccero, *Dante and the Poetics of Conversion*, Cambridge (Mass.), 1986, pp. 70–6. A description of the Oxford Aristotle manuscript can be found in Nigel Morgan, *Early Gothic Manuscripts 1250–1285*, Oxford, 1989, no. 156 (a), II, p. 148. Two similar thirteenth-century drawings from manuscripts of the same text but which invert the figure so it is upright on the page are reproduced in Francesco Gurrieri, *Disegni nei Manoscritti Laurenziani*, Florence, 1979, Figs. 40 and 42.

7 Nicole Oresme, *Le Livre du ciel et du monde*, ed. A. D. Menut and A. J. Denomy, Madison, 1968, pp. 309–11. For the importance of Oresme in fourteenth-century art and cosmology see David C. Lindberg, *The Beginnings of Western Science: The European Scientific Tradition in Philosophical, Religious and Institutional Context, 600 BC to AD 1450*, Chicago, 1992, pp. 258–61.

8 For the tradition of illustrating this text see Donal F. Byrne, 'The Boucicaut Master and the "Livre des Propriétés des choses" ', *Gazette des Beaux-Arts*, XCII, 1978, pp. 149–64.

9 F. Saxl, 'Macrocosm and Microcosm in Medieval Pictures', *Lectures*, London, 1957, especially plate 37(a), a twelfth-century drawing from Prüfening Abbey. For the rise of astrological thinking in the later Middle Ages see the essays by Krzystof Pomian 'Astrology as a Naturalistic Theology of History' and John D. North. 'Celestial Influence – the Major Premiss of Astrology' in *Astrologi hallucinati: Stars and the End of the World in Luther's Time*, ed. Paola Zambelli, New York, 1986, pp. 30–54.

10 Saint Bonaventure, *Commentaria in quattuor libros Sententiarum Magistri Petri Lombardi*, lib. 2, dist. 14, p. 2, art. 2, qu. 2 in *Opera omnia*, II, Quaracci, 1885, p. 360 col. 2. See Edward Grant, 'Medieval and Renaissance scholastic conceptions of the influence of the celestial region on the terrestrial', *Journal of Medieval and Renaissance Studies*, XVII, 1987, pp. 1–23.

11 Saxl, 'Macrocosm', p. 67 and see also the long study of the *homo signorum* in H. Bober, 'The Zodiacal Miniature of the *Très Riches Heures* of the Duke of Berry – its Sources and Meaning', *Journal of the Warburg and Courtauld Institutes*, XI, 1948, pp. 1–34.

12 This (and Figure 9) are from a French manuscript dating from *c*.1380–1422, Paris Bibl. Nat. lat. 11229, published by K. Sudhoff, in *Archiv für Geschichte der Medizin*, V, 1912. The best survey of medical images from this period is R. Herlinger, *History of Medical Illustration from Antiquity to AD 1600*, London, 1970, pp. 20–4.

13 For the complex iconography of the male sexual organs see D. Jacquart and C. Thomasset, *Sexuality and Medicine in the Middle Ages*, Cambridge, 1988, p. 182 and Michael Camille, *The Gothic Idol: Ideology and Image-Making in Medieval Art*, Cambridge, 1989, pp. 87–101.

14 John of Salisbury, *Policraticus [sive de nugis curialium et vestigiis philosophorum]*, ed. C. C. J. Webb, 2 vols, Oxford, 1909, reprinted Frankfurt, 1965, II, 1, p. 282. A useful modern translation is John of Salisbury, *Policraticus*, ed. J. Cary, Cambridge, 1990.

15 This unpublished manuscript is discussed and its patron and political context explored in M. Camille 'The King's New Bodies: An Illustrated Mirror for Princes in the Morgan Library', *XXVIII Internationaler Kongress für Kunstgeschichte*, Berlin, 1994, pp. 393–401. The text has been briefly discussed in D. M. Bell, *L'Idéal Ethique de la Royauté en France au Moyen Age*, Paris, 1962, pp. 42–9.

16 Jacques Le Goff, 'Head or Heart: Political Uses of the Body Metaphor in the Middle Ages', in *Fragments for the History of the Human Body*, New York, 1989, III, pp. 13–26. For useful discussion of political iconography see the remarks by Jeannine Quillet, 'Community, Counsel and Representation', in *The Cambridge History of Medieval Political Thought c.350–1450*, ed. J. H. Burns, Cambridge, 1988, pp. 520–45.

17 John of Salisbury, *Policraticus*, II, 1, p. 282, lines 14–22. See Tilman Struve, 'The Importance of the Organism in the Political Theory of John of Salisbury', in *The World of John of Salisbury*, ed. Michael Wilks, Oxford, 1984, pp. 303–17.

18 Suprisingly there is no study of the iconography of body and soul in medieval art, but for a good discussion of scholastic distinctions see James J. Bono, 'Medical Spirits and the Medieval Language of Life', *Traditio*, XL, 1984, pp. 91–129.

19 For the importance of the mouth see M.-C. Pouchelle, *The Body and Surgery in the Middle Ages*, Cambridge, 1990, pp. 182–3 and M. Camille 'Mouths and Meanings: Towards an Anti-Iconography of Medieval Art' in *Iconography at the Crossroads*, ed. B. Cassidy, Princeton, 1993. Lacan refers to the mouth as 'this something which properly speaking is unnameable, the back of this throat, the complex unlocatable form, which also makes it into the primitive object *par excellence*, the abyss of the feminine organ from which all life emerges, this gulf of the mouth, in which everything is swallowed up, and no less the image of death in which everything comes to its end'; Jacques Lacan, *The Seminar of Jacques Lacan, Book II: The Ego in Freud's Theory and in the Technique of Psychoanalysis 1954–55*, New York, 1988, p. 164.

20 Hostiensis' commentary on the fifth book of the Decretals, cited in P. Michaud Quantin, *Universitas: Expression de Mouvement Communitaire dans le moyen-âge latin*, Paris, 1970, p. 59.

21 Brigitte Bedos-Rezak, 'Medieval Seals and the Structure of Chivalric Society', *The Study of Chivalry: Resources and Approaches*, Kalamazoo, 1988, pp. 313–72.

22 For orthodox theological critiques of subjects like the three-headed Trinity and the 'Vierge Ouvrante' see Creighton Gilbert, 'The Archbishop and the Painters of Florence', *Art Bulletin*, XLI, 1959, pp. 79–87 and Camille, *The Gothic Idol*, pp. 232–3.

23 See M. Camille, *Image on the Edge: The Margins of Medieval Art*, London, 1992, with further bibliography.

24 This is one of the major theses of what remains the best study of political body iconography of the period, Ernst Kantorowicz, *The King's Two Bodies*, Princeton, 1957. See also G. B. Ladner, 'Aspects of Medieval Thought on Church and State', in *Images and Ideas in the Middle Ages: Selected Studies in the History of Art*, Rome, 1983, II, pp. 435–45 and for a contemporary analysis, Giles of Rome *On Ecclesiastical Power*, trans. Arthur P. Monahan, Lewiston, 1990.

25 See Miri Rubin, *Corpus Christi: the Eucharist in Late Medieval Culture*, Cambridge, 1991.

26 Hans Belting, *Bild und Kult: Eine Geschichte des Bildes vor dem Zeitalter der Kunst*, Munich, 1991 and *The Image and its Public in the Middle Ages: Form and Function of Early Paintings of the Passion*, New York, 1990.

27 See Belting, *The Image and its Public*, p. 36 and G. Schiller, *Iconography of Christian Art*, London, 1972, II, pp. 226–9.

28 For the wound/vagina, see the *Psalter and Hours of Bonne of Luxembourg*, Metropolitan Museum of Art, the Cloisters MS 69, fol. 331, reproduced in Lucy Freeman Sandler, 'Jean Pucelle and the Lost Miniatures of the Belleville Breviary', *Art Bulletin*, LXVI, 1984, pp. 73–96; Fig. 17, p. 86. In a paper delivered at the Medieval Academy of America in 1992, Karma Lochrie discussed this image in relation to medieval lesbian sexuality. For more on the feminised body of Christ see Caroline Walker Bynum, *Jesus as Mother: Studies in the Spirituality of the High Middle Ages*, Berkeley, 1982.

29 G. Duby, *A History of Private Life. II: Revelations of the Medieval World*, Cambridge, Mass., 1988, p. 526.

30 This is the case in the description of the manuscript by Peter Murray Jones, *Medieval Medical Miniatures*, London, 1984, plate IX and figures 25, 40, 46, 47.

31 For the vagina as 'the gates of Hell' in a French *fabliau* of the period and in a Ghent Book of Hours, see Camille, *Image on the Edge*, p. 141 and fig. 64.

32 Caroline Walker Bynum, *Holy Feast and Holy Fast: The Religious Significance of Food to Medieval Women*, Berkeley, 1987 is the most cogent account of this slightly 'new age' medieval position of the female body. Against this approach one can read R. Howard Bloch,

Medieval Misogyny and the Invention of Western Romantic Love, Chicago 1990 and the useful review and critique of Bynum's book by Kathleen Biddick, 'Genders, Bodies, Borders: Postmodern/Medieval' in *Speculum*, LXVIII, 1993, pp. 389–418.

33 For Jewish commentaries such as the Babylonian Talmud, alluding to sex with the serpent, see Peter Brown, *The Body and Society: Men, Women and Sexual Renunciation in Early Christianity*, New York, 1988, p. 95. Bynum's claim that 'Medieval images of the body have less to do with sexuality than with fertility and decay' ('The Female Body and Religious Practices in the Later Middle Ages', in *Fragments for a History of the Human Body*, I, New York, 1989, p. 162), effaces a whole realm of verbal and visual imagery, going back to St Augustine's discussion of the Fall in the *City of God*, in which death and decay are directly linked to the sexual organs of Adam and Eve.

34 Thomas Lacquer, *Making Sex: Body and Gender from the Greeks to Freud*, Cambridge (Mass.), 1990.

35 For an introduction and further references to the 'five figure series' see Boyd Hill Jr, 'The Grain and the Spirit in Medieval Anatomy', *Speculum*, XL, 1965, pp. 63–9.

36 K. Sudhoff, 'Die fünf anatomischen Abbildungen der Baseler provenzalischen Handschrift', *Studien zur Geschichte der Medizin*, IV, Leipzig, 1908, pp. 24–9, plates II–V and Ludwig Choulant, *History and Bibliography of Anatomic Illustration*, trans. M. Frank, Chicago, 1920, pp. 56–7.

37 For the vast literature on death and the body in the later Middle Ages, see Philippe Ariès, *The Hour of Our Death*, London, 1974 and the extensive bibliography by Jane Taylor in *Dies Illa: Death in the Middle Ages*, ed. A. R. W. James and Jane H. M. Taylor, Manchester, 1984. The best visual survey is still Emile Mâle, *L'Art religieux de la fin du Moyen Age en France*, first published Paris, 1908 and now available as *Religious Art at the End of the Middle Ages*, Princeton, 1989.

38 E. R. Brown 'Death and the Body in the Later Middle Ages: The Legislation of Boniface VIII on the division of the corpse', *Viator*, XII, 1981, pp. 221–71 and Caroline Walker Bynum, 'Material Continuity, Personal Survival and the Resurrection of the Body', in *Fragmentation and Redemption: Essays on Gender and the Human Body in Medieval Religion*, New York, 1991, pp. 239–97 are excellent discussions of the anxiety of bodily partition in the later Middle Ages.

39 See Karl Sudhoff, 'Ein Skelettbild in einer Handschrift der Bibliothèque Mazarine aus dem Anfang des 14. Jahrhunderts', in *Studien zur Geschichte der Medizin*, X, 1914, pp. 36–7.

40 This passage is translated in R. G. Salomon, 'A Newly Discovered Manuscript of Opicinus de Canistris', *Journal of the Warburg and Courtauld Institutes*, XVI, 1953, pp. 45–57, at pp. 46–7. See also R. Salomon, *Opicinus de Canistris. Weltbild und Bekenntnisse eines avignonesischen Klerikers des 14. Jahrhunderts*, Studies of the Warburg Institute 1, London, 1936, p. 213.

41 See Jorg-Geerd Arentzen, *Imago Mundi Cartographica: Studien zur Bildlichkeit Mittelalterlicher West und Okumenekarten unter besonderer berücksichtigung des Zusammenwirkens von Text und Bild*, Munich, 1984 pp. 296–316 for Opicinus and the map-making tradition. The best account of geometrical diagrams in medieval culture is Michael W. Evans, 'The geometry of the mind', in *Architectural Association Quarterly*, XII, no. 4, 1980, pp. 32–55 which discusses Opicinus on p. 46, n. 76.

42 Salomon, *Opicinus*, plates 23, 35, 37, 47. Opinicus is an adherent of the basic Aristotelian principle repeated by William of Auvergne that 'like engenders like' and that all the operations of nature occur 'by similitude', described in Bert Hansen 'Science and Magic' in *Science in the Middle Ages*, ed. David C. Lindberg, Chicago, 1978, p. 491.

43 'While I was working on this a simple priest from Lombardy came to see me; and I had to cover the abdomen of the woman with a piece of paper in order not to shock him', cited in Salomon, 'A Newly-discovered manuscript', p. 54. His obsessions with the reproductive organs are part of a general fear/fascination among scholastic writers concerning the nature of generation.

44 This circular face, labelled *sol* in one of Opicinus' most striking pages (Salomon Plate 38) is based upon the representation of the sun in Arabic astrological images from the Deccan. See Franz Boll, Karl Bezold and Wilhelm Gundil, *Sternglaube und Sterndeutung*, Darmstadt, 1966, plate V.10 and the reproduction of a late Persian MS in the Bibliothèque Nationale, in Walter Herdeg, *The Sun in Art*, Zurich, 1962, Fig. 8, p. 42.

45 Salomon, *Opicinus*, plate 43, p. 269.

46 E. Kris, *Psychoanalytic Explorations in Art*, New York, 1952, pp. 118–27.

47 G. Deleuze and F. Guattari, *Anti-Oedipus: Capitalism and Schizophrenia*, Minneapolis, 1983.

48 Deleuze and Guattari, *Anti-Oedipus*, pp. 280–1.

49 G. Deleuze, *Expressionism in Philosophy: Spinoza*, New York, 1992, p. 147. Gentile da Cingoli and other north Italian philosopher/physicians argued that the body itself is altered by impressions (*species*) existing in the sense or intellect, for which see Nancy G. Siraisi, *Taddeo Alderotti and his Pupils: Two Generations of Italian Medical Learning*, Princeton, 1981, p. 206. For a study of the changing theories of relationships between between light, vision and cognition which raises important issues for the art historian see Katherine H. Tachau, *Vision and Certitude in the Age of Ockham. Optics, Epistemology and the Foundation of Semantics 1250–1345*, Leiden, 1988.

50 Salomon, 'A Newly Discovered Manuscript', p. 47. The problem of constructing coherent meanings around the body in cultural studies and the relationship between creativity and corporeality highly relevant for medieval studies is discussed in Elaine Scarry, *The Body in Pain: The Making and Unmaking of the World*, Oxford, 1987.

The person in the form:
medieval challenges to bodily 'order'

> The human body is a more astonishing thing than an old soul.
> (Nietzsche, *The Will to Power*)

Bodies in ritual, bodies in dance, bodies at work, bodies in ecstasy, bodies processing, bodies adorned, have been the subject for analysis of those symbols and acts which give force and meaning to connectedness, to social relations, which transcend the personal. Bodies in pain, tortured, mutilated, neglected, have attracted attention as being the products of sin, victims of disease, as failures in a process of social and religious education. This paper challenges the boundaries and integrity of bodies in the Middle Ages in a way which will render any attempt at grounding, at claiming determinacy of them, not only impossible, but uninteresting. Medieval people were worried by contradictions within their bodies and between each other. Worries, some differing and some similar to those we confront-eating, reproduction, love, work-posed their towering challenges, in contexts constructed by age, wealth, gender, knowledge, status. But it is important to confront the possibility of body boundaries drawn not only differently but also less securely. Bodies, their pleasure and their pain, their daily routines and their heroic and traumatic moments, are constructed but also lived, they are never natural, never given, always made, experienced individually in ways too plentiful to capture. While I retrace discourses of bodies I shall engage with texts and learn from their affirmations, elisions and evasions – their usages, their silences and their emphases – some of the bodily troubles which made medieval lives. In Frances Barker's words 'the body in question is not a hypostatized object, still less a simple biological mechanism of given desires and needs acted on externally by controls and enticements, but a relation in a system of liaisons which are material, discursive, psychic, sexual, but without stop or centre.'[1] Those who believe in the ability of the past to offer visions of difference and horizons of possibility have been attracted to unravelling the body as historical construction, and to exploring the variety of experience and articulation to which the body gave rise, gave place. Thus, rather than celebrating the body's naturalness, its power to offer a resting-place, a shared haven from the difference and contexts of human relations, here I shall try to reveal its 'otherness' in medieval consciousness.

One way to do so is through a series of glances at the construction of gender in a variety of late medieval texts of differing genres and moods. I shall suggest the ways in which gender roles were made in a world which, as opposed to our own, possessed very fluid notions of sexuality and of bodily contours. Thus gender will be revealed as a complex system, not grounded in biology, but made of attempts to impose upon biological diversity a regulating dichotomy: feminine and masculine.[2] We will also encounter the body as it was lived and experienced, *in parts*, rather than as whole. Pain and disease could concentrate awareness of a single part, which in meaningful ways could come to represent the whole body. Sharpening such an understanding of the epistemology of Christ's body, and of its amazing eucharistic forms, will lend further resonance to the problem of wholeness and form. I shall also emphasise the sense of openness and liquidity which the body was felt to possess, in its vulnerability and pliability. This is, after all, the context within which a particularly privileged body – Christ's own – emerged, out of these corporeal anxieties of shapelessness and loss.

I

The *Annales Colmarienses Minores*, a chronicle compiled by Dominicans of the city of Colmar in Alsace in 1308–14,[3] records under the year 1300 among reports of royal deaths, the quality of harvest and the price of wine, the following interesting event:

> In a town near Bern . . . a woman lived for ten years with a man. Since she could not have sex with a man she was separated [from her partner] by the spiritual court. In Bologna (on her way to Rome), her vagina was cut open by a surgeon, and a penis and testicles came out. She returned home, married a wife, did hard [physical] labour, and had proper and adequate sexual congress with her wife.[4]

So a person who passed for a woman but who was unable to have a sexual relationship with her partner, was eventually recognised as an inadequate partner, and released from marriage. On her way to Rome (on hopeful pilgrimage?) she visited Bologna, Europe's foremost medical town, where a surgeon's scalpel came to reveal another pair of genitals. The chronicler then recounts a happy ending, as the person returned home to undertake a full and satisfying life, as a man.

The person of Bern was a hermaphrodite. We encounter them in numerous medieval discourses: in the literature of medicine and surgery, in the tales of travel and prodigies, in the transmission of the legend of Hermaphroditus from within the Ovidian corpus, and in anecdotal tales

such as the entry in the Annals of Colmar. In a text which was reused
by surgical writers of the later Middle Ages, Albucasis (d. after 1009)
described three types of hermaphrodites (two male and one female) and
recommended that the redundant genitals should be cut off.[5] Similarly, the
Canon of Avicenna (980–1037) recognised three types of hermaphrodites:
those in which both members were equally potent, those in which the
hidden ones were in fact dominant, and those in which the hidden ones
were also the least powerful. He recommended in the last case 'And
oftentimes it is cured by the cutting of the more hidden member, and it
is then treated after the manner of surgical wounds.'[6] In the case described by our annalist the hidden members were those which prevailed,
since the vagina was cut open to let out the virile members and allow the
hermaphrodite to become a social male.

Wondrous beings could also be encountered in the literature of marvels and exotic travel which circulated in the Middle Ages, based largely
on the Plinian corpus of monsters, and mediated through Isidore of Seville in the early Middle Ages.[7] An early medieval collection 'De monstris'
told of *androgini, mulieres barbatae* as well as a hermaphrodite *homo de
utriusque sexus* who seems more like an effeminate homosexual.[8] Such lore
was transmitted in medieval bestiaries and in texts based on Isidoran lore,
such as the twelfth-century 'De monstris', which describes androgynes: 'It
is written and read of a miserable prodigy who is of joint or mixed gender.
It reproduces, as father and as mother, bringing forth a single creature
which has both male and female members alike.'[9] From the thirteenth
century the powerful Aristotelian paradigm provided material for the
renewed observation of nature. Thus, Albert the Great (*c.*1200–80) considered the generation of hermaphrodites and other monsters in his comprehensive study *De animalibus* (written 1258–63), in which he defined the
existence of two sets of genitals as a case of superfluity caused by a su-
perabundance of matter. He used the analogy of the generation of twins,
with the difference that in the case of hermaphrodites the *virtutes* of the
sexes are equally matched:

> and if the force (*virtus*) is defeated in one way and triumphs in the other, it is
> generally a *hermaphrodite*. And sometimes the form of each member is so com-
> plete that it is impossible, either by sight or by touch, to decide which sex
> prevails. And it is not unfitting for such an offspring to have two bladders and
> to urinate from each of them, or that in coitus it should be both active and
> passive, lie on top or lie under. But I do not think that it can both impregnate
> and be impregnated. But the prevailing sex should definitely be the one gov-
> erned by the complexion of the heart.[10]

So even when there is perfect sexual doubling, Albert expects there to
be a marginally prevailing, 'principal' sex, one which is related to the
complexion of the heart.

Medical discourse even provided a site for the making of persons with such abundant genitals and identities. The *Anatomia magistri Nicolai phisici* of the second half of the twelfth century described the womb as seven-celled, with three cells on the right for the generation of boys and three on the left, where girls gestated, and a central cell for the generation of hermaphrodites.[11] But he also commented that other physicians saw all cells as capable of generating boys and girls, according to the balance and strength of the respective seeds and the side of the womb in which they settled.[12] In his *Anatomia* the Bolognese surgeon Mondino de' Liuzzi (c.1270–1326) expounded the theory of the seven-celled uterus, with three warmer cells on the right in which male foetuses would gestate, three colder cells on the left, producing females, and a single middle chamber, betwixt and between, from which hermaphrodites were born.[13] Similarly morally innocuous was the entry in the *Annales Colmarienses* under 1293: 'And a boy was born, that is a hermaphrodite infant, in the valley of Kaiserberg. That is to say, an infant who had both a male member and a female member.'[14] But the chronicler goes a long way in showing just how powerful was the intellectual drive in demystifying the world, and providing explanations for peculiar natural phenomena: 'A monstrosity occurred by some error in the operation of nature, because of abundance or because of lack, whether in the position or in the form of the members.'[15] This paradigm allows the world to be seen as fluid, in that it produces extra-ordinary creatures. This all the more calls for the control of education and socialisation. Even the hermaphrodite must choose his or her sex, and persist in it to become a productive and reproductive member of society.

The person who appeared to be a woman, with no protruding genitals, and who could not function sexually fell foul of the theological view of marriage, which turned sexual activity into a binding debt, where the inability to pay could provide sufficient grounds for separation.[16] This transformation of the 'woman' was so complete, so convincing, so effica-cious, that the new 'man' was able, for once, to fulfil the marriage debt and to partake in marital intercourse. In the annalist's account cited above we encounter the work of a number of discourses. Theological and can-onistic discourse could deal with the case as one of non-consummation, denying theoretical existence to the hermaphrodite; medical discourse had a surgical answer; the discourse of marvels and prodigies saw it as worthy of mention, a tale of human interest, one which dramatises the instability of the category of sexual identity.[17]

Theological discussion of hermaphrodites was not frequent, but by the twelfth century Peter the Chanter (d.1197) had developed a strict attitude. In the *Verbum abbreviatum* he demanded that the hermaphrodite choose his or her sex and persist in it:

If he is hotter, like a man, then he should be allowed to lead [in sexual intercourse]; if indeed he is effeminate, then he should be allowed to marry, as a bride. If, however, it is then the case that the organ (*instrumentum*) is deficient, none the less the use of the *other* organ should not be allowed, rather it should be repressed for ever, because [sexual] alternation is the sign of the vice of sodomy.[18]

Once the choice was made this was to be followed consistently, since movement between sexual personae would be disruptive, and worse, would necessarily produce occasions of sodomy, the vice addressed by Peter in this chapter.[19] The attitude betrays no moral outrage, simply the need to define a single sexual persona and impose on it a heterosexual orientation.[20] What is curious about the tale is its wholesomeness, as compared with the treatment it would receive in a popular publication today.[21] No moral deviance is suggested, only a rather uncomfortable and inconvenient social fact, a fact about identity.

Yet quite different in tone is the entry found only a few years earlier in the *Annales Colmarienses* under the year 1281: 'A hermaphrodite was blinded in Breisach, because he had violently tried to have sex with a woman.'[22] The violence exerted by the hermaphrodite forced into female behaviour, and who had behaved contrary to that designation, occasioned the counter-violence of public punishment. Here, a hermaphrodite must have been deemed to be more female than male, and did not contain himself, attacking a woman. Hermaphrodites were also frequently confused with homosexuals and when this happened, were treated harshly. Guido Guinicelli and his band who languish in Dante's purgatory declare 'our sin was hermaphrodite' but go on to describe their practice as 'we did not observe human law / following appetite like beasts', which may suggest homosexual practice rather than the dilemma of hermaphroditism.[23] The hermaphrodite identity was noteworthy, but not blameworthy. And in the case of the woman from the neighbourhood of Bern, there is a triumphant happy ending in the arrival and the exercise of a fully articulated sexual identity. Whatever the chosen sexual persona it had to be adhered to in the face of social and legal institutions. Roman law provided the basis for subsequent medieval usage in civil and canon law. Under the section 'De statu hominum' in the *Digesta* we read '*Ulpian*: Question: Whom do we consider an hermaphrodite? I believe that it is to be judged according to the sex which prevails in the person.'[24] In Bracton's *De legibus et consuetudinibus Angliae* after discussion of human types according to their relative freedom, he goes on to gender distinctions: '*Another division of persons.* There is another division of persons: some are male, some female, and others hermaphrodite.'[25] And in the next section the hermaphrodite is required to choose according to the principle of prevalence: '*Of the hermaphrodite.* The hermaphrodite is considered male or female according to the amount of heat of the prevailing sex.'[26] A collection of scholastic questions of c.1500 relating to the body resolved the problem of legal accountability by insisting that the church demand that a single 'member be used', and a single legal and social persona be presented to the world.[27] Foucault claimed that the process which forced hermaphrodites to choose a single identity was a long one, which was enforced together with other prescriptions in the eighteenth century, the century of the great 'closure':

> Biological theories of sexuality, juridical conceptions of the individual, forms of administrative control in modern nations, led little by little to rejecting the idea of a mixture of the two sexes in a single body, and consequently to limiting the free choice of indeterminate individuals. Henceforth, everybody was to have one and only one sex.[28]

As we have seen, medieval institutions required similar consistency and exclusivity in personal identity in all that touched the handling of property, entry into contract, and marriage. The whole theory of marriage was challenged by the hermaphrodite, who could fulfil the requirement for consent, while retaining ambiguity or lacking the ability to have fruitful intercourse.

Once chosen the gender roles must be strictly followed. Physical abundance may be the offering of nature, but it had to be managed in the social sphere. Aberrant appearances could lead to distrust, and even abuse. It is hard to judge the tone of Eustache Deschamps' (c.1346–c.1406) ballad *Contre les hermaphrodites*, but it does convey the sense of danger and repulsion which an ambiguous sexual appearance could incite, and the bodily anxieties it invoked:

A soft chin, son Hermaphrodite
Effeminate, a defect of nature,
Faint in heart, devoid of all virtues,
But full of vice, which tends towards nothing but filth.
A masculine name, a female body
who are wont to impose false names on others
I never read the books of such as them
who are not perfect in nature,
Corrupt in body, in thought, the pigs,
Untrustworthy, disloyal, evil.

. . . A woman out of a man, who should be bearded,
Man without hair, this is an insult to everyone.
To meet them is nothing but misfortune,
And their gaze can be pleasing to no one.
They make (sexual) use of both kinds,
I have known them in my time to be
Untrustworthy, disloyal, evil.[29]

Similar sentiments are expressed in the anonymous tract on manners of the late fifteenth century, the *Kalendrier des bergiers*. One should beware of improper characters, 'especially of beardless men, who have no beard, because they are inclined to various vices and evils and one should beware of them as of one's mortal enemy.'[30]

The humoral paradigm of the body meant that persons could be born in a wide range of shapes and with clusters of characteristics produced by the constellation of cosmic, climatic, spermatic, and humoral conditions of conception and generation.[31] In its section on the beard *Le propriétaire des choses* describes the phenomena of bearded women and beardless men as resulting from an abundance of heat in the former and coldness in the latter: 'And it sometimes happens that women have beards because they are of hot and moist complexion, and conversely, men of cold and dry complexion have no beard at all.'[32] Thus, the Aristotelian understanding of the human body allowed for the range of possible sexual identities.[33] The fluidity which underpins this made hermaphrodites natural, if interesting. Male and female were internally bound as manifestations of human sexuality, where the male was paradigmatic, and other forms fell short of that perfection. In that sense a woman, just like a hermaphrodite, was less than a perfect human form. Women were understood as inverted males. In the words of Henri of Mandeville (d. *c.*1320) 'the generative apparatus of women [is] similar to the generative apparatus of men, save that it is inverted'. The womb matched the scrotum, the vagina the penis, and the ovaries testicles.[34] In consequence, humours inflected a single humanity, fluid and open to variation. Here lay the explanation of the dizzying variety of imaginable and observable human forms.

This coexistence of a wide range of human attributes and physical material which was not amenable to strict sexual differentiation is also illustrated in the image favoured by the medical gaze in representing the paradigmatic 'sick person' as a crouching frog-like human which could be male or female. The 'disease-woman' in the fifteenth-century Wellcome Apocalypse has few specific female attributes except for a small pear-shaped space on her left side, neatly entitled 'embrio'.[35] The medical gaze did not concentrate on sexual organs, but sexual organs did indicate identity and social roles, and thus required clarification for use in the social sphere.[36] Once a clinical intervention could clear up the confusion, the person could develop the proper social personality. Powerful adherence to the rules of gendered grammar left no room for choices within the social and linguistic sphere. To confuse genders was a corruption of the nature of language. In Alan of Lille's usage grammatical gender must thus adhere strictly to a clear sexual identity, or else threaten to create barbarism, chaos.[37] By extension, the whole gamut of female characteristics, vanity, luxury, gossip, voluptuousness – which the variety of misogynistic discourses repeated *ad tedium* and in varying degrees of ferocity[38] – would follow from the psychosomatic whole, living in the proper degree of coldness and dryness which the female body and the female person inhabited. Yet the known existence of varied forms of body and sexuality regularly forced the collapsing and questioning of those schemes which organised binary hierarchial orders.[39]

The possibilities raised by the abundance of sexual forms were unsettling, and thus lent themselves to poetic reflection. The medieval reworking of the myth of Hermaphrodite, the son of Mercury and Venus, told in Ovid's *Metamorphoses* (4.285–388) was an occasion for such reflection. The story recounts how Hermaphrodite was pursued by a nymph who finally caught him in a pool where they united, after which he was transformed into a man–woman.[40] Classical interpretations saw the pool as the world, and understood the tale as a cautionary allegory about the effeminacy and loss of *virtus* which follow overindulgence in worldly things.[41] Following one of the traditions of the *Ovide moralisé*, Boccaccio (1313–75) chose a different interpretation, where dual sexuality represented concord and mutually beneficial influences. In the *Genealogy of the Pagan Gods* he likened the pool to a female womb, with one of its cells the birth-place of the hermaphrodite. Following Vitruvius' commentary he locates the story at the fountain of Salmacis near Halicarnassus, a place where barbarians met Greek influence and learned civilised behaviour. The resulting hermaphroditism, is 'feminised', civilised: 'It so happened that both because of the pleasure of water and the abundance of food, the savage barbarians came down into dwellings and gradually put aside their rudeness and began to cultivate the gentler and more humane habits of the Greeks.'[42] In a similar mood, and within a Christian exegetical frame, later in the century Pierre Bersuire (d.1362) provided the story with a Christian interpretation which saw Christ in Hermaphrodite, humanity in the nymph with whom He was joined, in a pool, clear and sparkling as the Virgin:

> Thus these can be represented and applied to the blessed incarnation. So this young man, the son of Mercury, is God's son and most elevated bridegroom, who from the beginning left his own forest, that is paradise, in order to come to this world and there to bathe himself in the water of mercy according to his father's order . . . This useless nymph could signify human nature, worthless and dragged down by idleness. The fountain can signify the glorious blessed Virgin, bright, clear and pure.[43]

The hermaphrodite was also appropriated as a spy, whose existence could explain and legitimate the acquisition of intimate feminine knowledge by men; doctors, priests, surgeons. Commentaries deriving from the *Metamorphoses* elaborate the myth of Hermaphrodite, who brought the secrets of women, known to him/her from life among them, to the world of men. The hermaphrodite had betrayed a part of himself and thus announced his rebirth as a man alone.[44] *Desloyal*, indeed!

II

So much which made a woman resided in the womb that it is not surprising to observe the danger and anxiety related to that nurturing part. A terrifying tale is recorded in the chronicle of Richer of Senones (d.1267), the *Gesta Senoniensis ecclesiae,* written around 1255. It relates a story of alleged Jewish atrocity which took place in the town of Saint-Dié, near Epinal:

> A certain poor young woman frequented this Jew's house and executed whatever chores were necessary to earn her livelihood. To be sure, on a certain day that same girl went into the Jew's house and he saw her, and rejoiced, because he was in fact alone in the house with her. Summoning her he said: 'Come and eat a little, because you must work.' And when she had eaten and drunk, she was thus enchanted, so that she looked as if she was sleeping and could feel nothing. And when the Jew saw that his incantations had had their effect, he locked the doors and took his tools, prepared for what he wished to do, and approached the young thing, he opened her legs, and extracted with his metal instruments that little sack which is called the womb (*matrix*), and in which infants are conceived, from the stomach in the natural way. Having done this, he kept it by him . . . That young thing lay there in that way for a while and that Jew did what he knew to be necessary for his own ends. She then arose and felt herself wounded inside, so she began to cry. And when indeed some Christian women saw her coming out of the Jew's house in tears they approached her and interrogated her as to why she was crying. And she answered them that she did not know what that Jew had done to her, which caused her pain in the stomach. The women . . . diligently examined her and found out what had happened to her.[45]

Here is a gory tale of a Jewish man and a young Christian woman, an explosive concoction of fantasies of rape and violence through the agency of the established murderous and demonised figure of the Jewish man. He was blind to Christian truth, untouched by saving grace, and different. This difference was particularly stark within high and late medieval culture which strove towards uniformity and homogeneity, in the pretence of togetherness and sameness which was offered as an image of a Christian society. The Jew came to carry all the pent up anxiety, shame and fear which Christians harboured about themselves, their bodies, their God, their doubts, their desires. From fantasies of child abuse told of Jews and retold as tale and edifying entertainment from the twelfth century,[46] to the host desecration fantasies of the thirteenth,[47] and the well-poisoning scares of the fourteenth,[48] narratives of horror could lend to the most daily and innocent exchanges and relations between Christian and Jewish neighbours a potential for danger and fear. The relationship of Jewish householder and Christian maid is one which was seen as particularly dangerous.[49] Christian–Jewish business partnerships, indebtedness to court–Jews on the part of lords and magnates, and the treatment by Jewish physicians of Christian patients were all sites of anxiety which offered scenarios for fantastic elaboration of fear of corruption, contamination, loss of identity and boundaries.

Our case is a story full of secrecy. In the privacy of his house the Jewish employer enticed the young woman (*juvencula*) to take some food before beginning her work; the food and drink he had poisoned sent her into a drugged 'enchanted' sleep. He checks that the doors were locked and proceeds with his operations. Using metal instruments, as surgeons do, he extracted from her the uterus, this all-important female part, which Richer defines in medical parlance, 'in which infants are conceived'.[50] The medical discourse greatly valued the womb as a singular part of the female body. In his encyclopaedic work of natural philosophy, Honorius Augustodunensis described the making of hermaphrodites in his description of the womb: 'The womb . . . has seven cells, impressed with a human shape, like coins are . . . And so it is, that a woman can never bear more than seven infants at one birth.'[51] The French translator of Bartholomeus Anglicus' *De proprietatibus rerum* likens the womb to a vessel charged with reception of the seed. Physician–magician the Jew enchants–operates, manipulates–dismembers the young woman, excising from her body the magical–medical uterus, the source of humours and moods, keeping it for himself (perhaps for future use?).[52] The girl wakes up in appalling pain, in tears, and rushes out of the house and into the hands of those alternative gynaecologists, adult women, women–mothers, who intuit her problems and examine her with authority. They reveal a body abused, invaded, amputated, bereft of its most important and defining organ. The Jew–male–physician–magician was duly caught and punished, an overdetermined culprit, whose violent end was the only possible resolution.

Meredith Lillich suggests that we have here an abortion gone wrong which produced the heinous tale;[53] a context–*habitus* for the elaboration of the horror story. Jewish surgeons definitely possessed elaborate knowledge of abortion practice,[54] as did Christian medicine, although canon law allowed it only in the case of a foetus less than forty days old.[55] Abortion was often effected in the context of magical practice, as was much of the medicine applied to women's bodies,[56] and was linked to magic and spells and to the use of particularly efficacious properties, such as the eucharistic host.[57] A case from Manosque in Provence in 1298 illustrates the dangerous context of rumour and suspicion which might surround the practice of a Jewish physician. In that year Isaac son of Resplenda was accused of having provided Uga (short for Astrugua) with an abortifacient potion. A series of witnesses testified that they had heard rumours of her pregnancy, and then had been told that Uga's mother had disposed of the infant after its death. Uga was unwed, and the circumstances of the newborn's disappearance induced rumour which led to the court proceedings; the Jew was said to have been seen with Uga before the alleged 'birth': 'One day she saw Master Isaac, Jew and physician, enter into the said house in which the said Uga was staying.'[58] He was not only seen in the house where Uga lived, according to another female witness, he was also seen talking with Uga on a number of occasions during her pregnancy: 'She saw the said Master Isaac speaking on many occasions with the said Uga, during the period when she was thought to be pregnant.'[59] In his defence Isaac claimed that she had died in the course of childbirth, but his claim was rejected and his family only secured his release by paying a stiff fine.[60]

Richer's account associates categories with no apology: the Jew, doctor or magician, doctor and magician?[61] The operation, an abortion gone wrong or the truncation of a uterus precious in magical use? and the *ferramenta*, nasty tools of violence or the professional tools of surgeon–craftsman? and the girl in tears, a woman any longer? The body is here a vulnerable thing which can be put to sleep and mutilated to produce an unwhole person, a most defective woman.

The Jew, that threatening arch-enemy, chose the body and its inner secrets as his point of abuse of innocence and trust, and of wilful denial of fertility.[62] Bodies were seen in the medical discourse as full of secrets and inner knowledge which a good physician must try to fathom and which surgical dissection was making increasingly familiar from the thirteenth century.[63] What went on in women's bodies was especially fascinating and dangerous. This curiosity caused the development of the vaginal speculum, like that drawn in a fourteenth-century Latin manuscript of Albucasis.[64] It also produced a taste for scenes such as that from the *Roman de la rose* where Nero watches as his mother Agrippina is dissected, a scene which was a favourite of medieval illuminators.[65]

The female body was a place of hollows, caverns, mysterious spaces, above all that private space, the womb, which *Le Propriétaire des choses* described as a chamber in a house.[66] Yet the female body, private and full of elusive secrets, was also tantalisingly adorned with apertures, from the privileged mouth[67] to the wild and terrifying anus.[68] The images of interiority created a corresponding desire for entry, penetration and discovery and the Jew in this tale had enacted the fantasy of violation, in the most brutal way, drugging away his victim's consciousness, denying her the chance of resistance or shame, using cold metal implements, and depriving her of her secret and fertile place.

The body presented opportunities for identity-making which contained a wide range of possibilities and forms, but it also courted danger in its vulnerability to attack and to fragmentation. Public judicial mutilation (such as that suffered by the hermaphrodite of Breisach) dramatised the relation between the body and its parts; religious practice concentrated contemplation on distinct body parts or body marks: wounds, heart, face. Images arising from the crucifixion, in the iconographic set known as *arma christi*, broke down the Passion scenes – protagonists, instruments – and then shuffled them and redistributed them in what would seem today to be a surrealistic scrambling of a powerful and naturalistic composition of the historical moment.[69] Similarly powerful is the ease of movement between discrete body parts and the creation of metaphors which use the very vibrancy of flesh and its radical vulnerability. The body could be thus rearranged in the order of a document possessing a totally different order to that of a biological body.

The body, like a legal charter or a book, unfolds only with the effort of engagement, but both have secrets to yield. Torture, love, surgery, translation, decoding, dizzying hermeneutic moves of empathy, enfold the engagement with the body of God and the promise that had come with it.[70]

III

This tense affinity between the fragmented body and perfect deity within this culture hinged powerfully on the particular eucharistic configuration elaborated so formatively and ubiquitously in the later Middle Ages. The eucharistic divine body was treated as a workaday body, in its regular accessibility, in the pain of its suffering; and yet it was quite different – it was glorious, eternal. It had been crucified but not destroyed; it could be eaten with impunity and bring benefit to the worthy, and it could taste like honey to the virtuous,[71] whereas those who received it unworthily were put in danger of damnation, and it could turn into raw flesh in their throats.[72] God's physicality could be reassuring in its similarity to that of mortals, but it could also be confusing when the beholder's sense of self and embodiment were ruptured and disturbed.

Aude Fauré was thus disturbed as she was trying to adapt to the life of a young married woman as wife to a prosperous farmer, Guillaume Fabre, in the village of Merviel, not far from Montaillou, in the first decades of the fourteenth century.[73] Falling ill after childbirth she summoned her aunt, Ermengarde, to be with her. Aude tried to be a good woman and wife, and to toe the line of religious probity which her husband and aunt expected. But she had always entertained doubt about the particular version of embodiment which eucharistic teaching required. She found it particularly hard to accept that the eucharist was God himself. When she confessed this with some torment to her aunt: 'Alas, Aunt, how can it be that I cannot believe in God, and cannot even believe that the host the chaplain raises on the altar is Christ's body?'[74] Aude was offered soothing prayers and fortifying miracle tales to allay her doubts, but the aunt's authoritative guidance within the patriarchal household was exercised through sanction and rebuff. When none of these worked, the husband himself intervened, and when she cried 'My Lord, how can it be that I cannot believe on our Lord?', he reproached her: 'You accursed creature, are you in your right mind?'[75] and threatened to send her away if she failed to confess properly. Neither her husband's threats nor the coaxing auntie-tales could quite settle the problem which an embodied God posed for Aude.

As the investigation continued and her husband, aunt and neighbours were examined, Aude was re-summoned, and told her inquisitors the root of her doubts, and her loss of faith in the eucharist. It all began some four (not seven or eight as she had alleged) years earlier, when her own body underwent the experience of childbirth, as she lived through that period of utmost physical awareness, producing a new body, and then through the enclosed seclusion of the period preceding ritual purification.[76] Now Aude was prone to bitter doubts more than ever. Her corporeal mutability, the sense of her body's changeability, of its ability to produce vile and unclean things, as well as a living throbbing child, heightened the tension which she felt towards that all too physical God. A recent event in the village induced a heightened experience of these emotions. A woman had given birth on the roadside, being too far from home:

> She heard from some women, whose names she claimed not to remember, that on the preceding night a woman had given birth to a daughter on the road leading into the castle of Merviel, because she could not reach her home. And having heard this, she was reminded of the filth (*turpitudo*) which women emit at birth; and when she saw Christ's body elevated at the altar, she was reminded of that filth which would have affected the Lord's body. And because of that thought she fell into an error of faith, that is, that the body of the Lord Jesus Christ was not there.[77]

The story raised a mirror to Aude's self: she was that woman, even if she had given birth in the comfort of a well-appointed peasant house. This created a chain of imaginings. If Christ was as human as can be, a re-deemer by virtue of that humanity, then he must have been born in similar 'filth' (*turpitudo*), having been nurtured in such a body as hers, and brought into the world as a vulnerable creature like the new-born on the road to Merviel.[78] This placenta was treated with care. Doctors were charged with supervising the birth, and especially the un-making of the womb's furnishings: the placenta (*secundina*) which must be induced to come out or it might imperil the mother's life. In the English translation of *De proprietatibus rerum* it is recorded: 'And if it happe in any case þat þe skyn abide stille in þe wombe aftir þat þe childe is ibore, þanne þe woman is in perile.'[79] Danger and promise, life and death, were thus attached to the womb, where the seeds of conceptions were nurtured, within the unique control of the pregnant woman.[80] The womb received specialised attention. A thirteenth-century pharmacological compendium, the *Areolae* of John of Saint-Amand, recommended preparations for the drawing out of the placenta and the foetus.[81] He must have, furthermore, brought forth the *filth* of birth, that redundant, useless, formless and bloody mess of the 'afterbirth' (the placenta) having been fed on the female inner organs for nine months, female blood which was just turning into mother's milk in his mother's breasts.[82] Aude had only recently given birth, her child's wet-nurse still resided with the family, when she experienced her moment of gravest doubt; the body struck her as so human – could Christ be embodied and be God?[83]

IV

It is interesting that Aude's anxieties were pinned on to the embodied Christ, not the embodied Virgin; on blood, not on mother's milk. Blood, the liquid of life, was a privileged signifier of the valences of life, material and spiritual. It invoked the sense of vulnerability, the ubiquity of pain, and the many other images of immolation, torture and dismemberment which were practised in late medieval towns. Blood flowed from tortured bodies as limbs were removed, 'loosened', and bodies disfigured in the course of judicial torture.[84]

Bodies were also dismembered and unmade in the context of burial, and the greater the person the more likely the fragmentation of the ca-daver. The church repeatedly enjoined the preservation of bodily whole-ness in burial from Boniface VIII's first bull *Detestandae feritatis* of 1299, based on the contemporary formulations of the psychosomatic understanding of the human person,[85] but dynastic aspirations demanded fragmentation of the body. Rituals of evisceration and ossification thus followed the death of the great, often far from their homes, and the piecemeal burial of the vital parts; heart, head, bones . . .[86] Fragments of the seigneurial body could mark family seats and, when distributed for burial among religious houses, could fulfil an elaborate programme of intercession.[87] In the same dec-ades medical autopsy and dissection was being practised, first in Italy, and then in France, using the bodies of criminals for furthering the knowledge of bodily secrets.[88] There was a definite economy of pain and parts, whereby relics of martyrs and saints, of bodies tormented and emaciated, were recovered and circulated as sources of health and healing, in uses magical, nutritive, affective.[89]

So the body in parts, broken, dismembered, fragmented was all too present, its significations threatening and troubling to the images of per-sonal and corporal wholeness which were promoted in the discourse of romance, in the efforts of physicians.[90] Christ's body of the Passion came to be represented as a series of wounds or wounded body parts surrounded by wounding instruments; hand, foot, side, sweaty brow. This was the way through which Christ's suffering body was apprehended, in the breaking up, in the *corps morcelé*.[91] Its threat was always there, and religious teaching tried to harness that fragmentation, to use that pain as a form of self-knowing which was only a minuscule analogue to that great outpouring of pain and love which Christ's Passion represented.[92] Pain was the very essence of human existence, and in the context of discussion of Christ's humanity the question was thus forced upon Thomas Aquinas (1224–74): 'Was Christ born without labour pains'?[93] There were reasons to think that pain was experienced by the Virgin, in her humanity, because midwives surrounded her, because all birth brought forth pain. But no, this birth was different to the extent that by the later thirteenth century Mary had become quite different from any ordinary woman, so Thomas objected: 'In the woman the pain of birth follows from intercourse with man. Hence *Genesis* says, *In pain you will bring forth children*, and, *you will be under your husband's power*. But, as Augustine says, from this sentence is excepted the Virgin mother of God.'[94] So pain in birth is related to a whole gender system which inscribes servility within marriage after the Fall. From this particular pain Mary was exempt, and Christ exited her womb without forcing his way, thus inducing no pain.[95]

The pain of the Passion, the most exalted pain, was powerfully linked to the spilling and loss of blood. And the blood-merchants *par excellence*, both past and present, were the Jews. They were said to drain the bodies of little boys and girls whom they killed (sometimes in crucifixion, sometimes also circumcised), using every possible cut and incision to drain the blood. This blood was said to be needed for a variety of applications; medical, cosmetic, ritual and magical. Devotional literature elaborated Christ's suffering at the hands of surgeons/magicians/executioners. The *Southern English Ministry and Passion of Christ* (*c.*1275–80) gives such a detailed account:

> Qwan þei þe rote of þi swete lyf [at þi herte ground] it souȝtte,
> Þat [i]s þe wil of euery mannys lyf – þer were loþ to leuyn owȝt.[96]

It presents a lurid discourse on the three types of human blood – flesh, veins and heart – all three of which Christ was made to shed:

> þe ferste betwen fel & flesch [clene] ouȝtt was brouȝt
> þe þou were rent with scourgis; þer belevyd in þe nouȝt.
> þe blood þat is her þ[e] lyf, þat in þe veynys is,
> wol clene þorwȝ þi fet & hadnys brouȝt was ouȝt iwis,
> & also þorw þe crounne of þornys þat in þe hed deþe woode;
> þese þre stremys out of þi veynys wol clene souȝtte þi bloode,
> for þer is no veyne in mannys body but it tillyþ to þat on ende.[97]

The death on the cross thus becomes a triple death, a thorough draining of Christ's body, as the Jews thus rendered Christ's sacrifice complete:

With the leste drope of þi blood þou my3ttyst us ha bou3t,
& þou 3eve for us euery drope þat þer belefte ty3t nou3t.[98]

The shedding of blood, the most complete unmaking of the body, was the ultimate offering, ultimate sacrifice, most complete pain.[99] In her visions Julian of Norwich (c.1343–1443) experienced the image of Christ's body bleeding 'hot and freshly and as lifelike as I had before seen . . . and this was shown me in the wounds of the scourging and it ran so plenteously'.[100]

Blood and body parts were part of a vast economy of salvation, a sort of symbolic cannibalism between generations which died for each other, and who all hoped to be saved through a single exemplary immolation. Out of pain came all that was comfort; St Ramon Nonat's mother died in childbirth, and the knowledge of this moved him to a life of bodily mortification, which in turn produced in his saintly body a relic comforting to women in labour and protective of infants.[101] That such images came to inhabit not the margins but the heart of representation – in paintings on church walls, above altars, in vernacular religious drama – is closely linked to the prevalent images of a fluid body already encountered. Bodies were not 'governed totalities' but vulnerable and non-reducible to a fixed order.[102] This disorder, this openness is often and necessarily linked with pain as the very susceptibility to violation.[103] It is the experience of pain, the knowledge of confusion, which subverted dichotomising efforts and could establish a scepticism about their validity. Man–woman, spirit–flesh, body–mind, health–sickness, sanity–madness, could not contain the variety of embodied experiences.

So bodies were created and lived between the authoritative discourses which endorsed order and hierarchy through binary classifications and schemes of practice, and experiences broad and divergent grounded in contact with other people, in connectedness and in imagination. Bodies could also be imagined and described, drawing out an audience's experience, as must have been the case with Chaucer's Wife of Bath, a body full of power and pleasure even when circumscribed by the limitations of law and the pain of desire. Figures like her remind us just how varied and localised, how deliberate, the production of notions of the body and the self could be.[104]

Historians may try to move in ways which allow the embodied nature of things to be revealed. To do so is to move between the variety of explanatory grids offered within the constraints of language and of context and situation; since the experience of *being in the world* never quite fits into the structures of discourse. The production of meaning is also where resistance and agency can be found. Thus we have seen how the ordered hierarchies of male–female, inner–outer, whole–part, were also escaped, subverted, torn, rent in practices and fantastic elaborations which look nothing like the binary gazes of current medicine nor like the embarrassment concerning the body which we find in religious teaching.[105] Biological aspects of the medieval body were only the beginning of elaboration of notions of selfhood and identity. The questions about generation, personality, selfhood – the sort of question which conundrums like Hume's sock or Theseus' ship explore – occupied medieval people; where does a man end and a woman begin? how does a painful or joyful part of the body relate to a consciousness, a self? could Christ's body be as vulnerable as oneself and yet divine and eternal? and can the body be linked by routines and disciplines to things outside it, eternal, and very different from its own pathetic and finite matter? We have come across some of the variety of *corporeal style* which could either be repeated in obedience to persuasion, in collusion, in ignorance, in submission, or else be subverted by unexpected moves, of parody, rebelliousness, through error, or misunderstanding, to perform otherwise than expected, and outside expected bodily 'order'.[106]

NOTES

I owe many thanks to Helen Phillips for stimulating 'bodily' conversations.

1 F. Barker, *The tremulous private body: essays on subjection*, London, 1984, p. 12. The book goes on to develop a disjointed and anarchic, ahistorical body-picture, but its early statement of embodied inquiry is worthy of attention.

2 I shall be working with the understanding that 'There is no gender identity behind the expressions of gender; that identity is performatively constituted by the very "expressions" that are said to be its results', (J. Butler, *Gender trouble: feminism and the subversion of identity*, New York and London, 1990, p. 25), paying attention to the historical nature of such 'expressions' and 'resulting' identities. See also *Gender/body/knowledge: feminist reconstructions of being and knowledge*, ed. A. M. Jaggar and S. R. Bordo, New Brunswick (NJ), 1989.

3 On its making see E. Kleinschmidt, 'Die Colmarer Dominikaner-Geschichtsschreibung im 13. und 14. Jahrhundert. Neue Handschriftenfunde und Forschung zur Uberlieferungsgeschichte', *Deutsches Archiv*, XXVIII, 1972, pp. 371–496.

4 'Prope Bernam in villa . . . mulier 10 annis viro cohabitat; quia cognosci a viro non potuit, iudicio spirituali a viro separatur; Romam proficiscens, Bononiae a chirurgo cunnus eius scinditur, egreditur virga virilis cum testiculis; domum reversa uxorem ducit, opera rustica facit, cum uxore congreditur legittime et sufficienter', *Monumenta Germaniae Historica. Scriptores* (henceforth *MGH.SS*), 17, p. 225. See on the same page another shorter version: 'Mulier prope Bernam, arta nata impotens ad cognoscendum, virum plus quam 10 annis habuit; fuit in virum, habentem magna virilia, transmutata.'

5 *Albucasis on surgery and instruments: a definitive edition of the Arabic text with English translation and commentary*, ed. M. S. Spink and G. L. Lewis, Berkeley (CA), 1973, c. 70, p. 454. Albucasis also recommended the cutting of an enlarged clitoris, *ibid.*, c. 71, p. 456.

6 'Et multotiens curantur per incisionem membris occultioris, et regimen vulneris eius', Avicenna, *Liber canonis*, Basle, 1556, book 3, fen. 20, tract 1, c. 43.

7 J. Friedman, *The monstrous races in medieval art and thought*, Cambridge (Mass.), 1981, p. 10; Isidore of Seville, *Isidori hispalensis episcopi etymologiarum sive originum libri XX*, ed. W. M. Lindsay, Oxford, 1911; II, 11.3.1: 'Hermaphroditae autem nuncupati eo quod eis uterque sexus appareat'.

8 *Traditions tératologiques ou récits de l'antiquité et du moyen-âge en occident*, ed. J. Berger de Xivrey, Paris, 1836, c. 1, p. 5; c. 22, p. 94; c. 25, p. 100.

9 'Communis generis vel mixti androgenus esse scribitur et legitur prodigum miserum. Ut pater et mater gignit, parit unus et idem utraque membra ferens vir mulierque simul', C. Hünemörder, 'Isidorus versificatus, ein anonymes Lehrgedicht über Monstra und Tiere aus dem 12. Jahrhundert', *Vivarium*, XIII, 1975, pp. 103–18.

10 'et si vincatur virtus in uno et vincat in alio, generaliter *ermafroditus*. Et aliquando est ita figura utriusque membri completa quod ad visum et tactum discerni non potest quis sexus praevaleat: et non est inconveniens quod talis partus etiam habeat duas vesicas et urinam emittat per utrumque et quod in coitu et agat et patiatur, et incumbat et succumbat: sed non puto quod et impraegnet et impraegnetur. Sed pro certo sexus erit principalior qui a cordis curatur complexione', Albert the Great, *De animalibus libri XXVI*, ed. H. Stadler, Beiträge zur Geschichte der Philosophie des Mittelalters – Texte und Untersuchungen 16, Münster, 1920, book 18, tract 2, c. 3; II, p. 1225. On the position in the womb and sex determination see also the English view of *c*.1200 cited in J. Cadden, *Meanings of sex difference in the Middle Ages*, Cambridge, 1993, pp. 202–3, and on the effect of heat or coldness see pp. 198–9. On twin lore see also D. Hüe, '*Ab ovo*: jumaux, siamois, hermaphrodites et leur mère', in *Les Relations de parenté dans le monde médiéval*, Sénéfiance XXVI, 1989, pp. 351–71. On attitudes to werewolves, who were not 'Plinian' monsters see C. Oates, 'Metamorphosis and lykanthropy in Franche-Comté, 1521–1643', in *Fragments for a history of the human body*, ed. M. Feher, R. Naddaff and N. Tazi, New York, 1989, I, pp. 304–63, at pp. 317–19.

11 On the womb see D. Jacquart and C. Thomasset, *Sexuality and medicine in the Middle Ages*, trans. M. Adamson, Cambridge, 1988, pp. 22–9.

12 *Ibid.*, pp. 34–50, 141.

13 This theory became popular in the twelfth century and was misattributed to Galen; see N. Siraisi, *Medieval and early Renaissance medicine: an introduction to knowledge and practice*, Chicago, 1990, pp. 91–6; F. Kudlein, 'The seven cells of the uterus: the doctrine and its roots', *Bulletin of the history of medicine*, XLIX, 1965, pp. 415–23, and for an image of a seven-celled womb see Jacquart and Thomasset, *Sexuality and medicine*, figure 1.4, p. 21.

14 'Item natus fuit puer scilicet infans hermafrodita in valle Kesirperch, id est qui membrum mulieris atque virilia continebat', *MGH.SS* 17, p. 220.

15 'Monstruositas enim accidit ex errore aliquo operationis naturae secundum habundantiam vel defectum aut positionem aut figuram membrorum', Albert the Great, *De animalibus*, book 18, tract 1, c. 6, p. 1217. See also Friedman, *The monstrous races*, p. 115. On monsters as natural wonders see K. Park and L. J. Daston, 'Unnatural conceptions: the study of monsters in France and England', *Past and present*, XCII, 1981, pp. 20–54, at pp. 35–6.

16 See J. A. Brundage, *Law, sex and Christian society in medieval Europe*, Chicago, 1987, pp. 199–201, 376–8, 415–16.

17 On the construction of gender as reflected in the treatment of hermaphrodites in a later period see O. Moscucci, 'Hermaphroditism and sex difference: the construction of gender in Victorian England', in *Science and sensibility: gender and scientific enquiry, 1780–1945*, ed. M. Benjamin, Oxford, 1991, pp. 174–99.

18 'Si magis calescit, ut vir, permittunt eum ducere; si vero magis mollescat, et mulier permittunt ei nubere. Si autem in illo instrumento defecerit, nunquam coincederetur ei usus reliqui instrumenti, sed perpetuo continebit, propter vestigia alternitatis vitii sodomitici', in 'Verbum abbreviatum', *Patrologiae latinae cursus completus* (henceforth *PL*) 205, c. 138, col. 334.

19 J. Boswell, *Christianity, social tolerance, and homosexuality: gay people in western Europe from the beginning of the Christian era to the end of the fourteenth century*, London, 1981, pp. 375–6.

20 A. R. Jones and P. Stallybrass, 'Fetishizing gender: constructing the hermaphrodite in Renaissance Europe, in *Body guards: the cultural politics of sexual ambiguity*, ed. J. Epstein and K. Straub, New York and London, 1991, pp. 80–111, at pp. 104–5.

21 C. Geertz, 'Common sense as a cultural system', in *Local knowledge: further essays in inter-pretive anthropology*, New York, 1983, pp. 73–93.

22 'Hermaphrodita exocculatur in Brisaco, pro eo quod violenter voluit cognoscere mulierem', *MGH.SS* 17, p. 208.

23 *Purgatory* 26.82–7:

> Nostro peccato fu ermafrodito,
> Ma perchè non servammo umana legge,
> Seguendo come bestie l'appetito,
> In obbrobrio di noi per noi si legge,
> Quando partiamci, il nome di colei
> Che s'imbestiò ne l'imbestiate schegge.

On 'hermaphrodite' as a category applied to homosexual men see Cadden, *Meanings of sex difference*, pp. 224–5.

24 '*Ulpianus*. Quaeritur: hermaphroditum cui comparamus? et magis puto ejus sexus aestimandum, qui in eo praevalet', *Corpus iuris civilis: Institutiones, Digesta*, ed. P. Krüger, 21st edn, Dublin and Zurich, 1971, book 1, tit. 5, 5, p. 35.

25 '*Alia divisio hominum*. Est autem alia divisio hominum quod alii sunt masculi, alii feminae, alii hermaphroditae.'

26 '*De hermaphrodito*. Hermaphroditus comparatur masculo tantum vel feminae tantum secundum praevalescentiam sexus incalescentis', Bracton, *De legibus et consuetudinibus Angliae*, ed. G. E. Woodbine, New Haven (CN), 1922, II, p. 31.

27 *Problemata varia anatomica*, ed. L. R. Lind, Lawrence (KS), 1968, p. 67; C. Thomasset, *Commentaire du dialogue de Placides et Timéo: une vision du monde à la fin du XIIIe siècle*, Publications romanes et françaises 161, Geneva, 1982, p. 38. On attempts to ascribe sex-types and the difficulties involved see Cadden, *Meanings of sex difference*, pp. 218–27.

28 M. Foucault, 'Introduction', in *Herculine Barbin; being the recently discovered memoirs of a nineteenth-century French hermaphrodite*, trans. R. McDougal, pp. vii–xvii, at p. viii. For a critique of Foucault's analysis of Herculine's diaries see Butler, *Gender trouble*, pp. 93–106.

29 Menton poncé, filz Hermofondricus,
> Effeminé, defaulte de nature,
> Couraige vain, vuit de toutes vertus,
> De vice plain, qui ne tent qu'a ordure,
> Non masculin, femenine figure,
> Qui imposer suelz faulx noms sur autruy;
> Ains es livres de telz gens bien ne luy
> Quant ilz ne sont en nature parfais,
> Corrups de corps, de pensée, les truy,
> Infeables, desloyaulx et mauvais
>
> . . . Femme d'omme, qui doit estre barbus,
> Homme sanz poil, c'est a chascun laidure.
> Eulx encontrer n'est que male adventure,
> Et leur regart ne doit plaire a nulluy.
> Usans des deux; de mon temps en congnuy,
> Infeables, desloyaulx et mauvais,

(*Oeuvres complètes d'Eustache Deschamps*, ed. Queux de Saint-Hilaire, Paris, 1889, VI, ballad 1129, pp. 49–50.)

30 'specialement de homme esbarbe, c'est qui n'a point de barbe, car telz sont enclins a plusieurs vices et mauvaistiez et s'en doit on garder comme de son ennemi mortel', *Le Compost et kalendrier des bergiers*, facsimile of edition of 1493, Paris, 1926.

31 See on the development of the embryo C. S. F. Burnett, 'The planets and the development of the embryo', in *The human embryo: Aristotle and the Arabic and European traditions*, ed. C. R. Dunstan, Exeter, 1990, pp. 95–112.

32 'Et advient aulcuneffoys que les femmes sont barbues car elles sont de complexion chaulde et moiste et au contraire les masces qui sont de complexion froide et seiche nont point de barbe', *Le Propriétaire des choses*, Paris, 1518, book 5, c. 15; see also P. Brown, *The body and society: men, women, and sexual renunciation in early Christianity*, New York, 1988, p. 11.

33 T. Laqueur, *Making sex: body and gender from the Greeks to Freud*, Cambridge (MA), 1990, pp. 25–62.

34 M.-C. Pouchelle, *The body and surgery in the Middle Ages*, trans. R. Morris, Cambridge, 1990, pp. 180–2. See also C. W. Bynum, 'The female body and religious practice in the later Middle Ages', in *Fragments for a history of the human body*, ed. M. Feher, R. Naddaff and N. Tazi, New York, 1989, I, pp. 160–219, at pp. 186–7; and for the classical origins see P. DuBois, *Sowing the body: psychoanalysis and ancient representations of women*, Chicago, 1988, pp. 184–5.

35 P. M. Murray, *Medieval medical miniatures*, London, 1984, plate II, facing p. 49; K. B. Roberts and J. D. W. Tomlinson, *The fabric of the body: European traditions of anatomical illustration*, Oxford, 1992, pp. 15–17; plate 1, p. 23.

36 See the representation of bodies without genitals in some margins of medieval manuscripts in M. Camille, *Images on the edge*, London, 1989, fig. 52, p. 96 (The Oscott Psalter, BL Add. 50000, fol. 173v).

37 See Alan of Lille's complaint in *The plaint of nature*, trans. J. Sheridan, Toronto, 1980, sec. 10, p. 162; J. Ziolkowski, *Alan of Lille's grammar of sex: the meaning of grammar to a twelfth-century intellectual*, Speculum anniversary monographs 10, 1985, pp. 22–3; A. Leupin, *Barbarolexis: medieval writing and sexuality*, trans. K. M. Cooper, Cambridge (MA), 1989, pp. 59–78.

38 On which R. Howard Bloch, *Medieval misogyny and the invention of western romantic love*, Chicago, 1991, especially the introduction, pp. 1–35.

39 C. Dinshaw, *Chaucer's sexual politics*, Madison (WN), p. 182.

40 On the transmission of the story see L. Silberman, 'Mythographic transformations of Ovid's Hermaphrodite', *The sixteenth century journal*, XIX, 1989, pp. 643–52, at pp. 643–4.

41 *Ibid.*, pp. 646–7.

42 'factum est ut tam aque dilectatione quam cibi opportunitate non nunquam barbari immanes descenderent in tabernam et consuetudine paulatim barbariem ponere, et Grecorum mollioribus moribus atque humanioribus adherere inciperent', G. Boccaccio, *Genealogie deorum gentilium libri*, ed. V. Romano, Bari, 1951, Scrittori d'Italia 200, I, pp. 140–2, at p. 141.

43 'Ista possunt allegari et applicari ad beatam incarnationem. Iste enim puer filius Mercurii est Dei filius super omnia sponsus, qui a principio propriam silvam i. paradisum deseriit, in quantum ad istud seculum venit et ibi in aqua misericordie se lavit iuxta mandatum patris . . . Ista nimpha ociosa potest signare humanam naturam ocio deductam atque vacuam. Fons iste potest signare beatam Virginem gloriosam, claram, limpidam, atque puram', F. Ghisalberti, 'L' "Ovidius moralizatus" di Pierre Bersuire', *Studi romanzi*, XXIII, 1933, pp. 5–136, at p. 116.

44 C. Thomasset, *Commentaire du dialogue de Placides et Timéo: une vision du monde à la fin du XIIIe siècle*, Publications romanes et françaises 161, Geneva, 1982, pp. 160–2.

45 'Huius Iudei domum quedam pauper iuvencula frequentabat et in eadem domo que agenda erant agebat, ut sustentationem victus ibi accipere posset. Enimvero cum quadam die ipsa iuvencula domum ipsius Iudei . . . intrasset et Iudeus ille iuvenculam illam vidisset, gavisus est valde, quia solus cum sola in domo erat. Et accersita ea, dixit ei: 'Veni et comede paululum, quia te opportet operari'. Et cum illa comedisset et bibisset, ita est incantata, ut dormire videretur nec aliquid sentiret; et cum Iudeus videret, incantationes suas effectum habere, obseratis hostiis accepit utensila sua ad hoc quod facere volebat preparata, et ad iuvenculam illam accedens, divaricatis cruribus eius, quibusdam ferramentis folliculum illum qui matrix appellatur, in quo infantes concipi solent,

de utero illius per naturam extraxit. Hoc facto, matricem illam sibi reservavit . . . Iuvencula vero illa cum per horam ita iacuisset et Iudeus ille quod sciebat ad hoc necessarium esse circa illam fecisset, iuvencula ipsa surrexit, et senciens se intus in corpore lesam, cepit flere. Mulieres vero christiane cum vidissent eam de domo Iudei exivisse iuta plorando, accesserunt ad eam et interrogaverunt eam, quare fleret. At illa respondit eis, quod Iudeus ille nescio quid cum ea egerat, unde in ventre torqueretur. Mulieres . . . studiose eam circumspexerunt et invenerunt quod ei acciderat', *MGH.SS* 25, c. 37, p. 323. This episode is discussed by M. P. Lillich, *Rainbow like an emerald: stained glass in Lorraine in the thirteenth and early fourteenth centuries,* University Park (PA), 1991, pp. 78–81.

46 G. I. Langmuir, 'Thomas of Monmouth: detector of ritual murder', *Speculum,* LIX, 1984, pp. 820–46; R. P. Hsia, *The myth of ritual murder,* New Haven (CN), 1988.

47 M. Rubin, 'Desecration of the host: the birth of an accusation', *Studies in church history,* XXIX, 1992, pp. 169–85.

48 J. Trachtenberg, *The devil and the Jews,* New York, 1943, pp. 97–108; C. Ginzburg, *Ecstasies: deciphering the witches' sabbath,* London, 1990, pp. 33–62, 63–8.

49 See ecclesiastical legislation prohibiting Jewish employment of Christian maids and the dwelling of servants in Jewish households: S. Grayzel, *The church and the Jews in the XIIIth century,* New York, 1966, pp. 106–7, 110–11, 114–17, 136–7, 198–9, 204–5, 252–3, 298–9, 300–7, 316–17, 322, 324–5, 330–1.

50 'in quo infantes concipi solent'. For elaborate discussions of the uterus see the medieval gynaecological text with extensive treatment of the uterus and its diseases in R. Barkaï, *Les Infortunes de Dinah ou la gynécologie juive au moyen-âge,* Paris, 1991, especially. pp. 164–74. See the plates between pages 160–1 for images of the uterus and for some drawings of gynaecological instruments.

51 'Matrix vero . . . septem obtinens cellulas, humana figura ut moneta compressas . . . Inde est, quod septem, nec unquam plures mulier uno lecto potest parare', Honorius Augustodunensis, 'De philosophia mundi', *PL* 172, c. 10 'De matrice', cols 88–9.

52 For the complex images and meanings of natural and unnatural births and the opening of the womb see R. Blumenfeld-Kosinksi, *Not of woman born: representations of Caesarean birth in medieval and Renaissance culture,* Ithaca (NY), 1990.

53 Lillich, *Rainbow like an emerald,* p. 81.

54 Barkaï, *Les Infortunes de Dinah,* pp. 93–4.

55 S. Shahar, *The fourth estate: a history of women in the Middle Ages,* London, 1983, pp. 123–5; M. Greilsammer, *L'Envers du tableau: mariage et maternité en Flandre médiévale,* Paris, 1990, pp. 294–302.

56 Barkaï, *Les Infortunes de Dinah,* pp. 102–4.

57 P. Browe, 'Die Eucharistie als Zaubermittel', *Archiv für Kirchengeschichte,* XX, 1930, pp. 134–54.

58 'vidit aliqua die intrante magistrum Ysac judeum et fisicum in dicta domo in qua morabatur una dicta Huga', J. Shatzmiller, *Médécine et justice en Provence médiévale. Documents de Manosque, 1262–1348,* Aix-en-Provence, 1989, no. 10, pp. 80–3, at p. 82.

59 'ipsa vidit dictum magistrum Ysacum loquentem pluries cum dicta Huga quando dicebatur quod esset pregnans', *Ibid.,* p. 83.

60 For other cases of accusation of malpractice against Jewish physicians see J. Shatzmiller, 'Doctors' fees and responsibility: evidence from notarial and court records', in *Sources of social history: private acts of the late Middle Ages,* ed. P. Brezzi and E. Lee, PIMS Papers in Mediaeval studies 5, Toronto, 1984, pp. 201–8, at pp. 206–8.

61 On the Jew as magician see Trachtenberg, *The devil and the Jews,* especially pp. 88–96.

62 On bodies and secrets see Siraisi, *Medieval and early Renaissance medicine,* pp. 79–80. On techniques for the extraction of truth from bodies in another period see P. DuBois, *Torture and truth,* New York and London, 1991, especially pp. 146–7.

63 Siraisi, *Medieval and early Renaissance medicine,* pp. 86–97.

64 London BL Add 36617, fol. 28v; on this manuscript see Jones, *Medieval medical miniatures*, p. 28.

65 *Ibid.*, plate III, facing p. 64.

66 'Ceste matris a deux chambrettes la dextre en quoy le filz est conceu et la senestre en quoy la fille est conceue et se ung enfant est conceu entre ces deux chambrettes il a nature de home et de femme. Le livre de anathomie dit quil ya trois chambrette en la matris pour les filz et trois pour les filles et une au milleu ou ce qui est conceu a la nature de filz et de fille et est apelle des philosophes hermafrodite', *Le Propriétaire des choses*, book 5, c. 44.

67 On the symbolism of the mouth see I. Toinet, 'La Parole incarnée: voir la parole dans les images des XIIe et XIIIe siècles', *Médiévales*, XXII–XXIII, 1992, pp. 13–30, at pp. 13–21.

68 Pouchelle, *The body and surgery*, pp. 135–6.

69 See images in E. Duffy, *The stripping of the altars: traditional religion in England, c.1400–c.1580*, New Haven (CN), 1992, pp. 233–48. For Passion iconography see J. H. Marrow, *Passion iconography and northern European art of the late Middle Ages and early Renaissance: a study of the transformation of sacred metaphor into descriptive narrative*, Ars Neerlandica 1, Kortrijk, 1979. On fragmentation and the concept of *imagos* see Barker, *The tremulous private body*, pp. 85–9.

70 A. Funkenstein, *Theology and the scientific imagination from the Middle Ages to the seventeenth century*, Princeton (NJ), 1986, pp. 42–57.

71 On the merits of the mass see M. Rubin, *Corpus Christi: the eucharist in late medieval culture*, Cambridge, 1991, pp. 62, 140, 153, 231.

72 On punishments for unworthy reception see *ibid.*, pp. 125–6.

73 On Aude see the penetrating analysis of P. Dronke, *Women writers of the Middle Ages: a critical study of texts from Perpetua (+203) to Marguerite Porète (+1310)*, Cambridge, 1984, pp. 213–15, 271–3, 317–18.

74 'Osta, cia, qualiter potest esse quod non possum credere Dominum, nec eciam possum credere quod hostia que elevatur in altari per capellanum sit corpus Christi?', *Le Registre d'inquisition de Jacques Fournier*, ed. J. Duvernoy, Toulouse, 1965, II, pp. 83–4; for the whole set of testimonies see pp. 82–105.

75 'Domine, quomodo potest esse hoc, quod non possum credere Dominum nostrum?' et tunc dictus maritus suus dixit sibi reprehendendo ut dixit, eam: 'Quomodo, maledicta? loqueris in bono sensu tuo?, que respondit quod sic', *Ibid.*, II, p. 83.

76 On churching see Greilsammer, *L'Envers du tableau*, pp. 216–22.

77 'audivit a quibusdam mulieribus, de quarum nominibus dixit se non recordari, quod nocte precedente quadam mulier quondam filiam [pepererat] in via intus castrum de Muro Veteri, ita quod non potuerat pervenisse ad hospicium, quo audito cogitavit turpiditudinem quam emittunt mulieres pariendo, et cum videret elevari in altari corpus Domini, habuit cogitationem ex illa turpitudine quod esset infectum corpus Domini, et quod ex hoc incidit in errorem credentie videlicet quod non esset ibi corpus Domini Ihesu Christi', investigation on 21 July 1318, *ibid.*, II, p. 94.

78 On repugnance towards the placenta see J. Gelis, *History of childbirth: fertility, pregnancy and birth in early modern Europe*, trans. R. Morris, Cambridge, 1991, pp. 166–7.

79 *John of Trevisa's translation of Bartholomeus Anglicus De proprietatibus rerum*, ed. M. C. Seymour, Oxford, 1975, I, p. 295.

80 *Le Propriétaire des choses*, book 5, c. 44.

81 '*Camomilla* utrumque provocat et educit secundinam et embryonem', *Die Areolae Johannes de Sancto Amando (13. Jahrhundert)*, ed. J. L. Pagel, Berlin, 1893, pp. 63–6, 68. Gelis, *History of childbirth*, pp. 166–7.

82 For some ideas about the placenta (*secundina*) as a nurturing and well-furnished home for the foetus see Pouchelle, *The body and surgery*, pp. 134–5. For the placenta's therapeutic powers see Gélis, *History of childbirth*, pp. 170–1.

83 On similar ideas of incarnation as humiliation see J. Le Goff, 'Corps et idéologie dans l'Occident médiévale', in *L'Imaginaire médiéval*, Paris, 1985, p. 124.

84 See descriptions of torture perpetrated by Galeazzo Visconti in 1362–63 in Milan in D. Wallace, 'Writing the tyrant's death: Chaucer, Bernabò Visconti and Richard II', in *Poetics: theory and practice in medieval English literature*, ed. P. Boitani and A. Torti, Woodbridge, 1991, pp. 122–3; on the medieval literature of torture see E. Peters, *Torture*, Oxford, 1985, pp. 54, 59–60.

85 E. Brown, 'Death and the human body in the later Middle Ages: the legislation of Boniface VIII on the division of the corpse', *Viator* 12 (1981), pp. 221–70; see on the intellectual background for the papal initiative F. Santi, 'Il cadavere e Bonifacio VIII, tra Stefano Tempier e Avicenna intorno ad un saggio di Elizabeth Brown', *Studi medievali*, third ser., XXVIII, 1987, pp. 861–78.

86 On the granting of exemption from the prohibition see Brown, 'Death and the human body', pp. 235–46, 256–67.

87 On tension between ecclesiastical and popular demands see A. Paravicini Bagliani, 'L'Eglise médiévale et la renaissance de l'anatomie', *Revue médicale de la Suisse romande*, CIX, 1989, pp. 987–91.

88 Roberts and Tomlinson, *The fabric of the body*, p. 406 (for an autopsy see Ashmole 399; figure 2.8, p. 21); Siraisi, *Medieval and early Renaissance medicine*, pp. 86–97.

89 On 'sacred cannibalism' as similarly beneficial see P. Camporesi, 'Sacred and profane cannibalism', in *Bread of dreams: food and fantasy in early modern Europe*, trans. D. Gentilcore, Cambridge, 1989, pp. 40–55.

90 M.-T. Lorcin, 'Le Corps a ses raisons dans les fabliaux: corps féminin, corps masculin, corps de vilain', *Le Moyen-Âge*, XC, 1984, pp. 433–53.

91 On the *corps morcelé* see J. Lacan, 'The mirror stage as formative of the function of the I as in psychoanalytic experience', in *Ecrits*, trans. A. Sheridan, New York, 1977, pp. 1–7; J. Gallop, *Reading Lacan*, Ithaca (NY), 1985, pp. 79–81, 86.

92 T. Asad, 'Notes on body pain and truth in medieval Christian ritual', *Economy and society*, XII, 1983, pp. 287–327, 310–13.

93 *Summa theologiae* III q. 35 a. 6: 'Utrum Christus fuerit natus sine dolore matris?'

94 *Ibid.*, ad primum.

95 *Ibid.*, q. 28 a. 2.

96 *The South English ministry and passion*, ed. O. S. Pickering, Heidelberg, 1984, p. 181, ll. 2580–1.

97 *Ibid.*, ll. 2587–93.

98 *Ibid.*, ll. 2603–4.

99 On attitudes to pain in Christianity see G. Deleuze, *Nietzsche and philosophy*, trans. H. Tomlinson, London, 1983, pp. 14–17.

100 F. Beer, *Women and mystical experience in the Middle Ages*, Woodbridge, 1992, pp. 139–40.

101 D. de Courcelles, 'Le Corps des saints dans les cantiques catalans de la fin du moyen-âge', *Médiévales*, VIII, 1985, pp. 43–56. See also B. Cazelles, *Le Corps de sainteté*, Geneva, 1982, pp. 55–6.

102 P. Travis, 'The social body of the dramatic Christ in medieval England', *Early drama to 1600, Acta*, XIII, 1985, pp. 17–36, especially pp. 33–4.

103 On bodies 'vibrant' with pain in the descriptions of the *Legenda aurea* see M.-C. Pouchelle, 'Représentations du corps dans la *Légende dorée*', *Ethnologie française*, new ser., VI, 1976, pp. 293–308.

104 This is noted in a different context by Jones and Stallybrass, 'Fetishizing gender', p. 88. I do not, however, agree (as is clear from the analysis above) that a Galenic or Aristotelian understanding of the body impedes the type of fluidity in body classification which we have already noted.

105 On such practice and on the limits of binary gender categories see Butler, *Gender trouble*, pp. 23–5. On classification and its subversion see B. Lincoln, *Discourse and the construction of society: comparative studies of myth, ritual, and classification*, New York and Oxford, 1989, pp. 166–9. On the challenges posed by 'anomalies' such as hermaphrodites to classification see Jones and Stallybrass, 'Fetishizing gender', p. 80.

106 Butler, *Gender trouble*, pp. 139–41.

Bodies in the Jewish–Christian debate

I

It is hardly customary to broach the topic of 'the body' in an analysis of the Jewish–Christian debate. Scholars of Jewish-Christian polemics usually concentrate on the clearly visible components of that debate. These are the disagreement between Jews and Christians about the true conception of God and the acrimony arising from the Christian doctrine of Incarnation; the competition between Jews and Christians for the cherished status of *Verus Israel* or the Chosen People; and the vituperative discussions concerning the correct method of interpreting the Holy Scriptures. Yet if one looks closely at the underlying issues of these components, one finds that the concept of 'the body' did in fact enter the debate in various guises. In its most obvious form 'the body' was an issue when the Incarnation and the Virgin Birth came up for discussion. In conjunction with the human bodies of Jesus Christ and his mother the humanity of the Jews, who did not believe in Jesus, became a subject of debate. Finally, the body of Christ in its relationship to the mystical body of Christian believers, the *communitas Christi*, is an issue of vital importance. The purpose of this essay is to see how these guises of 'the body' emerged in anti-Jewish polemics of the first half of the twelfth century. An attempt will be made to show that looking at that period's Jewish-Christian debate from the viewpoint of the body can actually help to explain how and why attitudes towards Jews deteriorated so much in the course of the twelfth century.[1]

II

Essential to twelfth-century theological enquiries into the doctrine of the Incarnation was the question how an ineffable, transcendent, majestic God could take on the body of a man. How did God become man and, even more pointedly, why should God have wanted to become man in the first place? The urgency of the Incarnation as a topic of debate in this period's Jewish–Christian polemics lies in the fact that Jews were denying a doctrine which Christians were at great pains to explain among themselves. And the reason why so much new work was needed to make that doctrine intelligible was that twelfth-century thinkers were rapidly taking on board large chunks of classical philosophy. This new pagan knowledge demanded a precise reconsideration of old Christian doctrine. Reason was hammering at the gates of the realm of faith.

One of the best minds to face this challenge was Anselm of Canterbury, who tackled the problem of the Incarnation in his *Cur Deus Homo* (1095–98).[2] Anselm believed that faithful and obedient Christians could perceive with their reason the necessity and the feasibility of the Incarnation. To Anselm faith was the prerequisite to understanding; without the light of faith showing the way, reason could not hope to solve any of the issues at hand. The logical inference of Anselm's approach to the relationship between faith and reason would be that no Jew (or any other non-Christian) could be convinced of the truth of Christianity through reason alone. None the less, a number of thinkers, who clearly bear the mark of Anselm's influence, did bring rational arguments into their anti-Jewish polemics.[3] Others, who developed their own ideas about the role of reason, did so too. But however much recourse these thinkers had to philosophy, they did continue to attach great weight to the value of scriptural arguments. The Bible retained its central role in the debate.

Odo, bishop of Cambrai, used many of Anselm's arguments in his anti-Jewish disputation which he wrote between 1106 and 1113. Yet he seemed to expect that these rational arguments should be able to convince Jews of their error, at least if they would be prepared to use their reason. The meaning of reason in the hands of Odo and of many of his contemporaries is a very stoical one. It denotes what was believed to be the innate faculty of human beings to perceive truth. To be human is to possess reason; the bond between men is their common possession of reason.[4] Odo's confidence in reason is particularly apparent in the second part of the disputation where he argues against what he understood the Jewish criticism of the Virgin Birth to be. Odo claims that anyone using their reason should be able to understand the spiritual dimensions of the doctrine. Even though their senses are repelled by the thought of a woman's belly and all the waste passages it contains, their reason would inform them that the Virgin Mary's body was spotless because it was free of sin. Its sublime purity made it the ideal place for God to assume man.[5] (Earlier in the disputation Odo had explained how the one person of Jesus Christ consisted of two natures, one human and one divine, with neither impinging on the other.)[6] Christians, as human beings who use their reason, understand all of this. Jews bear more resemblance to animals because they rely solely on their senses to teach them about what is true. Odo in fact does not stop short from wondering whether Jews are animals rather than human beings.[7]

Guibert, abbot of Nogent, who emphasised how much Anselm's teaching had meant to him, wrote a vicious attack on Jews and their Christian sympathisers in his treatise on the Incarnation (*c*.1111).[8] Much of what

Guibert wrote betrays his deep concern about his own body and about bodily impurities in general. In his tract against the Jews he scoffs at Jewish rejection of the idea that God could take on the baseness of a human form. Bodies are pure as long as they lack sin; unlike all other human beings, there was not even a hint of sin in Jesus Christ. His body was as pure as can be. No opprobrium can be attached to the fact that like other men he too covered his private parts by wearing breeches. And because he had to eat and drink, his body would have functioned in the same way as that of all humans. And in any case even in sinful bodies there is help at hand. Within the framework of faith, reason is there to curb appetite and to keep the material aspect of the body under tight control. Jews do not curb their material instincts; they are a carnal people who delight in the literal meaning of the Old Testament. When understood at that primitive level, the Old Testament has no spiritual message to offer. All it seems to offer are material rewards. Indeed, Jews are concerned solely with making money and crippling the poor with their usury. Their mouths, which they stuff with lies and the excesses of luxury, are filthy in comparison to the purity of the Virgin's privy parts.[9] Guibert was particularly devoted to the Virgin Mary. Indeed his devotion forms part of the history of the developing cult of the Virgin. Like Odo he was at great pains to dispel any possible doubts about the propriety of Mary's body as the place for God to become incarnate. Thus we see him here being so explicit in his assertion that the parts of Mary which engendered Jesus Christ were purer than the mouths of those whom he accuses of being her detractors.[10]

Peter the Venerable, abbot of Cluny, shakes off Jewish criticism of the Incarnation as being crude in his diatribe against the Jews, which he completed by 1147.[11] He asks whether Jews really believe Christians have not worked out for themselves that there is a gulf separating God's sublimity from man's humanity. But whereas Jews condemn the idea that God became man on account of the imponderability of such a thing ever happening, Christians seize on the element of wonder in the thought that God assumed flesh, and they believe in it. They do not believe that God laboured, was hungry and thirsty, suffered, died and was buried. To read that in the doctrine of the Incarnation is to approach it in a carnal, animal-like fashion. The essence of God was not affected by the impurities of the human condition. In Jesus Christ there was the unity of one person made up of diverse substances. Different actions of his belong to the properties of these different substances. Thus the assumption of human flesh did not compromise the deity of Christ. But his flesh was exalted by the fact that God had assumed it.[12]

Thus Odo of Cambrai, Guibert of Nogent and Peter the Venerable defended the doctrine of the Incarnation by pointing to its spiritual meaning. God did not simply change into man; human nature was assumed

by God without effecting a change in the divine nature of God. Because
the full implications of God becoming man go beyond anything human
beings can experience or see for themselves, these thinkers insisted that
only the spiritual side of man could grasp that the Incarnation truly happened. The bodily or sensual component of human beings on its own is
incapable of taking on board this mystery. Because Jews refused to accept
the doctrine, they were viewed by these Christians as lacking spiritual
qualities and being dominated by their bodies. But an interesting new
twist was brought to the discussion about God by Peter Alfonsi, a convert
from Judaism, which in turn was taken up by Peter the Venerable in the
final part of his work against the Jews.

As we have seen, the Jews accused Christians of demeaning God by
asserting that the man Jesus was the son of God. This, in Jewish eyes, was
tantamount to blasphemy. Peter Alfonsi and Peter the Venerable pro-
ceeded to turn the tables on the Jews by accusing them of blaspheming
God because they (and not Christians) gave God a body. The two Peters
did this by isolating anthropomorphic descriptions of God in rabbinic
literature and by assuming that all Jews took these words at face value.
Because Jews refused to accept the spiritual christological meaning that
Christians discovered in the Old Testament, Christians accused them of
having regard for the literal sense of Scripture only. The perceived dearth
of Jewish capacity for spiritual understanding led Peter Alfonsi and Peter
the Venerable to believe that Jews were incapable of reading any text
allegorically. In addition to this Peter Alfonsi, who had been a Jew, had
experience of anthropomorphic tendencies among some of his former
Spanish co-religionists.[13]

Peter Alfonsi composed his *Dialogue* between Peter (himself) and
Moses (his former Jewish self) between 1108 and 1110 in order to explain
and justify his motivations for converting.[14] Peter claimed that the Jewish
doctores err against God because they refuse to read the words of the
Prophets allegorically, even when those words, taken literally, clash with
reason. Reason, says Peter, dictates that there is a God, who is the prime
maker of all that exists. This creator must be simple and unchangeable.
It is therefore impossible to suppose that he bears any likeness to the
creatures he himself created. All of this means that it is nonsensical to
read passages of the Bible which refer to the body of God (e.g. Isaiah 62.8:
'The Lord hath sworn by his right hand, and by the arm of his strength')
literally. Even worse are the stories in the Talmud which have God weeping,
being angry, residing in a particular part of the heavens, and so on. All
this would mean that God is a composite corporeal substance behaving
in the same way as men do. This is patently absurd. People with any knowledge of the make-up of the created world would not dream of thinking
such unworthy things of God. Peter concludes that Jews clearly have no

understanding at all of the true nature of God and his world.[15] Peter goes on to say that where the Bible speaks of God as a man, Jesus Christ, who was God and man, is prefigured. His human nature did not impinge on the divine nature of his person.[16] Thus these passages bear no insult to God's majesty. On the contrary, they contain substantial truths, provided they are understood as they should be, i.e. on a spiritual level and not a carnal one. In other words, Peter has Jews making a nonsense of God by reading texts literally, while he has Christians making perfect sense precisely in that area where Jews accuse them of getting it so wrong: the belief that Jesus Christ is God and man.

Peter the Venerable devoted a whole section of his anti-Jewish polemic to an attack on the Talmud. Some of his material is similar to that of Peter Alfonsi, and it seems reasonable to suppose that he knew of Alfonsi's work. Yet Alfonsi could not have been Peter's only source, for his treatise contains more Talmudic material than Alfonsi's *Dialogue* does.[17] The Talmud serves to reinforce Peter the Venerable's conception of Jews as animal-like beings. In the first four chapters of his treatise he incessantly accuses Jews of being less than human. It is as if this is the only way he can put into words why it is that Jews refuse to understand that the words of the Bible tell them that Jesus Christ is God and man and the Messiah who was foretold by the prophets. According to Peter, any other reading of the text contradicts reason and authority. Peter writes:

> I really do not know whether a Jew is a man, given that he does not yield to human reason, nor does he assent to the divine authorities which are his own. I know not, say I, whether he is a man from whose flesh the stony heart has not yet been removed and to whom the heart of flesh has not yet been given and in whose midst the divine spirit has not yet been placed, without which no Jew can convert to Christ.[18]

Elsewhere Peter emphasises what he sees as the animal-like qualities of Jews by asking his imaginary Jewish opponent why he supposes the miracles of the Exodus from Egypt and the wonders related by the Prophets occurred:

> So that you, Jew, could . . . stuff your belly with a variety of foods? So that you could get drunk . . . and snore in a drunken stupor? Did these things happen so that you could give such great rein to your desires . . . [and] abandon yourselves to your lusts? So that you could abound so greatly in riches and fill chests with gold, silver and many treasures and so that you could elevate yourself with proud and dominating arrogance over inferiors? No! May this be far from human minds, may it be absent from souls capable of reason and may it be remote from all those who know God. Reason does not support this and justice herself denies that man, who was placed before all irrational creatures by the Creator, should be compared to animals in all things and made similar to them, even though in some things man and beast are connected . . . if God

had conferred only worldly goods on man, what more would puny man possess
than a cow, a donkey or the vilest worm?[19]

It is clear to Peter that reason, which demarcates man from animal, simply
does not operate in Jews. For in his eyes Jews are only interested in worldly
goods. But the crucial question still remains. *Why* does reason not function in Jews? What is it that shuts down the working of reason in a Jew's
mind? And it is here that Peter introduces the Talmud. According to him
the fables of what to him is a hideous, bestial book overshadow the hearts
of Jews and obliterate Jewish capacity for reason. Jews are somehow caught
up in a vicious circle of depravity. According to Peter, it is on account of
their sins and the crimes of their fathers that they are being punished by
having their minds taken over by the Talmud. The resulting insanity pro-
vokes them to blaspheme God and to be impervious to all reasonable
arguments proving that Jesus Christ is God. Without escaping the vice of
the Talmud no Jew can hope to glimpse the truth.[20]

The passages of the Talmud which Peter the Venerable ridicules are
again aggadic (i.e. narrative) sections in which the rabbis explored what
one might call the give and take relationship between God and his chosen
people. To illustrate their points the rabbis used anthropomorphic language
to describe God. Thus at one point God is seen to mourn the captivity of
his children. At another he is involved in a scholarly debate between
students of the Talmud and, as any wise father would be, he is proud when
his sons defeat him.[21] Peter, however, lacks any appreciation for these texts.
He does not doubt for a moment that all Jews read all these words in a
purely literal sense. According to him Jews reject metaphors and allegories
which make it possible to use anthropomorphic language when speaking
about God. Where the Bible uses such modes of speech, Jews pervert the
text by reading only the 'killing letter'.[22] According to Peter, Jews are the
stupidest of all peoples, because they believe their rabbinic legends to be
literally true. The Greeks and the Latins were much wiser; as rational
beings, they never believed the inanities of their myths. They, unlike the
Jews, interpreted their stories in a useful (*utilis*) way.[23]

Peter the Venerable does not only take the text of the rabbinic stories
which have come his way literally; he makes changes and twists their contents to prove his point even better.[24] In Peter's version of the tales the
rabbis are incredibly rude to God and treat him as if his wisdom is barely
on a par with their own. They even imply he is a fool and a liar.[25] In Peter's
hands, then, the legends of the Talmud prove that Jews have stripped God
of his omnipotence and transformed him into a vulnerable man, who can
cry and can be outsmarted in a debate. Peter wonders who except a Jew
would not shudder to think that God could be so wretched (*miser*)? He calls
the Jews a truly wretched people (*vere miserum genus*) because they imagine
the divine essence to be human, ascribing as they do to God human and

even animal-like roaring and weeping.[26] In other words, we could say that Peter accuses the Jews of regarding God in the same way that Jews thought Christians regarded him. For we now have both sides of the Christian–Jewish debate insisting that the other has encumbered God with a human body in a totally inappropriate way. In Jewish eyes Christians were the blasphemers because they claimed that God had a son, who was God and who suffered and died like a man. In Peter's eyes Jewish blasphemy against God has earned them the opprobrium of God and their fellow men. Their 'blaspheming mouth which constantly vomits out curses over men and pours out abuse over God' justly marks them for shame in this world and the next, where they can look forward to being a plaything for the demons of hell.[27]

III

We have seen how doctrinal differences between Christianity and Judaism encouraged twelfth-century Christian polemicists to transpose the generally accepted polarities of mind/body, spirit/flesh and man/beast on to the existing opposition between Christians and Jews. According to the developing paradigm, reason, which should control the mind, is what Christians care about; the body, with its bestial qualities, is the domain of Jews. We have seen how this theoretical doctrinal exclusion of Jews from the realm of reason presumed that Jews were concerned with material affairs only. It is therefore worth while to pause for a moment to consider Christian attitudes towards Jews which arose from the social and economic realities of the period.

The late eleventh and the twelfth centuries in north-western Europe were a period of rapid economic expansion. A society that had been primarily a gift economy began to reshape itself as a monetary one. The economic and social changes which took place were not beneficial to everyone. Those left out of the general increase of prosperity were bitter about the innovations they were experiencing. Beyond this Christian moralists were faced with the fundamental challenge of working out whether it was indeed a good thing for a Christian society to seek monetary profits rather than the poverty which the apostolic Church had extolled. All this affected Christian attitudes to Jews. The Jews of France, England and Germany were visible in this period as entrepreneurs and moneylenders. They were certainly not the only people occupied in this way, but there can be no doubt that their economic activities did boost the growing economy. Thus unease about the making of money was often expressed by Christians by attacking the Jews for doing just that. And the disappointment of those who were not as successful as they wanted to be was often translated into condemnation of any economic success Jews were seen or thought to have.[28] The economic stereotyping which grew out of these attacks was used to pinpoint what was seen to separate Jews from Christians. The similarities between economic anti-Jewish stereotypes and the doctrinal exclusion of Jews from matters spiritual is significant. For one thing the two types of stereotyping were mutually reinforcing. For another the overlap between the stereotypes served to marginalise the Jews even further.

Peter Abelard describes the economic position of the Jews rather sympathetically. In his *Dialogue of a philosopher with a Jew and a Christian* (written by the latter half of the 1130s)[29] he states that Jews are not permitted to own land and the only occupation they can have is that of lending money at interest. This leads Jews to be hated by those who feel oppressed by them.[30] Abelard's unbiased reporting of Jewish moneylending should not, however, blind us to the fact that one of the conclusions of his *Dialogue* is that Jews, however much they mean to, do not in fact serve God correctly. Jewish refusal to exchange the ceremonial details of the Law of Moses for a christological figurative signification means, in Abelard's eyes, that Jews do not have access to the inner spiritual truth which would direct them to true love of God.[31] And Abelard, too, resorts to animal imagery when he writes that Jews are 'animals and sensual and are imbued with no philosophy whereby they are able to discuss reasoned arguments'.[32]

We have already seen Guibert of Nogent connecting Jewish hermeneutics with Jewish morals. Just as Jews cannot rise above the letter of the law, so they do not seek anything in life that will not give them material gain. In his treatise against the Jews, the Jews are stereotyped especially as thieves and usurers. Bogged down as they are by these crimes they are incapable of perceiving something as spiritual as the Virgin Birth.[33]

Not surprisingly, Peter the Venerable had little sympathy for the economic position of the Jews. On a theoretical plane he saw Jews as so keen on material and ephemeral things that they cast aside the heavenly eternal goods on offer to them and everyone else.[34] Here, in a way not dissimilar to Guibert, Peter's view is informed by his conviction that Jews misread the Bible by taking it literally. But on a more practical level Peter is not less scathing. And here too his words are sparked off by religious fire. In his letter to Louis VII concerning preparations for the Second Crusade, he suggests to the king that the Jews should bear the brunt of the cost of the expedition. Peter writes that the Jews are far worse than the Saracens; Muslims and Christians have at least some beliefs about Jesus and the Virgin Mary in common. Jews believe Jesus was nothing special. They blaspheme him and his mother, rejecting and deriding all the sacraments of human redemption. The only reason they should not be wiped off the face of the earth is that God wishes them to live a fate worse than death. A good way to achieve this would be to take away from the Jews the money they make out of their reprobate business affairs. Instead of performing and holding useful and honest economic positions, Jews, according to Peter, function as 'fences' making a living from the stolen goods Christian thieves bring them from churches. 'The vessels of the body and blood of Christ [are divided] among the killers of that body and the spillers of the blood of Christ.' And to make matters worse, they desecrate the holy objects before making a profit out of them.[35] However much Peter's views were coloured by the difficult financial position of Cluny in this period, it is plain that his attitude to Jewish moneylending was inexorably bound up with his ideas about Jews as religious adversaries. The occasion of the Crusade, which he himself could ill afford to support, could only serve to bring out his feelings more strongly.[36]

IV

The question of otherness in the doctrinal and socio-economic spheres and the overlap between the concepts used in both spheres impinge in their turn on another facet of 'the body' in the Jewish–Christian debate. Jews were not only seen as a people denying that God assumed flesh; they were not only seen as a separate economic group. They stood accused of crucifying the very body through which God was supposed to have become incarnate.[37] Christians for their part not only venerated that body, they believed they had a share in that same body when they partook of the host. And it was through their participation in the Eucharist that they conceived themselves to be united in the body of Christ, becoming his holy Church.[38]

The expressions concerning Christian unity, which we find in our sources of the first half of the twelfth century, must be interpreted against the backdrop of the developing ideology of a universal Church or Christian society which was put forward so forcefully by papal reformers from the middle of the eleventh century onwards. One of the pressing questions of this period was to work out whose authority – the pope's or the emperor's – should have supremacy in this *respublica Christiana*. The problem became even more urgent in the course of the thirteenth century when temporal authority could use for its own purposes the political theory of Aristotle.[39] But whether temporal authority or ecclesiastical authority was given precedence in this notional body politic, the *respublica* remained Christian. And it seemed as if in that Christian society there could only be less and less room for Jews.

These sentiments emerge very clearly from the work of Rupert, abbot of Deutz, who was an outspoken protagonist of papal reform. In Rupert's work a direct connection is made between the Jewish rejection of Christ and the supposed enmity of Jews towards Christians. Rupert represents

Jewish hands as dripping with the very blood that serves Christians for their spiritual food and consequent salvation. He writes in his *Anulus sive Dialogus inter Christianum et Iudaeum* (1126) and elsewhere that the Jews conspired to and consented in the death of Christ and cruelly crucified him. But what is even worse than killing him is that they continue to malign Christ in their synagogues, which are part of the Synagogue of Satan. Thus Jews continue to be covered in Christ's blood because they do not distance themselves from the crime of their ancestors by recognising Christ as the son of God. The reason the prophets had to speak in such enigmas was that they would have been murdered if their Jewish listeners had been able to understand that they were preaching salvation to the nations through Christ. Rupert is adamant that Jews believe that only the circumcised can be saved. That is why he thinks Jews jealously keep circumcision to themselves. He sees the Jews as the antithesis of Christians. Where Christians are generous and do all they can to bring salvation to the whole of mankind, Jews are a mean and particularist people. They are the greediest nation on earth, dispersed throughout the world. Rupert is convinced that pride in their status as God's chosen people is what determines the attitude of Jews to non-Jews. They live in contempt of all non-Jews and are jealous of their salvation and plot against them.[40]

As far as Christians are concerned, Rupert's vision of the Church is a united one pivoting around the body of Christ. Rupert believes in a very literal way that partaking of the Eucharist gives the faithful the chance to be one with Christ.[41] He identifies himself explicitly with Christ, whose crucified body he adores on the cross.[42] Heterodoxically he asserts that the salvific Eucharist was instituted by Christ at the time of his passion.[43] In such a view it really does become hard to find a decent niche for Jews.

Peter the Venerable's *Weltanschauung* is not less Christian than Rupert's. But writing at a time when a second crusade had to be preached to buttress the victories of the first, Peter could not be unaware of the vast numbers of persons who were inimical to Christendom. In addition to this his visit to Spain in the early 1140s had exposed him to a society in which Judaism and Islam were still vibrant forces. Moreover his own writing against the Petrobrusian heretics betrays his awareness of the existence of heresy within Christendom.[44] None the less, in his polemic against the Jews he maintains first that Christendom is universal, both in theory and in reality, and second that Judaism is so in neither.

The universality of the Christian faith is of course based by Peter on the Gospel's message of salvation for all who believe in Christ. In Peter's eyes the universality of Christ's rule was presaged in the Old Testament. Peter tries to defend the reality of this by asserting that even though there are lots of Muslims, Jews and pagans about, they are not everywhere, whereas Christians are:

The Christian faith did not, in the manner of errors, subject to itself only bits of the world; because it is the truth, derived from ultimate truth, which is Christ, it conquered the whole world. I have said the whole world because although pagans or Saracens exercise dominion over some parts and although Jews skulk amongst Christians and pagans, there is not any part, or a significant part, of land, not of the remotest island of the Mediterranean or the ocean itself, where Christians do not live either as rulers or subjects. So it is shown to be true what Scripture says of Christ: 'And he shall rule from sea to sea, and from the river unto the ends of the earth' (Psalm 71.8); and what our Apostle says: 'In the name of Jesus every knee shall bow' (Philippians 2.10). So what if the Mohammedan error corrupted part of the world after the law was given by Christ? There were many heresies among the Jews after the law of Moses; after the Gospel of Christ many heresies were born in Christendom . . . There is no comparison between this Satanic falsehood and the divine truth of the Gospel, because although that prevailed among many, this . . . prevailed universally.[45]

According to Peter, Judaism not only lacks the universal appeal of Christianity, it does not have any universalistic ambitions. The only universalism it contains is the message of universal Christendom, and this is precisely what Jews resolutely deny. It is this denial that Peter must combat. For although Muslims constituted a formidable military challenge to Christian attempts to put their universal ideas into practice, it was the Jews who seemed to challenge the very content of that universal message. Thus we see Peter arguing that one must be stupid and 'thinking' like a beast of burden to imagine that God, the Creator of the whole world, would ignore everyone else and only look after the Jews, giving only them hope of salvation. Peter asks how one could imagine that God would narrowly confine his mercy by choosing this tiny quarrelsome ungrateful people while rejecting and damning the infinite number of other people. In the event he is convinced the opposite has occurred. The nations of the world have been saved, whilst it is the Jews who have been rejected and damned.[46]

It is clear that Peter sees the concepts which Jews possess about their own peoplehood and about the existence of a special bond between them and God as an affirmation that Jews are happy to see all non-Jews damned. To Peter, as to Rupert, this constitutes an affront to the all-embracing Christian faith. Thus he urges the Jews to stop being so arrogant and to cease bragging about the singularity of their law. They must understand that everyone is saved by the grace of Christ's Gospel and they must understand that this is exactly what the Hebrew Bible says.[47] In the eyes of Christian polemicists like Peter the Venerable the refusal by Jews to accept the role in which they were cast not only placed them outside the Christian body; Jews were seen as threatening that very body by blaspheming Christ and by steadfastly denying the salvation his body was supposed to bring to all those who believed in him.

V

The close of the eleventh century inaugurated a period in Western Christian thought that revealed a great fascination for the human nature and body of Jesus Christ. At one end of the spectrum we see this interest in theologians like Anselm and Abelard, who studied the Incarnation and its implications. At the other end we find it in the fervour of crusaders to win back for their Lord the land they believed he trod as a man. In all of this we sense that Christians concentrated on the special relationship they felt they had with God's son in order to feel closer to God. For in so many texts which expound the reason 'why God became man' a great deal of emphasis is put on the brotherly bond which was created between Christ and humanity on account of his willingness to die in order to save man. And that bond was made explicit again and again when Christians felt united in the body of Christ through their veneration of and participation in the Eucharist. Interwoven into these discussions was the attempt to explain how it was possible for a transcendent God to become man and how Jesus Christ could be both man and God. We have seen how these philosophical ramifications were discussed on the assumption that all human beings have a share in reason. And we have seen how this concept of human universality was made to overlap with the Christian one. Those who refused to have a share in the salvation universally offered to man by Christ were thought to lack a human share of reason. Refusing to enter the perimeters of 'true' belief, which was tantamount to refusing to become a member of Christ's body – for a time at least – became synonymous with quitting the perimeters of reason.

It will be patently obvious that the concept of universal Christendom was an illusion. But that did not make it any less real as a goal worth aspiring to. Jews were, of course, not the only people to run foul of this goal. Muslims, heretics and other social misfits joined them. But the Jews did hold a special position among what we might call the medieval outcasts.[48] Unlike Muslims living in Christendom, they had no autonomous Jewish territory they could ever turn to. Indeed the loss of their land was interpreted as a sign of their failure and obsolescence. Judaism, unlike Islam, was seen as a threatening negation of the very essence of Christianity. Unlike heretics Jews formed a self-perpetuating social group that defined itself not in opposition to the established Church, but without reference to the Church at all. As non-Christians, Jews not only could not play any part in the religious manifestations of the Church. They could not participate in the social activities generated by that religious ritual. To make matters worse that ritual often entailed a great deal of anti-Jewish sentiment. After all, each time the Eucharist was celebrated thoughts could easily turn to those who were accused of killing Christ.[49]

And in north-western Europe the special economic position of Jews could only marginalise them further.

One did not have to be a twelfth-century Jew to be called an animal. The wording of a number of biblical texts had encouraged Christians to use the word against Jews long before that. Moreover, Christians were happy to use the insult against their own co-religionists when it suited them.[50] But what we have seen in the anti-Jewish polemical material of the first half of the twelfth century is that the accusation was used against Jews as an all-encompassing reproach. Jews were not only being accused of reading the Bible literally as they always had been. Jews were being accused of blaspheming God and of being implacable enemies of Jesus Christ and his mother. Jews stood also accused of separating themselves from the domain of reason to which all other human beings belonged. And Jews were increasingly being accused of day-to-day animal-like behaviour. Examining the role of 'the body' in the Jewish–Christian debate of the first half of the twelfth century has helped us to uncover how and why these accusations began to interlock. And it is the interlocking of these different aspects of anti-Jewish feeling that, I believe, contributed to the deterioration of the position of the Jews in the course of that century and beyond.

NOTES

1 The writing of this article coincided with my supervision of David Behrman for his dissertation for the diploma of historical studies in Cambridge entitled 'Parallels between Christian critique of rabbinic literature and Jewish critique of the Christian faith in the twelfth and thirteenth centuries'. Thinking with him about the topic of his research has certainly contributed much to my thoughts for this paper.

2 S. Anselmi . . . Opera Omnia, ed. F. S. Schmitt, II, Edinburgh, 1946, pp. 37–133.

3 See my 'Christians disputing disbelief: St Anselm, Gilbert Crispin and Pseudo-Anselm', in Religionsgespräche in Mittelalter, ed. B. Lewis and F. Niewöhner, Wiesbaden, 1992, pp. 131–48. For R. W. Southern's view on the background to the Cur Deus Homo see his Saint Anselm. A portrait in a landscape, Cambridge, 1990, pp. 197–205.

4 See e.g. Cicero, De Officiis, 1.4, trans. W. Miller, Loeb Classical Library, Cambridge (Mass.), and London, 1975, pp. 12–17 and Cicero, De Legibus, 1.7.23, trans. C. W. Keyes, Loeb Classical Library, Cambridge (Mass.), and London, 1977, pp. 320–3. Both these texts were widely read in the twelfth century; see M. Lapidge, 'The Stoic inheritance', in P. Dronke, ed., A history of twelfth-century western philosophy, Cambridge, 1988, p. 92.

5 Patrologiae Latinae Cursus Completus (henceforth PL) CLX, cols 1110–12. Odo's obvious disgust for the female body is part of the story of medieval attitudes towards women.

6 PL CLX, col. 1108.

7 PL CLX, col. 1112; see my 'Christian imagery of Jews in the twelfth century: a look at Odo of Cambrai and Guibert of Nogent', Theoretische Geschiedenis, XVI, 1989, pp. 383–91.

8 De Incarnatione contra Iudeos, PL CLVI, cols 489–528.

9 Ibid., cols 489, 492, 496–7, 498, 519–24. See also my 'Theology and the commercial revolution: Guibert of Nogent, St Anselm and the Jews of Northern France', in Church and city, 1000–1500. Essays in honour of Christopher Brooke, ed. D. Abulafia, M. Franklin and M. Rubin, Cambridge, 1992, pp. 23–40.

10 In this matter too Guibert and Odo seem to have been under the influence of Anselm. See J. Pelikan, 'A First-generation Anselmian, Guibert of Nogent', in *Continuity and discontinuity in church history. Essays presented to G. H. Williams*, Leiden, 1979, pp. 71–82; 77 ff.

11 *Petri Venerabilis adversus Iudeorum inveteratam duritiem*, ed. Y. Friedman. Corpus Christianorum Continuatio Medievalis (hereafter CCCM), LVIII, Turnhout, 1985. See Friedman's introduction on the dating of the text, pp. lxiii–lxx.

12 *Ibid.*, 2, ll. 426–603, ed. Friedman, pp. 28–33.

13 M. Kniewasser, 'Die anti-jüdische Polemic des Petrus Alphonsi (getauft 1106) und des Abtes Petrus Venerabilis von Cluny (+1156)', *Kairos, Zeitschrift für Religionswissenschaft und Theologie*, XXII, 1980, pp. 47–9. See also N. Roth, 'Forgery and abrogation of the Torah: a theme in Muslim and Christian polemic in Spain', *Proceedings of the American Academy for Jewish Research*, LIV, 1987, pp. 203–36.

14 On Alfonsi see J. Tolan, *Petrus Alfonsi and his medieval readers*, Gainesville (FA), 1993.

15 *Dial.*, PL CLVII, cols 541–67.

16 *Ibid.*, cols 577, 617–19.

17 Friedman discusses the relationship between Peter the Venerable and Peter Alfonsi in her edition, pp. xiv–xx. See also Kniewasser, 'Die anti-jüdische Polemic', pp. 34–76.

18 *Adv. Iud.*, 3, ll. 564–70, ed. Friedman, pp. 57–8; cf. Ezechiel 36.26.

19 *Adv. Iud.*, 3, ll. 757–72, ed. Friedman, p. 63; cf. Psalm 48.13.

20 *Adv. Iud.*, 5, ll. 1–83, ed. Friedman, pp. 125–7. Peter speaks of the shadows which had cast Egypt into darkness now occupying the hearts of Jews.

21 On the content of some of these legends see Friedman, pp. xviii–xx.

22 *Ibid.*, 5, ll. 989–1002, p. 153; cf. 2 Corinthians 3.6.

23 *Ibid.*, 5, ll. 1106–40, pp. 157–8.

24 On Peter's use of the Talmud see Friedman, p. xx.

25 *Ibid.*, 5, ll. 357–9, p. 134.

26 *Ibid.*, 5, ll. 1022–32, p. 154.

27 *Ibid.*, 5, ll. 611–20, pp. 141–2.

28 L. K. Little, *Religious poverty and the profit economy in medieval Europe*, London, 1978, pp. 3–57.

29 E. M. Buytaert, 'Abelard's collationes', *Antonianum*, XLIV, 1969, pp. 33–9. There is disagreement about the dating of the dialogue; see my '*Intentio recta an erronea?* Peter Abelard's views on Judaism and the Jews', in a *Festschrift* for Prof. Avrom Saltman, ed. B. Albert, Y. Friedman and S. Schwarzfuchs (forthcoming).

30 *Dialogus inter philosophum, Judaeum et Christianum*, ed. R. Thomas, Stuttgart–Bad Cannstatt, 1970, pp. 50–1; trans. P. J. Payer, Mediaeval Sources in Translation, XX, Toronto, 1979, p. 33.

31 See my '*Intentio recta an erronea?*' (forthcoming).

32 *Dialogus*, ed. Thomas, p. 90; trans. Payer, p. 39.

33 *De Inc. contra Iudeos*. 2, 5, PL CLVI, col. 506.

34 *Adv. Iud.*, 3, ll. 19–25, ed. Friedman, p. 42.

35 G. Constable, ed., *The letters of Peter the Venerable*, 2, Harvard (Mass.), 1967, letter 130, pp. 327–30.

36 Y. Friedman, 'An anatomy of anti-semitism: Peter the Venerable's letter to Louis VII, king of France (1146), in: *Bar-Ilan studies in history*, ed. P. Artzi, Ramat-Gan, 1978, p. 100. See also J.-P. Torrell, 'Les Juifs dans l'œuvre de Pierre le Vénérable', *Cahiers de Civilisation Médiévale Xᵉ–XIIᵉ Siècles*, XXX, 1987, pp. 339–42. Friedman states that there is no proof that Peter borrowed money from the Jews (pp. 98–9); Torrell disputes this (pp. 332–3). See also G. I. Langmuir, 'Peter the Venerable', in *Toward a definition of antisemitism*, Berkeley and Los Angeles, 1990, pp. 200–3.

37 On the idea developing in the course of the twelfth century that Jews did not crucify Christ out of ignorance, see J. Cohen, 'The Jews as the killers of Christ in the Latin tradition, from Augustine to the friars', *Traditio*, XXXIX, 1983, pp. 1–27.

38 On the Eucharist see M. Rubin, *Corpus Christi. The eucharist in late medieval culture*, Cambridge, 1991.

39 W. Ullmann, *A history of political thought: the Middle Ages*, Harmondsworth, 1965, pp. 192–5. Ullmann stresses that the debate between *regnum* and *sacerdotium* could only move forwards when those defending temporal authority had non-biblical language at their disposal. But in my view the use of Aristotle did not make these polemicists and the society, in so far as it was their own, any less Christian.

40 Ed. R. Haacke in M. L. Arduini, *Ruperto di Deutz e la controversia tra Christiani ed Ebrei nel secolo XII*, Rome 1979, pp. 189–204, 238; *Comment. in XII Prophetas minores, in Amos Lib. III*, PL CLXVIII, cols 339–42; *De S. Trinitate, XXIX, In Hieremiam* 81, ed. R. Haacke, CCCM XXIII, pp. 1633–4; *In Iohannes Evangelium* 7, ed. R. Haacke, CCCM IX, p. 391; *In Genesim* 8.26, ed. R. Haacke, *De Sancta Trinitate et operibus eius*, CCCM XXI, p. 513; *De S. Trinitate, In Librum Psalmorum* 5, ed. R. Haacke, CCCM XXII, p. 1356; D. E. Timmer, 'The Religious significance of Judaism for twelfth-century monastic exegesis: a study of Rupert of Deutz c.1070–1129', Ph.D dissertation, Notre Dame, 1983 (UMI reprints), pp. 59–70. See also my 'The ideology of reform and changing ideas concerning Jews in the works of Rupert of Deutz and *Hermannus quondam Iudeus*', *Jewish History*, VII, 1993, pp. 44–50.

41 G. Macy, *The theologies of the Eucharist in the early scholastic period. A study of the salvific function of the sacrament according to the theologians c.1080–c.1220*, Oxford, 1984, pp. 66–7; J. H. van Engen, *Rupert of Deutz*, Berkeley/Los Angeles, 1983, p. 140.

42 Van Engen, pp. 105–16; *Anulus*, ed. Haacke, pp. 232–6.

43 *Anulus*, ed. Haacke, pp. 224–6; Van Engen, pp. 148–9.

44 Langmuir, 'Peter the Venerable', pp. 197–204.

45 *Adv. Iud.*, 4, ll. 1464–85, ed. Friedman, p. 109. See J. Muldoon, *Popes, lawyers and infidels*, Liverpool, 1979, pp. 119–25, 132–5, for what happened when Christians later discovered areas like the Canaries, which were untouched by Christianity.

46 *Ibid.*, 3, ll. 835–51, p. 65.

47 *Ibid.*, 4, ll. 1244–65, p. 103.

48 Essential for an understanding of the phenomenon of medieval outcasts is R. I. Moore, *The formation of a persecuting society*, Oxford, 1987.

49 In the late thirteenth century Jews were accused of desecrating the host in an attempt to make Christ suffer yet again at their hands; see G. Langmuir, *History, religion and antisemitism*, Berkeley/Los Angeles, 1990, pp. 300–1.

50 Torrell, 'Les Juifs', pp. 337–8; my 'Christian imagery', p. 388.

The Pardoner's body
and the disciplining of rhetoric

The term 'disciplining' in my title has a double value: it stands for the construction of rhetoric as an academic discipline, and it also suggests the way that rhetoric's disciplinary power has always been subject to the most severe kinds of institutional regulation, or 'discipline'. This double sense of discipline is dramatised in the figure of Chaucer's Pardoner, in the homologous relation of his rhetoric, with its ambiguous content and transgressive morality, and his sexuality, with its bodily ambiguity and its transgression of gender boundaries. The Pardoner's claims for the disciplinary autonomy of rhetoric are suppressed in the same way that his sexuality is subject to public correction through the Host's virtual threat of (re)castration. The linkage that I want to explore here between sexuality, disciplining of the body, and the discipline of rhetoric is not something that I have manufactured for the sake of (rhetorical) argument; it is a linkage that is already there in the history of rhetoric itself.

Just as there is no historically transcendent category of the body, so there is also no unitary discursive category of bodiliness. As a symbolic domain the body is the expressive language through which many cultural discourses, including intellectual relations, aesthetics and science, define themselves.[1] In this essay I will examine how scientific or disciplinary classification in antiquity and the Middle Ages constitutes one domain or category of the body, and how notions of violent physical correction or 'discipline' to be enacted on the human body are transferred metaphorically to the realm of intellectual disciplines. This has particular implications for the institutional history of rhetoric; I want to give the disciplinary body of rhetoric a history.[2] In locating this historical inquiry at the literary site of Chaucer's Pardoner I do not pretend here to advance on the innovative and important insights that recent work in feminist and gay theory have brought to Chaucerian texts, especially new readings of the *Pardoner's Tale* as a site for the discursive conflicts of gender.[3] Rather, what I offer is an attempt to understand how gender and sexuality are part of the political text of rhetoric's institutional history.

As a science, rhetoric – from antiquity onwards – has been suspect, subject to regulation and control by dominant institutional interests. Ancient and medieval (as well as modern) practitioners and theorists of rhetoric have always to answer to question, first posed by Socrates to Gorgias: 'does rhetoric constitute a legitimate study of its own?' I want to recast this question in the terms of its most radical implications: 'does rhetoric have a body?' This is the question to which the disciplinary legitimacy of rhetoric was (and indeed still is) linked; judgement of rhetoric's disciplinary status is articulated through a discourse about its bodily status.

To begin we can turn for illustration to two modern perspectives on medieval rhetoric, one which denies rhetoric any disciplinary autonomy in the Middle Ages by denying it a body, and one which denies medieval rhetoric a disciplinary legitimacy by giving it a transgressive, fragmented body. The first of these, which denies rhetoric any disciplinary status in history by denying it a body, is well exemplified through a recently published account of an extraordinary professional exchange. James J. Murphy, the foremost modern historian of medieval rhetoric, recounts how in 1960 he sent an article on medieval rhetoric to the journal *PMLA*. The article was rejected with this response from the reader: 'rhetoric is not a subject; and if it were, there would be no history of it'. Fifteen years later, after the appearance of Murphy's *Rhetoric in the Middle Ages*,[4] the reviewer was moved to apologise to Murphy and retract that opinion.[5] The view that the reviewer first expressed, that rhetoric is no subject itself and has no history of its own, is in metaphorical terms a denial of rhetoric's body, of its location in space or time; the reviewer's later admission of ignorance or shortsightedness was itself predicated on the 'embodiment' of rhetoric's disciplinary history in Murphy's substantial volume, a physical codex that the reviewer and others could see and touch as evidence of a body of historical facticity. One other notable example of the model of denying the disciplinary 'body' of rhetoric is Richard McKeon's influential article 'Rhetoric in the Middle Ages',[6] which also argues that medieval rhetoric has no history of its own, but can be known to us as the imprint of the many other intellectual (and specifically philosophical) practices with which it was associated. McKeon proposes to write a history of rhetoric that accounts for its multiple, shifting, and ephemeral nature:

> Such a history would not treat an art determined to a fixed subject matter (so conceived rhetoric is usually found to have little or no history, despite much talk about rhetoric and even more use of it, during the Middle Ages) nor on the other hand would it treat an art determined arbitrarily and variously by its place in classifications of the sciences (so conceived the whole scheme and philosophy of the sciences would be uncontrolled in their alterations and therefore empty) . . . Yet if rhetoric is defined in terms of a single subject matter – such as style, or literature, or discourse – it has no history during the Middle Ages.[7]

Very possibly the reviewer of Murphy's article (who was not, incidentally, McKeon himself) derived a point of view (as well as wording) from the *auctoritas* of McKeon's study. McKeon's language is virtually that of the body or bodily physics; rhetoric has no 'fixed' subject matter, nor does it have a 'place' in classifications of the sciences. Interestingly McKeon's language also betrays some anxiety about what would happen to the regulation of the sciences under classificatory schemes – a regulation that represents a coercive 'discipline' or control imposed on the sciences – if rhetoric were to be understood solely through its metamorphic and irregular appearances in those schemes; the entire system would be 'emptied' of its content and meaning and would no longer yield to our managerial control of its many and various parts. In other words, rhetoric shifts its position so often in medieval classifications of the sciences that it threatens to reduce the whole system to a meaningless jumble; rhetoric is so disruptive a force that it can only be historically and discursively managed, according to McKeon, by denying it a veritable scientific body of its own and treating its appearances in scientific classifications as merely suggestive illusions. The assumption behind this theoretical model that denies rhetoric a body is that rhetoric by its very nature defies the principles of solidity and stability attributed to the body; rhetoric is not substantive, it is not about or of anything, but is only a tool (in the Aristotelian sense of *organon*) that comes into being through application to other things.

The second modern perspective also challenges rhetoric's claims to disciplinary legitimacy, but in this case by giving it a body: an unruly, fragmented body that confirms rhetoric's illegitimacy. This is the view propounded quite explicitly by Brian Vickers in his recent book *In Defence of Rhetoric*,[8] which is argued through an unabashed bias of classical humanism. Vickers's chapter on the Middle Ages is entitled 'Medieval Fragmentation': the Middle Ages represent a falling away from rhetoric's integrity of purpose in antiquity, and are characterised by atrophy, reduction to mere tropology, a loss of the whole aesthetic picture, and a decline of function in favour of an endless pursuit of form. The Middle Ages fragment rhetoric into the repetitive mechanics of abbreviation and amplification. Medieval rhetoric is externally fragmented in that the classical rhetorical texts survive 'in a damaged and haphazard state'; it is internally fragmented in that 'readers atomized what had been transmitted to fit their own needs' (p. 220). The emergence in the Middle Ages of three specialised arts of rhetoric (*poetria*, *dictamen*, and the *ars praedicandi*) represents a 'dismemberment' (p. 236) of what had once been (in Vickers's humanist view) a coherent and homogeneous lore. This view (which Vickers also extends to poststructuralist criticism as a twentieth-century fragmentation of rhetoric) can be seen as a consequence of the logic of the 'bodiless' model exemplified by McKeon and the *PMLA* reviewer.

Rhetoric's transmutative heterogeneity makes it incapable of possessing a stable or healthy body; but those institutional interests that abhor a vacuum and that would manage that instability can nevertheless assign rhetoric a body, a body that symbolically confirms and justifies that imposition of coercive management. In the interests of institutional discipline rhetoric is given a body, a transgressive, atrophied or fragmented, illegitimate body that by its very nature invites corrective regulation. In the limited case of Vickers's book, the long-range project of institutional management of rhetoric is the moralised chronology that he aims to produce; here, operating in the same symbolic sphere of language that (as we will see) Quintilian also uses, Vickers invents a bodily image for rhetoric in order to discriminate between his ideal models of rhetoric (classical and Renaissance) and its fallen forms (medieval and modern). Thus the real purpose of giving rhetoric a body is to identify the transgressive tendencies of rhetoric when it is unguarded or unregulated (as Vickers believes it was during the Middle Ages), and to enclose it within a managerial paradigm of organic stability which can monitor its propensity for resistance.

These two modern perspectives on medieval rhetoric are very close to views of rhetoric that were propounded in antiquity and especially in the Middle Ages. In their views of medieval rhetoric, Vickers and McKeon actually voice the terms of censure that were used in the Middle Ages to vilify and marginalise rhetoric; indeed, their view of the Middle Ages is produced by the Middle Ages themselves, and through the institutional power of their voices is continually reproduced. In the metaphorical language about rhetoric from antiquity to the Middle Ages we see an opposition between a bodiless and an embodied rhetoric. These contradictory models reveal the enormous ideological stakes in this metaphorical discourse. Rhetoric by its very nature defies the principles that attached to ideas of the integrated body and, by extension, to ideas of a disciplinary body of knowledge. As I will argue here, rhetoric for this very reason had to come under some institutional and discursive regulation, and so a 'body' had to be invented for rhetoric to allow it to be 'disciplined'. The body invented for rhetoric was a transgressive, unlicensed body that would justify the severest regulation or discipline.

The relationship between scientific disciplinarity and the body as an object of punishment or discipline emerges in the history of the Latin word *disciplina*, which constitutes the larger framework for my investigation here. The extraordinary history of this word has been documented by Henri Marrou, to whose philological research my account here is indebted.[9] *Disciplina* is related to *discere*, 'to learn', although in classical usage it can also mean 'teaching', as in the teachings of a master. In classical antiquity, the broadest meaning of *disciplina* (in the plural) is intellectual culture or scientific knowledge. These meanings passed into patristic and early medieval use. Here we find the application of the word still familiar to moderns; *disciplina* designates a particular science, such as rhetoric, dialectic, astronomy, geometry, or music.[10] In the plural it designates all the various sciences together as a group.[11] Other words that are used synonymously with *disciplina* in this sense, sometimes with slightly different emphases, are *doctrina* (for which Marrou finds a more general and abstract connotation, the broader sense of study, intellectual work, or knowledge), *ars* (which early on was the preferred term for the elements of the *trivium*), and *scientia.*[12]

Thus in this application, *disciplina* is a particular body of knowledge. In signifying an individual branch of knowledge, it is a term for differentiating between kinds of scientific discourse and for delimiting and containing each branch of knowledge according to the rules that pertain to (or inhere within) a given discipline.[13] What *disciplina* really signifies is a set of rules which impose order. Here the rich semantic field of the word *disciplina* comes into play, for it has a much wider range of meaning than its synonyms, including *doctrina*. In classical use, *disciplina* is the Latin equivalent of the Greek *paideia*, acquiring the sense of rules imposed by a master on a student, especially moral rules aimed at the conduct of one's life. In this respect ancient usage is very informative. In classical Latin, *disciplina* is applied to military life, to designate the rules and principles that are used to maintain order, in other words, military discipline.[14] From this we need not look far to find the word used to designate the imposition of rules or order in the civil domain. Cicero speaks of '*disciplina civitatis*', and Tacitus speaks of the 'most severe discipline and laws' of Sparta and Crete.[15]

These various senses of *disciplina* were carried over into early Christian use. The practical, moral orientation of *disciplina* finds expression in the idea of a rule of Christian life: for Augustine, Christian discipline is the 'law of God', the wisdom and knowledge that constitute a rule of Christian living.[16] *Disciplina* is also the rule imposed by the Church on believers, and later by ecclesiastical authority on clergy. Along these lines we arrive at the notion of monastic discipline, the order and submission to authority that are required by observance of the rule within the monastic community.[17] Thus the discipline of civil law becomes the self-regulation of an enclosed religious community.

Finally, there is one meaning of *disciplina* unknown in classical usage, a meaning introduced in the language of the Septudgint and the New Testament: punishment, correction, pain inflicted for a transgression. Of course, ancient pedagogical practice involved corporal punishment, but the terms *paideia* in Greek and *disciplina* in Latin were not used to signify this aspect of instructive correction (even though corporal punishment would be understood as part of the educative system denoted by these terms).[18] In the Greek and Latin scriptures, however, the terms were extended to include this sense, taking on, moreover, the idea of the punishment that God reserves for correction of the sinner.[19] In the language of the Church Fathers, the punitive connotation of *disciplina* is associated with an educative function, corporal punishment as deterrent or correction. Here the term *disciplina* becomes linked with *verberare*, 'to flog', and with *vapulare*, 'to get a beating'.[20] The term inevitably acquires civil and legal dimensions: physical punishment by secular authority; the power to inflict punishment; and punitive law itself.[21] Out of its association with flogging and beating it also takes on the specialised meaning of flagellation, both in the sense of punishment under law and of self-inflicted scourging.[22] Thus by the early Middle Ages the idea of intellectual regulation, of observing a rule or scientific order, is identified semantically with the idea of physical punishment, *disciplina corporis*, disciplining of the body to correct or guard against vice, whether imposed by parent, teacher, monastic rule, civil law, or self.

From *disciplina* as a metaphorical body of knowledge we have arrived at *disciplina* as physical regulation and correction of the body. The implications of this semantic association for the discourse of scientific classification are readily apparent. To call a form or body of knowledge a discipline is to mark off its boundaries from another form of knowledge, and through this process of division to constitute that knowledge as an object. But it is not simply that disciplines create knowledge as a discursive object; as Foucault reminds us, the disciplinary order itself also becomes the object to be surveyed and regulated.[23] From antiquity onwards we see that discussions of the disciplinary relations between the sciences often carry corrective and restrictive overtones. In the *Institutio oratoria*, for example, Quintilian places firm restrictions on the territory of the grammarians, lest their work overlap with, or trespass into, the territory of the rhetoricians (1.9.6; 2.1.4–5).[24] Even Quintilian's attempts to promote a broad-based 'liberal' education for the orator are predicated on precise taxonomies and hierarchical differentiations between the domains of the various arts (1.10.1–12.7). We find similarly deterrent boundaries placed around the individual disciplines in Martianus Capella's *De nuptiis Philologiae et Mercurii*. Grammar's discourse is interrupted at the moment when she is about to discuss figures and tropes and introduce the question of metre (§ 326), subjects which are within the competence of grammatical teaching but which are normally governed by the disciplines of rhetoric and music respectively. Minerva also stops Dialectic from proceeding to the discussion of sophistic arguments, asserting that such a subject will dishonour the discipline of dialectic (§ 423). As these examples suggest, disciplinary structures function to contain and regulate bodies of knowledge, just as the human body is often subject to corrective discipline as a guard against moral or physical transgression. But disciplinary formations in turn are also subject to such corrective measures, so that it is not simply raw knowledge that is embodied as an object of control, but the construction of the discipline itself. The discourse of intellectual taxonomy, classification of the sciences, carries a clearly restrictive imperative that can be understood both in terms of the interests of territoriality, to mark off one intellectual property or domain from another, and of subjugation, to ensure the manageability of individual scientific systems.

The obvious link between *disciplina* as a science and *disciplina* as punishment is correction. But metaphorically the link is the body. It is this deep and secure metaphorical linkage that rhetoric, with its particular claims to disciplinary legitimacy, seems always to unfix. We see this in the important statements of Plato and Aristotle on rhetoric. In Plato's *Gorgias*, the sophist Gorgias argues that rhetoric's disciplinary power lies in its open borders; the art of persuasive speech comprises or overlaps all other arts. For Socrates the permeability of rhetoric makes it no science at all, but a mere knack gained from experience, a counterfeit of true science that panders (like cookery and cosmetics) to gratification and pleasure.[25] In identifying rhetoric with the temporal contingencies of experience and the arts of the pleasure-seeking body, Plato's text suggests that rhetoric is a kind of incontinent body that does not know its own boundaries. The discipline that Socrates imposes on the transgressive, permeable body of rhetoric is to condemn it to the realm of bodily provisionality from which it can make no claim to scientific integrity. Aristotle's rigorous programme of scientific classification recasts the Platonic hierarchy of knowledge in more pragmatic institutional terms. In the *Rhetoric* Aristotle says that rhetoric, like dialectic, is a tool (*organon*) of inquiry, not a science; rhetoric and dialectic 'are concerned with such things as are, to a certain extent, within the knowledge of all people and belong to no separately defined science'.[26] But for Aristotle, the permeability of rhetoric positions it, not only outside any disciplinary category, but in *opposition* to the body. Rhetoric is a system of artifice, of construction or invention of the modes of persuasion; the body is a *natural* site of truth which furnishes pre-existing ('inartificial' or 'extrinsic') proof in the form of evidence extracted from slaves under torture.[27] In Athenian judicial discourse, as Page duBois argues, the slave represents a primordial form of bodiliness, and the slave body is a secret repository of truth to be yielded up (and possessed by free men) through the application of torture.[28] In this context Aristotle uses the body to describe a coherent realm of truth in counterdistinction to the artificial system of representation that is rhetoric.[29]

In neither of these models is the body represented *within* the discipline of rhetoric. For Plato rhetoric is only body and thus a counterfeit discipline; for Aristotle, rhetoric is outside disciplinary order and in opposition to the body. It is Roman teaching on the art that places the body securely within the disciplinary order of rhetoric and judges rhetoric through its bodily manifestations. The political and pedagogical institutions of Roman culture confer on rhetoric a privileged status as the highest of the arts because of its application to the pragmatic interests of civic oratory. But because rhetoric holds so crucial a cultural position it is the more subject to severe containment, monitoring, or scrutiny. It is here that rhetoric is truly invented as a discipline; it becomes a body capable of yielding up valid knowledge provided that it is successfully managed. Most importantly, to regulate rhetoric is to control its artificial excesses; in this context artifice, and especially ornamentation, is identified with mere bodily form, comparable to Plato's notion of counterfeit gratification. Whereas for Aristotle artifice is bodiless, in Roman theory artifice is inscribed on the body, as the possibility of monstrous or corrupt disfigurement; it is only by subjecting rhetoric's body to a disciplinary regime that its transgressive potential can be channelled into the production of truth. Significantly rhetoric here registers its own unrestrained artifice and permeability in terms of the disfigured body and the sexually ambiguous body. The *Rhetorica ad Herennium*, which was to become the main authority on style in the Middle Ages, represents style that has gone out of control in terms of the tumorous or disjointed body:

> Nam ita ut corporis bonam habitudinem tumor imitatur saepe, item gravis oratio saepe inperitis videtur ea quae turget et inflata est, cum aut novis aut priscis verbis aut duriter aliunde translatis aut gravioribus quam res postulat aliquid dicitur ... Qui in mediocre genus orationis profecti sunt, si pervenire eo non potuerunt, errantes perveniunt ad confine genus eius generis, quod appellamus dissolutum, quod est sine nervis et articulis; ut hoc modo appellem fluctuans, eo quod fluctuat huc et illuc nec potest confirmate neque viriliter sese expedire.

> For just as a swelling often resembles a healthy condition of the body, so, to those who are inexperienced, turgid and inflated language often seems majestic – when a thought is expressed either in new or in archaic words, or in clumsy metaphors, or in diction more impressive than the theme demands ... Those setting out to attain the Middle style, if unsuccessful, stray from the course and arrive at an adjacent type, which we call the Slack because it is without sinews and joints; accordingly I may call it the Drifting, since it drifts to and fro, and cannot get under way with resolution and virility.[30]

As this example suggests, rhetoric can legitimise itself as a true discipline if it can expose – and thus subject to severe disciplinary scrutiny – its own capacity for distortion. In other words, rhetoric needs its own potential for transgression in order to demonstrate its capacity for self-discipline.

Quintilian's *Institutio oratoria* is even more explicit on this point, registering the threat of an unlicensed artifice in terms of the *sexually* permeable

body, the body that has crossed the acceptable bounds of gender identity
into a kind of monstrous spectacle:

> Corpora sana et integri sanguinis et exercitatione firmata ex iisdem his speciem
> accipiunt ex quibus vires, namque et colorata et adstricta et lacertis expressa
> sunt; at eadem si quis volsa atque fucata muliebriter comat, foedissima sint ipso
> formae labore. Et cultus concessus atque magnificus addit hominibus, ut Graeco
> versu testatum est, auctoritatem; at muliebris et luxuriosus non corpus exornat,
> sed detegit mentem. Similiter illa translucida et versicolor quorundam elocutio
> res ipsas effeminat, quae illo verborum volo esse sollicitudinem . . . Maiore animo
> aggredienda eloquentia est, quae si toto corpore valet, ungues polire et capillum
> reponere non existimabit ad curam suam pertinere.

> Healthy bodies, enjoying a good circulation and strengthened by exercise,
> acquire grace from the same source that gives them strength, for they have a
> healthy complexion, firm flesh and shapely thews. But, on the other hand, the
> man who attempts to enhance these physical graces by the effeminate use of
> depilatories and cosmetics, succeeds merely in defacing them by the very care
> which he bestows on them. Again, a tasteful and magnificent dress, as the
> Greek poet tells us, lends added dignity to its wearer; but effeminate and luxu-
> rious apparel fails to adorn the body and merely reveals the foulness of the
> mind. Similarly, a translucent and iridescent style merely serves to emasculate
> [translating *effeminat*] the subject which it arrays with such pomp of words. . . .
> It is with a more virile spirit [translating *maiore animo*] that we should pursue
> eloquence, who, if only her [for *eloquentia*, feminine noun] whole body be sound,
> will never think it her duty to polish her nails and tire her hair.[31]

This remarkable passage, from Quintilian's prologue to his lengthy discussion of style, gives expression to what was always implicit in the condemnation of rhetoric; that the undisciplined body is a sexually wayward body,
that pandering and gratification are tantamount to a weakening of sexual
identity, and that the disciplinary permeability of rhetoric is nothing less
than ambiguity of gender. Stylistic excrescence allows the well-trained,
masculine body to sink into effeminacy (not femininity), counterfeiting its
proper virility. It is interesting that rhetoric's anxiety about its corporeality
is given the most striking expression in relation to style, that rhetoric
admits its own propensity for unruly excess when it turns to consider its
most visible aspect, *elocutio*. Style is the part of rhetoric that can be seen,
and as such is always in danger of being considered merely deceptive
surface, whether as dress on the body or as the bodily exterior itself. It
thus also threatens to be taken for the body as a whole, to reduce by
perverse metonymy the art of *eloquentia* to pandering style, the body to its
appearance. But style is not an external excrescence that can be surgically
removed and expelled from the realm of rhetoric. It is a function inherent
to rhetoric. Rhetoric cannot deny or suppress the force of body as appearance, for it operates through the persuasive appeal of appearance. Thus
to constitute itself as a proper discipline, rhetoric repeatedly – almost

ritually – re-enacts and enforces its self-discipline by exposing its continual struggle with its wayward body.[32] It invents itself as a discipline by inventing a corrupt bodily image over which it can always be seen to be triumphing by determined self-discipline. And part of its self-discipline is to punish that counter-image of its body by exposing it to public condemnation as a kind of trophy of its agonistic victory over its own unruliness. This is borne out at wearisome length in nearly all rhetorical manuals from antiquity to the Middle Ages (and beyond), which illustrate precept through sharp castigation of defective practice.

Thus on the terms of its own construction, rhetoric, like the body, must be subjected to a healthy regimen, disciplined lest it lapse into license, disease, or disfigurement.[33] The most familiar image of rhetoric is female excess. Martianus Capella's allegorical depiction of Rhetoric as a garish, physically imposing woman in martial attire whose swollen speech threatens to overrun the time allotted to it is not far removed from representations of rhetoric as a richly arrayed mistress or even a female courtesan.[34] But the other common trope, which we have already seen in Quintilian, uses the male body to identify an undisciplined rhetoric with transgressive sexuality. In the Middle Ages, images of masculine licence are tied to the enforcement of social constraints on male clerical sexual behaviour.[35] The most familiar medieval example of this is Alan of Lille's *De planctu Naturae*, which describes the corruption of the language arts of the *trivium* in terms of proscribed sexual practice, representing the effect of rhetorical figuration in terms of bodily disfigurement:

> sic methonomicas rethorum positiones . . . Cypridis artificiis interdixi, ne si nimis dure translationis excursu a suo reclamante 'subiecto predicatum alienet in aliud, in facinus facetia, in rusticitatem urbanitas, tropus in uicium, in decolorationem color nimius conuertatur.

> so too I banned from the Cyprian's [i.e. Venus'] workshop the use of words by the rhetors in metonymy . . . lest, if she embark on too harsh a trope and transfer the predicate from its loudly protesting subject to something else, cleverness would turn into a blemish, refinement into boorishness, a figure of speech into a defect and excessive embellishment into disfigurement.[36]

The governing image of Alan's text (announced in metre 1) suggests that the vice of tropes, departing from the governance of grammar, has turned man into hermaphrodite.[37] In the passage above, the perversion of rhetoric results in the defilement of appearance. Here, as in the *Rhetorica ad Herennium* and Quintilian, rhetoric displays the effects of perverse figuration.

Alan's text represents an indictment of rhetoric from outside the borders of the discipline. But as we see elsewhere, the figural relationship of rhetoric to the transgressive body is so ingrained in discourse about the art that rhetoric even teaches its own precepts through this trope. In the

Ars versificatoria of Matthew of Vendôme, one of the models of rhetorical *descriptio* takes as its subject the depravities of Davus (a stock figure of ancient comedy). Here the pedagogical occasion of exemplifying rhetorical *descriptio* through the attributes of the person becomes the vehicle for exposing the vices of rhetoric:[38]

> Ne per se patiatur idem consordeat [*or* cum sordeat] intus
> Et foris, in Davo methonomia parit . . .
> Vergit ad incestum, Venus excitat aegra bilibres
> Fratres, membra tepent cetera, cauda riget.
> Metri dactilici prior intrat syllaba, crebro
> Impulsu quatiunt moenia foeda breves.
> Nequitia rabiem servilem praedicat, actu
> Enucleat servae conditionis onus.
> Urget blanda, furit in libera terga, rebellis
> Naturae vetito limite carpit iter.[39]

> Since he is foul both inside and out in Davus metonymy falls flat [literally: 'metonymy is made equal'][40] . . . He inclines to lewdness; his sickly libido (*Venus aegra*) excites the Brothers Testicles (they weigh two pounds), the related members warm up and he gets a hard on. The first syllable of the dactyl enters; with repeated batterings, the foul short syllables shake the ramparts. His baseness foretells his slavish frenzy and the act declares the work of a slave. He presses hard upon alluring backs and rages against the backs of freeborn men. A rebel to nature, he goes the route to forbidden borders.[41]

In this extraordinary and explicit passage, the body that knows no boundaries is one with a debilitated rhetoric; impossible metonomy is the attribute of Davus, and Davus embodies impossible metonymy. The ostensible subject here is not the nature of rhetoric, but the nature of Davus. The real subject, however, is the technique of rhetorical *descriptio* which this passage teaches through exemplification. But the vehicle of this particular pedagogy is the image of the incontinent sexual body, where the breaking of (hetero)sexual correctness is the sign of unlicensed permeability and of lawless metonymy (Davus is 'foul' outside and within, so that there are no borders between container and contained). Here the transgressive body is used to teach rhetorical *descriptio*, and within that corrective teaching is identified with an 'incorrect' rhetoric.

As these examples suggest, rhetoric is invented through constructions of sexual transgression. As a sexual body, rhetoric can be disciplined from within its own system through a kind of enforced purity, in which it is compelled to expose, and therefore be purged of, its excesses. This is the model that we see in Quintilian and Matthew of Vendôme, who teach rhetoric through the proscription of sexual–rhetorical vice. Or, as we see in Alan of Lille, rhetoric can be disciplined from outside its own system, through subordination to external governance, such as the balanced structure of the *trivium*, which maintains the 'body' of science in a 'normative' or prescriptive (sexual) order.[42] In both cases we see the operation of what Jonathan Dollimore has called, after Foucault, a 'politics of containment'.[43] Giving rhetoric a sexual body establishes a discursive construct through which institutional power can work. Rather than simply eliding the sexual body, the institutional powers of pedagogy, literature, and intellectual tradition continually stage their repression of the body, and it is in this drama of its own correction that rhetoric willingly participates.

This is the nexus of ideas that lies behind Chaucer's Pardoner. As Robert Payne has acutely recognised, the Pardoner is more than a figure of corrupt preaching in the particular context of late-medieval anti-fraternalism; in the form of corrupt preacher he is a figure out of long traditions of theoretical contest about rhetoric as a science, of debate going back to the *Gorgias* about rhetoric's appeal to appearances, contingency, appetite, will, and belief.[44] But it is the Pardoner's bodily presence, the sexual ambiguity of his bodily appearance, that most clearly associates him with the representation of rhetoric in the tradition that leads from Quintilian to the medieval language arts. The narrator's description of him in the *General Prologue* as either 'a geldyng or a mare' (1.691),[45] pointing either to a disfiguring absence or a transgression of gender boundaries, can be taken as a realisation, a making literal, of the figuring of rhetoric as an emasculated or effeminate male body. In this, of course, Chaucer's Pardoner has his most direct literary forebear in Faus Semblant of the *Roman de la Rose*, whose incarnation of false preaching takes the form of indeterminate gendering; as Carolyn Dinshaw points out, Faus Semblant is both man and woman.[46] Both Faus Semblant and the Pardoner are products of the metaphorical tradition of rhetoric as unregulated sexuality. But with the Pardoner's embodiment of rhetoric, the metaphors of rhetoric as body achieve a crucial and complex articulation. The social politics of sexuality and the institutional politics of rhetoric meet with renewed force in the performance of the Pardoner and the claims that he makes for the disciplinary autonomy of rhetoric.

The Pardoner's performance is realised through images of the disabled, fragmented body and unruly appetite. As recent readers of the text have pointed out, the Pardoner professionally associates himself with the purveying of false relics, which are merely fragments of animal bodies cut off from reference to any symbolic unity beyond themselves; he even submits his own body to a figurative dismemberment when he describes his physical gestures during his preaching in terms of a grotesque choreography of nodding neck and busy tongue and hands (6.395–9).[47] His own body, of course, is fragmented or dismembered, and the text continually plays with the linguistic and symbolic substitution of relics and other objects, such as the bag of pardons in his lap (*General Prologue*, 686–7), for the 'coillons' or testicles that the Pardoner apparently lacks.[48] But beyond the force of these visual emblems of fragmentation, the Pardoner's discourse is linked with and follows from the *Physician's Tale*, a story which offers the choice of a defiled maidenhead or a decapitation.[49] The *Physician's Tale* leaves us with the headless body of Virginia, the patriarchal vindication of Virginius, and the punishment of the lascivious judge Appius whose violent and wayward bodily appetites have moved him to violate the girl's virginity and the family honour that places so much emphasis on her intact virtue. There is not much left intact at the end of this story, save a rigid social code predicated on male power over the female body; the transgressive will of the prospective rapist and the violent defence of the girl's bodily integrity. Such a story scarcely brooks interpretative intervention from its listeners; their response is that of powerlessness. Indeed, the tale told by the Physician makes the audience sick. Harry Bailly says that the story so grieves him that he thinks it will almost give him cardiac arrest: 'But wel I woot thou doost myn herte to erme / That I almoost have caught a cardynacle' (6.312–13). Unless he has a drink or hears a merry tale, he tells us, 'myn herte is lost for pitee of this mayde' (6.317). Harry's threat-ened heart attack is as vivid a rhetorical response as we could want; both inside and outside the *Physician's Tale* there are bodies fragmented, dead, or dying, from the decapitated Virginia to Harry's 'cardynacle' or chest pains.

The Host's call to the Pardoner to supply a pleasant diversion, 'som myrthe or japes', and the protesting call from the 'gentils' of the company for 'som moral thyng' (6.319, 325), move us from the power, in the *Physician's Tale*, of an arbitrary and rigid law which requires obedience without interpretation, to the affective power of rhetoric, which requires only belief. Indeed, it is one of the powers traditionally ascribed to rhe-toric to be able to fulfil the opposing demands of mirth and morality, to offer something that is moral and edifying but at the same time pleasant and entertaining. The Pardoner's brief here is to offer something curative for the Host's disabled body, and by extension for the whole company, in this sense the social body constituting the audience and judge of a rhetori-cal performance. The Pardoner achieves his curative effects, however, not through his tale, but through his very presence as an embodiment – liter-ally a bodying forth – of the danger of rhetoric. If the horrible rigidity of the *Physician's Tale* strips the audience of its interpretative power and ethical leverage, of its capacity to make sense of an uncompromising law that permits (in Virginia's words), 'no grace . . . no remedye' (6.236), it seems that the community can regain its ethical and interpretative bear-ings when it learns how to govern and contain the force of rhetoric. The Pardoner's disquisition on rhetoric, his lecture on his own *techne* in his Prologue, teaches not just a body of rhetorical theory, but the means of controlling this body, how to make the body of rhetoric yield up its dangerous truths about itself so that it can be regulated from outside. The Pardoner's 'medicine' is to deliver up his professional secrets into the company's disciplinary control. As we know, it is in the act of threatening the Pardoner with corrective violence at the end of his tale that Harry Bailly springs back to life, miraculously cured.

My discussion here focuses on the Pardoner's Prologue. The Prologue dramatises in a very concentrated way something that I have described earlier in this essay as one of the key characteristics of rhetoric's discourse about itself: its compulsion to perform its disciplinary instabilities by performing the exposure of its own vices, thereby inviting (or establishing the need for) disciplinary correction. The Pardoner's Prologue is a consummate performance of rhetoric's self-exposure of its transgression and counterfeit. There are, of course, a number of ways in which the Pardoner's text differs in its dynamics from traditional rhetorical texts. Most obviously, the Pardoner does not himself demonstrate the self-governance of rhetoric from within its own text; unlike Quintilian, who stages rhetoric's vices in order to show how rhetoric can redeem itself by monitoring its own transgressions, the Pardoner simply stages the incontinence of his rhetoric, and leaves it to the dramatic response of his audience (in the person of Harry Bailly) to complete the work of punishing and containing his waywardness. Along more complex lines, the Pardoner's discourse does not need to make explicit the identification of a transgressive rhetoric with 'distortion' of the sexual body; this has already been accomplished dramatically through the person of the Pardoner, who embodies the sexual (dis)figuring of rhetoric. Thus while the Pardoner's discourse is yielding up the 'truth' about rhetoric's persuasive appeal to mere appearances, his bodily appearance and attributes – his high voice, his beardlessness, his playing at male fashion ('hym thoughte he rood al of the newe jet', *GP*.682), as well as his excessive 'stylistic' display of both hetero- and homosexual roles[50] – are yielding up or pointing to the 'truth' about his body, that is, his alienation from the masculine, heterosexual norm of patriarchal cultural power. One way of reading the truth about his body, as Dinshaw notes, is that we cannot know; the Pardoner may or may not be a eunuch, his exterior may or may not be consistent with his interior.[51] All we have is the narrator's judgment or belief, based on his appearance: '*I trowe* he were a geldyng or a mare' (*GP*.691). The appearance of the Pardoner's body produces, not conviction of truth, but mere belief. This is also the very mechanism by which the Pardoner, as a latter-day Gorgias, describes the efficacy of his rhetoric; as the sophist must admit to Socrates, oratory produces only belief based on provisional appearances, not conviction based on knowledge of truth.[52] But another way of reading the question of his 'truth' is that his body, in conjunction with his rhetoric, becomes a *locus* of truth for others to know and possess, that his body and rhetoric together confess or yield up the truth about themselves into the corrective possession of his audience. The 'truth' is that his body is permeable, without definable gender identity, just as his permeable and ambiguous rhetoric defies proper disciplinary identity; because he cannot be known, he must be contained the more severely. Thus at the end of his *Tale*, when the Pardoner singles out the Host as the one 'moost envoluped in synne' (6.942) and tries to purvey to Harry the very relics that he has just finished describing as false, the Host's threat of violent (re)castration, 'I wolde I hadde thy coillons in myn hon . . . Lat kutte hem of' (6.952–4), directs itself *at* the incontinence of the Pardoner's rhetoric *through* the ambiguity of the Pardoner's sexual body.

In his Prologue, the Pardoner describes how he gains the trust of gullible crowds by preying on their fears and displaying false relics, and he asserts the alienation of his own moral condition from the moral effect of his preaching:

> For though myself be a ful vicious man,
> A moral tale yet I yow telle kan
> Which I am wont to preche for to wynne.   (6.459–61)

From a technical point of view, the Pardoner's speech is a careful manifesto on *ethos* or ethical proof, the Aristotelian principle of a speaker's representation of his own character as part of his material for persuasion.[53] Aristotle's model of ethical proof survives in the Middle Ages in some attenuated forms in the *artes praedicandi* which recommend persuasive appeal to audiences.[54] But Robert Payne's crucial insight into the Pardoner's discourse is that it represents, within the terms of Chaucerian poetics, a forceful new articulation of the theory of character as a form of persuasion.[55] The Pardoner speaks *de arte*, that is, about the mechanics of his rhetoric, and describes in some detail how he invents an authoritative character for himself when he preaches, how he constructs a credible persona through his techniques of delivery and through his personal and professional display. When preaching in churches, he says, 'I peyne me to han an hauteyn speche / And rynge it out as round as gooth a belle' (6.330–1); he always announces from where he has come, shows his papal bulls along with the authorising seal on his letter patent (in order, he says, 'my body to warente' [6.338]), and then proceeds to display the paraphernalia of his trade (indulgences and relics), all the while sprinkling his speech with a few words of Latin to impress the crowds and 'stire hem to devocioun' (6.346). The construction of character for the purpose of persuasion is certainly efficacious, even on the terms of his vicious mockery of the enterprise: 'Thus spitte I out my venym under *hewe* / Of hoolynesse, to *semen* hooly and trewe' (6.422–3; my emphasis).

Through his articulation of appeal to *ethos* or character as a means of persuasion, the Pardoner makes a strong claim for the disciplinary autonomy of rhetoric. According to the Pardoner, the efficacy of rhetoric should depend on nothing except its own art; its success need be tied to no moral system, no verification of truth beyond the belief that it produces. The most immediate contexts for the Pardoner's pronouncement that 'many a predicacioun / Comth ofte tyme of yvel entencioun' (6.407–8) are scholastic debates about the efficacy of immoral preachers and the proper fulfilment of the office of preaching.[56] But his question, the relation of a speaker's character to his speech, has a much longer history in rhetorical theory, in the anxiety of rhetoricians such as Quintilian to differentiate a 'responsible' – that is, institutionally validated – rhetoric from the 'debased' or institutionally discredited theory of the sophists.[57] I would like to read the Pardoner's pronouncements about the autonomy of rhetorical *techne* as a kind of staging – however historically unlikely it may be – of the momentary possibility of a sophistic rhetoric. The Pardoner gives a view of rhetoric that is very much like that of the sophists, a view of a world to be negotiated through language and skilful argument rather than through a priori truth value, and in which there need be no coherence between the moral content of the message and the moral character of the speaker.[58] This is the epistemology of an autonomous rhetoric which emerged the loser in ancient debate, which Plato's institution of philosophy discredited, and the history of which came to be written by its adversaries.[59]

Whether or not Chaucer knew anything directly or indirectly about the sophists is not important here; the *mechanics of suppression*, Socrates (Plato) of Gorgias, the Host (or even Chaucer) of the Pardoner, are almost the same. Just as Socrates condemns Gorgias' rhetoric to the realm of mere bodily fragmentation from which it can make no claims to disciplinary integrity, so the Pardoner is condemned to make his claims for rhetoric in the person, in the body, of an unwhole man. It is here that his manifesto on *ethos* is subsumed by the dramatic *manifestatio* of the 'truth' about rhetoric that he is compelled to perform. More than a system of ethical proof, the Pardoner's Prologue is an exercise in rhetorical *descriptio* designed to manifest character, such as Matthew of Vendôme exemplifies in his description of Davus.[60] The corruption or moral vacuity of character that the Pardoner manifests – his pronouncements on his bald avarice, his indifference to the 'correccioun of synne' (6.404) – is metonymic for the deficiency or permeability of his sexual body and the incontinence of his rhetoric. The Pardoner's performance or *manifestatio* of his character is nothing less than a ritual exposure of the vices and transgressions of the body of rhetoric. Any claims for the disciplinary autonomy of rhetoric that the Pardoner may make through his exposition of *ethos* will be immediately invalidated by the self-admitted transgressiveness of the character that makes the claims.

Yet it is through his confessional exposure of his vices that the Pardoner's discourse stages the invention of rhetoric as a discipline. As a figure of rhetoric the Pardoner differs from Gorgias in one significant way: where the fragmentary body of rhetoric in the *Gorgias* consigns it to the sphere of non-science, of mere knack like cooking, the Pardoner represents the tradition of rhetoric that I have traced here from later antiquity to the Middle Ages, in which rhetoric comes into being as a discipline by offering up its corrupt or counterfeit body to be disciplined. The production of scientific truth here about the body and about rhetoric is enabled through the ritual of confession;[61] and the Pardoner's confession differs only in dramatic degree, not in kind, from the compulsive self-exposure that we have seen rhetoric undertake in its various pedagogical and technical appeals, from Quintilian to Matthew of Vendôme. At the end of his *Tale*, where the Pardoner turns to his audience and, as if mechanically compelled to complete his whole routine, invites the Host to kiss the relics that he has just proclaimed to be false, it is not that he has forgotten his audience; rather, it is that the dynamic of rhetoric is to confess and perform itself continually, to display and stage its wilful excess.

The Pardoner's manifesto on *ethos* and his larger *manifestatio* of rhetoric have already given the pilgrims the key to his *techne* by showing them how the art of persuasion works. Now that they understand how rhetoric works as a professional system they are in a position of power to regulate it. The Pardoner has theorised and performed a powerful rhetoric that threatens to exceed its proper limits; what is important is that the necessity to contain and thereby discipline rhetoric is expressed by the Host as a threat of violence against the Pardoner's body. The Host enacts the disciplining of rhetoric by naming the Pardoner's bodily deficiency. The Host, rebounding from his 'cardynacle', wishfully threatens to castrate the Pardoner, swearing in the optative mood that he would like to cut off the Pardoner's coillons:

> I wolde I hadde thy coillons in myn hond
> In stide of relikes or of seintuarie.
> Lat kutte hem of, I wol thee helpe hem carie;
> They shul be shryned in an hogges toord!   (6.952–5)

The denunciation and threatened assault is a public humiliation tantamount to public punishment. It is a punishment directed at the Pardoner's rhetoric through the Pardoner's body, for his body, ambiguous, transgressive, probably already emasculated, reproduces the nature of his crime, rhetoric. Foucault's observations about the value of public torture and execution are strikingly (if anachronistically) relevant here: through those public procedures of criminal discipline,

> the body . . . [produces] and [reproduces] the truth of the crime – or rather it constitutes the element which, through a whole set of rituals and trials, confesses that the crime took place, admits that the accused did indeed commit it, shows that he bore it inscribed in himself and on himself, supports the operation of punishment and manifests its effects in the most striking way.[62]

It is through this kind of public display at the end of the *Pardoner's Tale* that the containment of rhetoric, and thus its induction into disciplinary order, takes place. Just as the Pardoner has exposed the capacity of rhetoric for distortion, the Host now exposes the Pardoner's bodily disfigurement. For the Host to want to castrate a man who is already a eunuch is to want to punish him for the crime of monstrous distortion that his body has already committed, to reinscribe that crime in a public, ritual way. On the logic of its own tradition of self-representation, rhetoric does become a genuine discipline here; even the kiss that Harry gives to the Pardoner to mend their rupture inscribes the Pardoner and his rhetoric in a system of discursive control. Under this regime, rhetoric will produce the truth about itself.

Rhetoric and its disciplinary formation may be apprehended through intellectual history and textual analysis; but we cannot forget that rhetoric is a discourse of the real world, of temporality, circumstance, shifting interests and fragmented experience; in other words, a discourse of the body itself. The Pardoner and his sophistic forebears hold out the possibility of a critically detached knowledge 'in the subjunctive mode', as Nancy Struever has described rhetoric's shaping of language as contingent experience, feeling and desire.[63] But its very capacity for such a contingent detachment inevitably places rhetoric in conflict with hierarchical disciplinary interests that would seek to constrain its epistemological permeability. Thus in the Middle Ages, rhetoric's *techne* is channelled or pressed into the service of dominant interests; it is accessory to grammar in primary education, to logic in the cathedral schools and universities, or it is 'redeemed' through its harnessing to scriptural study and homiletics, as we see from Augustine to Bede and Aquinas. Even with its magnification, in the civic ideologies of Brunetto Latini and Dante, to the highest order of statecraft, it is still contained and delimited, its capacity for artifice and manufacturing of belief firmly regulated by the reigning institutional science of politics. The subjunctive autonomy that rhetoric would claim for itself, even today, to be a kind of metadiscipline, would also constitute a kind of science of the body in history, a science of provisionality, contingency, and even fragmentation. The legitimisation and 'disciplining' of rhetoric is inevitably its repression, a process in which rhetoric participates by naming its own bodiliness.

NOTES

1 See Peter Stallybrass and Allon White, *The Politics and Poetics of Transgression*, Ithaca, NY, 1986, which offers a materialist examination of the relationship between the 'cultural categories of high and low, social and aesthetic, . . . the physical body and geographical space' (p. 2).

2 My concern here is with the construction of rhetoric as a discipline in relation to external discourses of knowledge, not with the internal features of rhetorical theory. In this my project differs from the work of some recent critics who deal with the question of rhetoric and the body in terms of the elements and practices of rhetorical figuration as language use and as a form of cultural representation; see Patricia Parker, *Literary Fat Ladies: Rhetoric, Gender, Property*, London and New York, 1987; R. Howard Bloch, 'Medieval misogyny', *Representations*, XX, 1987, pp. 1–24 (the arguments of which are recast in larger terms in his book, *Medieval Misogyny and the Invention of Western Romantic Love*, Chicago and London, 1991); and Tzvetan Todorov, *Theories of the Symbol*, trans. Catherine Porter, Ithaca, NY, 1982.

3 See most importantly Carolyn Dinshaw, *Chaucer's Sexual Poetics*, Madison, Wisc., 1989. Other significant recent work includes Steven F. Kruger, 'Claiming the Pardoner: towards a gay reading of Chaucer's *Pardoner's Tale*', *Exemplaria*, VI, 1994, pp. 115–39. Glenn Burger, 'Kissing the Pardoner', *PMLA*, CVII, 1992, pp. 1143–56, and the ground-breaking article by Monica McAlpine, 'The Pardoner's homosexuality and how it matters', *PMLA*, XCV, 1980, pp. 8–22. I have also benefited from hearing presentations of new work on gay theory and the Pardoner that had not reached publication at the time that this essay was written; in particular I want to cite papers by Carolyn Dinshaw (New Chaucer Society, Seattle, 1992) and Allen J. Frantzen (International Congress on Medieval Studies, Kalamazoo, Michigan, 1991).

4 James J. Murphy, *Rhetoric in the Middle Ages*, Berkeley and Los Angeles, 1974.

5 This exchange is recounted by Murphy in the published transcript of a conference panel, James Berlin *et al.*, 'The politics of historiography', *Rhetoric Review*, VII, 1988, p. 33.

6 Richard McKeon, 'Rhetoric in the Middle Ages', *Speculum*, XVII, 1942, pp. 3–32.

7 McKeon, 'Rhetoric in the Middle Ages', pp. 3, 32.

8 Brian Vickers, *In Defence of Rhetoric*, Oxford, 1988.

9 H.-I. Marrou, ' "Doctrina" et "disciplina" dans la langue des Pères de l'Èglise', *Bulletin du Cange*, IX, 1934, pp. 5–25.

10 See, e.g., Martianus Capella, *De nuptiis Philologiae et Mercurii*, ed. A. Dick, Leipzig, 1925, § 362.

11 Marrou, ' "Doctrina" et "disciplina" ', p. 7.

12 Marrou, ' "Doctrina" et "disciplina" ', pp. 7–8.

13 See, e.g., Cassiodorus, *Institutiones*, ed. R. A. B. Mynors, Oxford, 1937, book 2, section 21, on the division of mathematics into four disciplines (arithmetic, music, geometry, astronomy).

14 Vegetius, *De re militari*, ed. C. Lang, Leipzing, 1885, 2.3; 2.9; 3.1; 3.10; cited by Marrou, ' "Doctrina" et "disciplina" ', p. 11.

15 Cicero, *Tusculan Disputations*, ed. M. Pohlenz, Leipzig, 1918, 4.1; Tacitus, *Dialogus de oratoribus*, ed. A. Baehrens, Leipzig, 1881, 40; citations from Marrou, ' "Doctrina" et "disciplina" ', p. 11.

16 Augustine, *De ordine*, ed. W. M. Green, Turnhout, 1970, 3.8.25; cited in Marrou, ' "Doctrina" et "disciplina" ', p. 18.

17 *Ibid.*, pp. 19–21.

18 *Ibid.*, pp. 21–2.

19 *Ibid.*, p. 23.

20 *Ibid.*, p. 24, and citation of Augustine, *Sermones* 83.7.8, *Patrologiae latinae* cursus completus (hence PL), XXXVIII, col. 518: 'Jam ergo obsecrant pueri indisciplinati, et nolunt vapulare, qui sic praescribunt nobis, quando volumus dare disciplinam: Peccavi, ignosce mihi.'

21 J. F. Niermeyer, *Mediae latinitatis lexicon minus*, Leiden, 1984, *s.v.* 'disciplina', 8, 10, 11.

22 Niermeyer, *s.v.* 'disciplina', 9 (citing, for example, 'disciplina corporis' in Merovingian law). On the term 'discipline' in relation to flagellation see also Giles Constable, *Attitudes Toward Self-Inflicted Suffering in the Middle Ages*, The Ninth Stephen J. Brademas Sr Lecture, Brookline, Mass., 1982.

23 Michel Foucault, *The Archaeology of Knowledge*, trans. A. M. Sheridan Smith, New York, 1972, pp. 40–9.

24 Quintilian, *Institutio oratoria*, text with translation by H. E. Butler, 4 vols, Loeb Classical Library, Cambridge, Mass. and London, 1921, repr. 1976.

25 *Gorgias*, trans. B. Jowett, *The Dialogues of Plato*, II, Oxford, 1953, pp. 544–54. On the disciplinary permeability of sophistic rhetoric before the constraints imposed on sciences by Platonic and Aristotelian epistemology, see Susan C. Jarratt, *Rereading the Sophists: Classical Rhetoric Reconfigured*, Carbondale and Edwardsville, 1991, p. 13.

26 *Rhetoric*, trans. George A. Kennedy, *Aristotle on Rhetoric; a Theory of Civic Discourse*, New York and Oxford, 1991, pp. 28–9.

27 Aristotle distinguishes between artificial proofs, which are provided by the rhetorician's art or *techne* and take the form of appeals to ethical, logical, or pathetic argument (*Rhetoric*, trans. Kennedy, pp. 36–47), and inartificial (extrinsic or 'nonartistic') proofs, which are furnished at the outset of the judicial case, not constructed by the speaker's *techne*; under inartificial proofs, Aristotle considers laws, the testimony of witnesses, contracts, oaths, and evidence or testimony extracted from slaves under torture (*Rhetoric*, pp. 109–18).

28 Page duBois, *Torture and Truth*, New York and London, 1991, especially pp. 63–8.

29 As duBois recognises, Aristotle also questions the reliability of evidence extracted under torture; see the *Rhetoric*, pp. 115–16, and duBois, *Torture and Truth*, p. 68. Jody Enders, in a forthcoming article entitled 'Rhetoric and Drama, Torture and Truth' (which posits and explores a striking relationship between judicial torture in classical rhetorical theory and the spectacle of torture in medieval drama), further suggests that the distinctions rhetorical theory preserves between torture as extrinsic proof and the intrinsic proofs supplied by the speaker's invention are not so firm; both *inventio* and torture are described in terms of verisimilitude and the appearance of plausibility. In other words, evidence derived from the body can also be 'fashioned' by the speaker's artifice to appear the more plausible to a case. I am grateful to Professor Enders for showing me the typescript of her important essay.

30 (Pseudo-Cicero), *Ad Herennium*, 4.10.15–16, text with translation by Harry Caplan, Loeb Classical Library, Cambridge, Mass. and London, 1954 (repr. 1977).

31 Text and translation from Butler, 8. Pr. 19–22. In reproducing Butler's translation of this passage I have indicated where the choice of English words develops the sexual metaphors that are implicit or at least more ambiguous in Quintilian's Latin.

32 Todorov has remarked that rhetoric, faced with the contradiction of presiding over stylistic art but having to prefer discourse without the appearance of stylisation, practises its art with a guilty conscience (*Theories of the Symbol*, pp. 72–3). I would say instead that rhetoric confesses its anxieties about its *techne* so publically, submits itself to such critical scrutiny, that it can hardly keep any secrets of which to be guilty.

33 The idea that within the text of rhetoric the disciplining of the body and of discourse 'configure' each other is treated at length by Susan E. Shapiro, 'Rhetoric as ideology critique: the Gadamer–Habermas debate reinvented', *Journal of the American Academy of Religion* (forthcoming).

34 See, for example, Patricia Parker, 'Literary Fat Ladies and the Generation of the Text', in Parker, *Literary Fat Ladies*, pp. 8–35. John Alford has recently shown how these feminine figures of rhetoric, ranging from the garrulous to the promiscuous, find their way into the portrait of the Wife of Bath as an image of rhetoric in opposition to the Clerk's

embodiment of dialectic. See 'The Wife of Bath versus the Clerk of Oxford: what their rivalry means', *The Chaucer Review*, XXI, 1986, pp. 108–32. Alford cites Lucian's *The Double Indictment* (second century AD) for an example of rhetoric depicted as a female courtesan. The image of rhetoric as a charming mistress is well exemplified in Dante's *Convivio*, book 2, where rhetoric as love poetry is identified with Venus. The more generalised image of rhetoric as a richly-adorned, beautiful (but not promiscuous) woman is also a medieval commonplace, from Alan of Lille's *Anti-Claudianus* to Stephen Hawes's *Pastime of Pleasure*. The medieval iconography of the Liberal Arts typically shows the influence of Martianus Capella's allegorical representation of Rhetoric in martial attire; see Philippe Verdier, 'L'Iconographie des arts libéraux dans l'art du moyen âge jusqu'à la fin du quinzième siècle', *Arts libéraux et philosophie au moyen âge*, Actes du quatrième congrès international de philosophie médiévale, Montreal and Paris, 1969, pp. 305–55.

35 See John Boswell, *Christianity, Social Tolerance, and Homosexuality: Gay People in Western Europe from the Beginning of the Christian Era to the Fourteenth Century*, Chicago, 1980, pp. 310–12 (with specific reference to Alan of Lille).

36 Text from Nikolaus M. Häring, ed., 'Alan of Lille, "De planctu Naturae"', *Studi medievali*, 3rd series, XIX, 1978, p. 848 (prose 5). Translation from James J. Sheridan, *Alan of Lille: The Plaint of Nature*, Toronto, 1980, p. 162 (section 10).

37 On grammar and its complex curricular relations in this text, see Jan Ziolkowski, *Alan of Lille's Grammar of Sex: The Meaning of Grammar to a Twelfth-Century Intellectual*, Cambridge, Mass., 1985.

38 In Ciceronian theory, the attributes of the person and the act supply the information that supports propositions in argument. These furnish topics for argumentation. Under attributes of persons Cicero considers name, nature, manner of life, fortune, disposition, feeling, interests, purposes, achievements, accidents, and speeches made. See *De inventione*, ed. and trans. H. M. Hubbell, Loeb Classical Library, Cambridge, Mass. and London, 1949 (repr. 1976), 1.24.34–36.

39 Text in Edmond Faral, ed., *Les Arts poétiques du XIIe et du XIIIe siècle*, Paris, 1962, p. 126, lines 53–4, 77–84. In line 53, Faral offers alternative readings: consordeat / cum sordeat.

40 The text is corrupt here, and I offer some alternatives for translation of this difficult but crucial passage: 'since he submits of himself just as he partners in filth (or: "even as he is befouled") both inside and out.'

41 Translation from Ernest Gallo, 'Matthew of Vendôme: Introductory Treatise on the Art of Poetry', *Proceedings of the American Philosophical Society*, CXVIII, 1974, p. 69.

42 Cf. John of Salibury's defence of rhetoric within the structured relations of the *trivium*: *Metalogicon*, ed. C. C. I. Webb, Oxford, 1929, 1.7, pp. 21–3 and 1.12, pp. 30–1.

43 Jonathan Dollimore, *Sexual Dissidence: Augustine to Wilde, Freud to Foucault*, Oxford, 1991, pp. 82–3.

44 Robert O. Payne, 'Chaucer's realization of himself as rhetor', in James J. Murphy, ed., *Medieval Eloquence: Studies in the Theory and Practice of Medieval Rhetoric*, Berkeley and Los Angeles, 1978, pp. 270–87.

45 All quotations of Chaucer's text are from *The Riverside Chaucer*, 3rd edn, ed. Larry D. Benson, Boston, 1987.

46 Dinshaw, *Chaucer's Sexual Poetics*, p. 175; *Roman de la Rose*, ed. Felix Lecoy, Paris, 1970–82, lines 11177–81. For a mythographical view of indeterminacy of form, see Jane Chance, '"Disfigured is thy face": Chaucer's Pardoner and the Protean Shape-shifter Fals-Semblant (a response to Britton Harwood)', *Philological Quarterly*, LXVII, 1988, pp. 423–37.

47 On these lines and the Pardoner's identification with relics, see Dinshaw, *Chaucer's Sexual Poetics*, pp. 162–8; see also Eugene Vance, 'Chaucer's Pardoner: relics, discourse, and frames of propriety', *New Literary History*, XX, 1989, pp. 723–45.

48 Dinshaw's chapter on the Pardoner presents comprehensive arguments about the problem of substitution and fetish, including the symbol and word 'relike' for 'coillon'. See also Dolores Warwick Frese, *An 'Ars Legendi' for Chaucer's 'Canterbury Tales': Reconstructive Reading*, Gainesville, Fla, 1991, pp. 23–57.

49 Lee Patterson has also argued, along very different lines, for the necessity of taking seriously the link between the *Physician's Tale* and the *Pardoner's Tale*. See *Chaucer and the Subject of History*, Madison, Wisc., 1991, pp. 368–74.

50 The Pardoner identifies himself with those 'yonge men' who would learn about wives and marriage from the Wife of Bath (3.163–87) and in his own Prologue claims to enjoy 'a joly wenche in every toun' (6.453); in the *General Prologue* he plays at a 'love duet' with the Summoner (*GP* 672–3).

51 Dinshaw, *Chaucer's Sexual Poetics*, pp. 157–8, especially on the significance of the Pardoner's identification within the terms of heterosexual, androcentric patriarchy.

52 *Gorgias*, trans. Jowett, pp. 542–3.

53 Aristotle, *Rhetoric*, trans. Kennedy, p. 38: '[There is persuasion] through character whenever the speech is spoken in such a way as to make the speaker worthy of credence . . . character is almost, so to speak, the controlling factor in persuasion'. Cf. the survival of this concept in Quintilian, *Institutio oratoria* 6.2.8–19; here the speaker can appeal to ethos as a quality of emotional moderation to characterise the persons of whom he speaks, and for such appeals to work the speaker must also embody the virtue of moderation. For Aristotle, the speaker need only project a credible character; for Quintilian the speaker must possess a good character.

54 See, for example, Margaret Jennings, CSJ, 'The *Ars componendi sermones* of Ranulph Higden', in Murphy, ed., *Medieval Eloquence*, pp. 112–26.

55 Payne, 'Chaucer's realization of himself as rhetor', especially pp. 274, 278–83.

56 See most recently Alastair Minnis, 'Chaucer's Pardoner and the "office of preacher" ', in Piero Boitani and Anna Torti, eds, *Intellectuals and Writers in Fourteenth-Century Europe*, The J. A. W. Bennett Memorial Lectures, Perugia, 1984 (Tübingen and Cambridge, 1986), pp. 88–119.

57 See, for example, *Institutio oratoria* 12.1.32 (ed. and trans. Butler): 'Hoc certe procul eximatur animo, rerum pulcherrimam eloquentiam cum vitiis mentis posse misceri. Facultas dicendi, si in malos incidit, et ipsa iudicanda est malum; peiores enim illos facit, quibus contigit' ('At any rate let us banish from our hearts the delusion that eloquence, the fairest of all things, can be combined with vice. The power of speaking is even to be accounted an evil when it is found in evil men; for it makes its possessors yet worse than they were before').

58 On sophistic epistemology see Richard Leo Enos, 'The epistemology of Gorgias' rhetoric: a re-examination', *Southern Speech Communications Journal*, XLII, 1976, pp. 35–51. On Gorgias' examination of the relation between truth and language see John Poulakos, 'Gorgias' *Encomium to Helen* and the defense of rhetoric', *Rhetorica*, I, 1983, pp. 1–16. See also Jarratt, *Rereading the Sophists*, pp. 49–61.

59 See Jarratt, *Rereading the Sophists*, pp. 1–29, and John Poulakos, 'Towards a sophistic definition of rhetoric', *Philosophy and Rhetoric*, XVI, 1983, pp. 35–48.

60 On the Pardoner's Prologue as an example of the rhetorical technique of *manifestatio* see Gallo's introduction to his 'Matthew of Vendôme', pp. 57–8.

61 Cf. Michel Foucault, *The History of Sexuality I: An Introduction*, trans. Robert Hurley, New York, 1980, pp. 58–9.

62 Michel Foucault, *Discipline and Punish: the Birth of the Prison*, trans. Alan Sheridan, New York, 1979, p. 47.

63 Nancy S. Struever, *The Language of History in the Renaissance: Rhetoric and Historical Consciousness in Florentine Humanism*, Princeton, 1970, pp. 145, 155; cf. Jarratt, *Rereading the Sophists*, pp. 11–12, who uses Struever's idea of rhetoric as a subjunctive mental mode to define a new historiography of rhetoric.

The old body in medieval culture

I knew the wonder of discovering once again my body, my body which cured
me from having a soul.
(Marguerite Yourcenar, *Alexis*, trans. W. Kaiser, New York, 1984, p. 104)

Discourse on the body, both from the physiological aspect and as a symbolic
representation, developed gradually from the twelfth century onwards.
Discourse on the individual body, and the prominence this gave to the
body of Christ, probably reached its peak between 1350 and 1500.[1] Interest
in the physiology of the body evolved as part of the preoccupation with
the concrete, with natural phenomena and with the laws of nature, and
from the thirteenth century onwards this interest was decisively influenced
by the philosophy of nature as propounded by Aristotle and his Arab
commentators. The partial rehabilitation of the body was based on the
acknowledgement that it was created by God, on the mystery of the Incarnation, and on belief in the resurrection of the body on Judgement Day.
As Hildegard of Bingen (1098–1179) writes: 'The body without soul is
naught; and the soul cannot operate without the body.' The soul is superior
to the body, but is dependent upon it. It is the microcosm in which the
soul dwells. Hildegard goes on to describe the beauty and intricacy of the
human body, which was also the body of Christ when he took human form.[2]

In the framework of discourse on the body and its use as metaphor, the
old body was also discussed. In descriptions of the process of ageing and
of old age itself, physical experience takes central place. Attitudes towards
the old were equivocal. Ageing was considered conducive to increased
wisdom, and to spiritual growth, as well as to liberation from passions and
earthly ambitions. But it was also a time of development of negative traits
of character, and even of vices, as well as of mental deterioration. In other
words there were two stereotypes of the old person – positive and negative. This was not true of the old body which had no positive valuation.
This negative stereotype can be found in all types of text (though emphasis may shift) from scientific texts through religious writings to works of
fiction. Both the advocates of the rehabilitation of the body, who considered
it legitimate to preserve its health, as well as those who perceived the body
as a prison in which mankind, in his folly and sinfulness, invests excessive
care and attention, employed the same stereotype in describing the old

body. In this context, they drew no distinctions between various social classes – the body was always the same. Those who lauded the beauty of the human body, created in the divine image, which was also Christ's body when he took on flesh, were not thinking of the old body. Only the protagonists of heroic epics, who transcend their age both spiritually and physically, are endowed with powerful and dignified old bodies. This was also the aspiration of those who dreamed of prolongevity and proposed ways of postponing ageing and increasing life expectancy. However, the meaning attributed to the old body was by no means unequivocal. Conflicting interpretations were advanced regarding its moral and spiritual significance, ways of treating it and what it harboured for the old person.

The present article examines the stereotype of the old body and its meanings in various discursive contexts.

THE NEUTRAL OLD MALE BODY

The neutral approach to the old body is characteristic of scientific and medical writings. Roger Bacon (1214–92) writes: 'All these accidents of old age and senility are white hair, pallor, wrinkling of the skin, excess of mucus, foul phlegm, inflammation of the eyes and general injury of the organs of sense, diminution of blood and spirits, weakness of motion and breathing in the whole body . . .'[3] A similar account is found in Vincent of Beauvais (c.1190–1264).[4] The neutral description by authors of medical and scientific texts was inserted either into theoretical discussions of the ageing process and diseases of old age, or into instructive texts on how to preserve the health of the old. These texts often include cautions to younger people who failed to guard their health and, as a result, were doomed to premature ageing. Discussions of ageing and the diseases of old age appear in compendia on pathology and therapeutics, which became popular from the second half of the twelfth century, when translations of Greek and Arabic medical texts began to appear in the West. General health manuals (regimen sanitatis) which offered advice, based on both medical theory and practice, on the various stages in human life from birth to old age, included advice to the old. The basic assumption of these works was that it was impossible to restore youth, or to revive impaired organs, since ageing is an irreversible decline of the organism. The objective of the regimen sanitatis, clearly reflecting the trend to rehabilitate the body and legitimise health care,[5] was to prevent, in so far as possible, deterioration of what was still healthy and unimpaired in the old body, to ensure a sense of well-being in the old person, and to guide his body through its natural span of life.[6] Authors of medical texts also distinguished between normal concomitants of old age and abnormal or diseased conditions, though they were unable to cure most of its ailments.[7]

It was commonly believed that mankind had forfeited immortality and been condemned to the subsequent process of ageing because of original sin. Opinions were divided as to whether, after the Deluge, the human life span was curtailed even further. But medical texts viewed both divine punishment for original sin and possible divine intervention after the Deluge as ultimate causes, preferring to focus on immediate causes and symptoms of ageing. The increase in external bad humours and the decrease of natural heat and innate radical moisture were regarded as the immediate causes of all the *accidentia senectutis*, both physical and mental. Roger Bacon, after enumerating the physical accidents, proceeds to describe the mental ones: 'failure of both the animal and natural powers of the soul, sleeplessness, anger and disquietude of mind and forgetfulness of which the royal Hali says that old age is the home of forgetfulness and Plato that it is the mother of lethargy'.[8] Physical and mental decline were not perceived as occurring at the same age. Aristotle believed that physical and intellectual ability peaked at different ages, the latter occurring later than the former.[9] According to most medieval medical and scientific authors who followed him, mental decline occurred in the later stage of old age (usually denoted *senium*). In extreme old age, man is in a state of both physical and mental decline. Because of the physiological changes occurring in his body, primarily the decrease in natural heat, he becomes once more like a child.[10]

The actual details of the regimen specified by medieval authors, which was inspired by Hippocrates, Galen and the Muslim physicians of the high Middle Ages, are beyond the scope of the present discussion. It is worth noting, however, that since they viewed man as a unity of body and soul and believed that by acting on the soul, one can act on the body, the authors included advice on how to prevent anger, anxiety and melancholy, which reduce the natural heat of the body. These feelings can be prevented by evoking emotion and joy through aesthetic pleasure, by encouraging intellectual discourse and, of course, through reading the Holy Scriptures.[11]

The *regimen sanitatis* genre, in both Latin and the vernaculars, became so popular that it inspired sceptical satires. In his *Ballade Farcie de Regimen Sanitatis*, Charles of Orléans (1394–1465) mocks medical advice in general, and in particular the advice that avoidance of over-indulgence in sexual intercourse could help postpone old age and extend the life span.[12]

The old body, its externality and interior, are described stereotypically in medical and scientific texts, but in matter-of-fact fashion, without moral connotations. Even when discussing the negative qualities, such as irritation and melancholy, which were attributed to old people, authors depict them as the inevitable outcome of physiological change in the body, over which the individual has no control.[13] Ageing of the body is part of the human condition. According to the laws of nature, the individual whose life proceeds in an uninterrupted line without being cut short prematurely will eventually arrive at the decrepitude of old age, which is the last stage in life.[14] As the poet Eustache Deschamps (c.1346–1406) wrote in one of his ballads: 'nature creates nothing stable and unchanging. Man is like a flower destined to fade and die.'[15] The death of an old man is not only natural but also easy, unlike the death of the young. According to Albert the Great (1200–80), the death of an old person is painless because of the total dwindling of the natural heat, the disappearance of the radical humours and the infiltration of bad humours from the outside. He now feels almost nothing, and is like a lamp about to go out. The death of a young person is bitter. It is like an unripe apple, which falls from the tree before its time, while the old person who dies is like a ripe apple that falls peacefully.[16]

THE HARMFUL OLD FEMALE BODY

It is not clear whether the authors subsumed women under the category of 'man' (homo) or were referring exclusively to men. Some of the components of the description of old age apply equally to both sexes, and none of the authors note explicitly that they are referring solely to the old male body. The impression is, however, that, as in the case of the schemes of the Ages of Man (etates hominis), the authors were thinking, if not exclusively, then primarily, of men.[17] But some writers did devote a separate discussion to one particular physiological change in the body of the old woman: the cessation of the menstrual flow. Here authors distinguished between the various social classes, a distinction never drawn in the case of men. They claimed that the destructive results attributed to this change were manifested mainly among old women from the poorer classes, the theory, implicit in scientific texts and explicit in some works of scientific popularisation, being that the old female body was capable of producing poison. As is well known, menstrual blood was considered impure, harmful and possessing destructive power.[18] After the menopause woman was even more dangerous because she had become incapable of eliminating the superfluous matter from her organism. As stated in De Secretis mulierum, attributed to Albert the Great, 'the retention of menses engenders many evil humours. The women being old have almost no natural heat left to consume and control this matter, especially poor women who live on nothing but coarse meat, which greatly contributes to this phenomenon. These women are more venomous than the others.'[19] The old hag, or panderer, who concocts philtres of love or death, is merely exercising an activity analogous to the transformation that physiology works on the female organism. Certain mental and psychological effects were attributed to the physiological changes in the old male body. But there was no parallel connection between such changes and actions in the case of old men.

Since medieval culture perceived a connection between the physical and the spiritual and insisted on their reciprocal influences, those who were considered to possess perverted or sinful souls were also perceived as physically repulsive. The appearance of the lepers indicated the corruptness of their souls and their loathsome deeds. The perverted soul of the heretics or Jews rendered them physically repulsive.[20] It is not clear whether it was the appearance of old, poor women which inspired the theory regarding their ability to generate poison, or whether the theory originated in the obsessive preoccupation with the contaminating and injurious effect of menstrual blood, but it was propounded in the most direct and blunt fashion.

THE OLD BODY AS A METAPHOR FOR THE TRANSIENCE AND VANITIES OF WORLDLY THINGS

In sermons focusing on the *Contemptus Mundi*, which denounced attraction to transient wordly vanities and called for repentance, the old body symbolises the impermanence and emptiness of the mundane life. It serves as a reminder that one must prepare for death, that is, detach oneself from this world and strive to save one's soul. Bernardino of Siena (1380–1444) describes the old body: the trembling of the head, quaking of the whole body, whiteness of head, swelling of the stomach, loss of teeth, dimming of sight and hearing, and cooling or end of libido.[21] An English preacher pictures the old man who still delays his repentance and refuses to accept the fact of his approaching death: 'see the wrinkled face, the snow-white head, the bent back, the failing of sight, hearing and limbs, the livid nose and nails, the evil breath, the hollow eye, the crazy mirth that seems to forget its approaching death'.[22]

Some of the details of this description echo scientific writings, but it is cruel and grotesque and the different context alters the significance. Innocent III (1160–1216), in a text influenced by Horace, and which itself had an impact on various later medieval texts, from sermons to literary works, depicts the vicissitudes of earthly life from conception to death. He devotes a detailed and unsparing description to the old body: the heart weakens and the head shakes; the spirits droop and the breath stinks; the face becomes wrinkled and the back bends; the eyes grow dim and the joints grow shaky; the nose runs and hair falls out; the hand trembles and makes awkward movements; teeth decay and ears grow deaf. And he adds: 'Young men, be not proud in the presence of a decaying old man; he was once that which you are; he is now what you in turn will be.'[23] The aim is not to evoke empathy but to caution against pride and arouse contempt for fleshly and earthly things. The old body here does not merely indicate the inevitable approaching biological end, as in medical works, but also symbolises the terrible judgement in the next world, which man, in his foolishness and sin, chooses to ignore. It is a symbol not so much of suffering as of the vanity and impermanence of the world.

De Remediis utriusque Fortune (*On the Two Kinds of Fortune*) by Petrarch (1304–1411) contains encyclopaedic knowledge, a catalogue of human situations and moral casuistry. In the first book, in the dialogue between Joy and Reason, the function of pessimistic Reason is to curb Joy and to bring home to him the folly of his happiness. The old body plays a central role in Reason's attempts to persuade Joy that all that now causes him happiness will become a source of evil and suffering. The good and the beautiful will rapidly pass away; the degeneration and increasing unloveliness of the body and the loss of bodily pleasures are indicators of the fragility, impermanence and insignificance of this world. Petrarch is making the same metaphoric use of the body as did the preachers (and he uses images and descriptions which appear in the sermons, accompanied by sarcastic comments).[24] The final words which Petrarch places in the mouth of Reason reflect a psychological truth; the sense of alienation of the old man from his body. The same sense of unfamiliarity was expressed by the fifteenth-century south Tyrolean poet, Oswald von Wolkenstein, in his song *Ich sich und hör* (*I see and hear*). The poet speaks to his old body as if to something outside himself.[25]

In the second half of Petrarch's work, in the dialogues between Reason and Sorrow, Reason explains to Sorrow that he must accept the situation with understanding and learn from the vicissitudes of fate such as old age. Sorrow complains at the loss of his teeth. Reason comforts him in an ironic tone: 'Now that you have lost your teeth, you shall eat less, speak less and bite less at another man's good name . . . and if chastity cause not thy old wanton affliction to refrain from unlawful kisses, then let shame restrain it.'[26] The old body, suffering from gout and scabies and constant fatigue, writes Petrarch, can no longer run, jump, play tennis or dance. The young body is like a flower, but a flower whose fading is inherent in its blossoming. Loyal to the concept of the unity of body and soul, after describing the changes in the old body and the diseases which are its lot, he depicts the dimming of understanding, the weakening of the memory and the disturbance of speech.[27] One might say that, for Petrarch, the old body is the symbol of the ephemerality of everything man enjoys in this world.

Reason, Joy and Sorrow are personified by male figures. The young and old bodies that are described are also male bodies. There is no reference in the text to the female body. Other authors of moralistic works did, however, depict the body of the old woman as the symbol of the ephemeral, stressing its loss of beauty as loss of the power to attract and so cause others to sin. Gerald of Wales (1147–1220) writes: 'The female body is so easily destroyed by sickness or old age ... Who could, for purposes of carnal intercourse, of licentious kisses so wantonly desire this skin (however much it was formerly desired) withered by sickness or shrivelled into an old woman's wrinkled by age.'[28] Gerald of Wales does not go into detail, and in general mention of the body of the old woman in sermons as a metaphor for the transience of earthly things is much rarer, and less detailed, than reference to the old male body. In didactic works, mention of the waning of beauty is usually accompanied by critical comments (sometimes quite sarcastic) on the vain efforts of old women to conceal this loss by lavish clothing, cosmetics and female wiles.[29]

THE YOUNG/OLD OPPOSITION

The young/old opposition is a binary one, whereby human thought tries to organise life and the world symbolically. Moreover, like that between male and female, that of young and old is prototypical and universal.

It appears implicitly in medical writings, and explicitly in Petrarch's *De Remediis*, but plays an even more central part in some literary and didactic works. In these texts, the old man (or woman) and the young man (or woman) appear as contrasts, both symbolised. One can discern in these texts Jungian archetypes, in which youth symbolises heat, blossoming, power, love, beauty, and its symbols are sunrise, sun, spring, whereas old age symbolises cold, weakness, ugliness, death, and is symbolised by darkness, winter, Father Time and the Grim Reaper.[30] Old men and women may symbolise the same phenomena but it is more common for women's bodies than men's to personify winter, evil traits, old age and death.

In the thirteenth-century *chantefable, Aucassin et Nicolette*, the two extremes of old age and youth are represented by Aucassin and his father. The old father, who is already weak but authoritative and cruel, is the source of suffering for the young couple. Whereas Aucassin is the perfect knight, his father employs the weapons of the weak – deception and manipulation. His death marks the end of the sufferings of the young and they can now marry. As in romances, the young are the victors, whereas a humorous passage consigns the old to hell.[31]

The seasons of the year symbolised the stages of life and the transition from youth to old age.[32] Conversely, the seasons were represented by images of women, and characteristically by the young woman/old woman contrast, as in this somewhat free version of the pseudo-Aristotelian text *Secretum Secretorum* by John Lydgate (fifteenth century). In spring 'the world becomes like a young girl adorned and resplendent before the onlookers'; in summer 'the earth becomes like a bride laden with riches and having many lovers'; in autumn it is like 'a mature matron who has passed the years of her youth'; and in winter 'the world becomes like a decrepit old woman for whom death draws near'.[33] In the *Pèlerinage de la Vie humaine*, written in the fourteenth century by Guillaume de Deguileville, virtues are personified by splendidly dressed young women while Sloth, Pride, Flattery, Hypocrisy, Envy, Treachery, Anger, Avarice, Gluttony and Lust as well as Tribulation, Heresy, Disease and Old Age itself are represented by ugly old ones. Unlike sermons, this text includes detailed and cruel descriptions of their bodies. Sloth is an ugly, hairy, dirty and stinking old woman. Pride is an old woman of monstrous obesity with swollen legs, who cannot walk alone. The image of Hypocrisy is not clear but she is covered by a cloak such as is worn by old women to hide their ugliness and infirmities. Pride crawls on her belly like a snake; she is shrivelled and dry, without flesh and blood. Disease leans on crutches and Old Age has legs of lead. But Mercy, leading the pilgrim to the infirmary, is a young woman, with one exposed breast so as to suckle the suffering:[34] the old woman also differs from the young one in her inability to nurse. She can never resemble the Holy Mother nursing her infant – the symbol of goodness, mercy and unstinting giving.

Fear of old age and oblivion were represented by the images of old women. In the Roussillon region, in the Middle Ages, two puppets, in the image of ugly old women, were fashioned during the Lent fast. At Easter the puppets were burnt at the stake. In rural areas of Italy and France, at the ceremony of banishing winter and death, two puppets in the image of the two oldest, ugliest women in the village were sawn in two. These puppets, like the masks worn at religious ceremonies in other cultures, gave an outlet to fear through protecting against it, and were a means of mitigating it. In Petrarch's *Trionfo della Morte*, the personification of death is an old woman dressed in black. 'With fury such as had perchance been seen when giants raged in the Phlegraean vale.'[35]

YOUTH – BEAUTY – LOVE; OLD AGE – UGLINESS – LOVE IMPROPER

Guillaume de Lorris, author of the first part of the *Roman de la Rose* (c.1230), describes in terms no less grotesque and cruel than Deguileville the images of old women excluded from the garden of love and representing Hate, Felony, Villainy, Covetousness, Avarice, Envy, Sorrow, Hypocrisy and Old Age. Like the preachers, he explicitly mentions the loss of beauty. Love is fitting for the young and beautiful and not for (ugly) old men and women, as Jean de Meun's Duenna confirms in the second half of the *Roman* (c.1279). Chaucer's Wife of Bath similarly declares:

For filthe and elde, al-so mote I thee
Been grete wardeyns up-on chastitee.[36]

Medieval authors were influenced by and borrowed from Roman writers like Horace, Juvenal and Maximian, who mocked at old men and women who still sought an amorous connection, or in softer and gloomier tone, described such conduct as unbecoming.[37] In the Middle Ages, medical, moral, social and aesthetic arguments combined to condemn the amorous old man. According to authors of medical and didactic works (who followed the physicians and philosophers of the classical world, like Seneca and Cicero), the sexual instinct dies down in old age and some lose their virility altogether.[38] It is unnatural for an old man to seek sexual relations, as Philippe de Novare writes: 'desire exists without need or capacity'.[39] And as for women, Christine de Pisan (1364–1430), exhorting older women not to criticise young women harshly and not to harass them, notes (though more delicately) that the sexual instinct abates with old age. Addressing older women, she says: 'if you no longer have the vices of youth, this is not out of virtue but because your nature no longer inclines you to them'.[40] An old man or woman who clings to youthful lusts is acting in unnatural fashion, as if mad. According to the physicians, sexual relations are even harmful to the health of the old man and hasten his end. In secular literature, he is presented as pathetic, comic or grotesque. In moral literature he is condemned for clinging to the sins of his youth instead of exploiting the opportunity to free himself of the sins of the flesh and repent.[41] The custom of young villagers in various regions of Western Europe to hold a *charivari* under the window of the widow or widower about to remarry expressed both feelings and attitudes. It reflected psychological concern for the children of the previous marriages as well as economic and social anxiety. It provided an outlet for hostility towards those who violated not only certain community rules but a natural law as well.[42]

The *charivari* was directed against both women and men. Like the *senex amans*, the old woman who wanted to continue her sexual life was condemned. Sometimes she is depicted as grotesque. But it is more characteristic to depict her as possessing secret knowledge which she uses to manipulate people, which makes her more threatening than grotesque. Unlike the *senex amans*, who is usually a man of standing and property, a rival for young men who are less prosperous than he, the old women, who are experts in the secrets of life and sex, belong to the lower classes. These old hags give advice on questions of love and sex, prepare potions and are procurers. Sometimes they disguise themselves and take the place of the young women with whom men have assignations. Other old women find satisfaction in luring young and innocent women to sin. This is their own substitute for an independent sexual life. In some *exempla*, the old woman plays the role of vampire; or the devil appears in the form of an old woman who plants malicious thoughts and tempts both men and women.[43] In the Middle Ages, descriptions of the old male body are no less cruel than depictions of the bodies of old women. But whereas the old male body was seen as pathetic, weak or grotesque, symbolising the negative traits of old age, and was used as a metaphor for the impermanence of life in this world and as pointing the way to death, the old female body was seen as possessing the power to do evil.

Only men wrote of their old age in the first person (or perhaps only what has been written by men has survived), and in such texts the body plays a central part. The prevailing tone in the ballad of Jean Régnier (1392–c.1468) is sadness. He is an old man of standing, but would prefer to be a young valet. He reminisces about his childhood and youth; how, as a child, he sought birds' nests and as a young man went out to hunt in spring. Now he must bid farewell to the sport he loved so much. He is weak, suffers from gout; his hand which grasps the goblet shakes. All he can eat is soup and milk. His nose runs; he suffers from cold and warms himself by the hearth. (Sensitivity to cold is the stereotype of the old man in the Icelandic saga as well.)[44] His amorous adventures are over; the joys of the past will never return. He is occupied in studying the theory of humours and is at the mercy of physicians.[45] As A. Planche has rightly noted, in descriptions of this kind, even though written in the first person, stereotyping is stronger than individualisation.[46] The ballad of Jean Régnier is marked by melancholy mixed with bitterness, but no grotesqueness. However, sometimes in first-person poetry the description is no less grotesque and cruel than are the descriptions of old women written by men. Eustache Deschamps, in his ballad *Regrets d'un Vieillard*, writes: 'I am bowed and hunched, tremble, my nose drips, my hair is white, my teeth are long, weak, sharp and yellow. My penis has become a soft tail which serves only for passing water.' And he adds the negative mental stereotype of the old man; impatient, miserly, quick to anger, irritable, bored and boring, hostile to new customs, laughter and merriment.[47]

The image of the upright, venerable white-haired sage, with eyes glowing with wisdom is not typical of the depiction of the old man in medieval texts, nor do we encounter white-haired old women whose countenance reflects goodness and understanding. Old Giannozzo in *I Libri della Famiglia* by Alberti (1404–72) is an impressive figure, but this is a personal description coloured by particular respect and not a stereotypical portrait.[48] (One of Alberti's objectives in his book was to exhort the young members of the family to respect the older members and to obey them.) The fifteenth-century Scots poet Robert Henryson, in *The Praise of Old Age*, depicts the singing of an old man who lists all the evils of youth and reiterates that he would not return to the days of his youth for all the money and honour in the world for 'the more of age, the nerar hevynnis blisse'. The poet's empathy for and identification with the old man are evident, but the only attractive physical attribute he mentions is a sweet and clear voice, and the first line of the poem introduces him as 'Ane old man and decrepit'.[49] Old men could be represented as having qualities such as wisdom, experience and religious piety, and we also find the stereotype of the respectable old woman, who is a faithful adviser and is worthy of chaperoning young women because of her sobriety and piety. But these positive stereotypes did not help create a dignified external image. When positive stereotypes of old men or women appear, bodies are not mentioned.

The external image of old men and women, whether neutral description, aspiring to realism, or indicative of symbolic or metaphoric meaning, was sustained by reality as well as literary convention. Taking into consideration the limited medical expertise of the time, the conditions of hygiene and the fact that many old people were also poor, it is reasonable to assume that many of those men and women who survived to old age must have been toothless. And probably many were decrepit, chronically maimed and also mentally impaired. But it is doubtful whether the poor mental and physical condition of many old people in the Middle Ages and the literary convention alone were responsible for the ugly and pathetic physical stereotype.

In the Middle Ages beauty was a knightly ideal. The heroes of epics and courtly literature, both young men and women, are distinguished by their outstanding beauty. Churchmen's admiration for it was more equivocal. Aelred of Rievaulx (1109–67) writes that the beautiful body is like a vase, a rustic or an urban one. A beautiful vase can contain bad food; and vice versa, an ugly vase can hold good food.[50] Stories intended to serve as *exempla* figure young men and women whose actions are described as praiseworthy, who not only discipline their bodies, but also mutilate their own beauty in order to avoid being tempted into sin, and in particular in order to restrain others from sinning, in deed or only in thought. The comely young men and women made a heroic sacrifice for love of God. The ugliness of the old man, however, is not the result of sacrifice. There is no sharp and dramatic transition from beauty to ugliness. The old body could serve as a symbol of the human condition and of suffering but not of heroic sacrifice.

YOUNG AND BEAUTIFUL: GOD THE SON AND THE RESURRECTED BODY

The image of God featured in medieval art was that of a handsome young man. God the Father appears only in Renaissance art (where there are also individual portraits of old men) as a venerable strong old man; but here too the dominant figure is God the Son.[51] In the Middle Ages, in both art and texts, the depicted God is Jesus (an infant or a handsome young man). Whether suffering or in triumph, he is always young. His beauty was described in sermons. Aelred of Rievaulx speaks of it as amazing the angels, the sun and the moon.[52] Mystics, in their devotion to Christ's body, blood, wounds and sacred heart, saw a young and beautiful God.[53] Whether the artists of the late Middle Ages emphasised Christ's sexuality as a symbol of his humanity, as Leo Steinberg argues, or depicted his body in a way that suggested that it was sometimes perceived as having female attributes as well, as Caroline Bynum argues,[54] it was always a young body. Similarly, Mary was depicted as a young and beautiful mother, nursing her infant or playing with him – the ideal of maternity in this world. In the fourteenth century, when there were more representations of the *Pietà*, showing the mother of all sorrows cradling in her arms her son who had been taken down from the cross, her face was marked by suffering, but it was often young.[55]

Those who entered Paradise were also supposed to be young (in contrast to the allegations in *Aucassin et Nicolette*). In a popular religious text, when the sage is asked if people will grow old in Paradise, he replies that they will be eternally young and merry as birds.[56]

As for the dead who were to rise up on Judgement Day, it was generally agreed, in the wake of Saint Augustine, that they would be resurrected as they were in their early thirties.[57] (Some sources are more precise, and specify thirty-two and two months.) Even if they died when older or younger, the bodies of the resurrected would be of just the same age at which Christ, who took on flesh, chose to die, in the bloom and vigour of youth. This belief was shared by orthodox theologians, authors of popular religious works and those heretics who believed in the resurrection of the body on Judgement Day.[58] In paintings and sculptures of the Judgement Day, as in the tympanum of the cathedral of Bourges, or in the painting by Signorelli in S. Brizio chapel in the cathedral of Orvieto, people could see the bodies of the just rising up again, young and beautiful. Old men and women could not serve as images of God the Son and his mother. Those who fostered the ideal of prolongevity, to whom I will refer later, strove to extend the span of youth in this world. This was not the teaching of religion, according to which old age must be accepted as part of the fate of the human race since the original sin. But it gave sanction to the dream of youth through the promise that it would be realised on Resurrection Day.

THE MALE TRANSCENDENCE IDEAL

The transcendence ideal was already found among the Epicureans, the Stoics and in early Christianity. It proposed that man, as a reasonable being, can overcome the *cursus aetatis*, the laws of nature and time, and manifest the ideal traits of all natural ages.[59] This is only spiritual transcendence, as Saint Augustine wrote: 'In your body, you cannot be both young and old. In your soul, however, you can: young through alacrity, old through gravity.'[60] But unlike St Augustine, who wrote of the blending of youth and age, the medieval Christian thinkers regarded the ideal transcendence as the manifestation of the traits of old age in the young and even in the child. In the *Vitae*, there often recurs the *topos* of the boy-old man (*puer-senex*). The boy-old man is serious, wise and displays religious piety from infancy. He personifies what are supposed to be the positive traits of old age; wisdom, control of instincts, and piety.[61] The concept of transcendence, as elaborated in religious literature, does not relate to the positive traits of the young. The ideal combination of alacrity and gravity, both in old age and in youth, as presented by Saint Augustine, has disappeared. There is no spiritual equalisation of ages; rather, by grace of God, a man is spiritually able to transcend his age upwards.

Yet the qualities of wisdom and spiritual maturity are not ascribed to all elderly people. Moreover, in both scholarly and popular literature, there was also a *topos* of 'the hundred-year-old boy' (*puer centum annorum*). This *topos* was based on Seneca's remark on the *puer elementarius*, and on an interpretation of Isaiah 20.65, as mistranslated in the Vulgate.[62] The greatest folly of the 'hundred-year-old boy' is his desire to continue his amorous activities, which is neither natural nor fitting for his age. To the extent that the traits of a younger age were attributed to the mature saint, these were the traits of childhood rather than youth. Authors of scientific works, it will be recalled, compared the very old man to a child, and in drawing this comparison they stressed the decline in intellectual powers in extreme old age. However, in religious literature it is sometimes the innocent child or the wise old man, the weak in body, who are privileged to discover a significant truth, hidden from the eyes of others. It is recounted of some saints that they were particularly fond of the company of children, because of their purity and innocence, which resembled their own, since they had preserved these traits in adulthood. And because of these qualities they were beloved by children, who felt a close affinity with them.[63] Despite such examples, however, the ideal transcendence in religious literature is towards old age. But the qualities of old age are mental, not physical.

According to Adalberon of Laon's *Carmen ad Robertum Regem* (composed *c.*1020), the symbolic king combines qualities of both youth and age, but his body realises the ideal of youth.[64] Similarly, the hero of the epic poem *La Chanson de Guillaume* embodies the qualities of youth in his physical strength and heroism. He is a mythical figure, 350 years old and mounted on his steed; he fights the Saracens like a lion.[65] This attribution of a youthful body to an older person is possible only with a mythical hero or symbolic king who is free of the constraints of the human attribution of a youthful body to an old person.

In the *Vitae*, the *topos* of the boy-old man is paralleled by that of the girl-old woman. The author of the Life of Saint Catherine of Siena described her at the age of six. 'From that hour, the little girl began to grow old. There was a wondrous maturity in her good qualities and her conduct. Her deeds were not those of a child, nor of a young woman, but were entirely in the spirit of old age.'[66] The image of the girl-old woman sometimes appears in literature as the personification of a positive trait, science or institution.[67] However, the religious literature, which presented the ideal of spiritual transcendence as something which a young man (and not only the child who was a future saint) could achieve, did not discuss young women. There is little room in the heroic epic for women either. The transcendence ideal was exclusively male.

POSTPONEMENT OF PHYSICAL AGEING AND PROLONGATION OF LIFE

The idea of prolongevity, as developed in various periods and cultures,[68] was based on the belief that, through human action, it was possible and desirable to prolong youth, and significantly extend the life span. The authors of health manuals set themselves the limited aim of protecting people from disease as far as possible and guiding the body to its natural life span. The advice directed at the young and middle-aged was intended to prevent premature ageing and death. The proponents of the idea of prolongevity, such as Roger Bacon and Arnold of Villanova,[69] recommended an ordinary regimen of health, but also raised the possibility of significantly extending the life span, postponing old age and even rejuvenating the old. This was to be achieved through special measures which are not included in the ordinary regimen. According to Roger Bacon, the signs of old age (*accidentia senectutis*) appear already at forty-five to fifty, a stage at which man should still be at the height of his powers. He specifies measures whereby a man can preserve his full powers to the age of one hundred, and only then will the first signs of ageing appear.[70] Reference is to ageing of both the body and the mind. Bacon and Arnold regarded the individual as a single psychosomatic entity, but emphasis is undoubtedly placed on the body, which should also remain young in appearance. Arnold of Villanova even promises those who have become impotent that if they adopt the measures he proposes, their virility will be restored.[71] (It seems that, as in medical works which dealt with ageing, authors who write about prolongevity and the postponement of ageing were thinking only of men.) In developing the idea of prolongevity, Roger Bacon was looking back to the past, to the recorded long lives of people in the antediluvian period.

He attributed the subsequent reduction in life span not to divine intervention, but to the foulness of the air, as well as to the debilitation of mankind due to folly and immorality. Each generation conducts itself like its
predecessor and so a weakened constitution passes from fathers to sons,
until a shortening of life results 'as is the case in these days'.[72] In order to
postpone ageing and extend the life span, Bacon asserts, the ordinary
regimen of health must be maintained at all stages of life from infancy
onwards. At a certain stage (he does not specify which) other measures
should be taken. These can be learned from the ancient tradition of
occult knowledge, found mainly in writings on astrology and alchemy
from the time of the Chaldeans, through the Greeks to the Arabs, now
forgotten or deliberately hidden.[73] In parallel, these proper measures can
be learned from experimental science. It is possible, among other things,
to observe the habits of various animals which use different herbs, stones
and metals to improve their bodies and rejuvenate themselves, and prolong their lives by natural action. The measures proposed by Roger Bacon
and Arnold of Villanova range from the drinking of a gold solution as an
elixir to the inhalation of the calorific and beneficial exhalation of young
and healthy girls, in order to create equilibrium between the opposite
poles of youth and old age.[74] Benoit-Lapierre has pointed out the parasitic
or vampiric associations of this practice, of which older men are apparently the only beneficiaries.[75] It is invoked, in more delicate fashion, by
the poet William of Aquitaine (1071–1127) in his poem *Mout jauzens me
prenc en amar* (*Full of joy I begin to love*). He yearns to cling to his young love
in order to remain young in body and spirit:

> To refresh my heart in her
> To renew my flesh in her
> So that I shall never grow old.[76]

The loved one is here a means of preserving youth.

Eternal youth and long life are ancient dreams of mankind and not
solely the aspiration of scientists.[77] In the fourteenth century, Mandeville's
Travel Book told of a well of youth located in the Indian jungle.[78] The
atmosphere of certain places was also believed to preserve youth and
guarantee eternal life, like the Isle of Avalon, where people neither grew
old nor died. An extended life without continued youth is, by contrast, an
affliction. The enigmatic old man in Chaucer's *Pardoner's Tale* seeks to die,
as does King Mordrain in *La Queste del Saint Graal.* He is condemned to
live for 400 years, old, blind and covered with sores as punishment for
having disregarded repeated divine warnings and come too close to the
Holy Grail. His long life, marked by suffering, is a punishment and a
means of atonement. His death is his redemption.[79]

Medieval advocates of prolongevity promised neither eternal life nor eternal youth. They sought only maximal postponement of ageing and death. Man had forfeited immortality and eternal youth as a result of original sin. He was meant to age because he was destined to die. Thomas Aquinas writes that our first parents lived many years after God passed his sentence but adds, quoting Saint Augustine: 'They began to die when they received the sentence of declining into old age.'[80] In the painting in the Sistine Chapel which represents the eating of the fruit of the Tree of Knowledge and the banishment from Eden, Michelangelo was faithful to the Christian conception of the history of mankind. Adam and Eve before the Expulsion are young, while afterwards Eve is an old woman, there is a heavy cloud over Adam's face and he has aged.

THE OLD BODY AS OPPORTUNITY FOR AND MEANS OF EXPIATION OF SIN AND SALVATION

The old body was weak. Hence, just as it served as a metaphor for the impermanence of worldly things, it was also perceived as an opportunity for expiation of sin, spiritual elevation and closeness to God.[81] The old body signals to its owner that he is not immortal and must prepare his soul for its fate in the next world, so that death, when it arrives, will find him ready. The old body is a means of drawing close to God because of its suffering and because it no longer has passions.[82] It is a special opportunity afforded man, who can choose to utilise it or not. The old man who clings to the sins of his youth, does not devote himself to saving his soul and does not accept his old age and approaching death, cannot approach God. The old have no need to discipline their bodies or to pray for sickness, as did young ascetics who sought disease in order to expiate their sins or even the sins of others, and in order to come close to God through their suffering.[83] Old age was seen as a source of physical suffering and almost as a disease. This view of the declining body as a means of spiritual elevation does not imply rejection of the theory which evolved gradually from the twelfth century onwards, that soul and body, though distinct entities, were linked. There is no dichotomy between body and soul, but they are perceived as developing in opposing directions. As John Bromyard, author of an encyclopaedia for preachers, asserted in the fourteenth century. 'To the extent that old age decreases the power of youth, it increases the devotion of the soul; what is suppressed in one is elevated in the other.'[84]

Some writers placed greater emphasis on the expiation of sin, others stressed spiritual elevation. Bernardino of Siena in his sermons denounced 'bad' old men who did not submit to fate and were resentful of their old age. With sarcasm reminiscent of Petrarch's De Remediis (and using some of his images and sayings), he elaborates on the theme of human inconsistency; everyone wishes to reach old age, but nobody wishes to be old. The old man is exhorted to accept his age and the possibility of his approaching death, to gaze into his own soul and to act for its salvation. Bernardino makes no mention, in this context, of spiritual elevation. On the other hand, he lists the sins which the old man can no longer commit because of his physical ageing and the decline of his powers. Having lost his teeth, he will laugh less, gnaw less at the good name of others, talk less and lie less. The weakening of sight will relieve him of gluttony, avarice and lust. If his hearing fails, he will be less able to listen to nonsense and instead will read learned works, write, gaze in silence at the works of God – at Heaven and Earth and all they contain.[85] Whether he wishes it or not, the old body is an expiation of sin as long as he accepts his lot uncomplainingly. In *Convivio* Dante's emphasis is on spiritual elevation. He compares the last stage of life to a ship gradually drawing in its sails before entering harbour. Like other thinkers and authors of medical manuals, Dante compares the death of the old man to the ripe apple falling from the tree.[86] In medical works, the emphasis is on naturalness and lack of pain; in Dante on the end of the road, acceptance and great peace.

Those who regarded the old body as an opportunity and means of spiritual elevation ignored the theory of humours, according to which the increase of external bad humours, and the decrease of natural heat and innate radical moisture, which were the main causes of ageing, led to mental as well as physical decline and even to the development of negative traits. The compiler Vincent of Beauvais notes the two different approaches to old age and, in this case, tries to reconcile them. He writes of the good in old age, stemming mainly from the increase in wisdom and decline in passions. He also repeats the words of Saint Jerome that the Christian man has no need of physical strength. At the same time, he lists the proper regimen for preserving the health of the old, and the means of preventing whitening and loss of hair, enumerating the manifestations of mental decline in old age: absence of energy, forgetfulness, gullibility. Aware of the inherent contradiction, he proposes a solution based on acknowledgement of the individual differences between people, on dissimilarity of personality; just as passions and wantonness are not characteristic of all *adolescentes*, so also senile folly (*stultia que deliratio dicitur senium*) is not evinced in all old people.[87]

The old man was envisaged as being in poor health, weak and often suffering from bodily pain. The relations between body and soul in disease resemble those in old age, according to those who considered the weakening of the body as an opportunity and means of elevating the soul. Bernard of Clairvaux, in his *Liber de Modo Vivendi* (a manual for nuns), writes that a healthy body may promote excessive fondness for this world. On the other hand, disease, which affects the body, purges and sanctifies the soul, and is to be welcomed. It is not a punishment for sin, and should be accepted uncomplainingly. In this world God sometimes takes pity on sinners and does not spare the righteous. Not so in the next world. Moreover, God chastises those he loves (2 Corinthians 12.9–10).[88]

About a century later, Humbert of Romans wrote that disease protects the sick man from many of the sins committed by the healthy. It is like a bridle (*frenum*).[89] And Bernardino of Siena wrote, concerning the weakening of physical faculties, that it prevents the old from committing various sins. According to the view that physical suffering was an intrinsic value, disease could be regarded as a special gift of God. Old age and its attendant physical decline (and often suffering as well) are part of the human condition, but in religious writings they were also depicted as a gift which man was privileged to receive. In popular sermons, however, the gift is the longevity which the old enjoy while so many others die prematurely in childhood or youth. The religious thinkers, on the other hand, who regarded the old body as an opportunity and means of spiritual elevation, in no way linked such elevation to the condition of the body. They did not hold out the promise of health in old age as a prize for living a moral life. No one could escape the suffering of an ageing, decaying body, and physical suffering facilitated expiation of sin and spiritual elevation. The authors of *Vitae* described the saints' physical frailty and suffering in old age and their strength of spirit. As Geoffrey of Clairvaux writes concerning the last days of Bernard of Clairvaux: 'His body, as it lay on the bed, suffered various pains, but his soul was free and strong.' Despite his physical distress, he continued to contemplate and to pray, dictated, guided others and consoled them.[90] About Saint Gilbert it is recounted that 'he derived new strength from his weakness and, in return for having lost light from the body, he received the illumination he merited from the greater and more important blessing of the spirit. Although he was infirm, sick and blind, he lost none of his mental energy.'[91]

Bernardino of Siena distinguishes between 'good' and 'bad' old people. He enumerates the spiritual calamities of old age: impatience, melancholy, ignorance, gloominess, perversity or vice, stupidity and mental blindness. He adds that these spiritual calamities are mostly found in 'bad' old people (*et maxime in senibus malis*). In order to forestall the development of these traits in old age, Bernardino writes,

> man should prepare from his youth for his old age, and for the possibility that he might die at any moment, and foster within himself the positive traits which offset the negative ones. When he grows old, he must accept his ageing with love, contemplate his soul and act to redeem it. Even if he did not turn to God before growing old, there is still hope for him and he can make amends.[92]

Bernardino was by no means promising the 'good' old man exemption from bodily calamity. In a certain section of his sermon, he compares

white hair to white lilies or the whiteness of the stork, as contrasted with
the black hair of the young man, which is like coal or the colour of the
raven. And he asks: who is he whose logic and judgement are so distorted
that he does not prefer the former to the latter, if he is destined to change?
But he adds that the old man's white hair is a figurative expression of the
wisdom of old age. If we interpret the white hair literally, it symbolises the
weakness of the old man as a result of the cooling of the humours and
the excessive fluids exuded by the old body, which are white in colour.[93]

The claim that the decline and suffering of the body provide an opportunity for spiritual elevation disregards the fact that a suffering body is an
obstacle. It preoccupies and troubles like an enemy who holds the sufferer
in his grip. The fifth-century poet Maximian, in his first *Elegy*, writes 'I am
conquered by an infirm body.'[94] A description in this vein appears in
Bernard's letter to his friend Arnold of Bonnevaux. He writes about his
stomach pains, about the fact that it is difficult for him to eat and drink,
to swallow and digest even the necessary minimum, particularly solid food.
He writes about his insomnia, caused by his pains, and describes his swollen
feet. The fact that so much space is devoted to description of his physical
discomfort is in itself an admission that his body gives him no peace, and
he adds 'I must say that nothing can give me pleasure now when all has
turned into bitterness.'[95] Geoffrey of Clairvaux included the letter in the
Vita but did not repeat this sentence in his own description of the last days
of Bernard of Clairvaux, since it did not fit into the hagiographical mode.[96]

THE EVER-YOUTHFUL SOUL

Those authors who perceived the old body as a means and opportunity for
drawing close to God emphasised spiritual development and the power of
the soul. But others wrote of the youthfulness of the soul within the old
body. In these texts, the youthfulness of the soul is a consolation and a
value. It is not the old soul but the young and constantly self-renewing
soul which is good, beautiful and desirable in the eyes of God, and its
youthfulness is the outcome of its proximity to God. Sometimes the youthfulness of the soul is discussed with relation to the body; sometimes the
body is not mentioned.

Aelred of Rievaulx, like many others, writes that one should not cling
to the body and trouble to preserve its health, just as one should not
adhere to this world and to worldly goods. Those who are concerned for
their body and who invest in it too much thought and attention tend to
forget that it is not always possible to find a cure for disease, and that
inevitable death can come suddenly when man is not awaiting it. He notes
that the weakness of the body is an opportunity for spiritual elevation, but

emphasises and elaborates the idea that the soul is totally free of the cycle and the suffering which afflict the body. The soul is wondrous and is surpassed in beauty only by the Creator himself, writes Aelred. Its beauty cannot be contaminated or harmed or dimmed by old age or poverty or disease or even by death.[97]

The full elaboration of the idea of the eternal youthfulness of the soul can be found in one of the sermons of Meister Eckhart (c.1260–c.1328), on Romans 6.4: 'Therefore we are buried with him by baptism into death; that like as Christ was raised up from the dead by the glory of the Father, even so we also should walk in newness of life.' God who created *ex nihilo*, writes Eckhart, who is always and who acts always, is new. Life and newness are his domain. All that is new comes from God and there is no other source of renewal. Come close to God, therefore, writes Eckhart: 'draw near, come back, turn round to God.' All those who draw near to God will be renewed (*innovantur*), purified; they will be good and sanctified, as in Psalm 103.5: 'thy youth is renewed like the eagle.' In a life of grace, man will always renew, and renewal is life. On the other hand, those who move away from God will grow old (*veterascunt*), sin and be lost, 'for the wages of sin is death' (Romans 6.23). The soul formed in the image of God is created young. It may have grown tired and feeble in bodily existence, but it can renew and purify itself. Only the material and visible are destined to age. Eckhart does not refer to the body, nor does he perceive the old body as an opportunity and means of spiritual purification through suffering, release from passions and expiation of sin. The possibility of the renewal of the soul is a constant factor, and this renewal is not a one-time act but is repeated. If a man delves into his inner resources, detaches himself from the world and concentrates on Divine Grace, he will be renewed. Only the soul of him who draws away from God will grow old, and the further away he moves, the more it will age (*antiquatur*).[98] Whereas for a writer such as Bromyard the physical and the spiritual are interconnected,[99] Eckhart does not refer to the body at all, whether young or old. All he says is that only the material and the visible are doomed to age. The young soul is free of the bonds of age, and the old soul is a metonym for drawing away from God, for sin and loss. In addition to quoting Saint Augustine, Eckhart often quotes from the Psalms in this sermon. It may be no accident that he omitted verse 14 of Psalm 92, since it refers to the body as well: 'They shall still bring forth fruit in old age; they shall be fat and flourishing.' Although the Vulgate does not give the Latin equivalent of 'fat' (which is the correct translation of the Hebrew), but uses the word *patientes*, which may be interpreted as referring to the spirit, Eckhart did not quote this verse.[100]

The idea of renewal has also endured in Western culture, and Goethe contributed to the concept of renewal of the soul. He considered renewal to be possible only for geniuses, possessed of a kind of entelechy (the condition whereby a potentiality becomes actuality):

> As with all men of natural genius, then it will, with its animating penetration of the body, not only strengthen and ennoble the organisation, but also endeavour, with its spiritual superiority, to confer the privilege of perpetual youth. Thence it comes that in men of superior endowments, even during their old age, we constantly perceive fresh epochs of singular productiveness; they seem constantly to grow young again for a time, and that is what I call repeated puberty.

Goethe, however, was also aware of the constraints imposed by the old body, as the weakened and sick body becomes the enemy of the spirit: 'Still youth is youth; and however powerful the entelechy prove, it will never become quite master of the corporeal; and it makes a wonderful difference whether it finds in the body an ally or an adversary.'[101]

Having examined the robust images of youth and old age as embodied, one wonders whether medieval culture could ever evoke youth or age without reference to their corresponding bodies. And it is dismaying to find that, then as now, old age is depreciated unless, in some way, it can simultaneously be conceived as youthful.

NOTES

1 See A. Boureau, *Le Simple corps du roi*, Paris, 1988, pp. 43–70.
2 Hildegard of Bingen, *Patrologiae latinae cursus completus*, CXCVII, *Liber Divinorum Operum Simplicis Hominis, Scivias*, A. Führkötter and A. Carlevaris eds, Turnholt, 1978, I, Part I, Vision 4, pp. 81–2; cols 813, 899.
3 Roger Bacon, *Opus Majus*, ed. J. H. Bridge, Frankfurt/Main, 1964, II, p. 206; English translation: Roger Bacon, *Opus Majus*, trans. B. B. Burke, Philadelphia, 1928, II, p. 619.
4 Vincent of Beauvais, *Speculum Naturale*, in *Bibliotheca Mundi seu Speculum*.
5 Though according to the rulings of thirteenth century church councils, a patient who wanted to see a physician had first to call a priest, since the soul was considered more precious than the body. At the same time a priest was often called 'physician of the soul', and in writings on penitence there is much use of medical metaphors; see J. D. Mansi, *Sacrorum Conciliorum Nova et Amplissima Collectio*, repr. Graz, 1961, XXII, C. 22, cols 1110–11; *Les Status synodaux francais du XIIIᵉ siècle*, ed. O. Pontal, Paris, 1971, I, pp. 184, 190, 191 and note 7; *Councils and Synods with other Documents relating to the English Church*, ed. M. Powicke, Oxford, 1964, II part 1, pp. 173, 705, part 2, pp. 1060–1; Humbert de Romans, *Sermones*, Venice, 1603, Sermo 66, pp. 65–6; Arnaldus de Villanova, *De Regimine Sanitatis*, in *Opera Omnia*, Basel, 1585, col. 838; John of Salisbury, *Policraticus*, ed. C. C. Webb, repr., Frankfurt, 1965, II, lib. 2, c. 29, p. 168. The fourteenth-century learned surgeon Henry of Mondeville implied that the surgeon's profession was more important than that of the priest. See M.-C. Pouchelle, *The Body and Surgery in the Middle Ages*, trans. R. Morris, Oxford, 1990, p. 46; there was also a biting criticism of physicians (just as of other professionals) which suggests that the medical profession was already well established. See for example the thirteenth-century text *La Bible de Guiot*, in C. Langlois, *La Vie en France au Moyen Age d'après quelques moralistes du temps*, Paris, 1907, pp. 67–8.
6 See for example Arnaldus de Villanova, *De Regimine Sanitatis*, cols 669–73, 819; Vincent of Beauvais, *Speculum Naturale*, lib. 31, c. 87, cols 2361–2.

7 See L. Demaitre, 'The Care and extension of old age in medieval medicine', in *Aging and the Aged in Medieval Europe*, ed. M. M. Sheehan, Toronto, 1990, pp. 3–22.

8 Roger Bacon, *Opus Majus*, II, p. 206; translation: II, p. 619; see also Roger Bacon, *De Retardatione Accidentium Senectutis cum aliis opusculis de Rebus Medicinalibus*, eds. A. G. Little and E. Withington, British Society of Franciscan Studies 14, Oxford, 1928, pp. 9, 29, 31, 80; there is a long discussion about the question whether human life was shortened after the Deluge because of divine intervention or due to natural causes in Engelbert of Admont (1250–133) *Liber de causis longevitatis hominum ante diluvium*, in *Thesaurus anecdotorum Novissimus*, ed. B. Pez, Augsburg, 1721, I, cols 439–502; the author finally attributes it to natural causes, mainly to the increased foulness of the air; Roger Bacon also attributed the regression in life expectancy to the foulness of the air, and also to neglect of the right regimen of health and to bad morals; Roger Bacon, *Opus Majus*, II, pp. 2205–6; trans. p. 618.

9 Aristotle, *Politica* 7.9; *Rhetorica* 2.12–14.

10 *Honorii Augustodunensis de Philosophia Mundi Libri quatuor*, PL, CLXXII, L, 4, C. 36, col. 99; Vincent of Beauvais, *Speculum Naturale*, lib. 31, c. 87, col. 2360; *Arnaldus de Villanova, De Regimine Sanitatis*, col. 372; Albertus Magnus, *Parva Naturalia. De Aetate sive de Juventute et Senectute*, in *Opera Omnia*, ed. A. Borgent, Pairs, 1890, IX, Tractatus 1, c. 6; G. Zerbi, *Gerontomacia: On the Care of the Aged and Maximianus' Elegies on Love and Old Age*, trans. L. R. Lind, Philadelphia, 1988, c. 1, pp. 30–1.

11 Roger Bacon, *De Retardatione*, pp. 9, 71, 178; Arnaldus de Villanova, *De Regimine Sanitatis*, cols 819, 821; Bernard de Gordon, *De conservatione Vitae Humanae seu de Regimine Sanitatis*, Leipzig, 1570, p. 121; see also Pouchelle, *Body and Surgery*, p. 65.

12 *Anthologie poétique française. Moyen Age*, ed. A. Mary, Paris, 1967, II, p. 217; an example of the scientific explanation of the injury caused to old people who do not avoid sexual relations: Albertus Magnus, *Parva Naturalia. De Morte et de Vita*, Tractatus 2, c. 8, p. 365; Arnaldus de Villanova, *De Regimine Sonitatis*, cols 823–4.

13 As Pierre Bersuire in the fourteenth century, for example, writes: 'Senes enim deficiunt in caloribus, et in spiritibus vitalibus, quae sunt causa dilatationis cordis et laetitiae, et ideo propter frigiditatem constringentem necesse est quod faciliter irascantur.' (Petrus Berthorius, *Dictionarium*, in *Opera Omnia*, Cologne, 1730, pars III, p. 86.)

14 Albertus Magnus, *Parva Naturalia. De Morte et Vita*, Tractatus 2, c. 12, p. 370.

15 Eustache Deschamps, *Ballade sur la vieillese*, in *Oeuvres complètes*, ed. Le Marquis de Queux de Saint-Hilaire, Paris, 1878, II, line 16, p. 131.

16 Albertus Magnus, *Parva Naturalia. De Morte et de Vita*, Tractatus 2, c. 7, p. 363; Vincent of Beauvais, *Speculum Naturale*, lib. 31, c. 87, col. 2360; Gabriele Zerbi, *Gerontomacia*, c. 56, p. 305; on the sources of the lamp metaphor and its uses, see P. H. Niebyl, 'Old age, fever, and the lamp metaphor', *Journal of the History of Medicine and Allied Sciences*, XXVI, 1971, pp. 351–68; the apple metaphor was adopted by authors of didactic, moralistic and philosophical works as well. See Dante, *Convivio in Le Opere di Dante*, ed. M. Barbi, Florence, 1921, c. 4, p. 28; *Francisci Petrarchae de Remediis utriusque Fortune*, Rotterdam, 1649, lib. 2, p. 563; this highly popular work was translated into English in the sixteenth century; *Phisick against Fortune by Francis Petrarch. Englished by Thomas Twyne*, London, 1572, f. 266v; Bernardino of Siena, Sermon 16, in *Opera Omnia*, eds Collegii S. Bonaventurae, Florence, 1959, VII, p. 262. Cf. the question posed by Vincent of Beauvais, 'Quid enim est senectus? Optatum malum, mors viventium, incolumis languor, spirans mors', *Speculum Naturale*, lib. 31, c. 88, col. 2361; and Jean Améry, *Du Vieillissement. Révolte et résignation*, trans. A. Yaiche, Paris, 1991, p. 181.

17 Also in modern gerontological research the ageing of men has received more study than that of women. See R. Barnet and G. Baruch, 'Women in the middle years: conceptions and misconceptions', in *Psychology of Women: Selected Readings*, ed. G. H. Williams, New York, 1979, pp. 479–87; S. Reinharz, 'Friends or Foes: Gerontological and feminist theory', in *Radical Voices*, eds R. D. Klein and D. L. Steinberg, New York, 1989, pp. 222–39.

18 It was not only woman's menstrual blood that was considered impure and harmful. According to both medical and popular conceptions the foetus in its mother's womb was nourished by her menstrual blood, which was not eliminated from her body during her pregnancy. The blood that served as nourishment for the foetus was thus also considered impure. According to Innocent III the menstrual blood of a woman which does not flow during her pregnancy is so vile and impure that its touch can cause a tree to wither, grass to shrivel, and the loss of fruit. Dogs which licked it would suffer from rabies, and a child conceived as a result of intercourse with a menstruating woman would be born a leper. See *Lotharii Cardinalis (Innocent III) De Miseria Humanae Conditionis*, ed. M. Maccarrone, Lugano, 1955, lib. 1, c. 4, pp. 11–12; in the *responsa* of the academic physicians of Salerno it was stated that the infant was incapable of standing, sitting, walking and talking immediately after birth because, unlike the animals, it was nurtured in its mother's womb on menstrual blood from which it was not easily cleansed, whilst animals were nurtured in the womb on purer food; *The Prose Salernitan Questions*, ed. B. Lawn, Oxford, 1979, Q. 228, p. 155; see also Bartholomaeus Anglicus, (*Lotharii De Miseria Humanae Conditionis*, lib. 6, c. 4), and *Summa de Magister Rufinus*, ed. H. Singer, Aalen, 1963, p. 16.

19 *De Secretis mulierum* in *Les Admirables Secrets de Magie du Grand et du Petit Albert*, cited in D. Jacquart and C. Thomasset, *Sexuality and Medicine in the Middle Ages*, trans. M. Adamson, Oxford, 1988, p. 75; on attitudes towards the menopause in non-Western cultures, see J. Griffen, 'A cross-cultural investigation of behavioral changes at menopause', in *Psychology of Women: Selected Readings*, ed. J. H. Williams, New York, 1979, pp. 488–95; in contemporary Western society, V. Skultans, 'The symbolic significance of menstruation and the menopause', *ibid.*, pp. 115–28; by the end of the fifteenth century when *fascinatio* (the process by which certain persons harmed others with the power of their sight) was brought into the academic medical domain, women were thought to acquire the power to fascinate in their natural process of ageing. The theory was developed by Diego Alvarez Chanca (*Tractatus de Fascinatione*, 1949) and by Antonio de Cartagena (*Libellus de Fascinatione*, 1529); according to these writers the actions of the old women were not controlled by will, but could be much worse if accompanied by bad intentions. The whole discourse in both treatises is based on the potential or actual venomousness of women's bodies, both while menstruating and after the cease of menses; however, old women whose menses had ceased, and thus always carried menstrual blood in their bodies, were considered especially prone to fascinate; their victims were generally children: F. Salmon and M. Cabré, 'Fascinating women: the evil eye in medical scholasticism', paper presented at the Barcelona Conference, Cambridge, September 1992 (forthcoming).

20 See on this M. Kriegel, 'Un Traité de psychologie sociale dans les pays mediterranéens du bas moyen age', *Annales*, XXXI, 1975, pp. 326–330.

21 Bernardino of Siena, *ibid.*, Sermon 16.7, pp. 254–6.

22 G. R. Owst, *Preaching in Medieval England*, Cambridge, 1926, p. 342.

23 Innocent III, *De Miseria*, lib. 1, c. 10, p. 16.

24 Petrarch, *De Remediis*, lib. 1, pp. 18 ff.; *Phisick against Fortune*, fol. 3v.

25 G. F. Jones, 'The signs of old age in Oswald von Wolkenstein's "Ich sich und hör"', *Modern Language Notes*, LXXXIV, 1974, pp. 767–87. Cf. G. Améry, *Du Vieillissment*, pp. 85, 190; see also Simone de Beauvoir, *The Woman Destroyed*, trans. P. O. Brian, London, 1984, p. 17.

26 Petrarch, *De Remediis*, lib. 2, pp. 597–9; *Phisick against Nature* fols. 284v–285v; Bernardino of Siena borrowed this passage from Petrarch.

27 Petrarch, *De Remediis*, lib. 2, pp. 94–95, 353, 564–6; *Phisick against Nature*, fols. 162r, 267r–268v.

28 Gerald of Wales, *Gemma Ecclesiastica*, ed. J. Brewer, Rolls Series XXIb, London, 1862, p. 182; translation: Gerald of Wales, *The Jewel of the Church*, trans. J. J. Hagen, Leiden, 1979, pp. 141–2.

29 Philippe de Novare, *Les Quatre Ages de l'Homme*, ed. M. de Fréville, Paris, 1888, p. 90; *Les Enseignements d'Anne de France à sa Fille Suzanne*, in A. A. Hentsch, *La Littérature didactique*

au Moyen Age s'adressant spécialement aux Femmes, repr., Geneva, 1975, p. 204; M. Laigle, *Le Livre de Trois Vertus de Christine de Pizan et son milieu historique et littéraire*, Paris, 1912, pp. 351–2. In popular medical texts it is often mentioned that the size of the womb of elderly women differed from that of young ones, as did those of more ardent women from those of less ardent ones; there were also writers who described the womb as a 'wild animal' circulating in the female body, with properties and desires of its own; see on this R. Barkaï, *Les Infortunes de Dinah ou la Gynécologie juive au Moyen Age*, Paris, 1991, p. 41 and note 20.

30 See on this D. J. Levinson, *The Seasons of Man's Life*, New York, 1979, p. 211.

31 *Aucassin et Nicolette. Chantefable du XIIIe siècle*, ed. M. Roques, Paris, 1954, p. 6; translation: *Aucassin and Nicolette*, trans. A. Lang, London, 1905, p. 13.

32 See, for example, Eustache Deschamps, *Adieux à la Jeunesse*, I, p. 250; *The Sermons of Thomas Brinton*, ed. M. A. Devlin, London, 1954, II, p. 286.

33 Cited in J. A. Burrow, *The Ages of Man*, Oxford, 1986, pp. 30–1; for other translations of this text, see, *Three Prose Versions of the Secretorum Secretorum*, ed. R.R. Steele, EETS ES 74, London, 1898.

34 William of Deguileville, *Le Pèlerinage de la Vie humaine*, ed. J. J. Stürzinger, London, 1893, especially pp. 229, 252–3, 255, 374, 407, 414.

35 Francesco Petrarca, *Trionfo della Morte*, in *Canzoniere, Trionfi, Rime varie E una scelta di versi Latini*, ed. G. Einandi, Rome, 1958, pp. 54–5; translation: Petrarch, *The Triumph of Death*, in *The Triumphs of Petrarch*, trans. E. H. Wilkins, Chicago, 1962, I, p. 54; G. Minois, *Histoire de la Vieillesse en Occident I: De l'Antiquité à la Renaissance*, Paris, 1987, p. 243; on the role of the masks: J. Delumeau, *La Peur en Occident XIVe–XVIIIe siècles*, Paris, 1978, p. 11.

36 Guillaume de Lorris et Jean de Meun, *Le Roman de la Rose*, ed. F. Lecoy, Paris, 1968, I, lines 338–60, 378–400, pp. 11–13; translation: *The Romance of the Rose by Guillaume de Lorris and Jean de Meun*, trans. Ch. W. Robbins, New York, 1962, pp. 9–10; on the loss of woman's beauty in old age, see also Conon de Béthune, *La Vieille amoureuse*, in *Anthologie poétique française*, I, *Moyen Age*, ed. A. Mary, Paris, 1967, pp. 216–18; *Le Roman de la Rose*, II, lines 14419–26; trans., p. 218; Geoffrey Chaucer, *The Canterbury Tales*, ed. W. W. Skeat, repr., London, 1947, pp. 31–322; see also Eustache Deschamps, *De la Demande d'une Vielle*, VI, pp. 224–5.

37 On the influence of classical literature and the borrowings from classical authors who wrote about old age see G. R. Coffman, 'Old age from Horace to Chaucer: some literary affinities and adventures of an idea', *Speculum*, IX, 1934, pp. 249–77; G. Zerbi, *Gerontocomia: On the Care of the Aged and Maximianus' Elegies on Old Age and Love*, trans. L. R. Lind, Philadelphia, 1988, pp. 309–18; in his first Elegy, after describing the beautiful girls he knew in his youth Maximian adds 'To mention these features once sought for is shameful for old men, and that which once was quite proper is now a sin.' *Ibid.*, lines 101–2, p. 321.

38 See for example Vincent of Beauvais, *Speculum Naturale*, lib. 31, c. 88; on the weakening of the libido and the changes it undergoes in old age according to psychoanalytical theory, see P. L. Assoun, 'Le Vieillissement saisi par la psychanalyse', *Communications*, XXXVII, 1983, pp. 167–79.

39 Philippe de Novare, *Les Quatres Ages de l'Homme*, p. 95.

40 M. Laigle, *Le Livre de Trois Vertus*, pp. 352–3.

41 On the *senex amans*, Petrarch, *De Remediis*, L. 1, pp. 220–1; *Phisick against Fortune*, f. 100v; *Les Quinze Joies de Mariage*, ed. J. Rychner, Paris, 1963, pp. 101–2; the story about January and May in The Merchant's Tale, Geoffrey Chaucer, *The Canterbury Tales*, pp. 391–417; see also the prologue of the Reeve's Tale, *ibid.*, pp. 100–1; on the resentment of young males towards old men marrying young girls, see D. Herlihy and C. Klapisch, *Les Toscans et leur Familles. Etude du Catasto florentin de 1427*, Paris, 1978, p. 607.

42 On the *charivari*, *Le Charivari*, eds J. Le Goff et J.-C. Schmitt, Paris, 1981.

43 *Le Roman de la Rose*, II, pp. 137–92; translation, pp. 258–307; *The Early English version of the Gesta Romanorum*, ed. S. T. Herrtage, London, 1879, Appendix XXVIII, p. 516; *Les Lamentations de Mathieu*, in C. Langlois, *La Vie en France au Moyen Age d'après quelques*

moralistes du temps, Paris, 1908, p. 250; see also A. K. Nitecki, 'Figures of old age, in fourteenth century English literature', in *Aging and the Aged in Medieval Europe*, ed. M. M. Sheehan, Toronto, 1990, pp. 1–116; *A Handbook of Medieval Religious Tales*, ed. F. C. Tubach, F. F. Communications, 204, Helsinki, 1981, 1552, 1553.

44 *Halldor Snorrarson*, in *Hrafnkel's Saga and other Stories*, trans. H. Pálsson, London, 1983, p. 120.

45 Jean Régnier, *Ballade de la Vieillesse*, in *Anthologie poétique française*, II, p. 205.

46 A. Planche, 'Le Corps en vieillesse. Regard sur la poésie du moyen-âge tardif', *Razo*, IV, 1984, p. 54.

47 Eustache Deschamps, *Regrets d'un Vieillard*, in *Œuvres complètes*, VI, pp. 225–30; see also Oswald von Wolkenstein's song written in the first person, note 27 above.

48 Leon Battista Alberti, *I Libri della Famiglia. The Family in Renaissance Florence*, trans. R. N. Watkins, New York, 1969.

49 *The Poems of Robert Henryson*, ed. D. Fox, Oxford, 1981, pp. 165–7; the title 'The Praise of Age' was given only in the eighteenth century; see pp. 449–52.

50 See J. Le Goff, 'Corps et idéologie dans l'Occident médiéval', in *l'Imaginaire médiéval*, Paris, 1985, pp. 123–48; Aelred of Rievalux, *Speculum Caritatis*, in *Aelredi Rievalensis Opera Omnia*, eds A. Hoste and C. H. Talbot, Corpus Christianorum Continuatio Medievalis, Turnhout, 1971, lib. 3, c. 19, p. 126; Vincent of Beauvais, *Speculum Naturale*, L. 31, C. 86, cols 2359 60.

51 See, for example, Tintoretto's *The Creation of the Animals* in the Galleria dell' Academia, Venice, and of course Michelangelo's *The Creation of Adam* in the Sistine Chapel; there are also painting of God the Father by Masaccio, Titian, Filippino Lippi, Raphael, Lucas Cranach, Cosimo Rosselli and some others; there were also statutes and paintings of 'The Throne of Grace', the seated Father sustaining the corpse of the Son; see L. Steinberg, *The Sexuality of Christ in Renaissance Art and in Modern Oblivion*, London, 1984, figs. 243–5; on the emergence of individual portraits of old males in Renaissance art, see G. Mino's, *Histoire de la Vieillesse*, pp. 336–7, 395–6.

52 Aelred of Rievalulx, *In annuntiatione Beate Marie de Tribus Tunicis Ioseph*, in *Sermones inediti B. Aelredi Abbatis Rievallensis*, ed. C. H. Talbot, Rome, 1952, p. 84.

53 *Le Héraut de l'Amour divin. Revelations de Sainte Gertrude*, trans. Pères benedictins de Solesmes, Paris–Poitiers, 1898, lib. 3, c. 15, p. 175; *Le Livre de l'Experience des Vrais Fidèles par Sainte Angèle de Foligno*, ed. and trans. J. Ferré and L. Baudry, Paris, 1927, p. 62.

54 L. Steinberg, *The Sexuality of Christ*; C. Walker Bynum, 'The Body of Christ in the later Middle Ages: A Reply to Leo Steinberg', in *Fragmentation and Redemption. Essays on Gender and the Human Body in Medieval Religion*, New York, 1991, pp. 79–117.

55 Examples of representations of the *Pietà* as a young woman, A Kutal, *Gothic Art in Bohemia and Moravia*, London, 1971, figs. 65, 128, 131; G. Ring, *A Century of French Painting 1400–1500*, London, 1949, plate 13.

56 *Le Roman de Sidrach*, in C. Langlois, *La Connaissance de la nature du Monde au Moyen Age d'après quelques écrits français à l'usage de Laïcs*, Paris, 1911, pp. 257–8.

57 St Augustine, *De Civitate Dei*, Corpus Christianorum Series Latina, 48, Turnhout, 1955, lib. 22, c. 15, p. 834.

58 See, for example, Albertus Magnus, *De Resurrectione*, in *Opera Omnia*, ed. W. Kübel, Aschendorff, Münster, Westf., 1958, XXVI, tractatus 2, Q. 6, p. 264; Petrus Lombardus, *Sententiae in IV Libros Distinctae*, eds Collegium S. Bonaventurae a Claras Aquas, Rome, 1981, L. 4, D. 44, pp. 516–19; *Lollard Sermons*, ed. G. Cigman, EETS, London, 1989, pp. 110, 238; on the Waldensians' belief in the resurrection in the bodies of thirty-three year olds, *Registre de l'Inquisition de Jacques Fournier (1318–25)*, ed. J. Duvernoy, Toulouse, 1965, I, p. 88; an example from popular didactic literature in the vernacular, Peter of Abernon, *La Lumière as Laïs*, in C. Langlois, *La Vie spirituelle. Enseignements, meditations et controverses*, Paris, 1928, p. 112.

59 See on this Burrow, *The Ages of Man*, pp. 95–134.

60 St Augustine, *Retractationum Libri II*, Corpus Christianorum Series Latina, Turnhout, 1984, I, c. 26, p. 80.

61 See S. Shahar, *Childhood in the Middle Ages*, London, 1990, pp. 15–16; Burrow, *Ages of Man*, pp. 137–42; on the boy–old man *topos* in classical literature and in the myths of certain religions, see E. R. Curtius, *European Literature and the Latin Middle Ages*, trans. W. R. Trask, New York, 1952, pp. 98–105. See also Bernard of Clairvaux, *De moribus et Officio Episcoporum seu Epistola XLII, PL*, CLXXXII, C. 7, cols 826–7; John of Salisbury, *Policraticus*, ed. C. C. Webb, London, 1.1, L. 5, C. 9, p. 321; translation, J. Dickinson, *The Statesman's Book of John of Salisbury*, New York, 1963, pp. 111–12; and Thomas Aquinas, *Summa Theologiae*, 3a, 9. 72, art. 8, Blackfriars, London, 1974, LVII, pp. 214–15; and according to Pierre Bersuire (fourteenth century): 'Sic vero moraliter possible est, quod homo sit iuvenis corpore, canus tamen, senex, prudens et maturus sit in mente.' (Petrus Berthorius, *Dictionarium*, in *Opera Omnia*, Cologne, 1730, pars 3, p. 86.)
62 An example from a compilation of commentaries on the Bible, *Walafridi Strabi Fuldensis Monachi Glossa Ordinaria, PL*, CXIII, col. 1311; from a popular didactic text, *The Book of Vices and Virtues. A fourteenth century English Translation of the Somme le Roi of Lorrens of Orléans*, ed. W. N. Francis, EETS 217, London, 1942, p. 287; see also Burrow, *Ages of Man*, pp. 141–62.
63 *Acta Sanctorum*, eds J. Bollandus and G. H. Henschenius, Paris–Rome, 1836–1940, March I, pp. 553, 574; March III, p. 193; *Liber Exemplorum ad usum Praedicantium*, ed. A. Little, British Society of Franciscan Studies, Aberdeen, 1908, p. 107; *Magna Vita Sancti Hugonis*, ed. and trans. D. Douie and H. Farmer, Nelson Series, London, 1961, I, p. 219.
64 *Carmen ad Robertum Regem*, ed. and trans. C. Carozzi, Paris, 1979, p. 2.
65 *La Chanson de Guillaume* ed. D. McMillan, Paris, 1949, I, lines 1436–43, p. 61.
66 *Acta Sanctorum*, April III, p. 870.
67 Curtius, *European Literature*, pp. 101–5.
68 See G. Gruman, *A History of Ideas about the Prolongation of Life*, Transactions of the American Philosophical Society, LVI, 9, Philadelphia, 1966.
69 Roger Bacon, *De Retardatione Accidentium Senectutis*, and his *Opus Majus*, II, pp. 207–13; translation, II, pp. 619–26; the treatise *Liber de Conservatione Juventutis et Retardatione Senectutis* was attributed to Arnold of Villanova; on the question to what extent Arnold of Villanova (or some other author) copied from Bacon's treatise see Roger Bacon, *De Retardatione*, pp. xlii–xliii; Arnold also inserted a number of chapters on the subject in his *De Regimine Sanitatis*, cols 817–35.
70 Roger Bacon, *De Retardatione*, pp. 10, 80; *Opus Majus*, II, p. 206, translation, II, p. 619.
71 Arnold of Villanova, *De Regimine Sanitatis*, cols 819, 825.
72 Roger Bacon, *De Retardatione*, II, pp. 205–6.
73 *Ibid.*, p. 3.
74 Arnold of Villanova in his chapter entitled 'Wine in which gold has been quenched' in his *Book on Wine* explains how to prepare potable gold; see *The Earliest Printed Book on Wine by Arnold of Villanova*, trans. H. E. Sigerist, with facsimile of the original German edition of 1478, New York, 1945, pp. 36–7.
75 N. Benoit-Lapierre, 'Guérir de Vieillesse', *Communication*, XXXVII, 1983, p. 15.
76 *Les Chansons de Guillaume IX, Duc d'Aquitaine 1071–1127*, ed. A. Jeanroy, Paris, 1913, lines 34–6, p. 23.
77 See on this Gruman, *History of Ideas*, pp. 24–8, G. Minois, *Histoire de la Vieillesse*, p. 205. Simone de Beauvoir, *La Vieillesse*, Paris, 1970, I, pp. 157, 219–20.
78 *Mandeville's Travels*, ed. P. Hamelius, EETS 153, London, 1919, p. 113.
79 *La Queste del Saint Graal*, ed. A. Pauphilet, Paris, 1923, pp. 82–7, 262–3.
80 Thomas Aquinas, *Summa Theologiae*, 2a, 2ae, Q. 164, art. 1, Blackfriars, London, 1971, XLIV, pp. 172–3.
81 See, for example, Innocent III, *De Miseria*, L. I, C. 20, pp. 28–9; Bernard of Cluny, *De Contemptu Mundi*, ed. H. C. Hoskier, London, 1929; Alan of Lille, *Summa de Arte Praedicatoria, PL*, vols 116–17 (in his *Anticlaudianus*, however, there is, to use the phrase of E. R. Curtius, a kind of 'optimistic naturalism'; E. R. Curtius, *European Literature*, pp. 117–22, 198); Bernard of Clairvaux, *Liber de Diligendo Deo, PL*, CLXXXII, C. 11, col. 993. See

also C. Walker Bynum, 'The body of Christ in the later Middle Ages: a reply to Leo Steinberg', in *Fragmentation and Redemption. Essays on Gender and the Human Body in Medieval Religion*, New York, 1991, pp. 79–117.

82 John Bromyard, *Summa Praedicantium*, Antwerp, 1614, pars 2, c. 5, p. 354; Vincent of Beauvais, *Speculum Naturale*, lib. 31, c. 87, col. 2360; he sees in old age an opportunity to aspire to salvation also due to greater wisdom and decline of desires that are not linked to the body, like greed and lust for honours and power.

83 See on this C. Walker Bynum, 'The female body and religious practice in the later Middle Ages', in *Fragments for a History of the Human Body*, ed. M. Feher, New York, 1989, I, p. 166.

84 'Ut quantum senectus a iuvenili vigore distrahit, hoc maior mentis devotio suppleat, et quod ille qui in uno gravatur, in alio sublevetur' John Bromyard, *Summa Praedicantium*, pars 2, c. 5, p. 355.

85 Bernardino of Siena, Sermon 16, in *Opera Omnia*, eds Collegii S. Bonaventurae, Florence, 1959, VII, pp. 253, 256–62.

86 Dante, *Convivio* in *Le Opere di Dante*, ed. M. Barbi, Florence, 1921, c. 4, p. 28; on the ripe apple metaphor, see note 17.

87 Vincent of Beauvais, *Speculum Naturale*, lib. 31, c. 89–90, cols 2359–61.

88 Bernard of Clairvaux, *Liber de Modo Bene Vivendi*, PL, CLXXXIV, C. 43, cols 1264–5.

89 Humbert de Romans, *Sermones*, Venice, 1603, Sermon 92, pp. 91–2.

90 *Vita Prima auctore Gaufrido*, PL, CLXXXV, lib. 5, c. 1, cols 351–5; see also William of St Thierry, *Vita Prima*, col. 225.

91 *The Book of St Gilbert*, ed. and trans. R. Foreville and G. Keir, Oxford, 1987, c. 27, pp. 86–9; see also *The Life of St Anselm Archbishop of Canterbury by Eadmer*, ed. and trans. R. W. Southern, Nelson Series, London, 1962, p. 141.

92 Bernardino of Siena, Sermon 16, p. 258.

93 *Ibid.*

94 G. Zerbi, *Gerontomacia: On the Care of the Aged and Maximianus' Elegies on Old Age and Love*, trans. L. R. Lind, Philadelphia, 1988, Elegy 1, line 257, p. 325.

95 'Quae enim voluptas ubi sibi totum vindicat amaritudo?' (Bernard of Clairvaux, *Epistola* 310, PL, CLXXXII, col. 514.

96 *Vita Prima auctore Gaufrido*, PL, CLXXXV, lib. 5, c. 2, col. 357; on the development of more individual *Vitae* see A. M. Kleinberg, *Prophets in their own Country. Living Saints and the Making of Sainthood in the Later Middle Ages*, Chicago, 1992, pp. 25–6.

97 Aelred of Rievaulx, *Speculum Caritatis*, in *Opera Omnia*, eds A. Hoste and C. H. Talbot, Corpus Christianorum Continuatio Medievalis, Turnhout, 1971, lib. 1, pp. 40–3.

98 Meister Eckhart, *In Novitate Ambulamus*, in *Die Deutschen und lateinischen Werke*, eds E. Benz, B. Decker and J. Koch, Stuttgart, 1956, IV, Sermo 15[2], pp. 145–54, especially pp. 149–50.

99 John Bromyard, *Summa Praedicantium*, pars 1, c. 3, p. 5; pars 2, c. 5, p. 356.

100 'Multiplicabantur in senecta uberi et bene patientes erunt ut annuncient.' Pierre Bersuire, describing the lot of the righteous old person, cites this verse (Petrus Berthorius, *Dictionarium*, in *Opera Omnia*, Cologne, 1730, pars 3, p. 86).

101 J. P. Eckerman, *Conversations with Goethe*, trans. J. Oxenford, London, 1930, repr. 1971, pp. 249–50.

The body in some Middle High German *Mären*: taming and maiming

I

A young and beautiful wife devises a stratagem to see her lover, the village priest. When she and her husband are in bed he is to steal into the house and announce himself by tugging on a rope which she has tied round her toes; at this signal she will creep out of the bedchamber and go to him. The plan goes awry when the husband wakes up in the night, discovers the rope and, sensing that his wife is up to no good, ties it round his own foot. He catches the priest after a struggle, and hands him over to his wife while he fetches a light to see who the nocturnal 'thief' is; she swiftly seizes the opportunity to dispose of her lover, substituting an ass in his place. Enraged, the husband throws her out on to the street. There she meets an old woman whom she bribes to take her place outside the house while she pays a visit to the priest. Aggravated by what he thinks is his wife's wailing, the husband cuts off the old woman's pigtails. The following day, in the presence of his kinsfolk, he accuses his wife of adultery and produces the grey hair to prove it. Since her hair, which is fair, is unharmed, the family believe her story, that she is the innocent object of persecution by her insane and unfaithful husband. The husband is made to suffer a painful exorcism of his evil spirits. Thus tamed, he never dares to challenge his wife again.

This, in outline, is the story of the priest and the rope (*Der Pfaffe mit der Schnur*). Its three versions[1] belong to the genre *Märe*, and its themes, cheating, cunning, sex, are fairly typical of these fabliau-like narratives in verse. They formed part of a European tradition, and were cultivated in Germany from the early thirteenth century to the beginning of the sixteenth. Yet in spite of their contents and their popularity the *Mären* were never literature of the people. They remained a literary form whose public was originally to be found among the nobility and higher clergy, though from the later fourteenth century the audience became increasingly urban.[2] One of the reasons why *Mären* have been considered to be popular literature is, doubtless, their representation of the human body, which certainly has affinities with the 'grotesque image of the body' and the

'material bodily lower stratum' famously identified by Bakhtin as key elements in folk culture.[3] However, it is not my intention in this essay to
reopen the debate about whether the *Mären* are popular; the literariness
of the genre has in any case been firmly established.[4] Rather my aim is to
examine the body in several *Mären* as a literary representation, and to relate
this representation, or bodily style, to the social experience of men with
power and influence, one of the groups in late medieval society where one
would expect to find literary activity.[5] More specifically I shall argue that
the bodily style of the *Mären* is a code by which men at the centre express
their perception of women on the social periphery.

The narrative of *Pfaffe* has three phases, from body to sign to body
again. The first begins with the lovers' stratagem to have sex, continues
with the physical struggle that follows when the priest, mistaking the
husband for his lover in the dark, makes to embrace him, and ends with
the victorious husband literally holding the body of the 'thief'. Throughout this phase, bodies couple, or desire to couple, in love-making and in
wrestling. The second phase narrates a pair of substitutions, ass for lover,
old woman's hair for wife's hair. That we are dealing with the substitution
of signs is clear from the words used for the pigtails when they are produced by the husband in evidence against his wife; *warzeichen* (A l. 386)
and *wortzeichen* (B l. 143, C l. 132) are here technical terms of the language
of law for what forensic rhetoric calls a *signum*, a material index of guilt
or innocence.[6] The substitution of one for another means that the innocent husband is incriminated by the signs with which he hoped to incriminate his guilty wife; she exploits to the full the incident with the ass and
the implications of another woman's hair in order to convince her kinsfolk
of her husband's madness, which has supposedly afflicted him for four (A
ll. 299, 355) or five (C l. 121) years, and to insinuate that he is the one
who is committing adultery. The third and final phase, the exorcism,
returns to the corporeal. Aided by her family the wife ties up her husband
in a kneading-trough, has him loaded on to a cart and wheeled screaming
to church; there his hair is shorn, he is drenched with holy water to the
point of drowning, and his head is burned with incense until the evil
spirits have been driven out of him.[7]

In fact the story does not stray far from the body even in its second
phase. The signs are bodies or parts of the body, and what they signify is
a bodily act or condition. The priest and the wife's hair, if the husband
had been able to produce them, would have been indices of adultery, an
illicit bodily union; the ass and the pigtails which, the wife argues, her
deluded husband has mistaken for her lover and her own hair, point to
madness, the possession of the body by evil spirits. Bodily acts and bodily
conditions are literally embodied in these signs. Moreover, it is noticeable
that the first phase of the story is concerned with the body in private,

whereas the third is about the body in public; the tale begins with the secret assignation of the lovers in a private place, the wife's house, at night, and ends with a ceremony witnessed by the community in a public place by day, the exorcism in church (AC; in B the priest is called to the house). Between the secret acts of the body and its communally sanctioned and institutionally enforced discipline come the signs, which encode the former and, once decoded, authorise the latter. The tale, therefore, moves from body to sign and back in order to demonstrate the effectiveness of symbols in transforming the private life of the body into an object of social control. Through the meanings they imply the signs map bodies on to the prevalent notions of what is licit or illicit, healthy or pathological. Since an illicit use of the body, such as adultery, or a pathological state, such as spirit possession, removes the body from normal social control, the signs of these acts and conditions are at the same time indices of the degree of social control over the body, bringing to light those bodies where discipline needs to be brought to bear.

The problem, and the source of the comedy, is that because the wrong signs are interpreted in the right way, the wrong body is disciplined. The original, and true, secret of the body (the wife is having an affair) is supplanted by a secondary and false one (the husband is mad) which, thanks to the general belief in the compelling nature of forensic *signa*, is accepted by everyone as bodily truth. The consequences are felt by the husband in his very body. The macabre humour of the tale of the priest and the rope demonstrates that the fate of bodies in society is determined not by factual truth, but by what the social group believes to be the truth of the body. This received truth is an effect of signification. But signs can be manipulated, as the story of their substitution shows. Precisely because they can speak false as well as true, but either way will be believed, how signs are used or abused becomes all-important.

Husband and wife confront each other as sign-users with the aim of having their bodily affairs settled in public; the husband hopes that his *warzeichen* will show his wife for the adulteress she is (B ll. 133–8, C ll. 112–13), even get him a separation (A l. 374), while she exploits the signs in order to have him tamed. The confrontation points to a broader gender division in the story: the fixity of the husband contrasts with the mobility of the wife. She moves about from one place to another, and from one man to another; she moves bodies round, substituting one for another. By contrast, her husband's sphere of action is confined to the house, and when he does leave it, bound tight in the trough, he is no longer a free agent; he does not cause anything to move round, but is left holding whatever comes into his hands. The contrast between fixity and mobility acquires nuance if we relate it to the distinction made by de Certeau between strategy and tactic:

I call a 'strategy' the calculus of force-relationships which becomes possible when a subject of will and power (a proprietor, an enterprise, a city, a scientific institution) can be isolated from an 'environment'. A strategy assumes a place that can be circumscribed as *proper* (*propre*) and thus serve as the basis for generating relations with an exterior distinct from it (competitors, adversaries, 'clienteles', 'targets', or 'objects' of research). Political, economic, and scientific rationality has been constructed on this strategic model. I call a 'tactic', on the other hand, a calculus which cannot count on a 'proper' (a spatial or institutional localization), nor thus on a borderline distinguishing the other as a visible totality. The place of a tactic belongs to the other. A tactic insinuates itself into the other's place, fragmentarily, without being able to keep it at a distance. It has at its disposal no base where it can capitalize on its advantages, prepare its expansions, and secure independence with respect to circumstances . . . On the contrary, because it does not have a place, a tactic depends on time – it is always on the watch for opportunities that must be seized 'on the wing'. Whatever it wins, it does not keep. It must constantly manipulate events in order to turn them into 'opportunities'.[8]

Strategies emanate from fixed centres, and are directed to the outside in pursuit of certain ends; tactics are the opportunistic, mobile responses of those without a place of their own. The husband of our tale has his proper place, the house, a fixed centre from where he plans his strategy for getting the better of his wife; he collects evidence and gathers his kin, all with the aim of punishing his wife. She, on the other hand, has no proper place from which to formulate strategies. Her mode of operation is precisely to be 'on the watch for opportunities that must be seized "on the wing"', manipulating events 'in order to turn them into "opportunities"'. The taming of her husband is not something she had planned in advance; initially she aims no further than to find a way of being with her lover; the ruse of the rope, which should enable her to do this undetected under her husband's roof, is a textbook example of tactical activity in the space of the other. Similarly, when she bribes the old woman, she is seizing an unexpected opportunity to see her lover. She cannot know at the time that her husband will cut off the other woman's pigtails. When she hears what has happened her response is: 'Now things will go how I want and the game will turn out well for me' (A ll. 284–5: 'so erget ez nach dem willen min / und wirt mir ein guot spil'). The wife sees herself as a player in a game, an activity that is all tactics, calling for quick-witted exploitation of whatever advantages are offered by the present state of play.[9]

The housebound husband is left holding whatever passes through his hands as a result of his wife's mobility; this is a powerful image of male strategy outmanoeuvred by female tactics. Such outmanoeuvring occurs regularly in the many *Mären* that narrate women's cunning subversions and circumventions of their husbands' authority.[10] In order to get round and get the better of their husbands wives manipulate signs; their language is not fixed to the truth. Moreover, this is no interest in language for its own sake; the mobile and tactical use of signs, which can take several forms in these stories, is shown to accompany and facilitate mobility in the life of bodies. In some *Mären* a smokescreen of linguistic ruses is thrown up round a temporary space where wives are free to do with their bodies what they will. In others the same dextrous manipulation can produce false knowledge about men's bodies, setting them up for the kind of treatment meted out to the hapless husband of *Pfaffe*. Either way, the usual subordination of wives to their husbands is suspended or reversed, and this is expressed in bodily misrule.

For all that *Mären* portray wives successfully tricking their husbands, yet they are not women's stories. Where the authors are known by name, they are without exception men, and their commentary on the narrative, in prologues and epilogues, is addressed by and large to other men: what are we men to do about women? Women, who doubtless were part of the public for these tales, may be addressed implicitly: male praise of good women and the curses heaped upon wicked ones suggest indirectly to women which roles they should take as their model; occasionally women are admonished directly.[11] Women's interest in the stories is acknowledged only in so far as it is a function of male needs. That is not to say that women could not have had their own response to the stories independently of men's concerns; they might for instance have admired and approved of the female characters and their ingeniously won victories over the menfolk, but this kind of response is outside the stated programme of the narrators. They are men, talking to other men, about women. At bottom these stories of cunning women are men's way of coping with their worries about being outflanked by female mobility. Male order would like to have women fixed in the place defined for them by men. Women's tactics undermine this fixity, challenging it with a mobility of signs and bodies which men experience as double infidelity, as lies and adultery.

The connection between the two kinds of infidelity is the theme of three *Mären*: the story of the chervil (*Das Kerbelkraut*),[12] Heinrich Kaufringer's tale of the forgotten breeches (*Die zurückgelassene Hose*),[13] and the variant of this *Märe* of the lover's breeches by Hans Folz, *Die Hose des Buhlers*.[14] In all three stories the evidence of a man's eyes is pitted against the linguistic tactics of his unfaithful wife, who goes scot-free thanks to the resourcefulness she shows in inventing new, innocent-seeming contexts for the incriminating sign her husband saw. In *Kerbelkraut* she convinces her husband that when he saw her with her lover he was deceived by an attack of double vision brought on by eating chervil (MHG *kervelkrut*); in *Die zurückgelassene Hose* the husband is persuaded that the breeches left behind on the bed by a hastily departing lover are intended as part of a shock therapy for the fever from which he supposedly suffers; while in

Folz's version the wife, her maid, and her nurse quickly collaborate in the pretence that the garment is left over from a game of forfeits they have been playing to amuse themselves during the husband's absence. Linguistic mobility consists in relocating the signs in a new context created entirely by women's speech. The true story of the body (the wife has been having sex) is supplanted by a false one (the husband is mentally confused, suffers from fever); the result is that the men no longer believe the evidence of their eyes. The wife in *Kerbelkraut* announces to her suspicious husband 'You should believe me rather than your own eyes' (ll. 20–1: 'du solt vil baz gelouben mir / dan dinen ougen'), and Hans Folz sums up: 'See, thus the husband was misled, even though he had first perceived the truth' (*Hose*, ll. 121–2: 'Secht, also ward der man verfüertt, / Wiewol er erst die warhaitt spürtt'). The attitude of the narrators to female cunning is one of resignation tinged with amusement and admiration. The story of the chervil begins by observing that women's guile knows no bounds, and then sets this in the context of linguistic and sexual infidelity; even if a man could prove his wife's adultery with the evidence of his own eyes, she would talk her way out of it, saying that he had not seen it at all (ll. 1–9). The moral of the story is that it is wasted effort for men to guard their wives (ll. 275–9). Folz concludes on the same note of helplessness, posing the rhetorical question 'Who can do anything about the guile of wicked women?' (*Hose*, l. 123: 'wer kan für böser weib gefeer?'); Kaufringer elaborates the lesson in a longer epilogue, reasoning that if men as strong, wise, and powerful as Samson, Solomon, David and Aristotle – the canonical *exempla* – were brought low by women's cunning, then there is no hope at all for ordinary men (ll. 82–116). Kaufringer's is in fact a comforting message for men: why worry if women outmanoeuvre us, since men far greater than we fared no better in the past?

The epilogue to *Die zurückgelassene Hose* may be interpreted in one of two ways, as a rationalisation of male inferiority, or as a joke about it. Men's helplessness in the face of female cunning is traced back by Kaufringer to a primal scene, the tricking of Aristotle by Phyllis, who rode the ancient philosopher like a horse. Ever since then, it has been the lot of all men to be women's dupes; they have inherited Aristotle's weakness (ll. 98–111). The outwitting of men by women would thus be no more than the repetition of the pattern of history and the iron laws of heredity. The function of such a rationalisation would be to relieve men of anxiety by allowing them to apprehend the disorder wrought by women's tactics as the workings of a law about which nothing can be done. There is nevertheless something frivolous about Kaufringer's epilogue which cannot be accounted for in terms of rationalisation. It is striking how he deflects his *exempla* from their traditional purpose – to establish the perennial wickedness of women – and uses them instead to prove that men

have never been equal to women's tactics.[15] I take this playful change of
emphasis to be a signal for comedy. There is certainly a comic lack of
proportion between the slightness of the incident of the breeches and the
energy expended on its exegesis (the epilogue occupies 35 lines out of
116), between the triviality – one might even say feebleness – of the story
and the seriousness of the exegetical schemata. The incongruities suggest
that the epilogue is intended as a joke. At this point it is important to
stress that the epilogue assumes an all-male circuit of communication;
Kaufringer adopts a 'we'-voice throughout to speak about men's problems
with women. Having heard a story about a woman playing a joke on a
man, the men now enjoy their own joke as Kaufringer invites them to
laugh at his laborious and inappropriate marshalling of all the ideological
hardware he can bring to bear on the rather silly anecdote of the breeches.
It is as though with their joke the men have gone one better than the
story, topping the joke enjoyed by the woman at the expense of their sex.
The formal structure of the entire text replicates the structure of the
narrative: as the wife triumphs over her husband, so the men's joke (the
epilogue) triumphs over the woman's joke (the narrative). In its own way,
the structural homology might be said to accomplish the same release
from anxiety as would result from a straight-faced reading of the epilogue;
not only do the men have the last laugh after all, but also, and perhaps
more fundamentally, they derive pleasure from the appreciation of the
homology between the form of the text and its content.[16]

The *Mären* of the chervil and the breeches maintain that men will
inevitably be women's dupes. *Der Zahn*, a story about a tooth,[17] has it
otherwise. Once again, the theme is the link between the linguistic and
the sexual infidelity of women. The wife, characterised as wanton and false
(ll. 8–9), is also a wily manipulator of language. With her sweet talk (l. 21:
'zartes kosen') she persuades her husband that he is ill and should stay in
bed, so that she can see her lover; when the latter asks her to bring him
one of her husband's teeth as a token of her love, she convinces the
unfortunate man that he has bad breath, and so what is in fact a perfectly
healthy tooth is pulled. The story exemplifies with pleasing economy all
the ways in which mobile sign-use can be related to bodily mobility; the
wife's deceitful words create a smokescreen for her extra-marital affairs,
and they produce false knowledge about her husband's body, setting him
up for a maiming that inverts the normal hierarchy. If a joke involves the
temporary subversion of the dominant pattern of relations by another
pattern that was hidden in it,[18] then the stories we have been telling up
to now satisfy the definition: a perverse, but none the less compelling logic
of signs subverts the normal claim of language to speak the truth, invented narratives supplant the facts, a disorderly mobility of bodies triumphs over fixed hierarchy. Although *Der Zahn* contains these elements,

it is ultimately unfunny. This is because mobility and fixity are not related
in a joke-structure, such that one triumphs over the other, but instead are
pressed into a moralising contrast between right and wrong. The story
begins in praise of 'well-bred, honourable, chaste women' (l. 1: 'zühtic
erbaer reine wip'), and ends on the same note, with the wish that God
may preserve good women (ll. 103–4). The wife is the contrasting type of
the 'wicked woman, full of evil' (l. 4: 'unwip vol von meine'); may the
Devil take her and her ilk (ll. 96–8). As there are two types of woman, so
there are two types of man, wise and foolish. The husband falls for his
wife's lies, but he is simple (ll. 5, 51: 'einvaltic'), guileless (l. 22: 'unlos'),
and foolish (l. 88: 'torhaft'); the lover on the other hand sees through the
woman's rhetoric, not believing her when she protests her love for him (ll.
34–8), and interpreting the tooth she brings him for what it really is, not
a token of her love, but a sign of her wickedness. When she brings him
the trophy, he recoils in horror; a woman who does not scruple to inflict
such pain on her husband might, he reasons, one day kill him, and so he
leaves her (ll. 80–5).

What the lover of *Der Zahn* voices as a fear becomes perverse reality in
Der Stricker's tale of the interred husband (*Der begrabene Ehemann*).[19] It is
the story of a husband who is buried alive after his wife has told him he
is dead. He loves her so much that he swears an oath to accept everything
she says as truth. Then he suffers one degradation after another: he is
forced to accept her word that it is midnight at midday, must uncomplainingly endure a cold bath, which she says is warm, and has to tolerate
her infidelity with a priest because any reproach he makes is denounced
by her as a lie. The climax is reached when the wife decides to get rid of
him in favour of her lover; she announces that he is dead and has him
buried. Like the stories of the chervil and the breeches, this *Märe* pits the
evidence of the husband's senses against his wife's word. But when he sees
her going from her lover (ll. 138–9) the wife does not even need to construct an alternative narrative to render innocent the evidence of adultery;
because the oath ensures that her word is accepted unconditionally, it is
enough for her to deny flatly what her husband has seen (l. 142). There
is no need for her to convince, nor does she; her husband does not
believe any of the things she asserts, but denies what he knows to be fact
in the hope that this will make her realise how much he loves her (ll. 86–
100, 118–23, 155–66, 189–94, 220–4). In other *Mären* women's sign-use
has a perverse plausibility, thanks to a context of interpretation that has
arisen by chance or by deliberate manipulation; women's mobility therefore represents the joking underside of the normal semiotic processes by
which we reach the truth of the world. *Der begrabene Ehemann* does not work
as a joke; in the place of ingenious subversion and deft circumvention of
convention and authority we have blunt assertion that black is white. The

story is not so much about mobility as mastery. The woman discovers that her absolute right to declare what is fact brings her new power over the body, her husband's and her own. The episode of the bath leads to the realisation that she is now her husband's master (ll. 113–14: 'si duhte an disem maere, / daz si sin meister waere'); it is not long before she takes a lover. As to the husband, his gruesome fate could not be otherwise, remarks Der Stricker in a laconic epilogue, for the reason 'that he set up a foolish woman as master over himself' (literally 'over his body') (ll. 246–7: 'daz er satzte ein tumbez wip / ze meister über sinen lip'). Implicitly, right and wrong behaviour are contrasted; the husband is an 'affe' (l. 220), a fool whose mistake is to love and trust his wife to such a pitch that he willingly relinquishes mastery over language and truth, and so over her and even himself. The moralising may be less heavy-handed than in *Der Zahn*, but this story too is not funny when all is said and done.

In *Der Zahn*, sex is given from the outset as the motive for all that follows: the woman is insatiable (l. 8: 'unbenüegic'), her linguistic infidelities flow from the need to cover her sexual ones. By contrast, the wife who buries her husband is not an adulteress from the beginning, nor is it clear that she has any intention of taking a lover until the priest presses her (ll. 133–7). Similarly, one of the wives in the story of the three cunning women (*Drei listige Frauen*) makes the discovery that linguistic infidelity creates opportunities for sexual infidelity. The story exists in three versions,[20] but its outline is as follows. Three peasant women hold a competition to see who can most ingeniously deceive her husband. One convinces hers that he is dead; the second that he is the priest who must say mass for his deceased neighbour; the third makes her naked husband believe that he is fully clothed, and in that state he goes to church for the funeral.[21] The first wife takes advantage of her husband's temporary lifelessness to have sex with one of the servants in full view of the 'corpse' who, in what is surely one of the most outstanding instances of grotesque humour in the *Mären*, remarks out loud that if he were not dead he would not tolerate this behaviour (A ll. 234–40, B ll. 269–80, C¹ ll. 41–4, C² ll. 29–32). The connection between linguistic and sexual infidelity could hardly be drawn more drastically, though, as we remarked, the linguistic trickery does not have its origins in sex. The motivation for the deception is to win a contest for honour (A ll. 33–6) or money (B ll. 37–42) or a belt (C¹ ll. 6–8, C² ll. 4–6).

Gesture and mimicry bulk large among the semiotic resources deployed by the women in this *Märe*. The first wife puts on a false show of lamentation for her dead husband. In version B she goes as far as to mime the whole ritual of dying, fetching a priest to hear confession and administer the last sacraments, lighting candles, covering the body and laying it out on the bier, admitting the mourners to the house (ll. 174–239); in C she wrings her hands, tears her hair and even paints the man's body with saffron and soot to make it look like a corpse (C^1 ll. 11–24, C^2 ll. 9–20). The second wife shaves a tonsure on her sleeping husband's head; he, doubting her word, is invited to feel it.[22] The antics of the third wife also vary across the versions: in A she measures her husband for his new suit of clothes, and mimes a fitting of the invisible garments (ll. 321–85); in B she swears oath after oath to her husband, who has just got out of bed, that he has his things on (ll. 443–5); in C she spits on her hands and makes as if to brush the feathers off the clothes in which he supposedly has been sleeping (C^1 ll. 101–3, C^2 ll. 65–7). The historian of medieval gesture Jean-Claude Schmitt has shown that theoretical reflection on gesture becomes more intense from the twelfth century. Among other things, there is concern to distinguish bad gestures from good. The body in Christian thought was ambivalent; on the one hand it was the prison of the soul, corrupt and sinful flesh, on the other it could, if tempered with discipline, be a sacrifice pleasing to God. Accordingly gestures could be wicked or virtuous; they could figure the carnality of fallen humankind or, by mortifying the flesh (through penitential exercises, for instance), lead to redemption. Whereas the word *gestus* can designate both kinds of gesture, good and bad, the term *gesticulatio* is reserved for bad ones. Gesticulations are associated with prostitutes, jesters, jugglers and mimes; they embody vice and sinfulness, transgress social custom and offend the ethical ideal of modesty.[23] Clearly the gesturings and mimicry of the three cunning women are *gesticulationes*. Indeed one of the two redactions of the C version concludes with an allegorical interpretation according to which the three women represent the temptations of the flesh, the devil, and the world (C^1 ll. 157–70).

Schmitt summarises medieval ideas about gesture under three heads: expressivity, communication and efficacy. Gestures were the outer, bodily expression of the inner movements of the soul; they communicated without words; they had effects, both practical and, in the case of ritual gestures, symbolic.[24] The revival of interest in gesture from the twelfth century onwards gave rise to 'the great question of symbolic efficacy . . . Some gestures seemed able to transform living beings or material things . . . Gestures used for ecclesiastical sacraments . . . were especially discussed'.[25] It is noticeable how integral to the tale of the three women are sacraments and sacramentals. Mass is to be said for the soul of the dead man (who in version B also receives the last rites); his 'priested' neighbour undergoes a mock ordination;[26] the naked husband makes an offering at the altar (and in B his wife swears oaths to him). The solemn gestures that should convey grace to the believer are here perverse gesticulations. The first of these episodes as it is told in B, and the second in both B and C seem to me to be joke interpretations of the doctrine of sacramental efficacy *ex opere operato*. The doctrine states that sacraments work in virtue of their objective performance alone. Here a perverse mechanism supplants the normal one: administer extreme unction, and your man is dead; give him a tonsure, and he is a priest. Nor can I help thinking that the episode of the naked husband in all three versions may also be a sacramental joke. Cyprian comments on the seamless coat of Christ (John 19.23–4) that it is a sacrament and a sign of the unity of the church: 'Sacramento vestis et signo declaravit ecclesiae unitatem.' The thing signified is itself a sacrament or mystery: 'Hoc unitatis sacramentum'.[27] Now a sacrament is, according to Augustine, the visible form of an invisible grace;[28] the seamless garment the sign of an invisible mystery, the indivisible church which, in a theological tradition following Paul, is conceived of as the body of Christ. In our story the visible and the invisible terms have been interchanged: the clothes are invisible, the body visible. Surely it is not far-fetched to interpret the three deceptions narrated in this late medieval *Märe* as joking subversions of the serious doctrine of sacramental efficacy?

Sacraments are signs, and if the *Märe* of the three cunning women is about anything, it is about how signs create beliefs about the body. That brings us back to *Der Pfaffe mit der Schnur*. But there the social group believes what the signs say, whereas the body concerned, the husband, does not; here the men, who in two cases are transformed into sheer corporeality, a naked body and a corpse, misrecognise themselves. They are betrayed by their own bodies which have become false signs of their bodily condition or identity. (Folz, the author of version C, even has the first wife hold up a mirror to her husband so that he can see his painted body; he believes her utterly (C¹ ll. 15–24, C² ll. 11–20).) Not that awareness of the social determination of belief is lacking, especially among the wives in version A. The first husband believes he is an abbot because his wife tells him that the prior and the monks have elected him at their assembly (ll. 61–3); the second that he is dead and must lie still because his wife insists that the priest, relatives and neighbours witnessed his death, and that if he does not remain still he will cause a scandal, as people will think his corpse is possessed by the devil (ll. 142–51, 167–82); the third husband is impressed by his wife's promise that his splendid new clothes will make him the talk of the whole village (ll. 282–7, 304–7). The women convince the men by appealing to social beliefs and norms.[29] This is less so in versions B and C, where belief is secured above all by gestural and sacramental means. Moreover, in these 'sacramentalist' versions the husbands finally wake up to the fact that they have been deceived (though in neither case do they plan revenge; Kaufringer, the author of version B, predicts that when they have come to their senses they will let the matter rest (ll. 543–50), and Folz gives us our parting glance at the three husbands as they propose to drown their misfortune in wine (C¹ l. 143, C² l. 107)). Perhaps this disillusioning

is necessary because the suggestion that joke sacraments might be perma-
nently effective is too uncomfortable for a Christian culture. Are jokes
about the sacred tolerable only if the rule of their logic is shown to have
its inevitable term? In A, where beliefs about the body are cemented by
reference to social values, no similar disillusioning occurs. The men remain
dupes to the last.

II

There is a well-established strain of criticism that hears in *Mären* the voice
of nature, in contrast to the voice of culture which speaks through high
courtly literature. In these texts, it is said, we have natural sexuality, un-
trammelled by the decorum and sublimation of courtly love. Whereas the
latter is a cultivating institution, an art with its proper rules and etiquette,
a form of service in which the sexual drive is channelled into morally
beneficial enterprises, the *Mären* show us desire at its most bodily and
instinctual, an elemental demand which proceeds directly to the goal of
physical gratification. For Bruno Barth the robust and earthy sensuality
('kräftige und derbe Sinnlichkeit') of these tales gave their audience a
welcome holiday from the idealism and over-refinement of courtly love;[30]
in a more censorious tone Gustav Ehrismann focused on what he felt to
be the natural eroticism and obscenity of the *Mären* in order to highlight
the gap separating their crude performances ('rohe Vorführungen') from
the cultivated 'Lebensgefühl' of courtly literature.[31] The same opposition
between nature and culture, between the 'raw' sex of the *Mären* and the
'cooked' love etiquette of high courtly literature, informs more recent
criticism. Heribert Hoven talks in the same terms as Barth and Ehrismann,
though with anything but the latter's disapproval: 'The over-refined culture of courtly love has a competitor in a love that insists on its origins in
nature.'[32] For Hoven, the genre *Märe* is constituted by its naturalness; *Mären*
are nothing more nor less than the embodiment of naked *eros*, stripped
of all the vestments of culture, anarchic, outside the constraints imposed
by social codes, and therefore subversive and laughter-provoking.[33]

Does the bodily mobility in the *Mären* we have been looking at confirm
the voice of nature hypothesis? Is women's promiscuity, the havoc they
make of fixed bodily order a carnivalesque celebration of sex and the
body outside the repressive constraints of civilisation? I think not. First let
it be emphasised once more that our stories are as concerned with sign-
use as they are with bodies; over and over again they demonstrate that
what people do with their bodies and what they believe about them is
determined by signs. Moreover, women's mobility is not located in some
utopia outside social relations; rather it involves tactical exploitation of
social beliefs and manipulation of conventional ways of reading signs. The

stories recount the triumph of mischievous versions of those beliefs and processes over what is normally admitted or expected; for instance, the frivolous interpretation of *ex opere operato*, or the absurd contexts invented for incriminating signs. What makes the stories funny is not just that perversity tilts against normality, but that this perversity also has a certain plausibility; given the belief that sacraments have some kind of automatic effect, why should they not work as they do in *Drei listige Frauen*? Precisely because these jokes exploit alternative patterns contained within the accepted ones, social conventions always provide the indispensable back-drop to the subversive humour. That brings us to a second consideration: in these *Mären* the characters are not just men and women, but husbands and wives; sex is never just sex, it is adultery. The sexes, and sex, are perceived through social roles and institutions. The same social deter-minination holds for the body.

In his seminal essay on the techniques of the body, Marcel Mauss ob-served that there is no bodily behaviour that is wholly innate or natural. Habitual ways of moving, resting, eating, sleeping, even the positions of the body in sex, vary with time and space, gender and generation, from one culture to another.[34] Mauss used the terms *habitus* and *exis* to express the idea that all comportment is acquired by learning and imitation; this *habitus* is produced by the techniques of the body, traditional and effica-cious acts whose purpose is to fit bodies to their uses.[35] Confining himself to techniques, which he was careful to distinguish from another kind of traditional and efficacious act, rite, Mauss did not enlarge upon the social symbolism of the human body. This is attempted by the anthropologist Mary Douglas in her study *Natural Symbols*.[36] She starts out from the premise that the body, which is common to us all, is the most obvious natural symbol for expressing social experience, which varies. Not only are per-ceptions of the body socially conditioned (this is what Douglas takes from Mauss), ideas of society are based on the physical body, which is a ready source of metaphors for the social organism. The two levels of experience, of the physical body and the social body, influence one another recipro-cally. Douglas writes: 'There is a continual exchange of meanings between the two kinds of bodily experience so that each reinforces the categories of the other. As a result of this interaction the body itself is a highly restricted medium of expression.'[37] Douglas maintains that it is a funda-mental principle of human cognition to seek consonance and abhor dis-sonance. The natural desire for harmonious and satisfying messages fuels a powerful drive to achieve consonance in all layers of experience. Thus experiences of body and society will be made concordant in a 'bodily style' that expresses the perceived social situation appropriately. It follows that bodily styles are subject to constraint: a certain style exists only if there is a corresponding social experience to be expressed; a style that did not have any foundation in the social situation would be dissonant. Consonant with social experience, and constrained by it, the culturally processed human body is a code.[38]

Bodily codes vary according to the underlying social experience. 'If there is no concern to preserve social boundaries, I would not expect to find concern with bodily boundaries . . . bodily control is an expression of social control.' Conversely, where social structure is weak, 'the inarticulateness of the social organisation in itself gains symbolic expression in bodily dissociation'.[39] In support of her thesis, Douglas calls on evidence gleaned from the comparative anthropology of a range of societies, traditional and industrial. Dissociation (the relaxation or loss of bodily control, manifested in trance, spirit possession, shaking, frenzy, sexual promiscuity) is viewed positively by societies with weakly defined roles and boundaries, and feared wherever the community is tightly structured and social categories are clearly drawn. Social systems are not always of a piece, however, and both controlled and uncontrolled bodily styles may be found within the same society, encoding the different experiences of its various segments. Many societies contain marginal groups, 'people who are peripheral to the central focus of power and authority . . . women subject to their husbands, serfs subject to their masters, indeed anyone in a state of subjection'.[40] For these groups, social control may principally be a matter of an outward relation of domination, which keeps the periphery pinned to the centre; the social categories and norms that are an internalised form of control at the centre have often not penetrated deep into the marginal group, which may then symbolise its correspondingly less articulate social experience in a dissociated bodily style. The centre, like any other society with an articulate organisation, views dissociation at its margins with fear and suspicion; the periphery, however, does not have the entirely positive attitude to dissociation found in weakly structured societies, but views it instead with ambivalence. A marginal group cannot escape being influenced by the views of the dominant class; yet it also exploits its masters' fears of bodily dissociation in order to secure advantages in the centre.[41]

What Douglas calls dissociation could include the bodily mischief that I have been discussing under the rubric mobility: promiscuity, gesticulation, mimicry; and her account of how the periphery manipulates its bodily dissociation brings to mind de Certeau's definition of tactics as the opportunism of the people who have no firm base in the social system. Add to this that women, frequently excluded by men from the seats of power and decision-making, are regarded by Douglas as a prime example of a peripheral group,[42] and we have the makings of a theory that will allow us to explain the mobility of women in our *Mären* by relating it to their social situation. However, there is a difference between the behaviour Douglas writes about and that narrated by the *Mären*. Douglas is concerned to relate symbolism of the body to the social experience of the owners of those same bodies; thus, for instance, she is able to propose peripherality as the explanation for why women so often figure prominently in millenarian and other effervescent religious movements.[43] The *Mären* on the other hand are not based on women's own social experience; they represent women as men imagine them to be. Bodily mobility in the *Mären* would thus be men's attempt at expressing their own perception of women's peripherality. Douglas remarks that 'the style appropriate to any message will coordinate all the channels along which it is given'.[44] In our stories social mobility (in the sense of being less fixed into the central structure) is re-expressed in the medium of the body and also of language. Men replicate their perception that women are not as fixed in the social system as they are by attributing to women both a mobile, incontinent use of the body and a mobile use of signs. The message about women is consonant, expressed in a total style whose every band reinforces and enhances the meaning of the others.

If the hypothesis that the body in the *Mären* is code for how men in the centre perceive women on the periphery is acceptable,[45] it follows that there is no voice of nature in these stories. Sexual promiscuity, often interpreted as nature's revolt against cultural repression of the body, expresses a particular social experience and is therefore no less culturally determined than bodily continence. Reading the body as code for social experience also allows us to historicise the misogyny of the *Mären*. There is no doubt that their representation of women draws on a long tradition of antifeminism.[46] Methodius, the third-century author of a dialogue in praise of virginity, might be describing the behaviour of women in the *Mären* when he admonishes the virgin not to 'give herself up to womanish weaknesses and laughter, exciting herself to wiles and foolish talking, which whirl the mind around and confuse it'.[47] He also makes the familiar connection between sexual and linguistic infidelity: 'It would be ridiculous to preserve the organs of generation pure, but not the tongue.'[48] Nor does Methodius stop at that; purity of the genitals must be accompanied not only by a pure tongue, but also by purity of the eyes, ears, hands, and mind.[49] It is hard to better this as an illustration of Douglas's principle of stylistic consonance; for 'purity' substitute 'infidelity' or 'mobility' and we are in the world of the *Mären*. But to point out the continuity begs the question: What is it that makes the image of woman in a dialogue written for the edification of a group of consecrated girls in the third century still expressive in a very different kind of text, for a very different public, in the late Middle Ages?[50]

I believe the answer has to be sought in the peripheral position of women in late medieval society, and the perception of that peripherality

by those men at the centre who told *Mären* and were their addressees. I
shall concentrate on the city, because information is more plentiful and
because *Mären* are to a considerable degree urban literature, especially in
the fourteenth and fifteenth centuries, though I think it is also possible to
make the centre–periphery hypothesis work for the countryside. Evidence
for the marginality, economic, legal and political, of women in late medieval urban society is not hard to come by. The view put forward in the last
century and often repeated since, that women could learn and practise a
trade on equal terms with men, has been called into question. There were
notable instances of women's guilds, such as the silkmakers in Cologne,[51]
but it was more common for women to be in guilds as wives, widows and
daughters of master craftsmen, entitled to certain social benefits and taking part in the religious activities of the organisation. Guild statutes generally make no provision for training women, so that they could not have
become masters; by and large their work was limited to retailing and
auxiliary jobs. Where craftswomen are mentioned, in tax records for example, it is probably a case of widows continuing their former husbands'
trade, which guild rules allowed them to do, though they imposed restrictions.[52] In commerce independent businesswomen existed, but were very
much the exception, and here too they were frequently daughters or
widows carrying on a business inherited from fathers or husbands.[53]
Women in service were regularly paid less than men, even if they did the
same work.[54] Overall, women's position in the urban economy was weaker
than men's; this is confirmed by the high proportion of women among
the poor.[55] In the countryside women were excluded from conducting their
own legal affairs by the *Sachsenspiegel* and the *Schwabenspiegel*, thirteenth-
century law codes, and by the customary law written down in the *Weistümer*
of the thirteenth to sixteenth centuries. All of these codes placed women
under the tutelage of men to a greater or lesser degree.[56] City statutes too
set limits to women's legal capacity and their power to act, and discriminated
against women in matters of marital property and inheritance, although
not all of them insisted on the husband's legal power over his wife.[57]
Women were excluded from the conduct of public affairs; they did not sit
in city councils, and had no vote in village assemblies. None of this is to
deny that there were women of considerable wealth and influence in the
society of the late Middle Ages, but they were the exception; the rule is
marginality. Men were bound to think of women as less fixed than
themselves into the central institutions and processes of social life. I suggest that this experience is the historical ground with which the notes
inherited from antifeminist tradition chime.

We can take the analysis in terms of centre and periphery further. Not
only are women peripheral to men; some men are peripheral to others,
artisans by comparison with patricians, for instance, or newcomers to the

city by comparison with their longer established and better integrated colleagues. The historian Erich Maschke has shown how all aspects of urban life were pervaded and underpinned by family ties. Central institutions, guilds, companies, ruling elites and religious fraternities were networks of allied families.[58] Not only were men at the centre joined by ties of marriage, but new men could be brought in from the periphery by allowing them to marry into the establishment. Of the numerous examples that Maschke cites of incomers whose social assimilation was furthered and completed by their marriages I select two. The weaver Hans Fugger, founder of what was to become the great financial dynasty, migrated from the countryside to Augsburg in 1367. He married twice, into guild families, and made the transition from craft to commerce. His son Jakob married the daughter of a mint-master, which gave him connections for dealing in precious metals and finance; six of his children married into patrician families. Thus in three generations the integration of the Fuggers into the centre of Augsburg society was accomplished.[59] Similarly, the rise of Hinrich Castorp (*c.*1420–88) from immigrant merchant to burgomaster of Lübeck is confirmed by his two marriages, first into a mercantile family, then to a daughter of the patrician Kerkrings.[60] Peripherality is relative; Fugger and Castorp were certainly not poor when they arrived in the city, but nor were they completely assimilated until they married into established families. In a less spectacular way, it was not uncommon for newcomers to acquire citizenship or membership of a guild through marriage: Maschke mentions that out of thirty-five grants of citizenship in Frankfurt in 1373 thirty were to men who married daughters or widows of citizens;[61] guild statutes allowed an outsider to obtain membership at a reduced rate if he married the daughter or widow of a master.[62]

Gratian called marriage a 'sociale vinculum',[63] and indeed it was 'the connective tissue of late medieval society',[64] bulking large in the experience of men. It was what joined them with women, and also to other men, creating and strengthening bonds of institutional as well as kinship solidarity. I think we can now see why *Mären* are so often stories about husbands and wives. Marriage is where centre and periphery meet, the institution in which women are made subject to men in accordance with the biblical teaching that the husband is the head of the wife (Ephesians 5.22–4). Medieval canonists and theologians, and also some municipal statutes reiterate Paul's teaching.[65] But marriage is also where the distinction between centre and periphery, lord and subject, is lost. Paul writes in another epistle that 'the wife hath not power of her own body, but her husband: and likewise also the husband hath not power of his own body, but the wife' (1 Corinthians 7.4); this was the basis of the canonists' insistence that in marriage husband and wife were completely equal in their right to demand the conjugal debt.[66] There were social experiences too where the peripherality of women became doubtful. Bonds between men often passed through their wives; it was for instance common for the associates of a company to be brothers-in-law.[67] In so far as men such as these acknowledged that their wives were the social cement that held them together, they were identifying women with a central function. In the case of hypergamy, where marriage with widows and daughters of established families conferred a more central status on relative outsiders, this identification would have been stronger still. Other everyday experiences could bring home to men the fact that marriage was about partnership as much as power. Teamwork was required for the successful running of a business, with the wives of merchants looking after the bookkeeping while their husbands travelled abroad; wives would also take on business responsibility in order to leave their husbands free to follow a political career. Against the background of such experiences, it is not surprising that husband and wife should regularly be portrayed in the visual arts as partners of equal status.[68]

The hypothesis that women are perceived as peripheral by men holds generally, but in marriage, where men's experience of women is closest and most continuous, this perception is blurred. All of this experience constitutes the ground of our stories. I have already suggested that the general perception finds appropriate symbolic expression in the mobility attributed to women in *Mären*. It remains to relate the ambiguous experience of centre and periphery within marriage to the bodily codes of a genre that is, after all, concerned with men and women in their roles of husband and wife. For a start, the obscuring of the centre–periphery distinction explains why *Mären* are so often jokes. Douglas maintains that

> all jokes are expressive of the social situations in which they occur. The one social condition necessary for a joke to be enjoyed is that the social group in which it is received should develop the formal characteristics of a 'told' joke: that is, a dominant pattern of relations is challenged by another. If there is no joke in the social structure, no other joking can appear.[69]

For the social group men, the dominant perception of women as peripheral is challenged by any number of everyday experiences in marriage, which call into doubt the axiom that all women are of no social importance. The social condition for jokes is given: *Mären* narrate hilarious subversions of the dominant order, with wives turning upside down hierarchies of meanings, beliefs and bodies. Douglas remarks that 'a successful subversion of one form by another completes or ends the joke, for it changes the balance of power'.[70] Whenever the wife in our stories triumphs, the result is a new, perverse fixity, expressed bodily: the husband tied in the trough, buried alive, lying on his death-bed quite still in the face of new infidelities. The taming of his body is frequently accompanied by its maiming. The outmanoeuvred husband of *Pfaffe* is burned and almost drowned, in *Der Zahn* he loses a tooth; the same tooth-pulling scenario is one of several grisly injuries inflicted by the wives in Kaufringer's macabre version of *Drei listige Frauen*: the 'dead' husband first has a couple of his teeth wrenched out, while his neighbour, naked in church, is castrated by his wife, who cuts off his 'purse' as he fumbles to make his offering.[71] The outcome of these stories is a new balance of power, but with women on top. A distinction between central and peripheral in marriage is drawn, where before it was obscure, with taming and maiming the embodied expression of that distinction's appearance.

Taming and maiming are bodily code for the creation of hierarchy in the place of ambiguity. But the indeterminateness of roles in marriage can be resolved in one of two ways, with women on top, or men. There are also *Mären* in which the husbands tame, and sometimes maim, their shrewish wives. *Die Zähmung der Widerspenstigen*, the 'taming of the shrew', is the story of a husband who subdues first his wife, by riding her like a horse, then her equally refractory mother, on whom he performs a surgical operation to remove her 'angry kidney'.[72] The tale of the woman as saddle-horse (*Die Frau als Reitpferd*)[73] speaks for itself; Der Stricker tells a story about a wife whose husband walls her in until her demons are driven out.[74] Just as the concrete and empirical categories of myths provide conceptual tools for handling contradictions and ambiguities that arise out of social experience,[75] so taming and maiming, which can be performed by either wife or husband, are concrete and embodied categories for expressing and working out the troubling experience of the lack of definition of marital roles. Bodily style, I suggest, is therefore not simply a static reflection of the social body; the code has a dynamic.

Of the stories that relate how husbands successfully turn the tables on their wives, I would like to end by telling one: Heinrich Kaufringer's tale of the husband's revenge (*Die Rache des Ehemannes*).[76] A knight whose concern for his chivalric reputation and prowess frequently takes him to tournaments away from home has a beautiful wife who is having an affair with a priest. One night the priest asks his mistress to prove her love for him by making him a present of two of her husband's molars. She resorts to the ruse we already know from *Der Zahn*: the husband, believing his wife's claim that she cannot bear to come near him because of the stench from his supposedly rotten teeth, allows two of his molars to be pulled. The priest has them made into two costly and ornate dice. One evening when he is visiting the knight, he produces these dice and in his drunkenness reveals how they were made. The husband, horrified, realises what has been going on and plans revenge. He tells his wife he will be away at a tournament for a month; during his absence the priest is to look after her. He steals back home unnoticed, hides in the bedchamber, and when he has observed the lovers *in flagrante delicto,* cuts off the priest's testicles and scrotum. These he has made into a magnificent purse. Once his month is up, he returns home openly, to be greeted by his wife who begs him to call on the suffering priest. He presents the priest with the purse, then discloses its origin. The priest is given a choice; either be killed there and then, or do the husband's bidding. He chooses to save his life, is forced to send for his mistress and, as she kisses him, bite out her tongue. Six months later the knight summons his friends and relatives and those of his wife to a gathering. The guests entertain themselves by telling stories, and the knight in his turn contributes the story of his own suffering and revenge, though he conceals his personal involvement in the events. His audience react as one; a wife who treats her husband in the manner recounted by the knight deserves to be put to death. Then the knight reveals that he and the husband in his story are one and the same; he is however willing to let his wife live on condition that they be separated. This is agreed, and the wife goes to live with her people.

We certainly have a dynamic of maiming here. The three mutilations, the extraction of the knight's teeth, the priest's castration, and the biting out of the wife's tongue, are organised as an exchange: the husband pays back the lovers in kind, returning the treatment they meted out to him. However, although each of the protagonists is wounded in an intimate part of the body, the mutilations returned by the husband are no equal currency. Only the maimings that he inflicts, or causes to be inflicted, have the effect of taming: the castrated priest, confined to his bed, his very life in the hands of the avenging husband, is compelled to carry out orders; the wife, whose wound leaves her able to utter only the syllable 'läll' (ll. 397–407, 514), is reduced to a mute object of the legal proceedings that settle her status. We are back where we began, in the world of *Der Pfaffe mit der Schnur.* That tale also ends after the husband has convoked his kith and kin with a view to obtaining their agreement to a separation. But this husband succeeds where his counterpart failed. The reason is that he has made sure to immobilise his wife. Her punishment fits her crime, for it was her skilful but deceptive rhetoric that convinced the husband of the need to have his teeth pulled (ll. 40–66), a point emphasised by the knight in his own retelling of the story, which identifies the wife's wicked chatter (l. 478: 'böses gespächt') as the cause of his suffering. Also, and crucially, the wife is eliminated as a speaking subject. The syllable 'läll' calls to mind the verb *lällen* (or *lallen*), 'to babble', a sound typically made by infants. The woman, mutilated, has become like a child, *in-fans,* unspeaking. In the final scene, the husband has language under control. As he tells his story, his infantilised and linguistically immobilised wife has no possibility of replying or manipulating the signs in her favour.

His retelling of the story is an appropriation; henceforth the story is his alone, not his wife's or her lover's, and he is able to use it strategically, in pursuit of his calculated end. For the separation is planned. After the wife has lost her tongue, her husband suspends conjugal relations with her (ll. 410–12); this is the separation of bed, followed by separation of board six months later (ll. 413, 506–8).[77] The avenging husband is more careful than his hapless counterpart in *Pfaffe*; above all he seems to have learned the lesson that signs produce the truth of the body, so that control of the former is a precondition for power over the latter. But the price of his success is laughter. This story, in which strategic fixity triumphs over tactical mobility, involves the victory of the generally dominant order over the subaltern one. Accordingly the tale which the wronged husband starts to relate for amusement's sake (l. 438: 'in schimpf weis') turns out to be no joke.

NOTES

1 Version A, Heinrich Niewöhner, ed., *Neues Gesamtabenteuer*, Dublin and Zurich, 1967 (henceforth NGA), no. 22; B, Hanns Fischer, ed., *Eine Schweizer Kleinepiksammlung des 15. Jahrhunderts*, Altdeutsche Textbibliothek, Tübingen, 1965, no. 10; C, Hanns Fischer, ed., *Die deutsche Märendichtung des 15. Jahrhunderts*, Münchener Texte und Untersuchungen, Munich, 1966, no. 44. For a detailed comparison of the versions see Rosemarie Moos, *Der Pfaffe mit der Schnur: Fallstudie eines Märes*, Europäische Hochschulschriften, Berne, 1986.

2 The fundamental handbook is Hanns Fischer, *Studien zur deutschen Märendichtung*, 2nd edn, Tübingen, 1983.

3 Mikhail Bakhtin, *Rabelais and His World*, Bloomington, 1984.

4 See especially Karl-Heinz Schirmer, *Stil- und Motivuntersuchungen zur mittelhochdeutschen Versnovelle*, Tübingen, 1969.

5 I do not want to suggest however that the upper classes participated *only* in high literary culture; the 'little tradition' of the people was also accessible to them. On the 'biculturalism' of the elite, see Peter Burke, *Popular Culture in Early Modern Europe*, Aldershot, 1988, pp. 24–9. Burke's observations are as valid for the late Middle Ages as they are for the early modern period.

6 See Grimm, *Deutsches Wörterbuch*, s.v. *Wahrzeichen*, *Wortzeichen*, for attestations of the legal use of these terms; at the time of writing neither the *Deutsches Rechtswörterbuch* nor the *Handwörterbuch zur deutschen Rechtsgeschichte* had reached the letter 'w'. For *signa* see Heinrich Lausberg, *Handbuch der literarischen Rhetorik*, 2 vols, Munich, 1973, pp. 195–7.

7 B omits these details.

8 Michel de Certeau, *The Practice of Everyday Life*, Berkeley, 1984, p. xix.

9 Gabrielle Marie Lyons, '*Avoir* and *savoir*: A Strategic Approach to the Old French Fabliaux', unpublished Ph.D. dissertation, Cambridge, 1992, approaches the related Old French genre in terms of strategy and tactics, although she does not use the term 'strategy' in exactly the way that I, following de Certeau, do.

10 See Fischer, *Studien*, pp. 94–6.

11 NGA, no. 1, ll. 821–6.

12 NGA, no. 14.

13 Heinrich Kaufringer, *Werke*, ed. Paul Sappler, Tübingen, 1972, no. 10.

14 Hans Folz, *Die Reimpaarsprüche*, ed. Hanns Fischer, Münchener Texte und Untersuchungen, Munich, 1961, no. 6.

15 The women who deceived Solomon and David are equated with the devil's snares, set to trap a man in deadly sin, by Heinrich von Langenstein, *Erchantnuzz der Sund*, ed. P. Rainer Rudolf SDS, Texte des späten Mittelalters und der frühen Neuzeit, Berlin, 1969, pp. 95, 99. This catechetical treatise, written *c.*1388, is contemporary with Kaufringer. The story of Aristotle and Phyllis was topical for women's wickedness in medieval literature and the visual arts. See Joachim Storost, 'Zur Aristoteles-Sage im Mittelalter: Geistesgeschichtliche, folkloristische und literarische Grundlagen zu ihrer Erforschung', in Hermann Nottarp, ed., *Monumentum Bambergense: Festgabe für Benedikt Kraft*, Munich, 1955, pp. 298–348; Wolfgang Stammler, *Wort und Bild: Studien zu den Wechselwirkungen zwischen Schrifttum und Bildkunst im Mittelalter*, Berlin, 1962, pp. 12–44; Hella Frühmorgen-Voss, 'Mittelhochdeutsche weltliche Literatur und ihre Illustration: Ein Beitrag zur Überlieferungsgeschichte', *Deutsche Vierteljahrsschrift für Literaturwissenschaft und Geistesgeschichte*, XLIII, 1969, pp. 69–70.

16 See Mary Douglas, 'Jokes', in *Implicit Meanings: Essays in Anthropology*, London, 1975, pp. 90–114, in particular pp. 101, 112.

17 NGA, no. 20.

18 Douglas, 'Jokes', pp. 96–8.

19 Der Stricker, *Verserzählungen I*, ed. Hanns Fischer, Altdeutsche Textbibliothek, Tübingen, 1973, no. 4.

20 Three versions: A, NGA, no. 18; B, Kaufringer, *Werke*, no. 11; C (two redactions), Folz, *Reimpaarsprüche*, nos. 10a and b. Comparative studies are offered by Francis Raas, *Die Wette der drei Frauen: Beiträge zur Motivgeschichte und zur literarischen Tradition der Schwankdichtung*, Baseler Studien zur deutschen Sprache und Literatur, Bern, 1983, and Jan-Dirk Müller, 'Noch einmal: Maere und Novelle. Zu den Versionen des Maere von den "Drei listigen Frauen"', in Alfred Ebenbauer, ed., *Philologische Untersuchungen: Gewidmet Elfriede Stutz zum 65. Geburtstag*, Vienna, 1984, pp. 289–311.

21 BC; in A the order varies: wife 1 convinces her husband he is an abbot, wife 2 hers that he is dead, wife 3 that he is fully clothed; and the three episodes are not linked by bringing together the menfolk in a final scene. See Müller, 'Noch einmal: Maere und Novelle', pp. 292–6.

22 BC; in A she shaves her husband's head, at his request, only after he has accepted her word that he is the abbot.

23 Jean-Claude Schmitt, ' "Gestus" – "gesticulatio": Contribution a l'étude du vocabulaire médiévale des gestes', in *La Lexicographie du latin médiéval et ses rapports avec les recherches actuelles sur la civilisation du Moyen Age*, Colloques internationaux du CNRS, Paris, 1981, pp. 377–90; also his 'The Ethics of Gesture', in Michel Feher, ed., *Fragments for a History of the Human Body*, II, New York, 1989, pp. 128–47; and his 'The Rationale of Gestures in the West', in Jan Bremmer and Herman Roodenburg, eds, *A Cultural History of Gesture*, Cambridge, 1991. The last is a summary of Schmitt's monograph *La Raison des gestes dans l'Occident médiéval*, Paris, 1990.

24 Schmitt, 'Rationale', pp. 64–5.

25 Ibid., pp. 68–9.

26 The ceremony of the tonsure did not itself constitute the form of the sacrament, but it was part of the ritual of ordination, and would have struck laymen as its most visible sign. The sacred symbolism of the tonsure and its supposed institution in the New Testament are asserted by Hugh of St Victor, *De sacramentis*, 2.3.1–3 (PL, CLXXVI, cols 421–2) and Peter Lombard, *Sententiae*, 4.24.2 (PL, CXCII, cols 900–1).

27 Cyprian, *De ecclesiae catholicae unitate*, ed. M. Bévenot, Corpus Christianorum, Series Latina, III, Turnhout, 1972, pp. 254–5.

28 *Epistulae*, ed. A. Goldbacher, Corpus Scriptorum Ecclesiasticorum Latinorum XXXIV, Vienna, 1898, p. 604 (*Ep.* 105.3.12).

29 See Müller, 'Noch einmal: Maere und Novelle', pp. 294–6.

30 Bruno Barth, *Liebe und Ehe im altfranzösischen Fablel und in der mittelhochdeutschen Novelle*, Berlin, 1910, p. 7, also pp. 244–6.

31 Gustav Ehrismann, *Geschichte der deutschen Literatur bis zum Ausgang des Mittelalters*, II, Schlußband, Munich, 1935, p. 115.

32 Heribert Hoven, *Studien zur Erotik in der deutschen Märendichtung*, Göppinger Arbeiten zur Germanistik, Göppingen, 1978, p. 388. The quotation is my translation of the German 'Gegen die überfeinerte Minne-Kultur tritt eine Liebe an, die auf ihre Ursprünge in der Natur pocht.'

33 Ibid., pp. 389–96.

34 Marcel Mauss, 'Les Techniques du corps', *Journal de Psychologie*, XXXII, 1935, pp. 271–93.

35 Ibid., pp. 275, 278, 281, 291–93.

36 Mary Douglas, *Natural Symbols: Explorations in Cosmology*, London, 1970.

37 Ibid., p. 65.

38 Ibid., pp. 67–72.

39 Ibid., pp. 70, 74.

40 Ibid., p. 83.

41 Ibid., p. 87.

42 Ibid., pp. 83–4.

43 Ibid., pp. 82–4.

44 Ibid., p. 67.

45 To suggest that the body may be used not only to symbolise one's own social situation but also to encode one's perception of others does not, I think, do violence to Douglas's theory. First it must be stressed that the theory relates bodily styles to social *experience*, not directly to the social structure itself; the experience of the centre surely includes its dealings with the periphery. Second, Douglas herself acknowledges that bodily styles can be attributed by the non-owners of those bodies. She writes of witchcraft beliefs that they

> flourish in small groups in which roles are ill-defined . . . the body politic tends to have a clear external boundary, and a confused internal state in which envy and favouritism flourish and continually confound the proper expectations of members. So the body of the witch, normal-seeming and apparently carrying the normal human limitations, is equipped with hidden and extraordinarily malevolent powers . . . A closer look at the symbolism of witchcraft shows the dominance of symbols of inside and outside. The witch himself is someone whose inside is corrupt; he works harm on his victims by attacking their pure, innocent insides.
>
> (Ibid., pp. 111–13)

Witchcraft accusations have a political rationale; they solve the group's structural inadequacies by blaming misfortune on malefactors who must be purged from the body politic. Clearly the image of the witch's own body is a function of that rationale, and of the social experience that gives rise to it, rather than a symbolisation of the experience of the witches themselves.

46 For this tradition see Katherine M. Rogers, *The Troublesome Helpmate: A History of Misogyny in Literature*, Seattle, 1966, and Katherine M. Wilson and Elizabeth M. Makowski, *Wykked Wyves and the Woes of Marriage: Misogamous Literature from Juvenal to Chaucer*, Albany, NY, 1990.

47 *The Banquet of the Ten Virgins*, trans. William R. Clark, Edinburgh, 1869, p. 49.

48 Ibid., p. 110.

49 Ibid.

50 On Methodius and his milieu see Peter Brown, *The Body and Society: Men, Women and Sexual Renunciation in Early Christianity*, London, 1989, pp. 183–9.

51 Margret Wensky, *Die Stellung der Frau in der stadtkölnischen Wirtschaft im Spätmittelalter*, Quellen und Darstellungen zur Hansischen Geschichte, Cologne and Vienna, 1980; Edith Ennen, *Frauen im Mittelalter*, Munich, 1984, pp. 157–61.

52 Peter Ketsch, *Frauen im Mittelalter*, 2 vols, Düsseldorf, 1983–84, I, pp. 111–224.

53 Ibid., pp. 225–8, 231–42; Erich Maschke, *Die Familie in der deutschen Stadt des späten Mittelalters*, Sitzungsberichte der Heidelberger Akademie der Wissenschaften, philosophisch-historische Klasse, Heidelberg, 1980, pp. 39–41.

210 Framing medieval bodies

54 Ketsch, *Frauen*, I, pp. 53, 58–65.
55 Ibid., pp. 30–1, 40–50; Ennen, pp. 181–2.
56 Ketsch, *Frauen*, II, pp. 162–6, 196–201.
57 Ibid., pp. 178–82; Gerhard Köbler, 'Familienrecht in der spätmittelalterlichen Stadt', in Alfred Haverkamp, ed., *Haus und Familie in der spätmittelalterlichen Stadt*, Städteforschung, Cologne and Vienna, 1984, pp. 136–60.
58 Maschke, *Die Familie in der deutschen Stadt*, especially concluding remarks, p. 97.
59 Ibid., pp. 61–2.
60 Ibid., pp. 76–7.
61 Ibid., p. 52.
62 Ibid., pp. 50–2, also Ketsch, *Frauen*, I, pp. 142–3.
63 *Decretum*, in *Corpus iuris canonici*, ed. Emil Friedberg, repr. Graz, 1959, vol. I, col. 1147 (C. 32 q. 7 c. 27).
64 James A. Brundage, *Law, Sex, and Christian Society in Medieval Europe*, Chicageo, 1987, p. 497.
65 Ibid., pp. 255, 426; Georges Duby, *The Knight, the Lady, and the Priest: The Making of Modern Marriage in Medieval France*, Harmondsworth, 1984, pp. 33, 65, 164; Ennen, p. 137.
66 Brundage, *Law, Sex, and Christian Society*, pp. 198, 241–2, 282–4, 368, 447, 505.
67 Maschke, p. 60.
68 Ibid., p. 34. On the visual arts see also Christopher Brooke, *The Medieval Idea of Marriage*, Oxford, 1989, pp. 280–6.
69 'Jokes', p. 98.
70 Ibid., p. 96.
71 On the sadism of this story, see Müller, 'Noch einmal: Maere und Novelle', pp. 297–301. He interprets the maimings as the sign of the irrational which can never be brought entirely under control.
72 NGA, no. 1.
73 NGA, no. 2.
74 *Die eingemauerte Frau, Verserzählungen I*, no. 6.
75 Claude Lévi-Strauss, 'The Structural Study of Myth', in *Structural Anthropology I*, Harmondsworth, 1977, p. 216, and 'The Story of Asdiwal', in *Structural Anthropology II*, Harmondsworth, 1978, pp. 170–5.
76 *Werke*, no. 13.
77 On *separatio a mensa et thoro* on grounds of adultery, which some municipalities granted without recourse to the courts Christian, see Köbler, pp. 147–8, and Rudolf Weigand, 'Ehe- und Familienrecht in der spätmittelalterlichen Stadt', in Haverkamp, *Haus und Familie*, pp. 188–9.

Women's body of knowledge: epistemology and misogyny in the *Romance of the Rose*

The argument of this paper is that changing attitudes towards the problem of knowledge between the twelfth and thirteenth centuries trouble the equations between femininity and carnality, and between masculinity and the mind or spirit, which are extensively invoked in classical and patristic writing to justify the subordination of women to men. The increasingly complex treatment of the mind–body dichotomy in this period, and the growing emphasis (under the influence of new translations and adaptations of Aristotle) on the senses as a source of knowledge, lead to the body figuring in intellectual discourses other than those propounding moral or theological hierarchies, and pose the threat that the alleged physicality of the feminine implies not women's inferiority, but the possibility that they might enjoy more immediate access to knowledge than men. This argument will be developed primarily with reference to the continuation of the *Romance of the Rose* by Jean de Meun (*c.*1276),[1] a text whose interpretation is very controversial, but which is universally acknowledged as unfolding a literary response to the intellectual and academic debates of the thirteenth century.

'Epistemology' may be an anachronistic term for speaking of medieval thought, since questions of knowledge are dispersed among a wide variety of different kinds of intellectual investigation. A major field to have epistemological implications is, for example, the study of the Trinity, whose persons are replicated in their human *imago*, the interlocking faculties of the mind.[2] A second, philosophical area of inquiry to raise epistemological questions is logic, since arguments over the status of universals, focused from the twelfth century onwards as a debate between nominalists and realists, associate language, ontology, and epistemology. Third, the impetus given to psychological investigation by medical, scientific and philosophical texts from antiquity leads to competing accounts of the role of man in nature, and of the 'powers' (*potentiae*) of the mind as they relate to sensory perception.

Disparate as these areas of academic study are, however, they are united in the literary form of the *Rose*, since on the one hand its anatomisation of psychic life deploys as 'characters' interacting faculties or inclinations (such as Amor and Raison),[3] and on the other, its reliance on personified abstractions each bearing the name of a common noun invites reflection on the reference of abstract vocabulary.[4] Furthermore, the framework of the poem, established by the author of the first part of the text which Jean continued and whom he names as Guillaume de Lorris, is that of the dream vision. In his prologue, Guillaume alludes to Macrobius' influential commentary on the *Somnium Scipionis* which categorises dreams according to their epistemological value. In its highest manifestation (that of the *somnium*), dreaming is a source of revelation; in its lowest (that of the *visum*), one of sensory delusion.[5] It is not known why Jean de Meun chose to continue Guillaume's apparently unfinished text which, the narrator claims, was composed forty years before Jean took it up. But given that Jean's continuation is in large measure composed of translations and adaptations of two famous Latin philosophical dream-vision texts, Boethius' *De Consolatione Philosophiae* and Alan of Lille's *De Planctu Naturae*, it is very likely that the possibility of exploiting parallels and divergences between them and the *Rose* inspired Jean's enterprise.[6] All three texts, as well as invoking the dream framework, and hence their own potentially educative function, play on a teacher–student relation within the dream itself. The dream-persona of Boethius, who appears to be the most autobiographical and least ironic of the three students, is lengthily instructed by Philosophia. The dream-persona of Alan, in a considerably more ambiguous text, listens to Natura's complaints against human misbehaviour. The figure of the lover in the *Rose*, initially inducted into the Ovidian labyrinth of courtship by Amor in Guillaume's poem, becomes an increasingly burlesque and unwilling recipient of a deluge of advice and information from Jean de Meun's protagonists, of whom Raison and Nature are inventive reworkings of Philosophia and Natura. Knowledge, its make-up, status, and how we come by it, is unmistakably a major motive force in this extraordinary poem.

The ostensible subject matter of the *Rose* is, however, the quest by the lover–dreamer for the mysterious but sensually alluring rose first seen (in Guillaume's text) in the well of Narcissus and confirmed as love-object by Amor. The theme of erotic love, vigorously kept in play by Jean de Meun, offers opportunity for interweaving the multiplicity of medieval discourses about women and the feminine (medical, moral, political); among these, misogynistic commonplaces recur with dismaying frequency. Misogyny thrives on repetition; it has been aptly described by Howard Bloch as a 'citational mode'.[7] In the celebrated passage where Jean's narrator defends the presence in his work of views that women might find disobliging, he does so by adducing the authority of his classical predecessors.[8] Yet to identify misogyny with textuality, and thus with literary representation in general, as Bloch does, is to lose its political significance for an uncertain gain in abstraction. Whilst misogyny may be endemic, it none the less manifests itself particularly strongly in specific historical outbreaks. It has been argued, against Bloch's position, that these correspond with anxieties created by political and economic conditions.[9] The argument presented here is a further attempt to historicise misogyny, by relating it to the intellectual climate in which it is produced.

MISOGYNY IN THE *ROSE*

The homology whereby the feminine is to the body as the masculine to the mind is discernible in Guillaume de Lorris's part of the *Rose*, which imposes a radical divide between lover and rose as between subject and object, person and thing, speaker and mute. The lover's interaction with Raison (even if he rejects her), and with Amor-as-mentor, is opposed to the Rose's subjection to the elemental force of Venus, who brandishes her torch but scarcely speaks a word. The lover may well be deluded when he thinks himself in a paradise garden, and learns the rules of love as deviant Decalogue. The appeal to Macrobius may similarly undermine rather than support the narrator's categorisation of his dream as an authoritative revelation. Nevertheless, his self-image is of one who breathes a rarefied air and experiences privileged illumination, whereas the rose just smells, and grows a little fatter.

If there is misogyny in this divide between 'feminine' body and 'masculine' mind, it remains implicit. But in Jean's continuation, which always errs on the side of explicitness, the identification of the feminine with the physical forms the basis of several misogynistic tirades. For the Vilain Jalous, a figure cited by Ami to denounce the ills of marriage, women are equated with their sexuality which, he lengthily laments, men are unable to control. Virtuous women are unnatural, rarer than the phoenix or white crows; if you find a chaste one, Juvenal says, then go and make offerings to the gods; if you choose one of the swarms of evil ones, you'll suffer for it (ll. 8687–926). Women are synonymous with sensual desire:

Toutes serés, estes ou fustes
de fait ou de volenté putes,
et qui bien vous encercheroit
toutes putains vous troveroit;
et qui peüst le fait estaindre,
volenté ne puet nus contraindre.
Tel avantage ont toutes dames
qu'eles sont de lor volentés dames;
l'en ne lor puet le cuer changier
por batre ne por ledengier.

All you women will be, are, or have been whores, either in deed or in desire, and anyone who were to investigate you would find you all whores; and even if he could prevent the deed, no one can extinguish the desire. Women have an advantage in being mistress of their desires; however much you beat them or insult them, you can't change their disposition.

(9155–62)

Although Ami cites the Jalous as an example of how *not* to treat your wife, his views on women are much the same. They are, he says, citing Juvenal again, just wall-to-wall appetite:

> Si sont eles voir presque toutes
> de prendre convoiteuses, et gloutes
> de ravir et de devorer,
> tant qu'il n'i puist rienz demorer
> a ceus qui plus loiaument les aiment;
> car Juvenaus si nous raconte
> qui de Berine tient son conte,
> que miex vosist un des yex perdre
> que soi a un seul homme aerdre,
> car nuls seus n'i peüst soffire
> tant estoit de chaude matire.

And truly they are almost all eager to take what they can, and greedy to snatch up and devour, so that they leave destitute those who most claim to be theirs and love them most loyally; for Juvenal relates in the story of Hibernia that she would rather lose one of her eyes than cling to one man, for no man on his own could satisfy her, she was made of such hot matter.

(8281–92)

Women's bodies are at once the site of their lust and, given the 'heat' of their 'matter', the explanation for it. Like matter, they lack stability. Ami complains that, like Solomon, he never met a woman who was 'ferme' (l. 9924).[10]

The second major misogynistic sequence in the text, which forms part of the exchanges between Genius and Nature, also equates the feminine with the instability of matter. Genius's strictures expand on Ami's point:

> Que ja feme n'iert tant estable
> qu'el ne soit diverse et muable.
> . . .
> Briement, en fame a tant de vice
> que nulz ne puet ses meurs parvers
> conter par rimes ne par vers;
> . . .
> tant sont decevables et nices,
> et de flechissable nature.

For woman can never be sufficiently stable as to prevent her from being various and changeable . . . In sum, there is so much wrong with woman that you couldn't recount all her perverse ways in rhyme or verse; ... they are easily deceived, stupid, and their nature is easily swayed.

(16327–8, 16334–6, 16342–3)

Their 'flechissable nature' aligns women with the material world of nature in general; for in her confession, Nature often refers to the contrast between the permanent or changeless, which is the domain of the supernatural, and her own, impermanent and subject to corruption:

Je ne fis onc riens pardurables;
quant que je fais est corrumpable.
Platon meïsmes le tesmoingne
. . .
Mi fait, ce dit, sont tuit soluble,
tant ai pooir povre et onuble.

I never made anything eternal; everything I make is subject to corruption. Plato himself bears witness ... My deeds, he says, can all be dissolved, so poor and shadowy is my power.

(19059–63, 19071–2)

Woman and Nature are analogues of each other, for if woman has the deficiencies of natural matter, Nature admits her feminine failings:

Ne si ne vuel or pas lasser
moi de parler ne vous d'oïr;
bon fait prolixité foïr,
si sont fames mout ennuieuses
et de parler contrarieuses;
si vous prise que ne vous desplese
por ce que du tout ne me tese,
se bien par la verité vois.

Fame sui, si ne me puis taire,
ains vuel de ja tout reveler,
car fame ne puet rienz celer.

Now I don't want to wear myself out with talking or you with listening; prolixity is best avoided and women are tedious and vexatious with their talking; I beg you not to be displeased that I'm not altogether silent, provided I am proceeding with the truth.

I am a woman, I cannot be silent, on the contrary I must tell all, for woman can conceal nothing.

(18296–303, 19218–20)

These passages, however, mark an important shift in the object of misogyny. Still present is the emphasis on women's uncontrollability, but now it is not appetite, but speech, that is incapable of restraint. And woman's speech – or Nature's at least – is an uninhibited torrent of truth. The line 'car fame ne puet rienz celer' refers us back to Genius's 'consolation' of the weeping Nature as she began her confession. For after his introductory comments on woman's 'flechissable nature', Genius warns at length against the dangers of confiding in women:

Nulz honz qui soit de mere nez,
s'il n'est yvres ne forcenés,
ne doit a fame reveler
nulle rienz qui face a celer,
se d'autrui ne la vuet oïr.

No one, unless he be drunk or mad, should reveal to a woman something that should be kept quiet, unless he wants to hear it on other people's lips.
(16349–53)

He continues with a fabliau-like bedroom scene where a wife bares her breasts and worms the secrets out her husband by a combination of nagging and sexual enticements. All Genius's sympathy goes out to the unfortunate wretch, who has merely committed some murder or other mishap (l. 16394), finding himself thus subjected to sexual harrassment. He launches into a specimen sermon designed to warn men against giving in. They can have sex with their wives, he says, but otherwise they should avoid them and never tell them anything that should be kept concealed (ll. 16618–40). Failure to comply with this advice will hand power over to women, and a woman with power 'is a vexation to her husband'. So the message is:

Quant entre les bras les tenés
et les acolés et baisiés,
taisiés, taisiés, taisiés, taisiés!
Taisiés, enfant, taisiés la jangle,
taisiés, ne savés qu'a en l'angle,
taisiés taisiés, vers tex oreilles,
taisiés, taisiés, ce sont merveilles!

When you hold them in your arms and embrace and kiss them, keep quiet, keep quiet, keep quiet, keep quiet! Keep quiet, children, keep quiet with your chatter, keep quiet, you don't know what may be skulking in the corner, keep quiet, keep quiet, so these ears don't hear, keep quiet, keep quiet, these are marvels!
(16658–60.04)[11]

Burlesque as this repetition is, it is also neurotic. Why has the character of misogyny changed from anxiety about maintaining possession of a woman-as-object to fear of her power as a knowing subject?

FEMALE AUTHORITY IN THE *ROSE*

The purveyors of information in the *Rose* are, as Gunn somewhat resentfully points out, nearly all feminine. 'One is grateful', he protests, 'for the presence of Ami'.[12] Raison is not above feminine coquetry; she is followed by a series of masculine speakers (Ami, Amor, and the *louche* figure of Fausemblant); but then there are some 7000 lines dominated by the Vielle and Nature, followed by the sermon preached by Genius to Amor's barons on behalf of Nature. Venus, representative of female sensuality, takes control of the *dénouement* and gains access to the rose for the lover. When Genius warns against women's loquacity and access to truth, he draws attention to the problem facing readers of the *Rose*. How do we respond to this marked pre-eminence of feminine authorities? The spectre of the uncontrollable woman – sexual and/or knowing – is raised throughout the discourses of Nature and the Vielle, though in very different ways. I shall look briefly at the Vielle first, before concentrating on the more philosophically interesting figure of Nature.

1. The Vielle addresses her advice to Bel Acuel. She wants to enlighten 'him' (as the expression of the rose's accessibility to the lover) regarding women's sexual experience, and train him to extort the maximum of material benefit from men, whilst conceding the least degree of personal freedom, in order to exact revenge for the ills she herself has suffered at their hands (ll. 12880–2) but is too old now to avenge in person (ll. 12893–923). Her speech is thus a counterpart to those of Ami and the Jalous, in that she is concerned with evading the possession which the Jalous seeks to assert, and with preserving women's 'natural' access to pleasure in the face of male exploitation. She is standardly read as the embodiment, and justification, of misogynistic prejudice.[13] And certainly, since much of what she says is an adaptation of Ovid's *Ars Amatoria* 3, she cannot be taken as a straightforward representation of 'a woman's point of view'. Her contention that the more lovers you have, the safer – and richer – you can be, followed up by tips on seductive behaviour, pander to a combination of male anxiety and titillation (ll. 13079 ff.), as do her suggestions for stage-managing lovers' and husbands' movements, so that they never coincide (ll. 14227 ff.).

Her advice also, however, contains some clear reversals of misogynistic *topoi*. You seduce men by appealing to *their* sensual desires. And you need many lovers because men are basically unreliable and untrustworthy:

Car il ont trop les cuers muables.
Jone genz ne sont pas estables.

Briement tuit les lobent et trichent,
tant sont ribaut, par tout se fichent,
si les doit l'en aussi trichier.

For their hearts are too changeable, young men are not stable.

In short, they all deceive and cheat [women], they are so lecherous, seeking advantage everywhere, and so they deserve to be cheated in return.

(13141–2, 13265–7)

This is the vocabulary of misogyny turned back against its authors. The Vielle's teaching overall is that women share the same material nature as men (and like them have a right to sexual pleasure) whilst their moral character stems from the need for self-defence against male exploitation. This last point is confirmed by the numerous parallels between her speech and those of Ami and the Jalous; hers mirrors theirs, just as women's moral choices are forced on them by men. In particular, the Vielle admits the necessity of marriage as a safeguard against rape (ll. 13907–16), thereby countering Ami's jaunty recommendation to the lover to 'take the rose by force and show that you're a man', since 'that's what women really like' (ll. 7690–4).

The Vielle's speech, then, plays a vital part in subverting the 'woman is to carnal as man is to mental' homology. More accurately, she deconstructs it by demonstrating that the meanings assigned to the lower term in each of the two oppositions in fact already inhere in the higher term. Women's allegedly characteristic 'instability' and 'lechery' are already present in men; the pressure of material and physical circumstances (such as male philandering) cannot be divorced from mental and moral behaviour.

If her words retrospectively subvert the misogyny of possession associated with Ami and the Jalous, they also anticipate the misogyny centring on language and knowledge voiced by Genius. Unlike any of the other speakers in the *Rose*, the Vielle identifies herself *as* a woman; although aware of prolixity (ll. 13904–5) she vaunts her authority. In his translation, Dahlberg refers to her speech as a 'sermon', but this is misleading; it is a university lecture. The Vielle's discourse alone mimics this academic genre; only she of all the text's would-be teachers is a qualified *mestre* (l. 13505). Her claim to her *chaire* (l. 12817) rests, it is true, on practical rather than theoretical studies:

> N'onc ne fui d'Amors a escole
> ou l'en leüst la theorique,
> mes je sai bien par la pratique.
> Experiment m'en ont fait sage
> que j'ai hantés tout mon aage.

> I was never at Love's school where the theoretical studies were lectured on, but I know through the practical ones. Experiences/experiments have made me wise, that I have pursued throughout my life.

(12802–6)

There is a play here between 'practical' meaning 'drawn from lived experience', and meaning the 'practical disciplines' which a conventional academic hierarchy distinguishes from theoretical ones;[14] a play which leaves the reader free to decide whether it involves a promotion for experience, a demotion of the practical sciences, or an irreducible incongruity. The Vielle's sleazy past, foundation of her 'authority', leaves a generous dose of irony in the passage however one interprets it. The joke is maintained throughout her address (rebuttal of the 'faus texte' of Amor's commands, ll. 13028–36; direction that her lecture be heard in other institutions, ll. 13497–8), culminating with her cocking a snook at the university authorities. Bel Acuel is to memorise the Vielle's lecture:

> Si en serés mestre cum gié
> et en lirés tout sanz congié,
> maugré tretouz les chanceliers,
> et par chambres et par celiers.

You will then be a *mestre* like I am and will be able to lecture without leave and despite the chancellors in bedrooms and cellars.

(13505–8)

This recalls the 1276 prohibition in the University of Paris against teaching in a private place any subject other than grammar or logic (which were both taught to the young, and presumably not thought to be inflammatory).[15] I shall return later to the condemnations of the 1270s which are often invoked as the immediate context of Jean de Meun's *Rose*. My point now is that the identification suggested by this passage between a raddled old woman and a university Master of Arts exacerbates the problem of interpreting the Vielle's address. Whether Jean is sneering at Arts Masters, or defending the claims of women's experience, or merely laughing at the gap his text opens up between the two, his readers find themselves already on the edge of Genius's misogynistic terrain: the possibility (or threat) of women having access to the language of knowledge.

2. If the comedy of the Vielle's lecture is somewhat uneasy, in Nature's confession the stakes soar. Nature is not 'a woman', but her material instability and loquacity identify her, as we have seen, with the 'feminine'. And yet her discourse ranges widely over the curricula of the two major faculties of the thirteenth-century University of Paris, Arts (represented primarily by her expositions of cosmology and natural science) and Theology. How are these elements brought together, and how do readers respond to their conjunction in a feminine speaker?

Unlike Alan of Lille's Natura, who lodges a complaint, Jean's Nature confesses – parodically, however, since the 'fault' is not hers – to Genius her priest (ll. 16285 ff.). Apologies for her tears prompt Genius to his virulent tirade against women for faults from which he admits Nature is exempt (ll. 16314–706), a speech referred to rather surprisingly as his 'comfort' of her (l. 16708). Nature has been represented as ceaselessly active at her forge, repairing the ravages of Death. The created world appears as a ferment of activity: Death chasing everywhere, catching any-one she can; individuals fleeing this way and that, trying desperately to avoid her clutches; and Nature, hammering away, producing new speci-mens so that however successful Death may be against individuals, she cannot put an end to species (ll. 15891–16016). Nature starts by describ-ing her role as 'chamberlain' of God's creation (l. 16772). As such, she acts as God's chief official and deputy (*connestable et viquere*, l. 16782). God devised the form, divisions and proportions of the universe, and entrusted their perpetuation to her. She watches over the 'beautiful golden chain that laces together the four elements' (ll. 16786–7), i.e. the whole inter-connecting fabric of material creation; and everything in it, except for one single creature, obeys her (l. 16800). Nature's role is thus presented in terms of twelfth-century Christianised Platonism; she is the material reflec-tion of God's spiritual intentions. So far, apart from the parodic elements, she closely follows her model in the *De Planctu Naturae*.[16]

Nature then proceeds to work through the various parts of the uni-verse, eliminating from her 'confession' the parts that are functioning as intended. In so doing, she is departing from the *De Planctu* to incorporate thirteenth-century science inspired by Aristotelian categories, as taught at the University of Paris by such masters as Albert the Great.[17] From the sky with the fixed stars (l. 16801) she quickly reaches the planets, whose movements detain her for over 2,000 lines (ll. 16833–18966). Inserted into this scientific treatise, however, is a protracted essay on why the planets do not control our destinies. Nature argues that reason can rise above and govern natural impulse (ll. 17087–100). Somewhat unexpectedly she raises the question, 'hard to explain to laymen', 'how predestination and divine foreknowledge, full of every foresight, can exist alongside free will' (ll. 17101–6). Imperceptibly Nature digresses into theology. Free will is com-patible with God's foreknowledge, since God sees everything in the pres-ence of eternity whereas man's perceptions are all located in time; man therefore has to work out the plot as he goes along, whilst God knows the story already. This is based on the teachings of Philosophia in Boethius' *De Consolatione Philosophiae*. Nature's defence of free will leads her back to the subject of man's ability, through reason, to dominate natural drives, but this time Nature also includes reason's capacity to rise above accidents of fortune, and resist sin (ll. 17527–78). If man can make sense of the movements of the stars, he can predict disasters and take preventive measures (ll. 17579–702). And if he can thus manage his body, what can he not achieve with his soul, which is so much more powerful (ll. 17703–14)? Regretfully, Nature admits that it would take too long to get to the bottom of these theological issues (ll. 17727–33). But she stresses their relevance to her theme, since man might wish to plead innocence on the grounds that his conduct is God's fault not his own (ll. 17774–6). On the contrary, she maintains, his folly arises from a failure of self-knowledge, which is caused by failure to keep his reason clear, which stems from vice, which is the result of a failure to exercise free will, which she has just demonstrated him to possess (ll. 17862–74).

Now, however, Nature leaves theology; it is time to return to the skies (l. 17880). The second part of her scientific treatise deals with the weather, optics, and delusions which include dreams remarkably reminiscent of that described in the *Romance of the Rose*. Superstitious belief in comets as signalling crises for kings or princes is combated; whereupon she expatiates on the futility of human belief in rank, and defends clerks as the most reasonable among men, and therefore the most capable of leading a moral life. At this point (ll. 18295–303) she worries in case she is falling into the feminine vice of prolixity, but none the less devotes 600 more lines to this section. The planets at last dealt with, she dispatches with alacrity the elements (l. 18967), plants (l. 18981) and living creatures, reaching (at long last) the guilty party at line 19021. Man alone, the pinnacle and epitome of created life, is worse than a wolf to her (l. 19054).

Here Nature again leaves the natural for the supernatural; the reasons for this are not clear at the time, and the transition is very abrupt. Admitting that she did not make man's understanding, she contrasts her own works, which are material and temporary, with those of God, which are spiritual and enduring. Citing Plato, Nature celebrates the eternal soul. She then tells of what even Plato, as a pagan, couldn't understand; only a virgin womb could comprehend God and know the marvels of the Trinity (ll. 19119–45). Nature concedes that the virgin birth is beyond her comprehension (ll. 19161–2), but this does not prevent her briefly expounding the incarnation, crucifixion and redemption. This excursus, it emerges, is an elaboration of the theme of man's sin; God having made man's reason, man used it to turn against him, thus making necessary Christ's redemption.

Reminding us once more than women cannot control their tongues (ll. 19218–20), Nature at last gets to the nub of her confession: she repents that she ever made man and proceeds to enumerate his faults. He is proud, murderous, thieving, treacherous, envious, and so on (ll. 19225–34) – a slave to all the vices. Evoking the pains of hell, she leaves it to God to punish him (l. 19325). One fault, however, is her particular concern: man's failure to do Amor's task with the 'tools' she provided. This 'naturalism' again marks a divergence from the Nature of Alan of Lille, the emphasis of whose plaint is ethical.[18] So Nature concludes her 'confession' by sending Genius to Amor's camp, with instructions to multiply on pain of excommunication (ll. 19378–88).

Nature's confession, then, is like a layer cake: alternating layers of science and theology, with an icing of Neoplatonism on top, and supported, as on a firm base, on the need for sexual reproduction. The 'naturalism' of this need sits oddly with her 'natural' cosmology (derived in part from Alan, in part from Albert) and her 'natural' theology (much of which comes from Boethius); and the parodic character of the confession, with its frequent misogynistic asides, draws attention to the bizarreness of the whole concoction. Not surprisingly, Nature has found admirers and detractors among *Rose* critics. My own preference goes to the view that different accounts of what nature might be are brought together so as to throw their discrepancies into relief, in a sceptical response to the multiplicity of academic discourses. I am in agreement here with Lucy Polak, who argues that Jean's Nature makes for herself the most spiritualising claims of twelfth-century Neoplatonism, whilst in fact occupying the most material and 'naturalistic' ground made available by thirteenth-century Aristotelianism.[19]

Yet however oddly they are put together, and making allowance for popularisation, both her science and her theology broadly conform to thirteenth-century university teaching.[20] Nature – the embodiment of the feminine, and the feminine as embodiment – does seem to know her stuff. It is no coincidence that anxiety about feminine access to knowledge characterises the misogynistic digressions of this part of the text. We have moved from a parodic university lecturer (the Vielle) to a figure disconcertingly like the real thing. Like the Vielle's, Nature's speech is both authoritative and self-undermining; but unlike the Vielle's, whose ramblings can be laughed off, the content of Nature's speech demands that we confront the question, what *are* the relations between the body, knowledge, and gender? I shall sketch answers to these questions by considering the *Rose* in comparison first with the *De Consolatione* and the *De Planctu*, and then with the subsequent philosophical tradition.

EPISTEMOLOGY AND THE BODY IN BOETHIUS AND ALAN OF LILLE

For Philosophia in the *De Consolatione*, the various faculties are ranged hierarchically, along with their corresponding objects. She first appears wearing a robe embroidered with a ladder usually interpreted as marking the progression from practical to theoretical knowledge (1.1).[21] From the end of book 1, and then in more detail in books 2 and 3, she teaches Boethius not to put his trust in material things, which come and go following the accidents of Fortune. When, in book 5.4, she reaches the more difficult subject of Divine Providence, a more comprehensive epistemological scheme is sketched.

Everything that is known is comprehended not according to its own nature, but according to the ability to know of those who do the knowing. Let us make it clear with a brief example; the same roundness of shape is recognised in one way by the sight and in another way by the touch . . . Similarly man himself is beheld in different ways by sense-perception (*sensus*), imagination (*imaginatio*), reason (*ratio*) and intelligence (*intellegentia*). The senses examine his shape as constituted in matter, while imagination considers his shape alone without matter. Reason transcends imagination, too, and with a universal consideration reflects upon the species inherent in individual instances. But there exists the more exalted eye of intelligence which passes beyond the sphere of the universe to behold the simple form itself with the pure vision of the mind.

Philosophia goes on to stress that the higher faculties are capable of the kinds of knowledge conveyed by the lower ones, whereas the reverse is not the case. Thus intelligence, for example, can achieve the whole range of knowledge available to the senses, imagination and reason; but imagination, whilst subsuming sensory perception, can get no higher than freeing sense data from their immediate realisation by matter. The purpose of Philosophia's teaching is to induce reason to raise itself to the heights of intelligence, in order to perceive the highest truths:

> Let us then, if we can, raise ourselves up to the heights of that supreme intelligence. There reason will be able to see what it cannot see by itself – it will be able to see how that which has no certain occurrence may be seen by a certain and fixed foreknowledge, a knowledge that is not opinion, but the boundless immediacy of the highest form of knowing.
>
> (5.5)

The visionary texts of the twelfth-century Neoplatonists, including the *De Planctu*, are inspired by Philosophia's prospect of an 'intellectual pilgrimage from the sensible world to the level of vision and theology'.[22] Citation of Boethius' list of faculties is widespread.[23] Alan of Lille is among those who draw upon it. In his *Summa Quoniam Homines*[24] he distinguishes *ratio* ('reasoning power which is exercised upon human and earthly things. Natural science or *naturalis philosophia* is its field')[25] from *intellectus* (understanding of spiritual beings, angels and souls) and *intelligentia* (by which man can have some comprehension of the Trinity). The *Quinque digressiones cogitationis*, a text of uncertain attribution but which could be by Alan, extends this hierarchy downwards by adding imagination and the senses, in conformity with the Boethian tradition.[26]

The relationship between soul and body is Natura's first major theme in the *De Planctu* (6),[27] where it is developed in a quasi-Boethian meditation on the hierarchy of faculties and their respective objects of knowledge. Natura describes how she disposed man's material body with its five senses to guard it (6.26–9; p. 117). Thus rendered less 'disgusting' (6.29–32; pp. 117–18), the body is married to the spirit as wife to husband. (Note the explicit gendering of the body as feminine and the spirit as masculine.) The spirit is then equipped with inner powers (*potentiae virtuales*) to match the external senses. Reason embraces virtue; yet on its own it is incapable of theological knowledge. For that, man needs wisdom (*Sapientia*) which rules over the inferior faculties. Nature stresses that the truths of theology are beyond her competence, and admonishes men to listen to its authoritative pronouncements, rather than to her reasoning (6.140–1; p. 124).

The body's place at the bottom of the hierarchy is moralised in both texts. The whole point of the *De Consolatione* is to console Boethius that, whilst he is confined in a literal prison, the prison he most needs to escape is that of the body. His mind can and must transcend it (1.5; 3.7).[28] Sensual pleasures figure among the material gifts of Fortune and are to be held in contempt (3.7–8). It is noteworthy that Alan gives pride of place to a personification which occupies a median position in the hierarchy of knowledge rather than to a figure of wisdom (like Boethius') who can move to its summit and thereby encompass it all; Natura is actually addressed by the dreamer of the *De Planctu* as *omnium rerum mediatrix* (8.108; p. 138). Her priest Genius who, as Wetherbee has argued, may be a figure of imagination, stands at an interface between visionary revelation and sensory perception.[29] Evans has suggested that Alan's interest is directed towards boundaries: 'the most important point he can show us [in the hierarchy of knowledge] is the threshold which divides the liberal arts from theology'.[30] Thus, Evans contends, although he accepts traditional hierarchies such as soul–body, heaven–earth, God–Nature, Divine–human, Alan chooses to explore the lower term,[31] the higher one being seen above all by comparison with what it is not.[32] Yet whilst Natura may be closer to the human body than Philosophia is, her representations of it are dominated by abstract and moral schemata which assimilate it to the cosmos (6.106–20; pp. 122–3), or to the state (6.27–99; pp. 117–22); irregular sexual behaviour is glossed in terms of work practices, or more consistently, of grammatical solecism and dialectical incompetence. The body becomes a text, where homosexuality threatens to destroy man's intended harmony with the universe, his capacity to represent its order. At times, then, it seems that for Natura the dichotomy between body and spirit is invoked primarily in order that the first term can be used as a metaphor for the malfunction of the second – as indeed it is in Boethius.

As a seat of appetite, however, Natura has nothing but contempt for the body. Its impulses are contrasted with those of reason:

> For the movement of reason, springing from a heavenly origin, escaping the destruction of things on earth, in its process of thought turns back again to the heavens. On the other hand, the movements of sensuality, going planet-like in opposition to the fixed sky of reason, with twisted course slip down to the destruction of earthly things.
>
> (6.55–8; p. 119)

Later in her lament, the notion of appetite provides a link between sexual and other vices. Gluttony anticipates lust (12.10–11; p. 169); other vices follow. Natura exhorts her listeners to abandon their subservience to the dictates of the flesh:

> Thus man's reason, trodden underfoot by greed, becomes a slave to the flesh and is forced to wait upon it as its handmaiden. Thus the eye of the heart, darkened by the fog of the flesh, grows weak and, suffering an eclipse, becomes isolated and inactive. Thus the shadow of the flesh debasingly cloaks the radiance of the human sense and the glory of the mind becomes exceedingly inglorious.
>
> (13.59–64; pp. 183–4)

She urges them to reverse this process by making the flesh the handmaid of the spirit (15.20; p. 194). The body conceived in abstract terms may be positively valued as subtending a network of illuminating analogies, but *qua* flesh it must be subdued and transcended.

If we compare these texts with the *Rose*, it is apparent, I think, that Jean is both invoking and flouting their epistemological (and moral) hierarchies. Much of the general pattern of Philosophia's argument is reproduced by Jean. But the teachings on Fortune are entrusted to Raison, whereas those on Providence are given to Nature. There is, then, in both texts an overall progression from seeing events from the limited perspective of man's perception of material things, to understanding his place in a theological scheme in which both divine predestination and free will have their place. But whereas in Boethius the movement up the ladder of enlightenment is matched by progression up a ladder of faculties, in Jean the movement up the scheme of knowledge is played off against a flagrantly transgressive shift downwards, from the mind (Raison) to the material world of Nature, and thence downwards again, to the genitals, manifested first in their admittedly problematic representation as Genius, then in Venus, and finally in the meeting of the dreamer with the rose (or, if we revert for a moment back to the upward hierarchy, of the pilgrim with the relics). Thus Jean's continuation is obedient to the Boethian tradition which works *up* a hierarchy of knowledge, but also reverses it by working *down* the faculties of perception. The two movements, one up, the other down, intersect in the figure of Nature whose speech, as we have seen, contains striking conjunctions of the material with the spiritual. Furthermore, unlike Natura, Jean's Nature does not condemn appetite but encourages it; the criticisms of desire pronounced by Natura in the *De Planctu* 9 are given to Raison in the *Rose*, whereas Nature throws her weight behind the lover. Her materiality and sensuality do not appear to inhibit her access to 'higher' forms of knowledge – *au contraire.*

Subsequently the divergence between the upwards and downwards movements in the poem becomes increasingly burlesque. Genius's sermon is a crazy miscellany of visionary theology and sexual exhortation, and the copulation of the 'pilgrim' with the rose an audacious exploration of the capacity (or incapacity) of the material and the spiritual to act as metaphors for each other. In Nature's discourse, however, the two movements, upwards and downwards, though they meet in an uneasy and unstable way, *do* meet. Her teachings are basically sound; it is the way they are combined that is so bizarre. Jean's text, then, is a tremendous challenge to the traditional Boethian hierarchy; it seems momentarily possible that the material *could* be a guide to the spiritual, and sensuality an impulse towards truth. Nature's speech is a provocation to a major philosophical tradition.

GENDER AND THE BODY IN ALAN

In the later sections of the *De Planctu* we are reminded of Natura's opening theme of the marriage of body to mind as of wife to husband. Natura's message is not only that man should not be dominated by the flesh, but that it is the *femininity* of the flesh that must be mastered. Degeneracy struck under the auspices of the female goddess Venus, to whom Natura foolishly entrusted the workings of the universe (8.235–46; p. 146). When Hymenaeus is introduced to restore order, his size and age are depicted as constantly varying, but not his gender: 'On his face there showed no signs of feminine softness; rather the authority of manly dignity alone held sway there . . . His hair lay in orderly fashion to prevent it from appearing to degenerate into feminine softness' (16.10–16; pp. 196–7). Alan's insistence on this steadfast masculinity casts light on his apparent homophobia; homosexuality is for him at once an example, and a metaphor, of man's 'effeminacy', the weakening of the masculine mind by 'feminine' bodily practice. His text itself is homosexual, in its desire to repress anything but the masculinity he admires.[33]

How is this denigration of the body as feminine compatible with the deployment of a female agent of revelation? In the *De Consolatione*, although Philosophia is feminine, her gender is not referred to after the opening prose section. She is more a voice than a fleshly body. Her authority does not seem to be compromised by any association between femininity and materiality; the problem may be raised *by her* when she describes Fortune as a fickle woman, but not in relation *to her*. Alan's text shows more brinkmanship. Natura is not beyond the feminine; it takes a man to fix her chariot for her, for example (4.11–14; p. 108). The narrator is at pains to point out that the dainty kiss she gives to Genius is reminiscent more of Cupid than of Venus (18.114–5; p. 219). But if it is the feminine that should be repressed, then it seems that Natura succeeds, by and large, in doing so. She aligns herself, as *mediatrix*, with reason in the middle of the hierarchy, rejecting the body as a material entity on the one hand, and deferring to the insights of theology – and the priestly authority of Genius – on the other.

In its treatment of this material, the *Rose* once more plays the hierarchical systems against each other. It follows – and exaggerates – Alan's misogyny, while at the same time promoting a figure of Nature who does not identify (as Alan's did) with reason against the flesh/the feminine, but with the material and the feminine together. The text's philosophical provocation is staged not just by the body, but by the feminine body; just as (as Nature says) a woman's body comprehended the incarnation. And Jean's Nature even goes so far as to recast her Latin model's warning that homosexuality leads to damnation as the surprising claim that heterosexual desire will lead to salvation. There is a good deal of deliberate outrageousness in Jean's representation of Nature.

EPISTEMOLOGY AFTER NEOPLATONISM

Whilst I do not think that Jean is aiming accurately to reflect any particular writer or text subsequent to the *De Planctu*, it is to this material we should look, in my view, for the catalyst to his remarkable overturning of Boethius and Alan. In the epistemology of Augustine,

> Intellection was the interior vision of things in their true reality, reality that was vitally and luminously present within the mind in Neoplatonic fashion as an intelligible object that was identified with each particular intelligible and yet was one intelligible. Augustine's use of this intelligible world to explain human thought is generally called today, as it was occasionally in the Middle Ages, the doctrine of 'divine illumination'. That doctrine obviated any need to explain how external things could get into the mind in order to be known. They were already there, since they really existed in the mind's interior light, God himself; indeed, they had a higher type of being in the divine Word than in the external world.[34]

In such an account, the body risks being an impediment to knowledge, since it 'fogs' or 'cloaks' the mind, reducing its capacity to be illumined. Qualified expressions of this view of the body are to be found, as we have seen, in the *De Consolatione* and the *De Planctu*. But Aristotle's work (especially the *De Anima*), which became available to Western scholars from the late twelfth century, reviews the contrary claim that all knowledge derives ultimately from sensory experience. Cognition, on this account, is not best described in terms of light, but of existence. Thought is not the same as sensory perception, but cannot take place without it, for the mind must operate on sensible images (*phantasmata*) which exist in the mind as the result of sense data. The clash between the Augustininan and Aristotelian epistemologies posed problems to thirteenth-century Western philosophers. They also had a further current of ideas to contend with; the pagan medical writings which had first surfaced in the mid-twelfth century, and which tried to give an account of the workings of the mind in purely physiological terms.[35] The radical dichotomy of body and soul, which the Augustinian and Neoplatonic epistemology had favoured, had to be bridged in order to account for relations between human and other forms of life, and to develop an account of cognition that recognised the embodiment of the human mind as an essential fact of human existence – at least as long as a person was alive. Christian thinkers had to try to reconcile their view of the soul as individual and immortal with pagan conceptions of it as that which, residing in the biological systems (common to other life forms) of respiration and the blood, informs matter with life.[36]

Aristotle's *De Anima* 3.5 provided a distinction which, perhaps because it was not very clearly drawn in the surviving text, proved a major impetus to philosophical speculation: that between the agent intellect and the potential intellect.[37] For Roger Bacon, 'The agent intellect illuminates phantasmata, dematerialized to some extent by sensitive powers, liberates them definitively from material conditions and impresses them upon the potential intellect as concepts, intentions, or universals.'[38] This view separates out two aspects of the mind in order to relate one (the agent intellect) more closely to sensory operations. Albert the Great similarly incorporates the distinction between agent and potential intellect among a range of internal *potentiae* that process, with increasing degrees of abstraction, the information transmitted to them by the external senses.[39] In his *De Anima*, Albert criticises the Neoplatonic division of faculties into rational and irrational, and their glossing as higher and lower, good and bad. His interest here is in how the psyche works, not what ends it should serve.[40]

The most considerable thinker to grapple with the Aristotelian epistemology is Aquinas. Like Albert, he maintains that information must necessarily pass through phantasms of sense data on the way to becoming intelligible to the agent intellect. He accepts the corollary of this that man's understanding of non-material beings such as God and the angels can be arrived at only by comparison with things of which he does have phantasms.[41] As Mahoney puts it:

> Unlike Albert, Thomas sees no need to postulate any divine illumination to account for man's natural knowledge, and unlike Bonaventure, he believes that the human intellect's own abstractive abilities are sufficient to account for its necessary and certain knowledge . . . Thomas is highly critical of any suggestion that during this life the human intellect can achieve an intuitive cognition of separated substances, whether they be intelligences, angels or God.[42]

The soul, for Aquinas, is immaterial; but it stands at the bottom of the immaterial hierarchy, below the angels and God. It was designed to be embodied; since 'the senses operate through bodily organs, the very condition of the soul's nature makes it appropriate for it to be united with a body' (*Quaestiones de Anima*, 7).[43] Far from being an impediment to human knowledge, the body, on this account, is the prerequisite for it. The senses are necessary to knowledge, but not sufficient for it, since before they are processed by the agent intellect they are not actually intelligible.[44] Aquinas was involved in a polemic with the more radical Aristotelian Siger of Brabant, who expounded (though may not have shared) the view of Averroes that there is only one intellect, with its two powers of agency and potentiality, which is divided out among men. As a Master in Arts, Siger maintained the right to independent philosophical inquiry, without regard to theology. Aquinas attacks the Averroistic position on two counts: (1) for not believing that the potential intellect is the substantial form of the human body; and (2) for believing that it is one for all men.[45] Aquinas's position here, designed to safeguard the status of the individual human soul, also stresses its necessary connection with an individual human body.

Marenbon stresses the degree to which, even when thinking 'philosophically', medieval writers did not lose sight of theological concerns.[46] Yet even so new ideas did not gain easy acceptance with traditional authorities. A period of repression in the early thirteenth century meant that Aristotle's *libri naturales* were not taught at Paris until Roger Bacon lectured there in the 1240s. Only thirty years later, in 1270, Bishop Tempier condemned a series of 13 propositions allegedly being promulgated at the university, and these were followed by a fresh list of 219 unacceptable doctrines in 1277. It seems that the condemnations were the result of pressure, possibly stemming from a neo-Augustinian conservative backlash,[47] against the teaching of some members of the Arts Faculty; though also censured were propositions that could be associated with Aquinas, who had died three years previously, and who had held a chair of Theology.[48] The *Rose* is dated on the strength of historical references to roughly this period, and scholars have long seen a connection between the condemnations and the problems of interpreting the poem. Most commonly cited is the 1277 proposition no. 205 that simple fornication between unmarried people is not a sin.[49] Some scholars have seen the *Rose* as defending what Tempier criticises in his preamble to the condemnations; the idea (imputed to Siger) that the truths arrived at philosophically may conflict with those of theology.[50] Also at stake in the condemnation, however, are numerous propositions relating to knowledge and the body.[51] Is there any evidence in Nature's speech that she is responding to the new epistemology? Is her basis in the material presented as a necessary, if not sufficient, source of truth?

As we might expect with Jean de Meun's tricky text, its answers to these questions are not altogether clear. Nature's scientific expositions are remarkable for their insistence on the inadequacy of sense perception. When she describes the faultless revolution of the sky she points out that 'it is not seen by man' but that 'reason demonstrates it by proofs' (ll. 16829–32). The section on the properties of mirrors (ll. 18034–286) compares their effects with other optical delusions caused by sickness or distance, and denounces the superstitious follies to which they give rise. Nature declines to explain the details of angles of reflection, or even to distinguish between those images arising from the external senses ('visions . . . forainnes', l. 18267) and those created by the *fantasie* (the *potentia animae* that produces *phantasmata*). Such matters, she says, would be too long and hard for her – and passes the burden of explanation on to clerks. She appears less preoccupied with physics or the psychology of sight than with marvelling at the funny things people see in mirrors, and speculating on unexpected uses for them; if Mars and Venus had only thought of using a mirror, they could have seen Vulcan's trap and avoided being caught in adultery (ll. 18060 ff.). This passage creates a link between Nature's speech and that of the Vielle, who also recounts the amours of Venus and Mars; it evokes misogynistic fears about women's infidelity, and aligns them with anxiety about women's knowledge, since Venus is imagined drawing on scientific expertise.

Just as Alan's Natura claims the terrain of reason but insists on its inadequacy in comparison with theology, so Jean's Nature, speaking from the site of material things, constantly defers to reason which she did not make (ll. 19059–60) and cannot comprehend. The body is a necessary, but not a sufficient condition for true and certain knowledge. The noblest, because most intellectually skilled, class of men are the clerks. Nature constantly invokes the need for the interpretation and control of her own gifts by the operations of reason. Whereas the Vielle had maintained that 'Nature is superior to Nurture' (*norreture*) (l. 14038), for Nature it is the other way round (ll. 17071–100). She stresses the order of the material universe, but looks beyond it to the intellect for understanding. Her description of the moon as in part luminous, in part shadowy (ll. 16879–80), sums up her view of how men see the world – and how readers struggle with her text.

Yet in talking of predestination, free will and providence, Nature speaks very differently from her counterpart in the *De Consolatione*, since she bases her case in the body, and argues from it by analogy. Meteorology allows men to make predictions about the weather and take preventive action. If the body is thus able to escape the effects of the skies, surely, she contends, the soul is even more capable of resisting their influence (ll. 17703–13). In the second of her theological passages, analogy is also crucial. Plato could not understand truths that were 'comprehended' by 'the womb of a maid' (ll. 19119–23). It is through the incarnation – the making flesh

– that the mysteries of the Trinity are made accessible to us. Our under-standing of how we can live in God's order is grounded, it would seem, in the body. Is Nature talking here, as Fleming maintains, as one who is necessarily excluded from the order of grace?[52] Or is she invoking proposition no. 2, condemned by Tempier in 1277, that 'our intellect by its own natural power [i.e. as embodied] can attain to a knowledge of the first cause [i.e. God]'?, of which Tempier complains 'This does not sound well and is erroneous if what is meant is immediate knowledge'?[53]

Most interesting of all, however, is Nature's disquisition on dreams, because it offers the prospect of a commentary on the poem (and its genre) as a whole. The ascetic way of life, she says, produces visions as delusory as those of Scipio (ll. 18357–67). The implied reference to Macrobius, and the rhyme *mençonge–songe*, refer us back to Guillaume de Lorris's prologue. The accounts of possible dreams that follow explicitly invite scepticism about visions of 'dances and carols' in idyllic landscapes, or amorous experiences featuring Jalousie and Malebouche (ll. 18383–404); allusion here to Guillaume's narrative is patent. Aquinas had held that dreams delude us because in sleep the *potentia* of the common sense is inoperative, and thus unable to assess the value of *phantasmata*.[54] Nature shows awareness of such teaching when she states that dreams are the products of *phantasmata* (l. 18498), and yet in the end she declines to judge 'whether they are true or whether they are lies' (l. 18500), whether they relate to people's temperament (*complexions*, l. 18506) or whether they are revelations sent by God. Between the psychology of Aquinas and the Neoplatonism of Macrobius, Nature is agnostic. Ultimately, it is difficult to untangle how far her association with the body confirms her authority, and how far it devalues it. As a principle of material order, Nature seems both alarmingly limited, and to have access to the highest truths.

We find, then, replayed in Jean's theme of the body and epistemology the same equivocation as inheres in his treatment of gender; Nature is both elevated (as God's chamberlain) and denigrated (as a foolish woman). How do his allusions to thirteenth-century philosophy connect with this issue of gender? The neo-Aristotelians, although less austere with respect to the body than those in the Augustinian tradition, are not remarkable for their pro-feminist pronouncements. In Aristotle, matter and form are gendered with matter as feminine and form as masculine, so that they constitute a hierarchy analogous to that of body and spirit. Aquinas does not suggest that women are wiser or more knowing than men because of their association with matter; such a suggestion would have been regarded as preposterous. In its equivocal treatment of the contradictions between traditional misogyny and the new epistemology, Jean's text is behaving just as outrageously towards the neo-Aristotelians as it does towards its more obvious sources in Boethius and Alan of Lille. Its inferential chain is a stupendous example of sophistry; if women are to body as man is to mind, and the body is a necessary source of knowledge, then women are a necessary source of knowledge. This is not serious philosophy but an elaborate joke – which does not stop it generating anxiety *against* women and their bodies, an anxiety rendered palpable in his text by its constant equivocations.[55]

CONCLUSIONS

In the case of the Vielle, the reader is confronted with the problem of how to interpret the gap between her representation, simultaneously, as a Master of Arts and an old *entremetteuse*. In the scenes with Nature, this gap widens vertiginously as we are faced by a principle of material order who is both a silly woman and a learned teacher, and who is furthermore posing as a participant in the sacrament of confession. Genius's sermon to Amor's barons, promising them salvation through reproduction, exacerbates this *aporia* between spiritual and bodily discourses.

Jean's continuation of the *Rose* poses constant problems of interpretation. His sense of controversy is expressed through patterns, images, and unspoken implications, and above all through the inventive (and subversive) recasting of other texts. The dramatic reversal of Boethian paradigms; the outrageous recasting of Alan of Lille's sexual preoccupations; the crazy confrontation of neo-Aristotelians with the 'conclusion' that their ideas are empowering of women – all these are poetic responses to, rather than explicit formulations of, the relationship on the one hand between knowledge and the body, and on the other between the body and femininity. The poem does not tell us whether Jean de Meun thought that misogyny was justified or not, or whether he was committed to one epistemology or another. What it does show, however, is that there is a relationship between the two issues. An alert poetic ear picks up and amplifies the subterranean tremor ignored by the academy but created by the collision between its discourses of gender and knowledge. The result is the provocative staging, defence, and disavowal of woman's body of knowledge in the *Romance of the Rose*.

NOTES

I should like to thank Leslie Turano and James Simpson for their help with this paper.

1 Guillaume de Lorris and Jean de Meun, *Le Roman de la Rose*, ed. D. Poirion, Paris, 1974. The translations are my own.
2 John Marenbon, *Later Medieval Philosophy (1150–1350). An Introduction*, London and New York, 1987, p. 94.
3 Charles Muscatine, 'The Emergence of a Psychological Allegory in Old French Romance', *PMLA*, LXVIII, 1953, pp. 1160–83.

4 The relation between language and epistemology in Jean de Meun is addressed by Daniel Poirion, 'Les Mots et les choses selon Jean de Meun', *Information Littéraire*, XXVI, 1974, pp. 7–11. This paper is attacked by Gustav Ineichen, 'Le Discours linguistique de Jean de Meun', in the Proceedings of the Göttingen 'Colloque sur le *Roman de la Rose*', *Romanistische Zeitschrift füt Literaturgeschichte*, II, 1978, pp. 245–53. Poirion is taken to task for his literary formulation of issues which are 'd'ordre logique' (p. 249); Ineichen asserts that 'le problème de Jean de Meun est celui de la connaissance', and identifies Jean's position as conservative relative to the new Aristotelianism. Poirion defends his position once more in 'De la Signification chez Jean de Meun', in *L'Archéologie du signe*, ed. Lucie Brind'Amour and Eugence Vance, Toronto, 1983, pp. 167–85.

5 Charles Dahlberg, 'Macrobius and the Unity of the *Roman de la Rose*', *Studies in Philology*, LVIII, 1961, pp. 573–82.

6 A somewhat similar suggestion is made by Michael D. Cherniss, 'Jean de Meun's Reson and Boethius', *Romance Notes*, XVI, 1974–75, pp. 678–85.

7 R. Howard Bloch, 'Medieval Misogyny', *Representations*, XX, 1987, pp. 1–24. Lionel J. Friedman, ' "Jean de Meun", Antifeminism and Bourgeois Realism', *Modern Philology*, LVII, 1959–60, pp. 13–23, was the first to point out that the speech by the Vilain Jalous is a tissue of quotation (pp. 20–3).

8 Ll. 15195 ff. Apologies to women are also a 'citational mode'; see Jill Mann, *Apologies to Women*. Inaugural lecture delivered 20 November 1990, Cambridge, 1991.

9 Roberta L. Krueger, *Women Readers and the Ideology of Gender in Old French Verse Romance*, Cambridge, 1993, pp. 105–111. See also Mark Chinca's essay in this volume.

10 This despite the fact that the 'heat' of women is still colder than the coolest men. See Marie-Thérèse d'Alverny, 'Comment les théologiens et les philosophes voient la femme', in *Actes du Colloque consacré à la femme dans les civilisations des Xe – XIIIe siècles*, *Cahiers de Civilisation Médiévale*, XX, 1977, pp. 105–28, pp. 123–4, for a discussion of this tradition of 'biological essentialism' in the Middle Ages.

11 The last four lines of this quotation are not present in all MSS.

12 Alan M. F. Gunn, 'Teacher and Student in the *Roman de la Rose*. A study in archetypal figures and patterns', *L'Esprit Créateur*, II, 1962, pp. 126–34, 101.

13 Edmond Faral, '*Le Roman de la Rose* et la pensée française au XIIIe siècle', *Revue des Deux Mondes*, XXXV, 1926, pp. 430–57, p. 439: 'Ainsi éclate la misogynie de Jean de Meung. C'est une belle occasion que lui offre, pour l'étaler, le personnage de la Vieille.'

14 'Practical and theoretical studies, that is the hierarchy of sciences already set out in Boethius's exegesis of Porphyry and again in scholastic form in his *De Trinitate*, ascending through the inferior disciplines of moral philosophy, politics and economics, up to the less practical, purer disciplines of natural sciences, mathematics, and theology' (Henry Chadwick, *Boethius. The Consolations of Music, Logic, Theology, and Philosophy*, Oxford, 1981, p. 226).

15 John F. Wippel, 'The Condemnations of 1270 and 1277 at Paris', *Journal of Medieval and Renaissance Studies*, VII, 1977, pp. 169–201, p. 185: 'on September 2, 1276, a university-wide decree was issued which prohibited teaching in secret or in private places, with the exception of logic and grammar'.

16 See Lucy Polak, 'Plato, Nature and Jean de Meun', *Reading Medieval Studies*, III, 1977, pp. 80–103, pp. 80–86.

17 Gérard Paré, *Le 'Roman de la Rose' et la scolastique courtoise*, Paris and Ottawa, 1941, pp. 53–86.

18 See G. Raynaud de Lage, *Alain de Lille, poète du XIIe siècle*, Paris and Montréal, 1951, p. 73; Marie-Dominique Chenu, *La Théologie au XIIe siècle*, Etudes de Philosophie Médiévale, XLV, Paris, 1957, p. 36.

19 Polak, 'Plato, Nature and Jean de Meun', pp. 90–3, 96–8.

20 Paré, *Le 'Roman de la Rose' et la scolastique courtoise*, pp. 52–86, 88–111, 183–203; *Les Idées et les lettres au XIIIe siècle. Le 'Roman de la Rose'*, Montréal, 1947, pp. 203–78.

21 Boethius, *Philosophiae Consolationis Libri Quinque* ed. Walter Berschin and Walther Bulst,

Editiones Heidelbergenses, XI, Heidelberg, 1977. The translation quoted is from *The Consolation of Philosophy*, trans. with an introduction by V. E. Watts, Harmondsworth, 1969. On this passage see Chadwick's comments, cited in note 14 above.

22 Winthrop Wetherbee, *Platonism and Poetry in the Twelfth Century. The Literary Influence of the School of Chartres*, Princeton, NJ, 1972, p. 90.

23 P. Michaud-Quantin, 'La Classification des puissances de l'âme au XIIe siècle', *Revue du Moyen Age Latin*, V, 1949, pp. 15–34, especially p. 16. See also Peter Dronke, 'Thierry of Chartres', in *A History of Twelfth-century Western Philosophy*, ed. Peter Dronke, Cambridge, 1988, pp. 358–85, especially pp. 370–1.

24 Marie-Thérèse d'Alverny, *Alain de Lille, textes inédits*, Paris, 1965, pp. 313–17.

25 G. R. Evans, *Alan of Lille. The Frontiers of Theology in the Later Twelfth Century*, Cambridge, 1983, p. 48.

26 Alverny, *Textes inédits*, pp. 313–17 for the text and pp. 181–3 for discussion of attribution.

27 Cited from N. M. Häring, 'Alan of Lille, *De Planctu naturae*', *Studi Medievali*, XIX, 1978, pp. 797–879; translations from *Alan of Lille. The Plaint of Nature*, translation and commentary by James J. Sheridan, Toronto, 1980.

28 Anna Crabbe, 'Literary Design in the *De Consolatione Philosophiae*', in *Boethius, his Life, Thought, and Influence*, ed. Margaret T. Gibson, Oxford, 1981, pp. 237–74, pp. 241–2. See also the opening of Boethius' *De institutione arithmetica*, praising the *quadrivium* for scholars 'whom a higher sense of purpose leads onward, away from those senses which are born with us, to more certain kinds of understanding. For there are certain definite stages and dimensions of advancement through which it is possible to rise and progress until the eye of the mind (that eye which, as Plato says, is far worthier of existence and preservation than all our organs of sensory perception, since only by its light may truth be sought or perceived) – until, I say, this eye, which has been submerged and blinded by our bodily senses, may be illumined once again by these disciplines' (cited by Winthrop Wetherbee, 'Philosophy, Cosmology, and the Twelfth-century Renaissance', in *Twelfth-century Philosophy*, p. 30).

29 Winthrop Wetherbee, 'The Theme of Imagination in Medieval Poetry and the Allegorical Figure "Genius"', *Mediaevalia et Humanistica*, VII, 1976, pp. 45–64.

30 Evans, *Alan of Lille*, p. 49.

31 *Ibid.*, p. 154.

32 Wetherbee, 'Philosophy, Cosmology, and the Twelfth-century Renaissance', pp. 50–1.

33 See Sarah Kay, 'Sexual Knowledge: the Once and Future Texts of the *Romance of the Rose*', in *Sexuality and Textuality*, ed. Judith Still and Michael Worton, Manchester, 1993, pp. 69–86, pp. 72–4.

34 Joseph Owens, 'Faith, Ideas, Illumination, and Experience', in *The Cambridge History of Later Medieval Philosophy*, eds Norman Kretzmann, Anthony Kenny and Jon Pinborg; associate editor Eleonore Stump; Cambridge, 1982, pp. 440–59.

35 P. Michaud-Quantin, 'Les Puissances de l'âme au XIIe siècle', pp. 17–19. Unfortunately in this passage the dates 1130, 1140 and 1150 have been misprinted as 1230, 1240 and 1250.

36 See also the essay by Robin Kirkpatrick in this volume.

37 Marenbon, *Later Medieval Philosophy*, pp. 99–108.

38 Z. Kuksewicz, 'The Potential and the Agent Intellect', in *The Cambridge History*, pp. 595–601.

39 Edward P. Mahoney, 'Sense, Intellect and Imagination in Albert, Thomas, and Siger', in *The Cambridge History*, pp. 602–22, pp. 602–5; P. Michaud-Quantin, 'Albert le Grand et les puissances de l'âme', *Revue du Moyen Age Latin*, XI, 1955, pp. 59–86.

40 Michaud-Quantin, 'Albert le Grand', pp. 66–7.

41 Mahoney, 'Sense, Intellect and Imagination', p. 609.

42 *Ibid.*, pp. 610–11.

43 Thomas Aquinas, *Quaestiones Diputatae*, vol. II, ed. R. M. Spazzi *et al.*, 10th edn, Marietti, Turin and Rome, 1965; cited by Marenbon, *Later Medieval Philosophy*, p. 124. See also Anthony Kenny, 'Intellect and Imagination in Aquinas', in *Aquinas: A Collection of Critical*

Essays, ed. Anthony Kenny, Notre Dame, Indiana, 1976, pp. 273–96 (first published in New York 1969).

44 Kenny, 'Intellect and Imagination', p. 284.

45 Mahoney, 'Sense, Intellect and Imagination', pp. 611–21.

46 Marenbon, *Later Medieval Philosophy*, p. 87.

47 Wippel, 'The Condemnations', pp. 177–8, 181, 195.

48 *Ibid.*, pp. 169–70.

49 David Hult, '1277, 7 March: Jean de Meun's *Roman de la Rose*', in *A New History of French Literature*, ed. Denis Hollier, Cambridge, Mass., 1989, pp. 97–102. The numbering of the propositions is that of the edition by P. Mandonnet, translated and presented by Ernest L. Fortin and Peter D. O'Neill, 'Condemnation of 219 Propositions', in *Medieval Political Philosophy: A Sourcebook*, eds Ralph Lerner and Muhsin Mahdi, New York, 1963, pp. 335–54.

50 Alan M. F. Gunn, *The Mirror of Love*, Lubbock, Texas, 1952, repr. 1982, p. 478: 'For Siger's doctrine of the double truth expanded into a doctrine of plural truths is the theory of life which the completed *Roman de la Rose*, with its formalized contradictions and divergent views, sometimes appears to express.' It is not clear that Siger held any such doctrine, but the condemned article 191 is an interesting example of what Tempier is against, since it maintains that reason persuades the natural philosopher that the world is eternal, whereas faith guided by supernatural causes insists that it is not.

51 For example, 'That the motions of the heaven are for the sake of the intellectual soul, and the intellectual soul or intellect cannot be educed except throught the mediation of a body', 119; that form is dependent on matter (120) and the soul on the body (128, 133); that individuation is by matter (42, 43, 110, 116) and the soul is not what makes a man a man (113); that there can be no change without matter (44) and that God is bound by physical laws (66, 67, 68, 69, 97, 108, 109), whilst our knowledge of him can be achieved by our natural power (8), i.e. without the need for revelation. See Fortin and O'Neill, 'Condemnation of 219 Propositions'.

52 John V. Fleming, *The Roman de la Rose. A Study in Allegory and Iconography*, Princeton, 1969, pp. 195–209, especially pp. 202–3.

53 Fortin and O'Neill, 'Condemnation of 219 Propositions', p. 339.

54 See Mahoney, 'Sense, Intellect and Imagination', p. 607.

55 Perhaps this ambivalent response to the possibility of there being an epistemology of the (feminine) body is also found in other thirteenth-century works, such as the fabliaux, themselves also responding (albeit at a distance) to philosophical changes. See Gabrielle Marie Lyons, *'Avoir' and 'Savoir': A Strategic Approach to the Old French Fabliaux*, unpublished Ph.D. thesis, Cambridge, 1992, fos. 141–57.

Dante and the body

The interest in the representation of the human body which the present volume shares with a great deal of recent literary criticism has in large part been stimulated by the writings of social historians, and additionally by those of Michel Foucault. There are many good reasons why this interest should be encouraged, especially in regard to medieval literature. It needs, for instance, to be recognised that the period conventionally described as the Middle Ages is many centuries long and cannot, on a historical view, be thought to have sustained a single or unaltering position in regard to matters such as the representation of the body. Equally, the medievalist is bound to emphasise that issues of this nature, which all too often are analysed as if they first arose in the eighteenth century, may plausibly be traced back far further than this. In this essay I shall be concerned with the ways in which, as regards the theme of the body, Dante's work asks questions of both the past and the future. Coming as Dante does at the end of the medieval period, we should expect his position to reflect at least something of the complexity of the foregoing debate. At the same time, we should not be surprised if Dante looks forward; just as his contemporary Giotto is credited with a revolutionary approach to the pictorial representation of bodies, so Dante, as is generally agreed, displays a markedly far-sighted concern with the individuality of human beings.[1] This concern is traditionally understood in terms of psychological realism; but it will be seen later that the body is allowed, in Dante's view, a position which is disconcertingly central to the human constitution.

On points such as these, the imaginative or intellectual 'frame' in which Dante places the body certainly deserves close attention. For all that, a principal part of my purpose will be to question whether it is adequate to speak, when dealing with Dante's work, in terms of sociological analysis. I also mean to suggest that the metaphor of a 'frame' (be that frame understood as an enclosure or as a deceit) may largely be inappropriate when considering Dante's representation of the body.

These objections are in part simply practical, and are intended to remedy the distortions which can occur – even among Dante scholars – when preconceptions about the status of the body in medieval thought are allowed to colour the reading of Dante's text. It may, for instance, seem natural, considering that the *Commedia* is set in the other world, to suppose that Dante's view of the body were in some way ascetic or dualistic in character. Yet many things go wrong on the level of practical reading when one allows that assumption to persist. For that reason, I shall pay particular attention to the second cantica of the *Commedia* where Dante's narrative describes conditions akin to the conditions of the temporal world and conducts a sustained meditation on bodily pain and pleasure.

Yet beyond the practical question there lies a question of theory which, in its most general form, leads one to doubt whether the frames which Foucault and similar historians have set up can ever be wholly adequate to the analysis of literary texts. In section II, I shall touch upon the outline of this argument. I do so, however, with the purpose of suggesting – as I return to Dante in sections III, IV and V – that his work both requires, and in some measure provides, an alternative to the view of the body cultivated recently in much historicist theory.

II

Charles Taylor in his essay 'Foucault on Freedom and Truth'[2] speaks of the contradictions which arise when the 'relativities' revealed by cultural history are subjected to a 'monolithic analysis' deriving, in Foucault's work as elsewhere, 'from the Nietzschean model of truth' whereby – to paraphrase Foucault's own words – truth is a thing of this world which is produced only by multiple forms of constraint.[3] It is notoriously hard to see how the validity of any such analysis can be established unless the analyst resorts to the very claims for truthfulness which his observations discredit. Or else, if these claims really have been abandoned, one would expect to find some admission in the work of the relativity inherent to the analysis itself. Taylor can discover no admission of this sort in Foucault's extant writings. On the contrary, whilst rejecting any conception of moral truth, Foucault often reveals conditions which are self-evidently evil and urgently need to be remedied. For Taylor, a concern over 'truth' – even if truth is understood in a weak sense as the reflection of human agreement – remains a constitutive feature of the attempts we make to free ourselves from evil. Thus, even on the plane of historical and social change it is, for Taylor, relevant to consider agencies which derive from and are readily observable upon the plane of personal rather than institutional history.

> Biographically, we see examples all the time. After long periods of stress and confusion, I come to see that I really love A or I really don't want to take that job. I now see retrospectively that the image of myself as quite free and uncommitted had a merely superficial hold on me. It did not correspond to a profound aspiration . . . What makes these biographical changes of outlook/life

possible, which seem to be steps towards the truth? Our sense of ourselves, of
our identity, of what we are. I see this change as a discovery of what I am, of
what really matters to me ... I see it as a step towards the truth (or perhaps
better put, it is a step out of error), and even in certain conditions a kind of
liberation.

(*Philosophy and the Human Sciences*, p. 180)

From arguments such as this,[4] it is possible to derive a further objection
to Foucault's account which will prove to be of particular importance in
dealing with questions of bodily identity. For instance, in his study of the
execution of Damiens,[5] Foucault invites one to see a prototypical example
of how institutions possess and speak through the body of a subject. Yet
nothing at all is said of how the regicide himself came in the first place
to perform the act of assassination. The intellectual purposes of Damiens
are ignored; just as importantly, no consideration is given to the physical
moves which led the assassin to carry a weapon and select an appropriate
place and time for the deed. In the innumerable physical actions which
preceded the event, there must have been some motivations which were
not determined by the institution which Damiens had set himself to attack.

Following Taylor, then, it appears that the historical descriptions which
Foucault encourages will always tend, in regard to method, to be insuffi-
ciently microscopic. What is more, this fault in method may well become
a fault of substance if one is led by the rules of a morally neutral – or
'monolithic' – description to suppose that there is no possibility of ethical
or physical agency. There is, however, a remedy; and this must lie in a
return to forms of discourse which are either capable of microscopy, or
else are themselves the product of such particular agencies. Philosophical
analysis (when conscious of its own methods) is one such form, as it
inspects the logical and ethical implications of particular propositions and
offers them for debate and adoption. But literary works are also, I shall
maintain, the result of and the object of a similar particularity of attention; dictate a theme to a poet and he still has to choose the words to
express it. Which is not, of course, to deny that the questions raised by
general historical description may be illuminating, particularly where they
identify evils, and particularly in the area of power and identity. Thus in
considering Dante's *Commedia* it will remain important to recognise that
individuality is presented as a problematical rather than a natural phenomenon; and Dante, certainly, is able to entertain the idea that bodily
identity may be regarded as an institutional construct – at least as an evil
to be resisted. But, as Taylor has shown, any response to such findings will
involve – as it does, without acknowledgement, in Foucault's own case –
a concern with questions of motivation, truth and change. And this is true
in the literary as well as in the moral or political sphere. For plainly in a
literary work one will seek to account for the particular stylistic decisions

which led the author to begin, say, *Surveiller et punir* with a deliberately – and shockingly – neutral account of Damiens's execution. Dante – as both philosopher and poet – consciously invites attention on both fronts.

The present essay stands in counterpoint rather than in opposition to Foucault's suggestions. At the same time, it proposes an alliance between literature and philosophy built upon three specific principles, all of which are especially important to Dante, and especially relevant to questions of bodily nature. The first concerns the power of both philosophy and of literature to generate – or regenerate – the terms of logical and ethical debate; the second concerns the power of such debate to contribute, as it were biographically, to changes of mind; and the third concerns the way in which such changes in both philosophical and literary understanding are the result of particular or 'microscopic' intentions.

On the first count, then, it would be entirely reasonable to ask what place Dante's thinking about the body holds in the history of ideas, and to consider what Dante may himself have drawn from the scholastic philosophies of his own time. Yet when a literary work is in question, such an inquiry is just as likely to reveal idiosyncrasy as conformity on the author's part, whilst on the reader's part the impulse to inquiry will characteristically be born of literary appreciation, seeking not so much to place the text in its historical perspective as to clarify or intensify a particular response. The interest, then, is likely to be prospective as well as retrospective, especially when ethical decisions as well as imaginative responses are involved. Thus it will quickly become apparent that the issues which Dante addresses are not resolved within their own historical period but rather descend from the Greeks and anticipate the issues of modern philosophical debate. For any discussion of the body must at some point decide whether to settle for a broadly dualistic view of the relations between body and mind or else for a broadly hylomorphic view in which the intimate connections between matter and form are emphasised. Clearly the decision we make will have profound consequences for our ethical and imaginative behaviour. Thus modern philosophers – following Ryle – have been eager to attack the view (associated both with Descartes and with Plato) that 'the careers of minds can be assumed to have one sort of existence, while those . . . of bodies have another sort';[6] and the search for an alternative to the dualistic fallacy has led in some cases to a vindication of the Aristotelian conception of mind and in others to a demand for a more adequate philosophy of the body itself:

> Are [minds] made of mind-stuff? . . . How are they created? can they perish? Can they be located? The prospect of getting clear enough about dualism to answer such questions is very dim indeed. The Aristotelian by contrast will say that these enquiries get off on the wrong foot. To have a mind is not like having a heart; it isn't to have a special sort of component or constituent;

rather it is to have a set of capacities, such as those of perception and action, belief and sensation.[7]

As will be seen later, Dante's position on this question, in common with that of his scholastic forebears, is already profoundly Aristotelian. But the obvious concern which his narrative shows with the anatomical detail and motivations of the body is also an indication of what may follow, on the imaginative plane, from a philosophical decision on this issue; and this leads to the question of how philosophy and literature may both be concerned to generate changes of mind through debate or persuasion. History, of course, can contribute very persuasive evidence indeed to this debate; it will by turns be shocking, stimulating or salutary to recognise that one's physical pleasures as well as one's intellectual constructs may at some level always be determined by institutional power. But once this has been recognised, the decision remains as to whether one should seek to alter or indulge (henceforth consciously) that state of affairs. Here, on behalf of philosophical analysis, Taylor would argue that liberating choices are possible precisely because institutional or cultural systems are not commensurable with each other, and that as a consequence it is intuitively right to speak of gains and losses in drawing comparisons between such systems.[8] But literature has a similar claim to make, as is notably the case whenever it touches on matters of sexual morality. Of course literary texts – understood in the widest sense – may easily be seen to reflect or even to pander to prevailing codes of marriage, romance or Hampstead adultery. None the less, one would need only to list names such as Petrarch, Donne, Flaubert, Tolstoy and Lawrence to see that the images, rhythms and rhetoric of a literary text can contribute directly to changes of perception. And Dante would occupy a peculiarly important place in that list. For in all of his writings his concern is love; and from his earliest complete work, the *Vita nuova*, onwards he consistently registers on the level both of biography and of cultural history the possibility that the acceptance of love, as word and as experience, may well be made to change. Moreover, the understanding of such change is pursued quite deliberately as part of a critical and stylistic programme; through a minute attention to terminology, lexicon and poetic rhythm, Dante progressively liberates himself from the vocabulary of sexual (and also at times political) experience which he had inherited from his Italian and Occitan forebears.

The *Vita nuova*, in its recalibration of sexual vocabulary, is the account of a conversion; the *Commedia* is written on the understanding that others too can be converted. But these considerations, in common with Taylor's criticism, all point to a central insufficiency in Foucault's thinking; the question of agency, in regard to physical as well as mental motivations, needs to be examined far more closely than he allows.[9] On this count the philosopher would characteristically argue a claim for the freedoms of rational debate so as to explain why anyone should possess an appetite for such debate. Literature might enter upon the coat-tails of that argument, as Dante certainly does in the *Convivio*. But literature has, in regard to freedom of motive, a specific and, arguably, a far stronger claim of its own to make.

For it is in the nature of a literary work not to be written under compulsion. Granted that the literary intertext, like the historical context, will always have some bearing on the formation of any work, these factors can never explain why a particular author considered it worthwhile at some particular time physically as well as mentally to take up the pen and write – or for that matter why, at another time, a reader hefted a particular book from the shelf. Writing is an *acte gratuit*. And this characteristic becomes the more obvious when one allows (as in the case of Damiens) that physical motivations are themselves essential if the task is to be accomplished. No one is obliged to manipulate a pen at all. But when someone does, the freedom which is asserted in that act is itself essentially subversive of all frames and institutions. For instance, it is a defining characteristic of Irina Ratushinskaya's work that she should have commanded not only the mental courage but also the physical means – which in this case distinctly were microscopic – to produce and transmit her poems beyond the wall. Prison literature – producing, at least since Boethius' time, results as different as the prisons have been different – is an essential model for all literature. And Dante's work – produced from within the invisible walls of exile – is itself a prime example. In exile, both his poetry and philosophy are motivated by a profound concern with the principles of justice; his personal freedom is consistently seen to depend upon persuading others that universal justice is possible, since in the establishment of universal justice the particular justice of his own case will also come to be recognised. Yet this attempt to subvert the malign institutions of his own day – Church and Mercantile City – is by no means conducted only in rational terms. At every point, Dante presents his own physical existence in exile to the reader as an object of attention, through images of a hard journey from place to place, or of the bitter ascent of 'another man's stair'.[10] Thus in the exile poem 'Tre Donne . . .' he not only speaks of the myth of Justice in the Golden Age but also lays before the reader the image of his own skeletal rib-cage in which death has put its key (ll. 85–7), as though the pity and the terror felt along the nerves could be as eloquent as any rational argument.

As we shall see, to read the *Commedia* in full means that we must attend to the body, discovering freedom in a cathartic concentration upon the particular. Nor is it irrelevant in this regard to note that Dante, throughout his poetic theory, places exceptional emphasis upon the materiality of the poetic medium: a poet is a maker who composes textures of rough and smooth, shaggy and combed; and words – as Dante himself emphasises – stand not only as rational but equally as sensuous signs.[11] Thus reading will involve not only mental process but also the tracing, at least in the sensuous appreciation of phonetic effect, of a continuing sequence of stylistic intentions and decisions. Moreover, our appreciation of this will itself contribute to the subversion of injustice; when Dante imagines himself returning to Florence, it is as a poet, since it is his poetry which will have vindicated the honour of the skeletal exile.[12] For this reason, it will be necessary, in section IV, to pay considerable attention to themes suggested in the imaginative structure of Dante's work and to the play of stylistic effect. But first I must return to a purely philosophical question and confirm – as will already be apparent – that Dante is no dualist.

III

The philosophical choices that Dante makes invariably lead him to assert the unity of body and rational soul in the human individual. Thus, resisting the claims of Averroes that the potential intellect is a substance separable from matter, Dante declares that God breathes into the work of physical nature an intellective power which in union with the material body forms a single soul that lives and breathes and circles upon itself:

> e perchè meno ammiri la parola,
> guarda il calor del sol che si fa vino,
> giunto a l'omor che de la vite cola.

> and so that you should wonder less at my words, look how the heat of the sun becomes wine when joined with the juice which flows from the vine.
>
> (*Purg.* 25, ll. 76–8)

In reading the twenty-fifth canto of *Purgatorio*, attention is now likely to fall upon the unremittingly Aristotelian nature of Dante's embryology – which insists that in procreation only the semen of the male is a truly active principle – or else upon Dante's precise identification of the moment at which human life begins. Regardless of how the argument on these matters might proceed, such attention is in itself enough to suggest how much may be at stake, as regards ethical choice, in the philosophical investigation of mind–body relationships; and for Dante himself the doctrine enunciated in this canto can plausibly be taken as the central principle not only in his religious thinking but also in his philosophy, politics and even – considering how corporeal is his representation of the other world – to the narrative construction of his poetry.

Philosophically, Dante is at one here with Aquinas, who attacks the superficiality of Plato's approach to the problem (thus anticipating the

modern philosopher who regards Platonic dualism as a 'savage supersti-
tion')[13] and firmly commits himself to the alternative view available in
Aristotle. On this understanding, soul is neither more nor less than the
animating principle of a particular form of life. To quote Jonathan Lear:

> Because soul is form, Aristotle thinks he has solved the problem of how soul
> and body fit together. Form and matter are not two distinct ingredients which,
> when mixed, constitute a living organism. An organism is itself a unity which
> in philosophical reflection can be seen to have formal and material aspects (De
> Anima 2.1.412b.6–9). Soul is not a special ingredient which breathes life into a
> lifeless body: it is a certain aspect of a living organism and a living organism is
> a paradigm of a functioning unity.[14]

This much Dante shared with his scholastic contemporaries (and their
modern inheritors). It is, however, characteristic of his own thinking on
the subject that this doctrine should be given a political application. For,
as Patrick Boyde has shown,[15] it is an emphasis upon the specifically
embodied nature of the human soul that leads Dante to insist, in De
Monarchia, that God intends human beings to achieve happiness in the
sphere of the temporal world, where they operate according to the specific characteristics of a constitution which is properly and uniquely both
spiritual and physical. Dante of course does not deny that the eternal
destiny of human beings is to enjoy contemplation of the Godhead. But
the peculiarity of his thought, in a medieval context, is to assert that
human beings are intended to enjoy two forms of beatitude – one in
eternity, the other in time. Thus in De Monarchia Dante argues, on
philosophical grounds, that God himself has directly appointed the Just
Emperor who will ensure, through a rational and equitable distribution of
goods, that humanity achieves its temporal end.[16]

Notions – and emotions – associated with this explicit argument can be
traced throughout Dante's writing. For instance, a comparable belief in
the value of physical environment leads Dante to assert in the Convivio that
human beings have this much in common with water plants: that they
thrive best in the place which is physically natural to them.[17] On this view,
exile would be a peculiarly unnatural punishment for Dante to suffer – a
literal deracination. And when in canto sixteen of the Paradiso Dante is
told what a perfect earthly city could be, by an ancestor who had shown
perfect devotion to the Empire, the city itself is depicted not as some
anonymously pure utopia but rather as a place in which wandering
Florentines could return to the streets, churches, tables, beds and ultimately the graves from which injustice had uprooted them.

What, though, will happen to the non-dualist after death? Here too
Dante persists in his position, in this case through a sustained and char-
acteristically strong insistence upon the concept of physical resurrection.
Thus it is emphasised at Paradiso canto 20, lines 132–8 that the purely

spiritual Heaven which Dante visits is itself a temporary condition until, at the Last Judgement, its spiritual inhabitants return to their proper – which is to say their physical – form; indeed, even the Christian philosophers of *Paradiso* 14 (lines 61–6) are shown to long for the recovery of the 'corpi morti' – the dead bodies – which they inhabited before being transformed into the apparently superior condition of sempiternal flames. Above all, however, it is through his representation of Beatrice that Dante enforces the notion of resurrection. This would be surprising if one assumed that Dante were some Neoplatonist, interested only in the spiritual beauty of Beatrice. Yet as recent criticism has increasingly been prepared to argue, the development which Dante records in the *Vita nuova* may certainly amount to an abdication of sexual love for Beatrice, but also leads to a disinterested love of embodied human nature, as expressed in her particular being.[18] The Christian understanding towards which Dante moves at the end of the work is one which ensures, through faith in the resurrection, the immortality of such a being; and in that perspective it is entirely appropriate that at a salient point in the *Paradiso* Beatrice should enunciate the doctrine that, where all other material beings are destined to pass away, the physical matter which is constitutive of the human individual should alone enjoy eternal existence (*Par.* 7, ll. 125–48).

Justice and resurrection, then, are the characteristic terms in Dante's myth of the body. Dante's interest in justice allows him to understand how far human beings may indeed be said to construct the frame of their own lives. At the same time, it is his interest in resurrection which leads him, as we shall see, to insist that the human body cannot be confined to any such frame. For the moment, however, before considering these self-evident goods, one is bound to acknowledge that there are implications in Dante's position which themselves verge on the self-evidently evil.

One such implication is familiar from the strictures of Sandra M. Gilbert and Susan Gubar, and suggests that the 'body' of Beatrice might be merely a projection of a possessively male imagination.[19] Of this I shall say nothing here, save to insist, as I believe Dante does through his representation of Beatrice, that bodies – to be understood realistically – need not be, and are not always, viewed in terms of their sexuality. Dante understands perfectly well how sexuality is itself determined, in human behaviour, by code and context,[20] but he also recognises that the sexual code can obsessively preclude a perception of all that bodies can otherwise achieve in acts of fetching, carrying, comforting and building.

A second difficulty, however, of a kind which Foucault's writing might well bring to light must concern us here. For Dante's Hell is itself constructed, it seems, according to an understanding of justice and resurrection. Thus the first doctrinal passage in the *Commedia* speaks of how the body will return, when justice is finally declared at the second coming, to its specific *carne* and *figura* – to its flesh and bodily form. At that time, human beings will become perfect and therefore, following Aristotle's logic, perfectly receptive to sense-impressions. But that in turn must mean that the damned will then suffer even more than now they do. In a word, the damned will move as the prisoners of Foucault's panopticon do (or else like those of Kafka's penal colony) from the external restraint and surveillance of an earlier age to an ultimate internalisation of their own submission.

Now there is very persuasive evidence throughout the *Inferno* to support this reading. Yet it is not, I believe, compatible with the view either of the body or of punishment which the *Commedia* as a whole develops. It is true that the infamous system of the *contrappasso* – of the punishment fitting the crime – anticipates in its detail the ritual tortures which Foucault describes. Yet equally there are signs, at least by the end of the *Inferno*, that Dante himself has begun to recognise the violence and moral inadequacy of the system he has himself built.[21] It is all too rarely noticed that the word *contrappasso*, which is used so confidently by Dantists to explain Dante's penal system, is in fact spoken by the sinner Bertran de Born who – absurdly swinging his own severed head in his hand – stands condemned for the attempts he made to imprison his fellows in a tit-for-tat cycle of violent revenge (*Inferno* 28). It is as if by now Dante were prepared to incriminate the very system of retributive justice which he himself had hitherto sought to construct. Or else a process of conversion has begun here in which Dante seeks a more minute and less possessive understanding of the human body that can appear in the institutions of justice. We have suggested that Dante shows himself capable of such changes in the *Vita nuova* – there, with the not dissimilar purpose of releasing himself from a sexually possessive view of Beatrice. Such a conversion would now not only free the body from the frame of punishment but also liberate the poet from the frame of his own mental habit; and for evidence to support this suggestion we must now turn to the *Purgatorio*, where the body, in the finest detail of movement and response, quickly becomes an object of disinterested love.

IV

Conversion is a central issue in both the moral themes and the poetic procedures of the *Purgatorio*. Thus a recent collection of essays on the cantica by John Freccero is entitled *The Poetics of Conversion*.[22] And yet, while this is an enviable title, the conversions which Freccero describes are wholly at odds with the view which has so far developed in the present essay.

Freccero – identified as a Platonist and Augustinian by his editor Rachel Jacoff[23] – persistently ignores Dante's emphasis upon physical particularity and, in speaking of conversion, envisages a movement away from rather than towards an attention to the human body. Nor is he prepared to see any radical difference between the *Inferno* and the *Purgatorio* in their representation of physical suffering: 'For all the apparently mimetic power of Dante's verse, there can be no doubt that corporeal representation in the poem is self-consciously symbolic. In this respect the *Purgatorio* does not differ greatly from the *Inferno*' (*Poetics of Conversion*, p. 199).

If, then, on Freccero's view, we do 'read bodies' in the *Commedia*, the purpose must be to convert our perception of particulars into an understanding of the divine plan and to reconcile all observations on the physical plane with the ideal book of the universe.

The particular episode which Freccero chooses to illustrate this argument is taken from canto 3 of the *Purgatorio*, where Dante encounters the figure of Manfred. Historically, Manfred represented the last effective hope that Imperial rule might prevail in Italy, and in Dante's narrative he appears heroically as a blond and handsome figure still bearing on his body the wounds, to chest and forehead, that he received during his final battle:

> Io mi volsi ver lui e guardail fiso:
> biondo era e bello e di gentil aspetto,
> ma l'un de' cigli un colpo avea diviso.
>   Quand'i' mi fui umilmente disdetto
> d'averlo visto mai, el disse: 'Or vedi';
> e mostrommi una piaga a sommo 'l petto.

> I turned to him and looked at him with fixed attention: he was fair-haired, and handsome and noble in appearance. But a blow had cleft one of his eyebrows. When humbly I had denied that I had ever seen him before, he said to me: 'Now behold': and he showed me a wound at the top of his chest.

> (ll. 106–11)

Now in Freccero's view these wounds are to be regarded as a 'baptism' (*Poetics of Conversion*, p. 197) – though he might have said as 'stigmata' – representing rebirth into a Christian order; indeed, the scene should be read as a reminiscence of Christ's appearance to doubting Thomas. Yet to Freccero Manfred's wounds are essentially the same as the wounds of punishments depicted, as he himself suggests, in the canto of Bertan de Born, *Inferno* 28. Both are a form of writing 'which progressively disfigures the page in order paradoxically to make it clear' (p. 205). The process of purgation, however, 'like the process of interpretation . . . is an assimilation and gradual *effacement* of the marks . . . ending in the vision of God's Book' (*Poetics of Conversion*, p. 205).

If all of this were true, then certainly we could speak of the frame to which Dante's God insists that we conform. Yet the *Paradiso* does not in fact end with a vision of God's book but rather with a vision of a human face that eludes all attempt at framing. Thus in the final moments of the

Commedia Dante sees God in the human form of 'nostra effige'; and the result is a bafflement – comparable to that of 'a geometer who seeks to square the circle' (*Par.* 33, l. 131) – in which no principle or description can be written around the face. It is, I suggest, towards a similar realisation that no human being – fashioned in the image of God – can be contained within the descriptions of another that Dante is advancing in the *Purgatorio* – or else he is returning to his origins; for in the *Vita nuova* he has already demonstrated that Beatrice's person cannot be contained in words.[24]

With many similar examples in mind, I would therefore argue, against Freccero, that the narrative tactics of *Purgatorio* 3 as a whole are designed precisely to resist both the moral closures typical of the *Inferno* and also any kind of symbolic assimilation to an ideal script. Let us first admit that Manfred may indeed have represented for the increasingly Imperialist Dante the hope of Imperial rule. Admit also that the wound in Manfred's side does assimilate him to the resurrected Christ. Surely, however, the upshot of these two admissions is nothing like clarity but rather an astonishment at the conjunction of political and Christian perceptions. And this astonishment will be further increased when one recalls that Manfred was the illegitimate son of a father known as Antichrist to the Church and that Manfred himself had been excommunicated no less than twice. In spite of all this, Dante chooses on his own discretion to promote such a figure to Purgatory. At the very least we have here a highly subversive claim on Dante's part against the presumption of the Church to decide authoritatively on the fate of any individual. More positively, we have Dante's own recognition – filtered through doubts (l. 97) which abdicate any right to final judgement – of the surprising and mysteriously irreducible presence of another being. The marks on Manfred's body are the marks of a particularity which persists despite the determined efforts of the Church to erase Manfred from human (or, through excommunication, divine) memory. Notably at Manfred's death his followers erect a cairn over his corpse, thus using the materiality of rock to express their reverence for the fallen body beneath (l. 129). But the Church now desecrates his grave; Manfred's corpse is removed from its cairn – 'a lume spento' ('with torches extinguished') – in a vain attempt to remove it also from human regard. Conversely, *Purgatorio* 3 is an attempt, as it were, to re-erect that cairn so that Manfred can return to the reader in all his historical particularity. In the canto Manfred does not speak to God but turns 'smiling' to human memory – 'I am Manfred, grandson of the Empress Costanza' (ll. 112–13) – asking that news of his salvation should be reported to his living daughter.

On this view, to read bodies is to read not meanings but rather the degrees of density or opacity in which the particular presence of another being impinges upon us. Thus a fully developed reading of *Purgatorio* 3 would, I suggest, reveal the extent to which Dante – escaping from hermeneutic conclusions – renders more complex and ambiguous the imaginative structure of the canto. At the very least, such a reading would need to reveal the play of parallels between the figure of Manfred in its second half and the figure of Virgil in its first: Manfred, as Imperial representative, is unexpectedly saved, despite the desecration of his body by the Church; Virgil, another representative of Empire, speaks (ll. 25–7), of how *his* body was moved – though in reverence – by Augustus from Brindisi to Naples, and yet Virgil, by God's judgement, must remain in the shadows of Limbo. There may at some level be a programme behind these parallels. But if there is, it cannot be allowed to dissipate the extraordinarily fine texture of emotions and images – shifting at every point from melancholy to social humour, from outrage to amazement – which constitutes the body of the canto itself. Neither judgment nor symbolism will be able to deliver a final sentence on that structure.

v

By now it may be obvious how far Dante has himself shifted from the attitude to the body which he adopted in the *Inferno*. In the *Purgatorio* the body is conceived not as a passive page for others to possess or write upon but as itself an expressive medium. Body indeed has become, as the Tolnudic philosopher Emmanuel Levinas would have it, all face.[25] Indeed, if one now seeks a theoretical statement of the position to which this essay is pointing, then Levinas could supply it:

> The incarnation of human subjectivity guarantees its spirituality. I analyse the inter-human relationship as if in proximity with the Other – beyond the image I myself make of the other being – the face, the expressiveness in the other (and the whole human body is in this sense more or less face) were what ordains me to serve him.

Here the aspects of existence which we describe as spiritual are themselves seen as secondary to, and generated by, the primal fact of our relationship to the Other; indeed we only exist at all in response to the questioning reality of that Other. This is not, however, to say – as commonly is said – that we define ourselves by an aggressive exclusion of others. On the contrary, the existence of each depends upon a continual re-enactment of the commandment 'Thou shalt not kill', since existence is grounded in the expressive reciprocations of face recognising face. Thus, says Levinas, 'one comes not into the world but into question'; and any attempt to resolve that question in power, in knowledge or even in words will be a violation of the ground on which the subject itself is constituted.[26] In the primal moment, existence is an ethical relationship where each allows to each its own opacity or expressive strangeness; as Levinas puts it – in terms which reveal both the subversiveness of his view and also its relevance to the case of the exiled Dante – the self is essentially

> a presence afraid of presence, afraid of the insistence of the identical ego, stripped of all qualities ... It has not yet been invested with any attributes or justified in any way. And this creates the reserve of the stranger – or sojourner on earth, as it says in the Psalms.[27]

One need not here emphasise the similarities which exist between this understanding and the final canto of the *Paradiso*. But a final example from the *Purgatorio* will demonstrate the application of such theory to the reading in Dante's text of what I shall now call face rather than body.

Purgatorio 23 deals with the most corporeal of sins, that of gluttony. And at first sight the penance which the gluttons endure seems to be a classic instance of the *contrappasso*. In ritual fashion, the penitents constantly encircle a tree transplanted from the Garden of Eden. The tree gives off exquisite aromas but the gluttons cannot pluck its fruit and the hectic appetite which they experience turns them to living skeletons; as Dante puts it in line 32, it was possible to read the Italian word for Man – OMO – on their countenance, the two letters O being formed from sunken eye-sockets and the M from the bones of the nose and forehead. It is true that, unlike the sinners in Hell, the penitents actually consent to their punishment. Indeed this canto contains one of the clearest expressions of the difference in this respect between penance and damnation when in line 72 a penitent declares that he speaks of pain when he ought to speak of solace; his pain is a pleasure, in so far as his new appetite for penance is identical with the desire which led Christ to martyrdom on the cross. Yet such an affirmation, on Foucault's view, would only confirm the sense that the demands of the institution have now been subtly interiorised.[28] This, too, would seem to be the implication of the word OMO, branded as it is on the forehead of each penitent. For it is a part of Dante's concept of justice – which is the essential virtue of human community – that there never can be justice where there is any spot of greed; it follows from this that, in the present case, the repatriation of the gluttons into the communal world of Purgatory should rightly be expressed in their submission to the word 'humanity' itself.

For all that, there is a movement in this canto – just as there is between the *Inferno* and *Purgatorio* – which leads to a displacement of any such judgemental construct. Thus in line 40, Dante, whose living body has already been viewed with amazement by the penitents, is recognised personally by one of their number. To begin with, Dante is prevented, by the disfigurement of the penitent, from any reciprocal act of recognition. But then the spoken word sparks a memory, and in Dante's mind the disfigurement dissolves so that he can now see, reassembled beyond it, the familiar features of a man whose name he knows:

> Questa favilla tutta mi raccese
> mia conoscenza a la cangiata labbia,
> e ravvisai la faccia di Forese.

> This spark rekindled in me my knowledge of the altered features; and I recognised the face of Forese.

(ll. 46–8)

At the centre of the canto, then, the violent frame built of generalisation – and written script – is broken, to be replaced in its remaining two sections by a mode of minute perception which is focused almost entirely upon physical, biographical or behavioural particulars.

The first of these sections evokes the friendship which existed between Dante and Forese and begins with a moving evocation of how Dante wept over the face of his companion on his death-bed – just as now he grieves at the sight of Forese's distorted features. But then as now the moment is cathartic; and then as now the catharsis – in its concentration on particularities – may also be seen as a contributory factor in conversion. For there was, it seems, something reprehensible about the relationship between the two Florentines. Dante himself suggests this obliquely in line 115; and what is certainly known is that the two men at one point exchanged scurrilous poems in which the parentage, sexual life and physical characteristics of each were held up to ridicule: according to Dante, Forese is a scar-faced bastard who knew as little of his own father as Joseph did of Jesus; as for Forese's wife Nella, all she could do at night was sniffle from a perpetual cold. Now there are refreshing signs here of Dantean humanity. But to be solemn about them, the poems of this *tenzone* stand as a demonstration of how much violence the judgemental word, in the degenerate mode of gossip and caricature, may do to the human body. And there is every reason to think that Dante – himself returning to solemnity in canto 23 of the *Purgatorio* – is seeking here to remedy the truculence, blasphemy and obscenity of his earlier work. For what replaces all this is a subtle (and subtly qualified) act of praise in honour of a scarred individual whose scars are now the mark, in Dante's eye, of his fitness for redemption. Stylistically too there is a conversion here, from a strident harshness of vocabulary – which in the *tenzone* anticipates the *Inferno* – towards a style in which sweetness of rhythm combines with a precise observation of detail and a Keatsian sensuality of image. Here, as I suggested earlier, one can simultaneously read Dante's skill – and also the body of his text – in a way which might be taken to justify his own return as poet to the applause of his fellow Florentines. Thus Forese is allowed to describe his situation in these terms:

Tutta esta gente che piangendo canta
perseguitar la gola oltre misura,
in fame e'n sete qui si rifà santa.
  Di ber e di mangiar n'accende cura
l'odor ch'esce del pomo e de lo sprazzo
che si distende su per sua verdura.

All these people who go weeping as they sing, having followed appetite beyond
good measure, here make themselves holy again in hunger and thirst. The
aroma which comes from the apple and from the spray which spreads over the
greenery, kindles in them an urge to eat and drink.

(ll. 64–70)

One may note that even Forese's rheumy wife, Nella, participates in this
great conversion; it is her prayers which are said to have secured Forese's
salvation. And yet how in that case is one to read the final section of the
canto? This centres upon an invidious comparison which Forese makes
between his own pious wife and the 'sfacciate donne fiorentine' – the
brazen women of modern Florence – who delight in the wearing of low-
cut dresses. For a moment the canto seems to return to the harsh style of
tenzone, projecting viciously misogynistic judgements against these women;
and in this light the canto stirs familiar arguments which might have been
the subject of this whole essay. Certainly one cannot avoid making a thematic connection between the bodily exposure that these women choose
and the images of bodily submission which appear elsewhere in the canto.
But this, crucially, is a canto of faces; and these women have deprived
themselves of faces: they are 'sfacciate' – offensively without a sense of
'face'. In that one word, one sees how attention might have been dis-
tracted from the expressive features of a human body to its sexual functions, and also how the imposition of, as it were, a sexual sumptuary code
might frame the object as much for attack as for attention. That would
not, now, justify the attack. But the canto itself does not leave it there. Its
final lines break through even the interlocking frameworks of misogyny
and titillation, to recall the names of persons, as Dante speaks with complete simplicity of Beatrice; soon Virgil, his rational guide, will leave him:
'che io sarò là dove fia Beatrice' ('I will be there where Beatrice is') (l.
128). In that meeting (*Purg.* 30), the frames which Dante himself most
values – those of history, discourse and justice, all represented by Virgil –
will fall away as, in the Earthly Paradise, Dante meets Beatrice face to face,
and responds not in words but only (and supremely) in the psychosomatic
language of sighs, tears, sobs and childlike tremblings.

VI

Erving Goffman has spoken of how, to be a competent agent, it is necessary for the individual to exert constant control over its own bodily

actions, and goes on to insist that the competence exercised by the agent must always be seen and recognised as such by others. In Goffman's view, the growth of such competence is intrinsic to the development of the individual, and constitutes the foundation of individuality as recognised in 'public relations':

> To walk, to cross a road, to utter a complete sentence, to wear long pants, to tie one's own shoes, to add a column of figures – all these routines that allow the individual unthinking, competent performance were attained through an acquisition process whose early stages were negotiated in a cold sweat.[29]

This process of acquisition will, of course, involve much that only an institution can teach; and much of what an institution might in fact teach will need to be examined closely if that programme is not to become a channel of tyranny. None the less Goffman does encourage the microscopic attention which we have been looking for throughout this essay. Certainly the words cited above could well be applied to the processes of education which Dante depicts in the narrative of his own physical journey in the *Commedia*. In the *Commedia*, however, a point arrives in the course of the *Purgatorio* at which, beneath the level of competence, the vulnerability or fragility of the agent – at the moment of the 'cold sweat' – is also revealed. Here, too, that moment may well be observed by others, as a phase in the development of agency. But the regard which is called for at this stage will not be judgemental or institutional. It will rather be a moment of pity or of love which looks more to the motivations revealed in the face of the individual than to the results which the individual might subsequently achieve. It is this same regard for face which Dante directs upon Manfred and upon Forese in the course of the *Purgatorio*, and which Beatrice will direct upon Dante himself at the conclusion of the *cantica*. If institutional frames are to be questioned, then constant reference must be made to moments such as these.

NOTES

1 See E. Auerbach in *Mimesis: The Representation of Reality in Western Literature*, trans. W. R. Trask, Princeton, 1953, also A. Thorlby in *Literature and Western Civilisation*, vol. II, ed. D. Daiches and A. Thorlby, London, 1972.
2 *Philosophy and the Human Sciences*, Cambridge, 1985, pp. 152–84.
3 Cf. M. Foucault *Power/Knowledge*, New York, 1980, p. 131.
4 Cf. Anthony Giddens, *Modernity and Self-Identity: Self and Society in the Late Modern Age*, Cambridge, 1991, p. 57, who cites Charles Taylor's *Sources of the Self*, Cambridge, 1989, on p. 234.
5 *Surveiller et punir: Naissance de la prison*, Paris, 1975; published in an English translation by Alan Sheridan, London, 1977, p. 3.
6 G. Ryle, *The Concept of Mind*, London, 1949, IV. See also Stuart E. Spicker, ed., *The Philosophy of the Body: Rejections of Cartesian Dualism*, Chicago, 1970.
7 Peter Smith and O. R. Jones, *The Philosophy of Mind*, Cambridge, 1986, p. 83.

8 'Foucault on Freedom and Truth', p. 182.
9 Cf. Giddens *Modernity and Self-Identity*, p. 57.
10 *Par.* 17, ll. 55–60.
11 See *De Vulgari Eloquentia* 2.7 and 1.3.
12 See *Par.* canto 25, ll. 1–9.
13 Peter Geach, *God and the Soul*, London, 1969, p. 38.
14 *Aristotle: The Desire to Understand*, Cambridge, 1988, p. 97.
15 *Dante Philomythes and Philosopher*, Cambridge, 1981, p. 204.
16 *De Monarchia*, especially 1.11; see also E. Gilson, *Dante and Philosophy*, trans. David Moore, repr. London, 1948.
17 *Convivio* 3.3.
18 See Thomas Pogue Harrison, *The Body of Beatrice*, Baltimore, 1988, and J. H. Potter, 'Beatrice Dead or Alive: Love in the *Vita nuova*', *Texas Studies in Literature and Language*, XXXII, 1990, pp. 62–84.
19 *The Madwoman in the Attic: The Woman Writer and the Nineteenth Century Literary Imagination*, New Haven, 1979, p. 25.
20 See especially *Inferno* canto 5.
21 An argument more fully developed in my *Dante's Inferno. Difficulty and Dead Poetry*, Cambridge, 1987, especially pp. 367–77.
22 *Dante: The Poetics of Conversion*, ed. with an introduction by Rachel Jacoff, Cambridge, Mass. and London, 1986.
23 *Ibid.*, p. xii.
24 *Vita nuova* cap. 19: 'Donne ch'avete . . .' (ll. 1–14).
25 On Levinas see especially Jacques Derrida, *L'Ecriture et la différance*, Paris, 1967, translated as *Writing and Difference* by Alan Bass, London, 1978. Also S. Hands, *The Levinas Reader*, Oxford, 1989. Here see Derrida, *L'Ecriture*, pp. 100–1.
26 E. Levinas in conversation with Philippe Nemo in *Ethics and Infinity*, trans. Richard A. Cohen, Pittsburgh, PA, 1985, p. 72.
27 *Justification de l'éthique*, Brussels, 1984, pp. 41–51, quoted here from Hands *The Levinas Reader*, p. 81.
28 Cf. Elaine Scarry: 'The self-flagellation of the religious ascetic is not an act of denying the body, eliminating its claims for attention, but a way of so emphasising the body that the contents of the world are cancelled and the path is clear for the entry of an unworldly contentless force', *The Body in Pain: the Making and Unmaking of the World*, Oxford, 1985, p. 34.
29 *Relations in Public*, London, 1971, p. 248.

Making the world in York
and the York cycle

The body of Christ was self-consciously elaborated in the late Middle Ages
as the very meeting place of the sacred and the profane. In the eucharist
it was at once the rationale and the centre point of what has come to be
known as medieval sacramentalism. As disseminated in the vernacular
devotional writings of the late Middle Ages it offered itself in postures of
love, sacrifice and suffering as the object of passionate identification. Its
precise relation to the Godhead (sign, figure, representation, Real Presence,
accident, substance) was furiously debated in the fourteenth and early
fifteenth centuries; the understanding of this relation informed and affected
attitudes towards the ecclesiastical establishment, particularly in the peculiarly English heresy – Lollardy. In the cities, towns and villages of England
a complex celebration of Corpus Christi was enacted in the Corpus Christi
procession which perambulated the host around the boundaries of the
city, blessing and delineating its borders.[1] In York the procession developed to incorporate the pageants staged and financed by the trade-guilds.[2]

Corpus Christi was a major symbolic resource for the religious culture
of the late Middle Ages. As the privileged *locus* for the divine and human,
it was the site of a two-way transference of sacrality. The body of Christ was
God made man; through the operation of grace and faith, men and women
could be made one in God.[3] Although theoretically the monopoly of the
clerical establishment, in practice Corpus Christi was made available to
and appropriated by many other factions and competing interests in late
medieval society. By far the most sophisticated, reflexive and textured set
of practices associated with Corpus Christi are the performances developed in the Corpus Christi pageants.[4] They proffer cultural critics an
invitation to analyse the constitutive interrelations of urban, theatrical and
ritual forms. For the Corpus Christi procession and theatre do not merely
reflect the shape and function of the medieval town and city whose borders they articulate, but mould and recreate urban topography in ways
both fantastical and material. City and actors are not then the mere instruments of the coherent and cohering 'message' of Corpus Christi. For a
start, its shape can never be guaranteed in advance. Cowling, for example,

points out that in York the parochial clergy and the laity celebrated Corpus Christi with the city fathers, independently of the monastic and cathedral foundations, so that there were sometimes competing processions on the same day.[5] Moreover, the route (and so the shape of the city and the body that are mutually implicated) was subject to argument which had a direct bearing on who was able to control and profit from a ritual forum intended to encompass all of its citizens. The positioning of the stations which determined the route of the pageants was regularly argued over.[6] In 1399, the commons presented a petition requesting that the stations of performance be positioned at the doors of the important civic officials as well as other more obviously public places.[7] Later, in 1417, at a meeting described as 'the most representative meeting of the community that the Memorandum Book has registered',[8] the populace complained about the profit made by those before whose houses the plays were performed:

> And it was ordained that in all the years following while this play is played, it must be played before the doors and holdings of those who have paid better and more generously to the Chamber and are willing to do more for the benefit of the whole commons for having this play there, not giving favour to anyone for his individual benefit, but rather that the public utility of the whole of the commons of York ought to be considered.[9]

The shape and timing and positioning of the performance of the Corpus Christi pageants, then, were subject to local bargaining in which the interests of private property and profit competed with the interests of 'tocius communitatis'.[10]

Criticism of the York cycle has characteristically insisted on its doctrinal, theological meanings as if it were merely a sermon in drama, as if all its meanings could be subsumed or explained in relation to some universally held and understood monolithic ecclesiastical dogma.[11] Such a stubbornly idealist mode of approach is unlikely to be able to conceive of the constitutive, performative means by which meanings are made and constructed through ritual knowledge and cultural enactment, nor to be able to read the multiply determined mechanisms through which the body is continuously implicated as the vehicle, simultaneously pursuer and subverter of cultural significations. This paper will be concerned with sketching out one strand of the York cycle's rich articulation of a politics of embodiment: its theatrical exploration of labour and its divisions, transformations, praxis and political regulation. York had a disproportionately large percentage of its population involved in manufacturing[12] and the pageants seem curiously interested in the theme of labour. How is work understood, then, as York itself is remade on Corpus Christi day? How does the political representation of the city connect with its cultural forms?[13]

In a recent Gary Larsen cartoon, God is to be found with a large lump of Plasticine on one side of him, and a series of Plasticine snakes on the

other. He sits in the middle gleefully rolling out one of the more conse-
quential of his creations. 'Boy,' he says, 'these are a cinch.'[14] Larsen's visual
humour works off an ancient theological axiom which insists that there
could be nothing approximating human effort, the labour of work, in the
act of divine creation. When God as 'maker unmade', as alpha and omega,
as the most primal of movers, creates the world in the York cycle, his act
is to be understood as an act of creation, rather than a production of
labour. And the subsequent fall of his creation is the originary myth of the
necessity of human labour, to be understood both as the pain of parturi-
tion and as the inauguration of a relentlessly finite existence: the rupture
of culture from nature. Labour will be the end of a process in which
reproduction – birth – will ineradicably be tied to death, and serve as a
reminder of the sundering of will and flesh. Furthermore, labour, in the
sense of work, will be necessitated by the new relationship of man and his
environment. Nature is henceforth the medium which will have to be
tended, worked and cultivated for sustenance.

However, it is not merely a regime of hard labour and sexual inequality
that is inaugurated by the fall of God's creation, but a sacramental culture.
For the architects of the sacramental system

> The time of the institution of the sacraments is believed to have begun from
> the moment when the first parent, on being expelled by merit of disobedience
> from the joys of paradise into the exile of this mortal life, is held with all
> posterity liable to the first corruption even to the end. For from the time when
> man, having fallen from the state of first incorruption, began to ail in body
> through mortality and in soul through iniquity, God at once prepared a remedy
> for restoring man.[15]

The sacramental system is part of the way in which fallen nature can be
recuperated as redeemed culture. Sexual reproduction itself, for example,
becomes part of that system through the sacraments of marriage, baptism
and confession.

But if the York cycle is concerned with the moment of the fall as the
inauguration of work, the subordination of woman to man through her
sexual and maternal nature, and ecclesiastically sanctioned and adminis-
tered sacramental culture, it is also concerned with the inauguration of
shameful and acute self-consciousness. 'Allas, what have I done, for shame!
... Me shames with my lyghame', utters Adam after he has eaten the apple
in the Fall of Adam and Eve pageant.[16] The central moment of this pageant
is not the transgression of eating the apple, that heinous and almost
unthinkable act of disobedience, but an appalled understanding of self-
consciousness as the facticity of the body itself. The staging makes this
moment quite central. For we have seen Adam and Eve naked in the Garden
of Eden throughout the pageant. All of a sudden we see them again,
mediated by their own profound shame. Nakedness becomes before our

very eyes the sign of sin and self-disgust. Though nothing has in fact changed in outward appearance, everything has changed in a new post-lapsarian world, a world where costume and covering are an intrinsic part of human appearance.

In Hugh of St Victor's *Didascalion*, Adam and Eve's shameful 'aprons', sewn together from fig-leaves, are the very first art objects.[17] It is not merely self-consciousness, work, sexual inequality and sacramentality, then, that are the densely interwoven story of embodiedness as told in the creation sequences of the York cycle, but the necessity of mediation and representation associated with covering, disguise and pitiful lack. The careful attention of the York plays to the world of making, and the world as made, is part and parcel of the cycle's elaboration of a politics of embodiment, its interest in the political regulation of the body, in a bodily epistemology, a theology of incarnation, and a community created through praxis and self-representation, not creation *ex nihilo*. What is at stake in the attention given to the body throughout this cycle? No longer the absolute and orthodox dividing line separating God from his creation, the act of making, although necessitated by the Fall, produces the framework in terms of which the world can be understood. Involved in this process, not simply at the theological level of the necessary reparation of incarnate humanity for sin, is the understanding of the body as the creative agency of knowing and doing. In York, this is no mere celebration of the physicality of humanity, but an acute investigation of the kinds of identification enabled by Corpus Christi, and of the kinds of political regulation necessitated by the body as a central mechanism of imaginary social order.

In his recent work *The Ideology of the Aesthetic*, Terry Eagleton has made the following statement:

> Paradoxically, a certain open-endedness and transformability is part of our natures, built into what we are; that the human animal is able to 'go beyond', make something creative and unpredictable of what makes it, is the condition of historicity and the consequence of a 'lack' in our biological structure which culture, if we are to survive at all, has at all costs to fill. But such creative self-making is carried out within given limits, which are finally those of the body itself. Human societies, by virtue of the biological structure of the body, all need to engage in some form of labour and some kind of sexual reproduction; all human beings require warmth, rest, nourishment and shelter, and are inevitably implicated by the necessities of labour and sexuality in various forms of social association, the regulation of which we name the political.[18]

Here Eagleton is extending the central Marxist understanding of praxis, by which, through creative activity and work, humanity changes its environment, its historical, human world, and hence itself.[19] For Marx, our epistemology is worked through and derived from our way of engaging the world through work: 'all social life is essentially practical'.[20] It is labour, in this view, that makes fluid the boundary between nature and culture, for it will vary according to the social and historical character of labour.

Standard commentaries on the creation of the world were in the habit of pointing out that God did not make the world as a craftsman makes an object:

> For the builder does not make the wood, but makes something from the wood, and so it is with all other craftsmen of this kind. But almighty God needed the help of nothing that he had not already made himself for carrying out his will. For if he was helped in making the things he willed to make by some other things that he had not made, he was not almighty; and to believe that is blasphemy.[21]

In the Fall of Angels pageant, God describes his own creation as 'warke' with a repetitious insistence that can hardly be accidental:

> To all I shall wirke be 3he wysshyng.
> This day warke es done ilke a dele,
> And all þis warke lykes me ryght wele,
> And baynely I 3yf it my blessyng.[22]

This insistence on work is repeated with greater point and elaboration in the Building of the Ark pageant where God becomes the master craftsman teaching the ignorant Noah the tricks of the trade of ship-building.[23] 'Warke' that has itself until this moment signified God's work of making the world, now comes to mean both the botched-up object of his work, man, and simultaneously, the necessity to redo the work all over again: 'Bot wirke þis werke I wille al newe.'[24] The significance is worked alliteratively also in lines 35–6, where God says to Noah:

> I wyll þou wyrke withowten weyn
> A warke to saffe þiselfe wythall.

The notion of God's creation in the Augustinian and Anselmian sense is increasingly compromised by the analogy of God as master-craftsman teaching Noah his trade. Noah knows nothing about 'shippe-craft', but God advises him in some detail (line 66). The work references continue insistently throughout lines 70, 87, 93, 95, 110, 115, 120, and with a newly charged meaning when it comes to mean the work of salvation, line 147. The reference to God as master-craftsman is made quite explicit at the very end of the pageant:

> He þat to me þis Crafte has kende
> He wysshe us with his worthy wille.[25]

The meaning of the word for 'work' then is densely encoded to mean at once humanity as the object of God's work, the work of making him, the work of restoring him, and Noah's work of ark-building and salvation. The hierarchies of creation insisted upon by Augustine and Anselm are here collapsed to foreground an activity seen in human and anthropomorphic terms.[26]

Compare this dense undercutting of standard theological readings with the treatment that links the creation story to Corpus Christi in the sermon which introduces the ordinances to the York Corpus Christi guild.[27] This guild, founded in 1408, included august members such as the Archbishop of York, the abbots of St Mary's in York, Richard, Duke of Gloucester (later Richard III) as well as nearly every citizen who could afford the 2d annual torch fee.[28] The sermon is based on Matthew 26.26, 'Hoc est enim corpus meum', conventionally read as the biblical inscription of the *sacrum convivium*, the eucharistic feast, and it links the creation of the body of Adam to the ideology of Corpus Christi as a sacramental unity: 'Likewise, having created, ruled, governed and endowed with a variety of virtues that same first body, the Lord was able to fulfill the words of this saying [that is, "This is my body"], as a special presage of unity.'[29] Creation is linked here with order, and with the formation of humanity not as an object of difference but as an extension of sameness, unity and the immaculate reduplication of a perfectly conceived social system. Where reproduction threatens or hints at the production of difference, pre-lapsarian procreation ensures the mere iteration of a hermetic integrity: 'Thus, through the act of procreation, the harmoniously formed body of every rational creature was to perpetuate in itself the primal unity of creation, the concord of the state of innocence; all distinction or rebellion being dug out by the roots.'[30]

These glosses not only link the creation story with sacramentality in a very overt way, winding both meanings around the scriptural precedent for the institution of the 'sacrum convivium', but also betray a concern with preoccupations of cohesion and the spectre of difference and distinction opened up by the formation of such a social body as the guild of Corpus Christi.[31] Central to the ideology of Corpus Christi as it is overtly articulated here is unity. All the metaphors which proliferate are about reproduction without difference.[32]

When Corpus Christi, the little host under clerical jurisdiction and subject to strict ritual control and construction, is extended into the drama of the town it risks its own meanings, finding them difficult to guarantee. If it is supposed to hold together the parts that ideally come to make up the whole, then the parts threaten to move in different directions. In extending 'God's flesh' over and around and through the city of York the hegemony of the host is as much threatened as confirmed. The ability of Christ's body to be a synecdoche for the composite society of York, for example, is questioned by the stresses on the borders and boundaries of that society. A bill presented to York council by a group of artisans excluded from the political governance of the life of their city, for example, reveals how thoroughly contested was the nominal community of council and commonality, but also how interrelated was the symbolic language of the body with arguments concerning the political structure of the polity:[33] 'for alsmuch as we ben all one bodye corporate, we thynke that we be all inlike prevaliged of the comonalte, which has borne none office in the city'.[34]

Political power in the late medieval town, as Rosser and Holt have recently reminded us, was 'largely an expression of economic influence'.[35] The medieval economy of the urban town was characterised by a complex and intricate division of labour in a small-scale economy. The power the merchant had over the craftsman was not the ownership of capital, but the control of the system of exchange.[36] As John Merrington has recently described it:

> So long as the market depended on price disparities between separate spheres of production in which the producers were not separated from the means of production and subsistence, trade only existed in the interstices of the system, monopolising the supply of a limited range of goods, and was dependent on political indulgence.[37]

The chief economic division in urban life was thus the one between the merchant and the manufacturing guilds. The division of labour imposed on the craft-guilds was partly an expression of mercantile anxiety which feared 'any situation in which a chain of operations, from the acquisition of the raw material to the marketing of the final product could be undertaken by the craftsmen themselves'.[38] Tanners and butchers, for example, had easy access to raw materials, and they supplied other crafts with the raw material for their own production. It was therefore essential to maintain commercial dominance to separate, for example, butchers, tanners, and cordwainers, just as it was important to separate millers and bakers, or for that matter, weavers, fullers and dyers.[39] But because economic status alone (unlike the capitalist relations of production) could not sufficiently secure mercantile power, the system of crafts organisations developed to divide and control the non-mercantile body.

This view of the craft-guilds is a very recent one among historians.[40] Long viewed as a form of voluntary self-policing fraternal organisation, recent research has indicated that they may be considered part and parcel of the repressive legislation of the late fourteenth century, part of a reaction to the rising power and costs of labour.[41]

The economy was organised in terms of the household; it is partly the erasure of this fact in so many accounts of the socio-economic life of late medieval towns that has tempted historians to see the mercantile-enforced fantasy of a division of labour as late medieval reality.[42] York's guild system underwent considerable expansion in the late fourteenth and early fifteenth centuries when the guilds became institutionalised as agents of the council. The labour statutes of 1363–64 introduced the principle of one person, one trade: 'artificers handicraft people, hold them every one to one mystery, which he will chose betwixt this and the said feast of Candlemas; and two of every craft shall be chosen to survey, that none use other craft than the same which he hath chosen'.[43] Swanson sees this 1363 statute as being a composite part of the repressive labour legislation instituted in the 1351 Statute of Labourers, and re-enacted throughout the late fourteenth and fifteenth centuries.[44] The drive behind such legislation was simple: seigneurial and mercantile reaction.[45] The legislation constituted an attempt to keep labour rates down to pre-plague levels, before labour scarcity had caused them to mount. By setting up a system whereby master-craftsmen were in control of an artificially divided labour force, 'the authorities effectively undermined the corporate identity which might develop amongst the artisans as a whole'.[46] 'It was not', according to Swanson 'a monopoly of manufacture that the council feared so much as a monopoly of distribution', because this was the very source of wealth-creation in the towns.[47]

The select body of York consisted in the mayor and the council of twelve, and a council of twenty-four. There was also a council of forty-eight, which it seems was rarely consulted. This was also known as the 'commonalty'. Where the identity of the 'forty-eight' seems capable of determination, it seems that the forty-eight were representative of the crafts of the city, referred to in the *York Memorandum Book* as 'les artificers'.[48] As Palliser points out, during the fifteenth century this wider body came to consist of the searchers of the city's craft-guilds.[49] Swanson points out that it is likely that as the searchers, whose task was to supervise the products of the manufacturing guilds, increased in authority as more powers were delegated to them by the council, 'it must have seemed logical for them to take on a representative function'.[50] The system of representation by guild hardly represented the power of the guilds. It is rather an assessment of the authority of the council. Usually it is clear from the York records that the group of forty-eight was largely excluded from the political process. This political system was in constant turmoil virtually throughout the staging of the Corpus Christi cycles. In the revised constitution of 1517, a new common council was appointed whereby the role of the merchant body increased at the expense of the manufacturing guilds.[51]

In a recent article Richard Homan has argued that there is one exception to this gradual and persistent process of exclusion. In the production of the Corpus Christi pageants, the group of forty-eight was regularly included in the decisions, and he therefore reads this as an instance of a ritualised compensation for an actual political exclusion. The many instances of craft-guilds protesting over their contribution to the production of the Corpus Christi pageants, he says

can only be understood if the festival is looked at as a microcosm of the political and social structure of the town in which economic inequalities, unresolvable
in fact, could be resolved, and most important, in which the central monopoly
of the city government could be ritualistically put right.

However, Maud Sellers does provide us with the crucial information,
omitted by Homan, that the forty-eight were actually fined for their non-
attendance at these meetings at which the organisation of the Corpus
Christi pageants were discussed. Their participation in the very meeting in
which one ideal form of the body of Christ was going to be constituted was
therefore financially and legally enforced.[52]

The instances of quarrels over payment for the pageants are indeed
emblematic of certain divisions between the trade-guilds. But those divisions tend to concern the dispute over the artificial division of labour
through which their manufacturing activities were framed. So, for example, the sausage-makers protested that they would not put on their pageant because they could not afford the expense, unless they received help
from those who made candles.[53] The mayor agreed that all those who made
candles for retail should henceforth be compelled to contribute to the
York Corpus Christi pageants. In this respect the sausage-makers ensured
that those who encroached upon one of their sidelines, the making of
Paris candles from tallow, would be forced to share the cost of the pageant. Swanson goes so far as to suggest that the guild of sausage-makers may
have been fabricated just so that they could bear the burden of a pageant.[54]
If this is the case then their protests expand the numbers of those who
should be liable to payment by demanding that all members from other
crafts who are not sausage-makers yet who sell sausages or their by-products,
and all those butchers and butchers' wives who sell candles made of tallow, one of the main by-products of the butcher's trade, should be forced
to contribute to the pageant.[55] On the one hand this may be seen as a
victory for the sausage-makers in revealing the artificiality (and injustice?)
of the divisions imposed by the civic oligarchy. The production, they insist,
will be mounted by all who actually make and sell sausages. At the same
time, it is, if not a recognition of the validity of the nonsensical category
of sausage-makers, a necessary subjugation to the power of the definitions
of the town government, and their ability to draw the lines delineating
(and constructing) the crafts.

The articificiality of the divisions of the civic body was thereby renego-
tiated, but only by acceding to a system of divide and rule, whereby the
artisanate were forced to compete with one another rather than perceive
their common structural interests.

The crafts system designed by the urban oligarchy was in this way a
piece of political machinery designed to prevent such a dangerous alternative body from forming.[56] The butcher's trade was in fact subject to the

closest of regulation because butchers, as well as supplying the vital food-stuff to the city, were also in a position to supply and participate in many other trades (leather-work, candle-making etc.) and so transgression of the boundaries established by the city seemed to be almost routine.[57] The particular ideological battle which the sausage-makers fought over their part in the pageant in 1417 was in fact lost, in that the pageant for which the sausage-makers had hitherto been responsible was amalgamated with several others in 1422.[58] Carrying the name of neither of the guilds nominally responsible for its payment and production, this pageant was to carry the arms of the city. Stevens reads this as a paradigm for the functioning of the cycle; individual sponsorship of the trades guilds could change, but the management of the city endured.[59] But it could also be seen as an ongoing strategic battle in which the guilds were constantly redefining the very nature of the parts they were to play, and for which they were to pay. It is indeed remarkable how much of the money financing the plays comes from infractions of the artificial division of labour set up by the mercantile oligarchy.[60] Regrators were fined and their fines went to the very craft-guild they had undercut. Where craftsmen poached on the nominal craft of another, their fines went to support the injured guild's craft pageant.[61] The plays were in many ways actually financed by the persistent and sys-tematic breaking of the lines of division established by the mercantile ruling body to separate one craft from another. If, as Heather Swanson has said, 'the burden of the pageants was instrumental in forcing a more rigid organization on the system of craft-guilds',[62] one could also say, paradoxically, that the display of the wholesome and holistic corporate body of the town had been partly put together through the transgressive but systematic reordering of the mercantile drawing of, and fantasy about, this corporate body and its constituents.

If this logic is pursued it follows that it was in the interests of the town government to increase artificial divisions between the guilds; the more guilds, the more searchers, the more searchers, the more fines.[63] Fines went usually to the council and to the pageant,[64] and it was in this way that the production of the pageants was so intimately linked to the political regu-lation of work.[65] The craft system which emerges from Heather Swanson's work suggests that although the records indicate a system in which a craft-guild exists to transmit the skills of the trade in a master–apprentice struc-ture, to maintain an actual distinction in function and control of craft, and to perform and organise monopolies in manufacture, the craft system actually is revised by the mercantile body in the late fifteenth and early sixteenth centuries to protect the mercantile group whose own economic status is threatened.[66] The timing of the commitment of the 'originals' (the play texts owned by the craft-guilds) to the Register between 1463 and 1477 coincides with recession, and with the decline in the York merchants' hold over overseas trade.[67] Merchants lost their hold over the overseas markets, and diversifying away from wool they invested in the market much more as regional distributors of manufactured goods.[68] This must have put them into a much more directly competitive position in relation to the craft-guilds. The increased level of control over the production of the Corpus Christi pageants consequent on its transmission to the Register is in line with the intensified polarisation in the relations of merchant and artisan in the recession of the post-1450s. Once again it was the organisation of the pageants that operated as one of the vehicles of that polarisation.[69]

This version of the interrelation of political and economic structure in the city of York should inform a different kind of cultural history of medieval theatrical production, as well, specifically, as a different account of the York plays themselves. For the conceptualisation of late medieval towns as 'non-feudal islands in a feudal sea',[70] as defined by their putative exemption and immunity from feudal relations, has meant that the products of late medieval urban theatre have been read as precursors of a Whig historiography, making of them a drama of bourgeois triumphalism. But as Rodney Hilton points out, the differing interpretations of the relation of urban life to feudalism derive from different conceptualisations of the nature of the structure of feudal social relations. If the determining features of feudalism are understood to be lord–vassal relations, characterised by private jurisdictions, then the town as an entity is consequently conceived as organised around the necessity to be free of seigneurial jurisdiction. But if, as for Hilton, feudalism is understood as a mode of production, the key relation is not within the governing class but between the landowning aristocracy, the expropriating class, and the peasantry who offer up surplus value in the form of rent, money or labour. In this definition, as Merrington puts it, 'urban "capitalism" was both internal and external to the feudal mode – or more precisely, the latter was the *condition* for the former', since it was corporate urban autonomy that functioned like a 'collective seigneur'.[71]

The Marxist historiography of the feudal relations of medieval urban life informed by Swanson's detailed and precise articulation of mercantile–artisanal relations in York should render not only possible but imperative a reconsideration of the kind of culture ritually celebrated in the Corpus Christi plays.[72] In particular we need to develop a better way of thinking about the interrelation of the socio-economic and the cultural. For our very conceptualisation of culture is frequently 'a-historical, non-processual and totalising'.[73] Because it is so often understood as all-inclusive, culture has to be conceptualised as either autonomous or independent, or merely dependent, superstructural. But as Ellen Meiskins Wood has argued, in pre-capitalist societies, 'extra-economic powers, political authority, and juridical privilege had special importance because the economic power of appropriation was inseparable from them'.[74] Cultural questions, then, are economic ones, and the distinction between base and superstructure that has been the source of such urgent debates, debates which intimately concern the relation of culture to the social, has to be reformulated.[75] Culture can no longer be the expression of a whole way of life, but must rather be conceived as the 'very terrain of the political struggle over the reproduction or the transformation of the social relations of <pre>-capitalism'.[76] If, as I have argued here, the Corpus Christi pageants are themselves the very mechanism for the regulation of labour, trade and manufacture in the city, then it is no longer possible to make the case that they are a cultural resolution of economic problems, at once the aesthetic mirror for York society and its ideal form. Neither are they an expression, a homology of the central mechanism of the 'market' conceived in its quintessentially urban 'function'.[77] Rather they are the cultural vehicles of socio-political life and the central means of their mutual articulation.[78]

How can this different understanding of the emphasis on work be re-read in the plays themselves in the light of this account? My contention in this paper is that many of the pageants reveal and help to articulate an artisanal ideology which placed importance on manufacture, or on making, rather than on the control of exchange mechanisms through the manipulation of networks of supply and distribution. The very public ceremonial designed to figure forth the body of the city as the wish-fulfilment of its most illustrious members is therefore undercut by an emergent structure of feeling which will precisely emphasise manufacture as central.

It is the Crucifixion pageant that most articulates these themes of making, and of division and wholeness, in ways that have a very close bearing on the interaction between the city's political regulation and the sacramentalism that supposedly underwrote it. The Crucifixion pageant, mounted at the time of recording in the Register by the pinners, is famously a pageant about making: the making of the central icon of late medieval Christianity, the body of Christ. If we take seriously Beadle and King's stage notes, it is possible to see the play first of all working visually along a horizontal axis. As the pinners playing the soldiers nail Christ to the cross, we cannot really see what they are doing. We know from their words that they are botching their job. They make Christ fit the cross, rather than the other way around. The apocryphal story that the tree out of which the cross was made buckles and moves in an effort to prevent the horrors of its destined use is brought into play here. Only when Christ is laboriously stuck in the mortice, in the vertical axis, suddenly on display to the audience, can we see the fruit of their labours. The twin axes of the play ask us first of all to divorce means from ends, and then to see them brutally reunited. The pageant constantly refers us to the crucifixion as work, and outrageously prolongs that work.[79] The soldiers understood to be acting under the aegis of an uncontestable authority[80] can conceive of their task only in blind relation to this authority. They cannot see the whole picture, and in not seeing it, they re-enact the crucifixion itself as they reproduce the very image of corporate holism signified by Christ's mutilated body. The job of pinners is of course to make the joins, the pivotal points which both link and articulate the structure of the made object. Their work is in fact to join things strongly and usefully together. When Christ in the second speech that cuts across the soldiers to address the audience says 'What þei wirke wotte þai noght', the costs of such a division are made to speak.[81]

The picture held up to York is the intimately familiar one that has reproached them from the walls of churches, from altarpieces and retables, in flat and plastic form. Here it is seen again, but re-conceived theatrically as the very product of human agency.[82] This is in striking contrast to both the affective Christ of the devotional tradition and in contrast too to the little wafer handled between priestly hands, synecdoche for the whole of Christian society. Here it is understood in particular and intimate relation to the divisions enforced on the artisan body.

Rather than being the place in which the social and political polity could re-imagine itself, the body of Christ, ideally the universal Church and all of Christian society, was the ritual object, administered by a closed caste which differentiated itself precisely by means of such administration. Some of the York Corpus Christi pageants nominally inscribe within them such an understanding of the sacrament. But they fundamentally revise their understanding of sacramental culture; the sacrament is no longer the little wafer distributed to the laity. It is what the clergy represented it as being: the social world of York. But it is that world, not as an object, but as a process of relation, and in taking the sacrament at its word, some of these plays succeed in unlocking the emancipatory critique that is always the other side of that sacrament's potent ideological force. Through the culture's central symbol of desire and suffering, the very limits of the satisfaction that the given system of social labour provides, are marked.[83]

For if it is the necessity of labour (rendered imperative by culture in the first place) that makes of humanity the creature who in transforming itself also transforms its environment, then it is this always excessive and non-self-identical creature who will permanently inhabit the gap between the actual and the possible. It is this gap between the actual and the possible that renders both inevitable and compelling the political struggle to 're-deem what is possible from what is real, our reality being but the system-atic obstruction of the possible'.[84] That is also why we might celebrate the fig-leaf, first art object, not so much as a deficiency, but as the very sign of human making.

NOTES

I would like to thank my new colleagues at the University of Pittsburgh for their responses to the very first draft of this paper, given under the auspices of the Medieval Studies Committee, and to the students of my 'Drama of Labour, Drama of Power' graduate class in the Fall of 1992 who helped me move towards, defend and modify, many of the formulations at work here. Special thanks to Tom Hahn for the chance to give this paper an airing at Rochester and to benefit from his enthusiasm, intellectual generosity and cogent advice. Thanks too to Sarah Kay and Miri Rubin for their editorial work. I thank Barrie Dobson and Heather Swanson for their knowledgable responses. John Twyning read this essay and came back with characteristically trenchant criticism and help.

1 For an excellent recent discussion of Corpus Christi processions, see Miri Rubin, *Corpus Christi: The Eucharist in Medieval Culture*, Cambridge, 1991, pp. 243–71. Rubin's book is an important revisionist account of medieval sacramentalism. See also Mervyn James's classic article, 'Ritual, Drama and Social Body in the Late Medieval Town', *Past and Present*, XCVIII, 1983, pp. 3–29.

2 The number of pageants corresponding each to a trade-guild given in the second list that comes after the *Ordo paginarum* of 1415–33 in the A/Y Memorandum Book is 56. The Register which contains the text of the plays provides for 48. For details of the *Ordo* and the later history of the cycle, see Richard Beadle, ed., *The York Plays*, London, 1982, pp. 23–8 (henceforth *York Plays*). For an account of the civic documents which contain the play manuscript and other crucial information relating to the structuring, history and performance of the plays, especially the civic memorandum books, see *Records of Early English Drama: York*, ed. A. F. Johnston and M. Rogerson, 2 vols, Toronto, 1979, I, pp. xix–xx (henceforth, REED: York). Beadle points out the inadvisability of reifying the text of the Register, in synchronic isolation from the wealth of other material, as the essential form of the York Corpus Christi Cycle: 'It need hardly be said that this constitutes a situation impossibly resistant to the conventional objects of modern textual criticism, with its yearning towards definitive and unitary notions such as authorial intention, the authorized text of a work, and the act of publication. Here, even the primary document, the Register, bears witness to the existence of the text evolving over a lengthy time span, during which the processes of change were as unsystematic as they were continuous', 'The York Cycle: Texts, Performances and the Bases for Critical Enquiry', in Tim William Machan, ed., *Medieval Literature: Texts and Interpretation, Medieval and Renaissance Texts and Studies*, LXXIX, Binghamton, New York, 1991, p. 111.

3 I have examined some of the cultural implications and significations of the body of Christ in this cultural transaction as it operates through late medieval devotional English writings in my *Christ's Body: Identity, Culture and Society in Late Medieval Writings*, London, 1993.

4 In a recent paper, Alexandra Johnson has reminded us that although the York Corpus Christi cycle is probably the only civic cycle (because the Chester cycle was performed at Whitsun, and N-town and Towneley are possibly literary constructs whose dramatic status and history is unclear), it does not form a pattern. The episodic biblical drama follows a very haphazard pattern, and not a transferable schema from the Creation to the Last Judgement. Indeed, it is the passion play rather than the cyclical form which is the most common form of biblical drama in the late Middle Ages in England. See her 'The Continental Connection: A Reconsideration', delivered at a conference organised by the Centre for Medieval Studies, The Pennsylvania State University, March, 1993, 'The Stage as Mirror: Civic Theatre in Late Medieval Europe.'

5 Douglas Cowling, 'The Liturgical Celebration of Corpus Christi in Medieval York', *Reed Newsletter*, I, 1976, p. 7.

6 For further details on the positioning of the stations see A. J. Mill, 'The Stations of the York Corpus Christi Play', *Yorkshire Archeological Journal*, XXXVII, 1951, pp. 492–502, and Meg Twycross, ' "Places to Hear the Play": Pageant Stations at York, 1398–1572', *REED Newsletter*, II, 1978, pp. 10–33. And the route was altered in other ways as well, for the very

topography of the city, the 'stage' of the pageants, profoundly altered during the course of its performance. P. J. P. Goldberg finds for example in his analysis of poll tax returns that in general bigger households with larger proportions of servants tended to be concentrated in the prosperous central districts of York, while many households (frequently female) with only one member were to be found in poorer suburban districts. See his 'Urban Identity and the Poll Taxes of 1377, 1379, and 181', *Economic History Review*, 2nd ser., XLIII, 2, 1990, p. 197. More graphically in his book *Women, Work and Life-Cycle in a Medieval Economy: Women in York and Yorkshire c.1300–1520*, Oxford, 1992, Goldberg describes the location of some of those peripheral suburban districts; St Saviour's Parish, for example, where many women gathered in cheap tenements, was near the Hungate district where butcher's offal and other waste was habitually discarded (p. 317). Before it is theatricalised in the Corpus Christi festivities, then, certain patterns of inclusion and exclusion, of core and periphery have already been firmly established. See also Goldberg's section on the occupational topography of later medieval York in which he locates many of the trade designations (pp. 64–71). By about 1450–1500, the 'commercial sector', comprising the mercers and drapers who clustered in Fossgate, and the parishes of St Crux and All Saints, Pavement, shrinks and becomes more closely defined. 'There was consequently an increasing polarization between this commercial quarter and other areas where trade and industrial activities were located' (p. 70). The point here is to point out the possibilities (and limitations) of the conception of the city as stage, rather than to see the city as a static reflection of a preconceived model of wholeness imposed on the city, simultaneously its reflection and its ideal form. Martin Stevens includes a chapter on the York Cycle and the city as stage in his *Four Middle English Mystery Cycles: Textual, Contextual and Critical Interpretations*, Princeton, 1986. Much detailed work on spatial location in relation to theatrical form remains to be done. I attempt a preliminary mapping in my article, 'Ritualizing the Body in the York Corpus Christi Cycle', University of Minnesota (forthcoming, 1995), in a volume based on the 'Intersections' conference organised by David Wallace and Barbara Hanawalt at the Centre for Medieval Studies, University of Minnesota, April, 1993.

7 Described by Maud Sellers in her edition of *The York Memorandum Book: II (1388–1419)*, Surtees Society, CXXV, 1914, p. xliv (henceforth *YMB*, II). The theory of the staging in multiple locations has been hotly debated. For a succinct analysis by a firm protagonist of the multiple staging argument, see Alexandra Johnston, 'The York Corpus Christi Play: A Dramatic Structure Based on Performance Practice', in H. Braet, J. Nowe and G. Tournoy, eds., *The Theatre in the Middle Ages*, Leuven, 1985, pp. 362–73.

8 *YMB*, II, 1914, p. xliv.

9 REED: York, p. 714. For the Latin original see *YMB*, II, 1914, p. 64. Johannes Morton, the man who became mayor the following year, initially opposed the motion, as the owner of a house in Micklegate, but eventually submitted to the ruling of mayor and council (pp. xlv, 64–5).

10 It seems that the scaffolds erected before the houses of the eminent in front of which some of the stations were to be located, functioned virtually like private theatres in the public city space for which those who could afford it might pay. See REED: York, p. 713: 'Nevertheless the mayor, the honourable men, and the whole said commons, by their unanimous consent and assent, order <that> all those who receive money for scaffolds which they may build in the aforesaid places before their doors on public property at the aforesaid sites from those sitting on them shall pay the third penny of the money so received to the chamberlains of the city to be applied to the use of the same commons', *YMB*, II, p. 63.

11 For criticism of the 'remarkably uniform' attribution of religious instruction to the plays, see Kathleen Ashley, 'Medieval Courtesy Literature and Dramatic Mirrors of Female Conduct', in *The Ideology of Conduct: Essays in Literature and the History of Sexuality*, edited by Nancy Armstrong and Leonard Tennenhouse, New York and London, 1987, p. 25.

12 For the comparative figures, see Nigel Goose, 'English Pre-Industrial Urban Economies',

Urban History Yearbook, 1982, pp. 24–5 and Charles Phythian Adams, *The Fabric of the Traditional Community*, 1977, p. 16, fig. 5. Goldberg estimates that roughly one fifth of the 'economically active population' was employed in the manufacture and sale of food and drink, and more than half in occupations associated with leather or metal crafts, textiles, clothing, or mercantile trades collectively; see his 'Urban Identity', p. 213, and tab. 8, p. 211. See also D. M. Palliser, 'The Trades Guilds of Tudor York' in Peter Clark and Paul Slack, eds, *Crisis and Order in English Towns 1500–1700*, London, 1972. It is, of course, not, strictly speaking, possible to treat manufacture as a specialism separate from trade in the urban market of the late Middle Ages, but it is in the interests of the merchant class to separate them as much as possible, since mercantile dominance establishes itself on the basis of establishing a position as both suppliers of raw materials and distributors of products. The handicraftsmen and retailers did not necessarily concede the point of view of mercantile wholesalers. David Harris Sacks describes the viewpoint of Bristol's craftsmen who 'rather than seeing the conduct of trade as a separate craft, . . . saw it as an aspect of every craft', 'The Corporate Town and the English State: Bristol's "Little Businesses" 1625–1641', *Past and Present*, CX, 1988, p. 92. For them, the freedom of the city precisely meant the freedom to trade, and they regarded mercantile monopolising as a usurpation of their ancient rights of citizenship. Although there is no purely economic separation, then, between trade and manufacture, the increasingly wide gap yawning between mercantile and trade-guilds in York is central to articulating the class relations of the pre-capitalist economy of the city and to the role of the Corpus Christi productions in that articulation.

13 Peter Travis has written about the interconnection of the social, political and economic through the figure of the body of Christ in his article, 'The Social Body of the Dramatic Christ in Medieval England', *Early English Drama, Acta*, XIII, 1985, pp. 17–36. On the interrelation between the cultural form of the Corpus Christi cycles and their socio-economic status, see also John Coldeway, 'Some Economic Aspects of the Late Medieval Drama', in Marian Briscoe and John Coldeway, eds, *Contexts for Early English Drama*, Bloomington, 1989, pp. 77–101, and Lawrence Clopper, 'Lay and Clerical Impact on Civic Religious Drama and Ceremony', *Contexts*, pp. 102–36.

14 *The Far Side Gallery*, Gary Larsen.

15 Hugh of St Victor, *De Sacramentis*, ed, R. J. Deferrari, Cambridge, Mass, 1951, p. 150.

16 *York Plays*, p. 67, l. 110.

17 *The Didascalion of Hugh of St Victor*, ed. J. Taylor, New York, 1961, ch. 9, p. 55; see Michael Camille, *The Gothic Idol: Ideology and Image Making in Medieval Art*, Cambridge, 1991, p. 40 for a discussion pertinent to the issues discussed here (see pp. 27–73).

18 Terry Eagleton, *Ideology of the Aesthetic*, Oxford, 1990, pp. 409–10. Eagleton importantly defends such a view against 'various reactionary brands of biologism' as well as 'metaphysical notions of a static human nature', (p. 409).

19 Karl Marx, *Capital*, 1974, p. 173: 'by acting on the external world and changing it, he at the same time changes his own nature'. For a fuller account of the dense history and significance of praxis in Marxist analysis, see the entry in *A Dictionary of Marxist Thought* edited by Tom Bottomore, Oxford, 1983, pp. 384–89. See also Raymond Williams's comment: 'At the very centre of Marxism is an extraordinary emphasis on human creativity and self-creation. Extraordinary because most of the systems with which it contends stress the derivation of most human activity from an external cause: from God, from an abstracted Nature or human nature, from permanent instinctual systems, or from an animal inheritance. The notion of self-creation, extended to civil society and to language by pre-Marxist thinkers, was radically extended by Marxism to the basic work processes and thence to a deeply (creatively) altered physical world and a self-created humanity' (*Marxism and Literature*, Oxford, 1977, p. 207).

20 *Theses on Feuerbach* in Economic and Philosophical Manuscripts of 1844, in *Writings of the Young Marx on Philosophy and Society*, translated and edited by Loyd D. Easton and Kurt H. Guddat, New York, 1967, p. 402.

21 *City of God* 12.26, quoted in Christopher Kirwan, *Augustine*, London, 1989. Augustine is
    partly responding to Plato's statement in the *Timaeus* that 'every cause that is an agent
    must be a craftsman'. In the *City of God*, the problem of creation brings in train the
    difficult problem of origins: why did God decide to create the world when he did, for
    example, or to phrase the question in the magnificent formulation of the *Confessions*: 'What
    was God doing before he made heaven and earth?' (*Confessions*, translated by R. S. Pine-
    Coffin, Harmondsworth, 1961, 11.10, p. 261). The problem of origin here inevitably entails
    the question of finitude, for to posit a beginning is to posit a point where God is not. See
    also Anselm's denial that God could be a craftsman (in the *Monologium*, translated by Sidney
    Norton Deane, La Salle, Illinois, 1951, p. 58, and Camille, pp. 27 ff.), and for a treatment
    which deals specifically with the issue of mimesis and fabrication in the mystery cycles as
    inaugurated in the Fall of Angels pageants, see Robert Hanning, 'You Have Begun a
    Parlous Play: The Nature and limits of Dramatic Mimesis as a Theme in Four Middle
    English "Fall of Lucifer" Cycle Plays', *Comparative Drama*, vol. VII, 1973, pp. 22–50. It is
    also worth remarking at this stage the way in which the Gospel of John echoes the
    opening lines of Genesis: 'In the beginning was the Word, and the Word was with God,
    and the Word was God. The same was in the beginning with God. All things were made
    by him; and without him was not anything made that was made' (John 1.1–3). John is
    here suggesting that Christ also had no beginning, being coextensive with God. See David
    Lawton's comments in his *Faith, Text and History: The Bible in English*, Charlottesville, 1990,
    p. 9.
22 *York Plays*, p. 53, ll. 158–9. Other references to 'warke' occur in the same pageant at ll.
    15–17. In the Creation pageant, the word occurs in one variation or another at ll. 49, 53,
    94, 124, and 125.
23 See the comments made by Richard Beadle and Pamela King remarking the puns on
    'mark(s)' (ll. 64, 68) and 'craft' (l. 150) in *York Mystery Plays: A Selection in Modern Spelling*,
    Oxford, 1984, p. 15. My own sense of the linguistic slippage at work here is that it works
    to blur rather than to preserve the distinction between divine arti-ficer and medieval
    craftsman.
24 *York Plays*, p. 79, l. 24.
25 *York Plays*, p. 82, ll. 150–1.
26 See the reference to Hugh of St Victor's hierarchy of creation/creativity that was to
    become standard, in Camille, p. 35.
27 This guild had nothing to do with the official Corpus Christi pageants, but they did put
    on their own 'pater noster' plays, etc. See A. F. Johnston, 'The Guild of Corpus Christi and
    the Procession of Corpus Christi in York', *Medieval Studies*, XXXVIII, 1976, pp. 372–84.
28 Alexandra Johnston, 'The Guild', pp. 372–3.
29 'quapropter creatione, possessione et gubernatione de ipso primo corpore humano
    virtutem varietate sic dotato poterit dominus thematis verba verificare velut singulare
    vnitatis presagium videlicet. *hoc est corpus meum*', 'The "Prologue" to the Ordinances of
    the York Corpus Christi Guild' transcribed and translated by Paula Lozar, *Allegorica*, I, 1976,
    p. 100, translation, p. 101.
30 'cuiuslibet creature rationalis per propagacionem genite primordiale principium
    omnimodam vnitatem et concordiam creatam pro statu innocencie in se gerendo omnem
    discreciam seu rebellionem radicitus extirpando', Lozar, p. 100, translation, p. 101.
31 See Theresa Coletti, 'Reading REED: History and Records of Early English Drama' in Lee
    Patterson, ed., *Literary Practice and Social Change in Britain: 1380–1530*, Berkeley and Los
    Angeles, Calif., 1990, p. 275, for an examination of the interrelations between the guild
    and city in relation to shared access to a Corpus Christi shrine whose keys were held by
    the guild.
32 My reading here differs from Theresa Coletti who sees such metaphors as expressing the
    'paradoxical relation of wholeness and differentiation . . . central to the civic mythology
    of Corpus Christi' (p. 276).

33 For the meaning of the frequent term 'communitas' in the civic documentation, see Maud Seller's comment, *York Memorandum Book: I (1376–1419)*, Surtees Society, CXX, 1911, p. iv, hence *YMB*, I. Susan Reynolds has criticised the way in which 'communitas' is readily translated by the term 'corporation' by constitutional historians, and sees this as a function of nineteenth-century struggles for municipal reform and popular government; see her 'Medieval Urban History and the History of Political Thought', *Urban History Yearbook*, 1982, pp. 14, 17. However, at stake for Reynolds is perhaps an even more deep-rootedly organicist notion of medievalism, for 'unlike people in the middle ages (so far as I understand the middle ages) we live in an age of ideological conflict about political principles' (p. 20). For two recent cogent critiques of the conceptions of community, medieval and modern, see R. M. Smith, ' "Modernization" and the Corporate Village Community in England: Some Sceptical Reflections', in A. R. H. Baker and D. Gregory, eds, *Explorations in Historical Geography*, Cambridge, 1984, pp. 140–79, 234–45, and Miri Rubin, 'Small Groups: Identity and Solidarity in the Late Middle Ages', in Jennifer Kermode, ed., *Enterprise and Individuals in Fifteenth Century England*, Stroud, 1991, pp. 132–50. And finally, for a recent examination of the organic analogy as it develops around the concept of 'communitas', see Anthony Black, *Political Thought in Europe: 1250–1450*, Cambridge, 1992, pp. 14–24.

34 Cited in Heather Swanson, *Medieval Artisans: An Urban Class in Late Medieval England*, Oxford, 1989, p. 123. See also Dobson's article, 'The Risings in York, Beverley and Scarborough, 1380–81', in *The English Rising of 1381*, Cambridge, 1984, ed. R. H. Hilton and T. H. Aston, p. 130, where he mentions the representatives of nearly all the craft-guilds uniting in 1381 in opposition to the *probi homines* to create a formidable if temporary coalition of 'all craftsmen, sellers of victuals and workmen (omnes artifices, victualium venditores et operarii) in the town'. 1381 could only have been a ghastly spectre of the kinds of corporate bodies that could form around political alliances utterly at odds with the fantasies of the ruling oligarchic body.

35 Richard Holt and Gervase Rosser (Introduction), *The English Medieval Town: A Reader in English Urban History 1200–1540*, London and New York, 1990. See John Merrington, 'Town and Country in the Transition to Capitalism' in *The Transition from Feudalism to Capitalism*, P. Sweezy, ed., introduction by Rodney Hilton, London, 1978, p. 178, who characterises such 'co-incidence of political and economic relations of subordination' as being grounded on and limited by 'the overall parcellisation of sovereignty . . . which defined the feudal mode'. On the relationship of the political and the economic generally within pre-capitalist societies see Ellen Meiksins Wood, 'Capitalism and Human Emancipation', *New Left Review*, CLXVII, 1988, pp. 3–20, and below.

36 So Marx in *Capital*, III, ch. 48: 'Capital is not a thing, but rather a definite social production relation, belonging to a definite historical formation of society, which is manifested in a thing and lends this thing a specific social character . . . It is the means of production monopolised by a certain section of society, confronting living labour power as products and working conditions rendered independent of this very labour power, which are personified through this antithesis in capital' (p. 60, Bottomore). 'Merchant capital', however, according to Marx, 'cannot determine the basic nature of society, but rather superimposes itself upon societies whose essential character is determined independently of it. Merchant capitalism is not a definitive social and economic system, but rather a mechanism of control over the exchange of products for money' (p. 333). These distinctions are crucial in the Marxist historiography of the 'transition from feudalism to capitalism'. See Maurice Dobb, *Studies in the Development of Capitalism*, London, 1946, 1963 rev. edn; the debate published in Hilton, ed., *The Transition*, and Robert Brenner's important articles with the ensuing arguments reprinted in *The Brenner Debate: Agrarian Class Structure and Economic Development in Pre-Industrial Europe*, edited by T. H. Aston and C. H. E. Philpin, Cambridge, 1985.

37 Merrington, *Transition*, p. 181.

38 Rodney Hilton, *English and French Towns in Feudal Society: A Comparative Study*, Cambridge, 1992, p. 101.

39 Ibid.

40 Swanson puts the case most forcefully, and with the most detailed attention to York, but the view is also articulated in Hilton, *English and French Towns in Feudal Society*, pp. 72, 101. Barrie Dobson, in a recent paper which I heard only after this article was drafted, is in substantial agreement with Swanson, but believes that craft guilds could retain some political influence in the city, ' "Artificers Belonging to Corpus Christi Plaie": The Social Context of the York Mystery Plays', delivered at 'The Stage as Mirror' conference, Pennsylvania State University, March, 1993. The literature on guilds is complex and conflicted, not least because of the difficulty in semantics – guild was not a self-ascribed term for the crafts guilds. The conventional criticism defines three types of guild; mercantile guilds controlled trade; crafts guilds oversaw industry; and religious guilds spiritually sustained their members. For these distinctions see Ben McRee, 'Religious Guilds and Civic Order: The Case of Norwich in the Late Middle Ages', *Speculum*, LXVII, 1992, p. 70, n. 2. The standard earlier works of reference are J. Toulmin Smith, *English Gilds*, Early English Text Society, Original Series, no. 40, London, 1870; C. Gross, *The Gild Merchant: A Contribution to British Municipal History*, 2 vols, Oxford, 1890; Stella Kramer, *The English Craft Gilds: Studies in their Progress and Decline*, New York, 1927. See also A. Black, *Guilds and Civil Society in European Political Thought from the Twelfth Century to the Present*, Ithaca, NY, 1984. I am grateful to Virginia Bainbridge for allowing me to read the opening chapter of her dissertation, 'Gild and Parish in Late Medieval Cambridgeshire c.1350–1558', in which guild historiography is discussed.

41 Swanson, p. 114. Swanson's book, a dense and detailed account of artisanal activities and relations in York, provides rich new material for any future readers of the York cycle. The argument is also made in succinct and abbreviated form in her article, 'The Illusion of Economic Structure: Craft Guilds in Late Medieval English Towns', *Past and Present*, CXXI, 1988, pp. 29–48. Swanson establishes a prehistory for her argument in the work of Maurice Dobb, *Studies in the Development of Capitalism*, London, 1946, p. 97, and Mrs J. R. Green, *Town Life in the Fifteenth Century*, 2 vols, London, 1894, II, pp. 145–57; 'The Illusion', p. 30.

42 It is, as Swanson emphasises, the erasure of the 'vital role of women in the domestic production unit' that has been historically invisible and that partially accounts for the willingness to read the official civic version as economic reality (p. 6). Swanson stresses that the division of labour imposed by the merchant elite was everywhere transgressed: 'Artisans worked in the service industries, kept livestock, ventured into the victualling trades, in short took every opportunity they could to make a little extra money. The diversity of their work disappears in official records, perhaps intentionally, for the civic authorities fully recognized that it was by trade and not by manufacture that even a modest fortune was to be made' (*ibid.*). See Martha Howell, *Women, Production and Patriarchy in Late Medieval Cities*, Chicago, 1986, for the positioning of women in the economies of late medieval urban life.

43 *Statutes of the Realm* i, London, 1810–28, p. 379; Swanson, p. 112. In his paper, ' "Artificers belonging to Corpus Christi" ', Dobson suggests that the York mayor and aldermen were coming under increasing governmental pressure to rationalise crafts guilds, partly as a response to the engrossing activities of the London grocers who were developing a monopoly over foodstuffs.

44 Swanson, p. 114. See also the excerpts from Knighton in *The Peasant's Revolt of 1381* edited by R. B. Dobson, London, 1970, pp. 59 ff. N. B. Goldberg comments that women were specifically exempted from the statute of 1363; *Women, Work and Life-Cycle*, p. 336.

45 The terminology here should make it plain that such a view works against the understanding of medieval towns as 'non-feudal islands in a feudal sea' (M. M. Postan, *The Medieval Economy and Society*, Harmondsworth, 1975, p. 239), a view which, as Merrington says, reads 'the progressive role of the urban bourgeoisie backwards into history' and

poses the market as 'the *only* dynamic force, the principle behind all movement, all change', (*Transition*, p. 173).

46 Swanson, p. 113, and see her further comments on p. 3 and p. 172: 'Ultimately artisans have to be seen in terms of their relations with the merchants who formed the ruling elite; by organizing artisans into formal guilds, by excluding them from political power, the merchants gave definition to the artisan class.' As Dobson points out, from the 1370s and 1380s onwards, the governing body begins systematically to call in the ordinances of as many crafts as possible ('"Artificers belonging to Corpus Christi"'). Examples of such ordinances registered in the *YMB* by the civic clerk are printed in *YMB*, I and II. See also Swanson, p. 112.

47 Swanson, 'The Illusion', p. 43.

48 YMB, I, pp. 35–6, 39, ix; Swanson, p. 121; REED: York, pp. x–xiii.

49 Palliser, *Tudor York*, Oxford, 1979, p. 68. See also introduction to REED: York.

50 Swanson, p. 121. See also the comments of Champion in 'The Gilds of Medieval Beverley', in *The Medieval Town in Britain* ed. P. Riden, Cardiff Papers in Local History, I, 1980, pp. 58–9, for further comments on the roles of the searchers in articulating the guilds as agents of town government.

51 Swanson, p. 123. See also Jennifer Kermode, 'Urban Decline? The Flight from Office in Late Medieval York', *Economic History Review*, XXXV, 1982, who discovers that the putative 'flight from office' is less a symptom of 'urban decline' than an example of a council 'keeping the lower orders out of high civic office and making a profit at the same time' (p. 195).

52 Richard Homan, 'Ritual Aspects of the York Cycle,' *Theatre Journal*, XXXIII, 1981, p. 121. It is quite unclear how the unresolvable 'in fact' could be resolved in ritual. See also Mervyn James for an articulation of this view. For a recent critique of such an account of ritual consensus see Claire Sponsler, 'The Culture of the Spectator: Conformity and Resistance to Medieval Performances', *Theatre Journal*, XLIV, 1992, pp. 15–29; see also Kathy Ashley's recent investigations of ritual theory in her introduction to a special issue of the *Journal of Ritual Studies* and the essay by Ashley and Pamela Sheingorn in that collection, 'An Unsentimental View of Ritual in the Middle Ages Or, Sainte Foy was no Snow White', *Journal of Ritual Studies*, VI, Winter 1992, pp. 63–85. See also Miri Rubin's comments on James in her 'Small Groups and Identity', p. 145, and my article, 'Ritualising the Body in the York Corpus Christi Cycle' (forthcoming); *YMB* part 2, p. xliv.

53 There is no extant version of the sausage-makers' pageant, but there is an entry for 1432 in the YMB which mentions their pageant, 'The Hanging of Judas', 'in qua representatur quod Judas Scarioth se suspendit et crepuit medius' (YMB, I, p. 155). It appears that the sausage-makers may have gone in for a bit of facetious and grotesque advertising for their trade by representing Judas's guts as a string of sausages. For further details of such 'advertising' see Alan Justice, 'Trade Symbolism in the York Cycle', *Theatre Journal*, XXXI, 1979, pp. 47–58.

54 Swanson, 'The Illusion', p. 44, and see *YMB*, I, pp. 155–6.

55 REED: York, pp. 715–16. As Goldberg points out the manufacture of tallow candles appears to be a 'feminised craft', citing evidence from Coventry that wives manufacturing and selling candles in Coventry are also requested to make a contribution towards the smiths' pageant (*Women, Work and Life-Cycle*, p. 133).

56 See Swanson, p. 173, and Dobson, 'The Risings'.

57 For the fluctuating fortunes of the victualling industry in relation to the mercantile élite, see Swanson, pp. 24–5. By the late fifteenth century it was in fact impossible to keep the butchers out of office altogether.

58 YMB, II, p. xlvii.

59 Martin Stevens, *Four Mystery Cycles*, p. 23. This episode becomes for Stevens emblematic of the 'self-perpetuating civic institution' generated by the Corpus Christi pageants (p. 24).

60 Beadle describes the sources of funding: 'yearly contributions from non-members of gilds

who gained income from practising the skills of the play-owning craft; special payments made on becoming a master in a play-owning craft, or on becoming a member of a gild: a percentage of fines levied for infringement of guild ordinances; and contributions from crafts which did not have plays in the cycle' (*York Plays*, p. 31), and see M. Rogerson, 'The York Corpus Christi Play: Some Practical Details', *Leeds Studies in English*, NS, X, 1978, pp. 97–101.

61 See for example YMB, I, pp. 66, 155–6, 185–6, vol. 2, pp. 102–4, 123–4, 167, 179, 297. *York Civic Records*, vols 1–8, ed. A. Raine, (York Archeological Society Record Series, XCVIII, CIII, CVI, CVII, CX, CXII, CXV, CXIX, 1938–52) vol. 3, pp. 14, 47, 61, 65–6. See also Swanson, p. 120.

62 Swanson, p. 120.

63 Swanson points out, for example, that the bowstringers in York seem to have existed as a craft simply to make provision for the searchers ('The Illusion', p. 43).

64 Swanson, 'The Illusion', p. 44 and *YMB*, vol. 2, p. 104.

65 Dobson cites the example of Durham, where the town craftsmen were not formally organised at all before the middle of the fifteenth century. It was the organisation of the Corpus Christi pageant that was the mechanism by which they were regulated and formalised, (' "Artificers Belonging to Corpus Christi" '). He notes the similarity to the York case and suggests that between 1370 and 1470 the gradual internal consolidation of the structure of guilds is coincident with the development of the Corpus Christi plays.

66 Swanson, 'The Illusion', p. 47 for details. The common council was henceforth to be constituted by major and minor crafts, the major crafts having two representatives and the minor crafts one. Swanson points out that 'major' and 'minor' are in this instance 'social and not economic distinctions', that is, political manipulations disguised as social categories to ensure economic dominance (p. 47). Dobson believes that Swanson overstates her case in arguing for the political rather than the economic function of the guilds (verbal response given at Stage as Mirror conference), but such arguments indicate that we need to think through the relations between these two categories whose separation might itself be seen as a product of a capitalist social formation (see below).

67 For details about the Register see *York Plays* (introduction). Jennifer Kermode describes the transitions in import–export patterns of the merchant oligarchy in 'Merchants, Overseas Trade, and Urban Decline: York, Beverley and Hull *c*.1380–1500', *Northern History*, XXIII, 1988, pp. 51–73.

68 Kermode, 'Merchants and Overseas Trade', p. 58.

69 Beadle points out that we are aware of the activity of the Common Clerk in 'keeping' the Register from between 1527 and 1554, and his presence at the first station of Corpus Christi from as early as 1501 ('The York Cycle', p. 107). His role was to check the plays he actually saw against the now authoritative Register, so it may be surmised that the commitment of the play texts to the Register is very much in the interests of oligarchic control, exploiting the fixity and authority of written texts over the habits of extempore performance and traditions of improvisation.

70 See above, n. 42.

71 *Transition*, p. 178.

72 Lee Patterson is one of the few literary scholars who has incorporated the Marxist historiography of feudal relations into his map of late medieval literature; see Chapter 5, 'The *Miller's Tale* and the Politics of Laughter' in his *Chaucer and the Subject of History*, Madison, 1991, pp. 247–54.

73 Gerald Sider, *Culture and Class in Anthropology and History: A Newfoundland Illustration*, Cambridge, 1986, pp. 4–8 for an examination of the anthropological concept of culture, also cited in *Christ's Body*, Introduction, n. 11, from which I extrapolate the comments here; and see my article, 'Ritual, Church and Theatre: Medieval Dramas of the Sacramental Body' in David Aers, ed., *Culture and History: Essays on English Communities, Identities and Writing*, Hemel Hempstead, 1992, pp. 65–90, for an attempt at an account of *The Croxton*

Play of the Sacrament in socio-cultural terms, and a critique of the nostalgic sacramentalist holism that so often comes into play when the concepts Corpus Christi, culture, ritual and 'medieval' are put together.

74 In E. M. Wood, 'Capitalism and Human Emancipation', p. 12. Ellen Meiksins Wood's most dense, brilliant and careful arguing of these points takes place in an earlier article, 'The Separation of the Economic and the Political in Capitalism', *New Left Review*, CXXVII, 1981, pp. 66–95. The 'rigid conceptual separation of the "economic" and the "political"', she says, has 'served *bourgeois* ideology so well ever since the classical economists discovered the "economy" in the abstract and began emptying capitalism of its social and political content' (p. 66). Her reconsideration of the relation between base and superstructure is avowedly indebted to the 'political' Marxism elucidated by Robert Brenner, whose articulation of 'the origins of capitalism' emerges out of his consideration of 'the unintended consequences of relations between non-capitalist classes, the outcome of which was the subjection of direct producers to the *imperatives* of competition, as they were *obliged* to enter the market for access to their means of subsistence and reproduction' (Ellen Meiksins Wood, *The Pristine Culture of Capitalism: A Historical Essay on Old Regimes and Modern States*, London, 1991, p. 10). For a further consideration of the relation between base and superstructure in relation specifically to the questions of class raised by E. P. Thompson, see Ellen Meiksins Wood, 'Falling through the Cracks: E. P. Thompson and the Debate on Base and Superstructure', in *E. P. Thompson: Critical Perspectives*, eds Harvey Kaye and Keith McClelland, Philadelphia, 1990, pp. 125–52.

75 See Stephen Rigby's discussion of the 'fundamentalist' and 'dialectical' version of 'base and superstructure' (pp. 182–6), and his comments at the end of his book *Marxism and History* (Manchester, 1987, p. 301): 'whilst much of the most interesting Marxist historical work is concerned with pre-industrial society, it is precisely in this area of historiography that Marxism, with its emphasis on the social constraints on politics and ideology, has had least impact'. Raymond Williams in his seminal essay 'Base and Superstructure in Marxist Cultural Theory' has put the matter best when he says: 'One of the unexpected consequences of the base/superstructure model has been the too easy acceptance of models which appear less crude – models of totality or of the complex whole – but which exclude the facts of social intention, the class character of a particular society and so on' (*Problems in Materialism and Culture: Selected Essays*, London, 1980, p. 36).

76 John Brenkman's formulation in 'Theses on Cultural Marxism', p. 25. See also the debate on economism, 'cultural Marxism' and socialist humanism, inaugurated by Richard Johnson's essay, 'Thompson, Genovese, and Socialist–Humanist History', *History Workshop Journal*, VI, 1978, pp. 79–110, and the ensuing debates, especially Simon Clarke, 'Socialist Humanism and the Critique of Economism', *History Workshop Journal*, VIII, 1979, pp. 137–56. See also Harvey Kaye's account of this argument and its implications in his *The British Marxist Historians: An Introductory Analysis*, Cambridge, 1984, pp. 18–22, and his chapters on Maurice Dobb and Rodney Hilton, pp. 23–69, 70–98, where both are read in terms of their contribution not only to historical studies, but also to a tradition of theoretical work. Kaye refutes Johnson's analysis of the break between economistic and cultural Marxism, and Dobb is a key figure in that refutation.

77 Miri Rubin has examined the historiography of medieval urbanity, questioning both the understanding of towns as 'natural ceremonial spaces' and our conceptual reduction of them to a function and nature conceived along the lines of either 'mentality' or market in her 'Religious Culture in Town and Country: Reflections on a Great Divide', in *Church and City: Essays in Honour of Christopher Brooke*, eds D. Abulafia, M. Franklin and Miri Rubin, Cambridge, 1992, pp. 10, 20, 21.

78 For a discussion of the conceptualisation of the interrelations of class, gender and the concept of culture in British historical work, see Stuart Hall, 'Marxism and Culture', *Radical History Review*, XVIII, Fall 1978, pp. 5–14. In surveying the work of *History Workshop* as well as the contribution of the Centre for Contemporary Cultural Studies, he reminds

us that 'one of the most serious theoretical and intellectual problems confronting the new concern with culture is how to conceptualize the areas of ideology, culture and consciousness without giving way, slipping back, to idealism' (p. 8).

79 *York Plays*, line references to work: ll. 25, 26, 47, 66, 127, 143, 153, 181, 240, 250, 261, and 'trauayle', l. 300.

80 *York Plays*, p. 315, Pageant XXXV, l. 5.

81 *York Plays*, l. 261.

82 It is striking how in the world of devotional prose there are only two actors, Christ and the human worshipper of Christ. Though we are asked to identify with the suffering of Christ, we are never asked to look at the social agents of brutality as we are here in the York pageant of the crucifixion.

83 John Brenkman, 'Theses on Cultural Marxism', p. 30.

84 The formulation is again Brenkman's (p. 27).

Index

This index is intended primarily to draw together scattered information and to draw attention to topics, or aspects of topics, which the reader might otherwise overlook.

References in italics are to illustrations. Where information is to be found in an end-of-chapter note and this is not apparent from reading the text, the note itself has been indexed; other references should be understood to include the end-of-chapter notes.